OTTO KAISER

ISAIAH 1–12

OTTO KAISER

ISAIAH 1-12

A Commentary

Second Edition
completely rewritten

SCM PRESS LTD

FOR GERTRUD

Translated by John Bowden from the German
Das Buch des Propheten Jesaja, Kapitel 1–12
(Das Alte Testament Deutsch 17)
fifth edition 1981
published by Vandenhoeck and Ruprecht,
Göttingen

Translation © John Bowden 1983

334 00744 5
First published in English 1983
by SCM Press Ltd
26–30 Tottenham Road, London N1
Phototypeset by Input Typesetting Ltd
and printed in Great Britain by
Redwood Burn Ltd
Trowbridge, Wiltshire.

CONTENTS

PREFACE

This commentary follows a consistent course in the critical approach which it adopts. Over a decade I have arrived at a view which differs fundamentally from previous literary assessments of the book of Isaiah. My understanding of the so-called memorial of the prophet Isaiah on his activity at the time of the Syro-Ephraimite war (6.1–9.6) is fundamental in this respect. Once one allows that this is a composition aimed at coming to terms with the exile in the sixth century, the rest follows almost automatically. Perhaps, therefore, I may be excused for having paid special attention to the elucidation of these chapters.

Only occasionally can I indicate how the insights into the development of the book of Isaiah presented in this commentary affect an understanding of Isa. 13–39. That calls for a further, separate investigation; however, it should be noted that I now put the essential process of editing this book in the pre-Hellenistic period. The limitations of this series and the fact that in discussing the memorial I have almost gone beyond them restricted my discussion of other points of view, and has largely ruled out even a discussion of the main evidence. Readers familiar with the results of modern scholarship will recognize the degree to which this commentary is indebted to its predecessors and will still be able to unravel this evidence; those who are uninterested in scholarly discussion will hardly miss what I have omitted.[1]

At this point it is only natural that I should remember in gratitude my old teacher and fatherly friend, Artur Weiser, the former editor of Das Alte Testament Deutsch, who has now died. He assigned the commentary on Isaiah to me twenty years ago, and the publisher, Herr Günther Ruprecht, endorsed that trust, though I was only a young lecturer in Tübingen. I am very happy that the collaboration has continued under Herr Ruprecht's son and successor, Dr Arndt Ruprecht. I am also grateful to Professor Hans-Christoph Schmitt, in Augsburg, for his kindness in reading through the manuscript, and to Herr Christian Wildberg, from Flensburg, not only for help with the proofs and revision of the map which is again included in

---

[1] I can only regret having missed G. Brunet, *Essai sur l'Isaïe de l'histoire*, Paris 1975, and that the second volume of Vermeylen's large-scale study has so far not become available.

connection with the exegesis of 10.28ff., but also for his critical reflections on passages which are decisive for an understanding of the book as a whole. If I single out from the audience at my Marburg lectures on Isaiah Pastors Martin Rösch and Bernhard Würfel from Lahr in Baden, they will know why! I must also express thanks to the Ministry of Culture in Hesse for granting me a sabbatical year to complete this book. And finally, the dedication expresses public thanks to my wife, without whose understanding and constant encouragement the book would never have been written.

Marburg an der Lahn, OTTO KAISER
Late summer 1979

Preface to the English Edition

I am particularly grateful to John Bowden, Managing Director of SCM Press, for honouring me on two counts: for including the new edition of my commentary in the Old Testament Library and for being so kind as to take upon himself the laborious task of translating it. I also owe a word of thanks to Matthias Missfeldt of Lichtenau in Westphalia, for working on the proofs of the English edition.

I would ask the reader not to pass judgment on what I have written until he has read the commentary on Isaiah 6–8; indeed, I would prefer that this part of the commentary should be read first of all.

I hope that in its new edition this book may fulfil two aims: that it may help in understanding the book of Isaiah better, and that it may show the way in which God seeks to have himself discovered by us human beings, a way of trust in his never-ending presence as the ground of our future.

Marburg an der Lahn, OTTO KAISER
Late summer 1982

ABBREVIATIONS

General Abbreviations

AAeg	Analecta Aegyptiaca, Copenhagen
AASF	Annales Academiae Scientiarum Fennicae, Helsinki
AcOr	Acta Orientalia Havania, Leiden
AfO	Archiv für Orientforschung, Graz, etc.
AGSU	Arbeiten zur Geschichte des Spätjudentums und Ur-christentums, Leiden
AHw	Wolfram von Soden, *Akkadisches Handwörterbuch*, Wiesbaden
AJSL	*American Journal of Semitic Languages and Literatures*, Chicago
AnBib	Analecta Biblica, Rome
ANET²⁻³	*Ancient Near Eastern Texts relating to the Old Testament*, ed. J. B. Pritchard, Princeton ²1954, ³1969
AOAT	Alter Orient und Altes Testament, Kevelaer and Neukirchen-Vluyn
AOT²	*Altorientalische Texte zum Alten Testament*, ed. H. Gressmann, Berlin and Leipzig ²1926
ArOr	Archiv Orientální, Prague
ATD	Das Alte Testament Deutsch, Göttingen
ATANT	Abhandlungen zur Theologie des Alten und Neuen Testaments, Zurich
AzT	Arbeiten zur Theologie, Stuttgart
BA	*The Biblical Archaeologist*, New Haven; Cambridge, Mass.
BASOR	*Bulletin of the American School of Oriental Research*, South Hadley, Mass.; Baltimore, Maryland
BAT	Die Botschaft des Alten Testaments, Stuttgart
BBB	Bonner Biblische Beiträge, Bonn
BC	Biblischer Commentar über das Alte Testament, Leipzig
BEvTh	Beiträge zur *Evangelische Theologie*, Munich
BFChTh	Beiträge zur Forderung Christlicher Theologie, Gütersloh
BHH	*Biblisch-historisches Handwörterbuch*, Göttingen
Bib	*Biblica*, Rome
BibOr	*Biblica et Orientalia*, Rome

BJRL   *Bulletin of the John Rylands Library*, Manchester
BK   Biblischer Kommentar. Altes Testament, Neukirchen-Vluyn
B–L   H. Bauer and P. Leander, *Historische Grammatik der Hebräischen Sprache des Alten Testaments*, Halle 1922=Hildesheim 1961
BRL²   *Biblisches Reallexikon*, ed. K. Galling, HAT 1, 2, Tübingen ²1977
BS   Biblische Studien, Neukirchen-Vluyn
BVSAW   Berichte über die Verhandlungen der Sächsischen Akademie der Wissenschaften zu Leipzig, Berlin
BWANT   Beiträge zur Wissenschaft vom Alten und Neuen Testament, Stuttgart
BZAW   Beihefte zur *Zeitschrift für die alttestamentliche Wissenschaft*, Giessen/Berlin and Berlin/New York
BZ NF   *Biblische Zeitschrift*, Neue Folge, Paderborn
CAH   *The Cambridge Ancient History*, Cambridge
CBL   *Calwer Bibellexikon*, ed. T. Schlatter, Stuttgart 1967
CBQ   *Catholic Biblical Quarterly*, Washington DC
CBQM   Catholic Biblical Quarterly Monograph Series, Washington DC
CRB   Cahiers de la Revue Biblique, Paris
CTA   *Corpus des tablettes en cunéiformes alphabétiques découvertes à Ras Shamra-Ugarit de 1929 à 1939 par André Herdner*, Paris 1963
CTh   Cahiers théologiques, Neuchâtel, etc.
DOTT   *Documents from Old Testament Times*, ed. D. Winton Thomas, London 1956
EHAT   Exegetisches Handbuch zum Alten Testament, Münster
EtB   Études Bibliques, Paris
EvTh   *Evangelische Theologie*, Munich
FRLANT   Forschungen zur Religion und Literatur des Alten und Neuen Testaments, Göttingen
FS   Festschrift
FzB   Forschung zur Bibel, Wûrzburg
G–K²⁸   E. Kautzsch, W. *Gesenius Hebräische Grammatik*, Leipzig²⁸ 1909, ET *Gesenius' Hebrew Grammar as edited and expanded by the late E. Kautzsch*, ed. A. E. Cowley, Oxford ²1910.
HAL   W. Baumgartner, *Hebräisches und Aramäisches Lexikon zum Alten Testament*, Leiden I 1964, II 1974
HAT   Handbuch zum Alten Testament, Tübingen
HK   Handkommentar zum Alten Testament, Göttingen

HSAT	Die Heilige Schrift des Alten Testaments, ed. F. Feldmann and H. Herkenne, Bonn
HSAT.E	Die Heilige Schrift des Alten Testament, ed. F. Feldmann and H. Herkenne, Ergänzungsband, Bonn
HSAT(K)	Die Heilige Schrift des Alten Testaments übersetzt von E. Kautzsch, ed. A. Bertholet, Tübingen ⁴1923
HTR	*Harvard Theological Review*, Cambridge, Mass.
ICC	International Critical Commentary of the Holy Scriptures, Edinburgh
IEJ	*Israel Exploration Journal*, Jerusalem
JBL	*Journal of Biblical Literature*, New Haven; Philadelphia; Missoula, Montana
JEA	*Journal of Egyptian Archaeology*, London
JNES	*Journal of Near Eastern Studies*, Chicago
JSS	*Journal of Semitic Studies*, Manchester
JTS	*Journal of Theological Studies*, Oxford
KAI	H. Donner and W. Röllig, *Kanaanäische und Aramäische Inschriften* I–III, Wiesbaden ²1968/69
KAT	Kommentar zum Alten Testament, Leipzig, ²Gütersloh
KBL	L. Koehler and W. Baumgartner, *Lexicon in Veteris Testamenti Libros*, Leiden 1953
KeH	Kurzgefasstes exegetisches Handbuch zum Alten Testament, Leipzig
KHC	Kurzer Hand-Commentar zum Alten Testament, Freiburg im Breisgau, Leipzig and Tübingen
KK	Kurzgefasster Kommentar zu den heiligen Schriften Alten und Neuen Testamentes sowie zu den Apokryphen, Nordlingen
KP	*Der Kleine Pauly*, Lexikon der Antike, Stuttgart and Munich
KS	*Kleine Schriften*
LCL	Loeb Classical Library, London and New York
LTK	*Lexicon für Theologie und Kirche*, Freiburg
MÄS	Münchener Ägyptologische Studien, Berlin
MSSOTS	Monograph Series. Society for Old Testament Studies, London
NF	Neue Folge
NTD	Das Neue Testament Deutsch, Göttingen
NZST	*Neue Zeitschrift für Systematische Theologie und Religionsphilosophie*, Berlin and New York
OrAnt	*Oriens Antiquus*, Rome
OTL	Old Testament Library, London
PEQ	*Palestine Exploration Quarterly*, London

PJB	*Palästinajahrbuch des Deutschen Evangelischen Instituts*, Berlin
PL	Patrologiae Cursus Completus, accurante J.-P. Migne, Series Latina, Paris
POS	Pretoria Oriental Series, Leiden
RivBib	*Rivista Biblica*, Rome
RLA	*Reallexikon der Assyriologie*, Berlin/Leipzig and New York
RM	Die Religionen der Menschheit, Stuttgart
RTP	*Revue de Théologie et de Philosophie*, Lausanne
SAT	Die Schriften des Alten Testaments, Göttingen
SB	Sources Bibliques, Paris
SBS	Stuttgarter Bibelstudien, Stuttgart
SB(T)	La Sacra Bibbia, Turin and Rome
SBT	Studies in Biblical Theology, London
SGV	Sammlung gemeinverständlicher Vorträge und Schriften, Tübingen
SKGG	Schriften der Königsberger Gelehrter Gesellschaft. Geisteswissenschaftliche Klasse, Halle
SMHVL	Scripta Minora. K. Humanistiska Vetenskapssamfundet i. Lund, Lund
SSAW	Sitzungsberichte der Sächsischen Akademie der Wissenchaften zu Leipzig
ST	Studia Theologica, Lund, etc.
SVT	Supplements to *Vetus Testamentum*, Leiden
TGI²	*Textbuch zur Geschichte Israels*, ed. K. Galling, Tübingen ²1968
THAT	*Theologisches Handwörterbuch zum Alten Testament*, ed. E. Jenni and C. Westermann, Munich
ThB	Theologische Bibliothek, Munich
TLZ	*Theologische Literaturzeitung*, Leipzig
ThSt(B)	Theologische Studien, ed. K. Barth, later by M. Geiger, E. Jüngel and R. Smend, Zurich
TDOT	*Theological Dictionary of the Old Testament*, ed. G. J. Botterweck and H. Ringgren, ET of *TWAT*, Grand Rapids, Michigan
TDNT	*Theological Dictionary of the New Testament*, ed. G. Kittel und G. Friedrich, ET of *TWNT*, Grand Rapids, Michigan
TWAT	*Theologisches Wörterbuch zum Alten Testament*, ed G. J. Botterweck and H. Ringgren, Stuttgart
TW	Theologische Wissenschaft, Stuttgart
TWNT	*Theologisches Wörterbuch zum Neuen Testament*, ed. G. Kittel and G. Friedrich, Stuttgart
TZ	*Theologische Zeitschrift*, Basle
TTS	Trierer Theologische Studien, Trier

UB	Urban-Bücher/Taschenbücher, Stuttgart
UF	*Ugarit-Forschungen*, Kevelaer and Neukirchen-Vluyn
UUÅ	Uppsala Universitets Årsskrift, Uppsala
VT	*Vetus Testamentum*, Leiden
WdF	Wege der Forschung, Darmstadt
WMANT	Wissenschaftliche Monographien zum Alten und Neuen Testament, Neukirchen-Vluyn
WUNT	Wissenschaftliche Untersuchungen zum Neuen Testament, Tübingen
ZAW	*Zeitschrift für die alttestamentliche Wissenschaft*, Giessen and Berlin or Berlin and New York
ZBK	Zürcher Bibelkommentare, Zurich
ZDPV	*Zeitschrift des Deutschen Palästina-Vereins*, Leipzig and Wiesbaden
ZRGG	*Zeitschrift für Religions- und Geistesgeschichte*, Leiden
ZTK	*Zeitschrift für Theologie und Kirche*, Tübingen

Abbreviations of works cited frequently

Barth, *Jesaja-Worte*	H. Barth, *Die Jesaja-Worte der Josiazeit*, WMANT 48, Neukirchen 1977
Becker, *Isaias*	J. Becker, *Isaias – der Prophet und sein Buch*, SBS 30, Stuttgart 1968
Bobzin	H. Bobzin, *Die 'Tempora' im Hiobdialog*, Diss. phil. Marburg/Lahn 1974
Brockelmann	C. Brockelmann, *Hebräische Syntax*, Neukirchen 1956
Budde, *Jesaja's Erleben*	K. Budde, *Jesaja's Erleben*, Gotha 1928
Cheyne, *Introduction*	T. K. Cheyne, *Introduction to the Book of Isaiah*, London 1895
Davidson	A. B. Davidson, *Hebrew Syntax*, Edinburgh ³1901 (1973)
Dietrich, *Jesaja und die Politik*	W. Dietrich, *Jesaja und die Politik*, BEvTh 74, Munich 1976
Donner, *Israel unter den Völkern*	H. Donner, *Israel unter den Völkern*, SVT 11, Leiden 1964
Fey, *Amos und Jesaja*	R. Fey, *Amos und Jesaja, Abhängigkeit und Eigenständigkeit des Jesaja*, WMANT 12, Neukirchen 1963
Gordon	C. H. Gordon, *Ugaritic Textbook*, AnOr 38, Rome 1965

Hoffmann, *Intention*	H. W. Hoffmann, *Die Intention der Verkündigung Jesajas*, BZAW 136, Berlin and New York 1974
Huber, *Völker*	F. Huber, *Jahwe, Juda und die anderen Völker beim Propheten Jesaja*, BZAW 137, Berlin and New York 1976
Jastrow	M. Jastrow, *A Dictionary of the Targum, the Targum Babli and Yerushalmi, and the Midrashic Literature* I–II, New York (1903) 1950
Joüon	P. Joüon, *Grammaire de l'Hébreu biblique*, Rome (1923) 1965
Kaiser, *Introduction*	O. Kaiser, *Introduction to the Old Testament*, ET Oxford 1975
Kaiser, *Isaiah 13–39*	O. Kaiser, *Isaiah 13–39*, OTL, London 1974
Luckenbill, *Ancient Records*	D. D. Luckenbill, *Ancient Records of Assyria and Babylonia* I–II, Chicago 1926–1927=New York 1968
Meyer[3]	R. Meyer, *Hebräische Grammatik* I–III, Berlin 1966–[3]1972
Rehm, *Messias*	M. Rehm, *Der königliche Messias im Licht der Immanuel-Weissagungen des Buches Jesaja*, Eichstätter Studien NF 1, Kevelaer, 1968
Schedl, *Rufer des Heils*	C. Schedl, *Rufer des Heils in heilloser Zeit*, Paderborn 1973
Vermeylen I	J. Vermeylen, *Du prophète Isaïe à l'apocalyptique* I, EtB, Paris 1977
Vollmer, *Geschichtliche Rückblicke*	J. Vollmer, *Geschichtliche Rückblicke und Motive in der Prophetie des Amos, Hosea und Jesaja*, BZAW 119, Berlin 1971
Whedbee, *Isaiah and Wisdom*	J. W. Whedbee, *Isaiah and Wisdom*, Nashville and New York 1971
Zorell	F. Zorell and E. Vogt, *Lexicon Hebraicum et Aramaicum Veteris Testamenti*, Rome 1968 and 1971

Commentaries
usually cited by author's name only

P. Auvray, SB 1972; Franz Delitzsch, BC III, 1, [2]1869; A. Dillmann and R. Kittel, KeH 5, 1898; B. Duhm, HK III, 1 (1892), [4]1922 ([5]1968);

Eichrodt, BAT 17, I, 1960 (^{2}1976); F. Feldmann, EHAT 14, 1, 1925; J. Fischer, HSAT VII, 1, 1, 1937; G. Fohrer, ZBK 19, 1, 1960 (^{2}1967); G. B. Gray, ICC, 1912 (1956); H. Guthe, HSAT(K), ^{4}1922; V. Herntrich, ATD 17, 1950; O. Kaiser, ATD, 1960: OTL, 1972; O. Kaiser, *Isaiah 13–39*, OTL ^{2}1980; E. J. Kissane I, 1941; E. König, 1926; K. Marti, KHC X, 1900; C. v. Orelli, KK. A 4, 1887; A. Penna, SB (T) 1957 (1964); O. Procksch, KAT^1 IX, 1930; C. Schedl, 1973; H. Schmidt, SAT 2, 2, ^{2}1923; J. Steinmann, Lectio divina, ^{2}1955; J. Ziegler, Echter Bibel 1948 (1954); H. Wildberger, BK X, 1, 1972.

Editions of the text

BHS   *Biblia Hebraica Stuttgartensia*, ed. K. Elliger et W. Rudolph, 7. *Liber Jesaiae*, praep. D. Winton Thomas, Stuttgart 1968
The Hebrew University Bible. The Book of Isaiah, ed. M. H. Goshen-Gottstein, I–II, Jerusalem 1975
M = Massoretic text
LXX is cited from the *Septuaginta auct. soc.litt. Gottingensis editum*, Vol. XIV, *Isaias*, ed. J. Ziegler, Göttingen 1939; T from *The Targum of Isaiah*, ed. J. Stenning, Oxford 1953, and V from *Biblia Sacra juxta Vulgatam versionem rec. R. Weber*, I–II, Stuttgart ^{2}1975.

Square brackets in references indicate the Hebrew text where its numbering differs from the English versions.

COMMENTARY

CHAPTER 1.1

The Formation of the Book of Isaiah: The Heading

1 **The vision of Isaiah the son of Amoz, which he saw concerning Judah and Jerusalem in the days of Uzziah, Jotham, Ahaz and Hezekiah, kings of Judah.**

[1] As it stands, the heading gives the impression that all sixty-six chapters of the book come from the prophet Isaiah, son of Amoz, who was working in Jerusalem in the second half of the eighth century BC. However, the man who once placed it at the beginning of a collection of prophetic sayings which he had made is only indirectly responsible for this impression. The anonymous collections to be found in chs. 40–55 and 56–66, and described as Deutero-Isaiah and Trito-Isaiah simply because they were incorporated into the book of Isaiah as a result of the tradition by which they were handed down, were only attached to the collection in chs. 1–39 at a secondary stage, causing this collection to be known as Proto-Isaiah.[1] Furthermore, even the first collection is not an original literary unit.

1. The commentary which follows indicates that the foundation of the collection may be seen as a smaller collection of prophetic sayings, presumably first made at the beginning of the fifth century, and influenced by the theology of the Deuteronomistic History.[2] It begins with the earliest sayings, contained in ch. 1, and is continued in the basic material of chs. 28–31. It was at one with Deuteronomistic theology in its concern to interpret the collapse of the kingdom of Judah, with the destruction of Jerusalem and the deportation of the royal family and the upper classes, in 587, as a consequence of the

---

[1] The words Proto-, Deutero– and Trito– are of Greek derivation, meaning first, second and third. In this case they refer to Isaiah. See Kaiser, *Introduction*, 220ff., 223, 260ff., 268ff.

[2] For this see Kaiser, *Introduction*, 169ff.

people's refusal to listen to the prophet and to trust Yahweh instead of Egypt (cf. 30.12ff.; 30.1ff.; 31.1ff.). At the same time it called upon the survivors to abandon their own resistance to Yahweh (cf. 1.22f., 4ff., 18ff.). Further clarification is needed as to whether the prophecies which form the basis of chs. 28–31 were originally regarded as Isaianic tradition or whether they were only interpreted in this way at a later stage. It was possible to ascribe an anonymous prophecy from the last years of the kingdom of Judah, with its warnings against trusting in Egypt, to the prophet Isaiah, and therefore make him see beyond his own time to the downfall of the kingdom, because the situations of 703–701 and 589–587 were essentially similar: at the end of the eighth century Hezekiah (715?–697) had rebelled against Sennacherib, king of Assyria (705–681), and was only able to save Jerusalem, already besieged by its enemies, by surrendering.[3] In the early years of the second decade of the sixth century, Zedekiah (597–586) had rebelled against his Babylonian master Nebuchadnezzar II (604–562) and paid for this by being deposed from the throne and imprisoned.[4] Given that Isaiah was on Hezekiah's side during the decisive years, as the Isaiah narratives of chs. 36–39, taken from the Deuteronomistic II Kings, indicate, it was easy to assume that at that point he had warned against the policy which proved so disastrous for the kingdom and forecast its consequences as the punishment of Yahweh. In this case the Isaiah narratives would have proved responsible for the formation of the whole of the tradition handed down in the prophet's name. However, whether or not this is the case, in the last resort the whole process of tradition, which caused the collection continually to expand, can only be understood against the background of the loss of living authorities in post-exilic Judaism and the consequent enhancing of the reputation of antiquity, as being well-tried and fundamental.

2. I think that this commentary demonstrates that the so-called 'memorial of the prophet Isaiah concerning his activity at the time of the Syro-Ephraimite War' (6.1–8.18) at all events presupposes that the earliest prophecies, contained in chs. 28–31, should be identified with sayings of Isaiah. In turn, the authors of this memorial were influenced by Deuteronomistic theology. On the basis of the accounts contained in the book of Kings, they recognized the significance for the whole of the future history of the kingdom of Judah of the voluntary submission of Ahaz king of Judah (734–715) to Tiglath-pileser III, king of Assyria (745–727), in the face of the

[3] See also Kaiser, *Isaiah 13–39*, 374f., and II Kings 18.13–16.
[4] Cf. e.g. A. H. J. Gunneweg, *Geschichte Israels bis Bar Kochba*, TW 2, Stuttgart [3]1979, 122ff.

threat posed by Israel and the kingdom of Damascus in the so-called Syro-Ephraimite war (734–732). From this they drew the conclusion that at that time the prophet Isaiah had already tried to dissuade the king from this faithless decision and prophesied the downfall of the kingdom.[5] In this way the authors sought to convince their own contemporaries that Yahweh had in fact shown himself to be Lord of history in the catastrophe which befell the people in 587, and accordingly had continued to remain the master of all possibilities, even now.

The heading could only be given its present form, setting the activity of the prophet Isaiah in the reigns of the kings from Uzziah to Hezekiah, after the memorial had been inserted into the original scroll. In this connection, 6.1 may have proved the starting point and the Isaiah narratives in chs. 36–39 the conclusion. The direct influence of the Deuteronomistic history is reflected in the insertion of Jotham between Uzziah and Ahaz,[6] which is historically correct, and probably also in the mention of Judah before Jerusalem.[7] The heading uses the terms for vision and seeing, ḥāzōn and ḥāzā, in quite a weak sense, denoting the receiving of revelation generally; this usage can also be found elsewhere in the headings to the earlier prophetic books and in the titles of the later ones,[8] and need not be taken to mark the prophet out as a visionary.

3. Like the basic material in 28–31, the memorial is based on the belief and trust that Yahweh shows his faithfulness and power by saving his people, and it requires the same belief from the people of its own time. It is obvious that this message called for amplification, indeed demanded it, considering the causes of the catastrophe. In the eyes of the prophets and the Deuteronomistic theology of history, the faithlessness and ingratitude of the people towards their God had manifested themselves not only in a faithless form of politics but also, as a glance at the present could recall, in the social and personal behaviour of the upper classes, who were in a special way responsible for the fate of the people. It is therefore understandable that when the memorial was incorporated in the prophetic scroll it was given a prologue and also an epilogue to underline its message of judgment. The so-called 'Song of the Vineyard' (5.1–7) castigates

[5] See below, 114ff.
[6] Cf. also II Kings 15.32ff.
[7] See also the statistics provided by D. Jones, 'The Tradition of the Oracles of Isaiah of Jerusalem', ZAW 67, 1955, 239 n. 61, and e.g. II Kings 23.1.24; 25.22; also below 69 n. 12.
[8] Cf. Amos 1.1; Micah 1.1 and also Ina Willi-Plein, *Vorformen der Schriftexegese innerhalb des Alten Testaments*, BZAW 123, Berlin and New York 1971, 15, 70, 115; also Hab. 1.1; Obad. 1 and Nahum 1.1; but also Isa. 2.1; 13.1. For the terms see also A. Jepsen, *TWAT* II, cols. 822ff. (*TDOT* 4, 280ff.).

breaches of the law and the suffering that this brings upon ordinary people. The woes contained in 5.8–24 + 10.1–3* specify in detail the general charges made in the Song of the Vineyard, so that the two together show the other causes of the earlier catastrophe and at the same time raise indirectly the question of the future fate of the people. The epilogue, the poem with a refrain mentioning the outstretched hand of Yahweh (9.8–21 [7–20] + 5.26–29), demonstrates in its retrospective survey of the disastrous history of the people and its announcement of the inescapable downfall of the kingdom of Judah, set in the context of Isaiah, that the fate of the two kingdoms of Israel and Judah is the just punishment of Yahweh, at the same time again calling for responsibility on the part of both the rulers and the ruled. This concern for the social dimension can also be found in the instructions about sacrifice in 1.10–17, which denounce as worthless all sacrifice which is not preceded by moral obedience concerned for the well-being of all members of the people. The lament about the faithlessness of Jerusalem expressed in the corruption of the judgment of the rulers (1.21–23a) is a comparable passage and raises for the people the question of the future of their city.

4. The next generation already had the judgment of the world in view, a judgment which was suggested by astronomically based beliefs coming powerfully to the fore in the West, according to which the world-cycle was nearing its end.[9] This belief found expression within chs. 1–12 only at 2.12–17, the announcement of the great Day of Yahweh, and then comes to determine above all the basic stratum of the so-called Isaiah apocalypse in chs. 24–27.[10] Another expectation came to maturity in the shadow of the first, that of the onslaught of the nations against Jerusalem and Judah, which broke over them like a storm, provoked by the arrogance and injustice of the upper classes. Thus 1.21–23a was expanded by vv. 23b–25; in the shade of the announcement of the outbreak of divine wrath against all pride upon the earth (3.1–4.1), the new message of judgment is formulated, and the woes in 5.9f., 12, 14, 17, 19 and 10.3 are accentuated accordingly. At the same time 6.12–13abα; 7.23b, 24, 25a; 8.19–23a, and presumably also 10.28–34*, were probably also added, so that this proclamation then came to underlie 5.26–29. This line can then presumably be traced further through 22.1–14* as far as chs. 28–31, where e.g. 29.1–4 and 32.9–14 take up this message.

5. However, the believer could not be content with the thought that Yahweh had resolved finally to abandon his people, to retreat

[9] Cf. B. L. van der Waerden, 'Das grosse Jahr und die ewige Wiederkehr', *Hermes* 80, 1952, 130ff.; id., *Die Pythagoräer*, Zurich and Munich 1979, 252ff.
[10] Cf. *Isaiah 13–39*, 173ff.

into his initial hiddenness and to give up the promises that he had made. 8.18 was seen as the prophetic declaration of trust, the announcement of hope in the God who dwells on Zion. And in the Deuteronomic history, II Sam. 7 contained the promise made to David that his dynasty would last for ever. So a generation later, attention was again directed to the saving action of Yahweh for his people beyond the future catastrophe, which would leave that of 587 far behind. The Immanuel prophecies in 7.14b–16ba*; 7.21f.; 8.8b*, 9–10 and the messianic prophecies of 9.2–7 [1–6]; 11.1–5 know that the saviour will be born in the time of distress, and that he will renew the dynasty and found the kingdom of eternal peace.

6. Wonder at the past and veneration for the ancient, which increased as time went on, strengthed the pseudepigraphical traits which are evident, at any rate, from the memorial and its setting in the Isaiah scroll. The preservation of Jerusalem in the year 701, presented in highly stylized form so that it becomes the antitype, the counterpart, of the catastrophe of 587,[11] now offered the possibility of speaking of the arrogance of Assyria, the danger posed to Jerusalem by the nations and the saving of the city through the latter's annihilation in a way that was innocuous to outsiders and clear enough to those in the know. It was a way of understanding the collapse of the world power and the peoples who were once again raging against the city of God. This Assyrian revision, with which we may have reached the end of the fifth century, begins in 10.5–15* and is continued in 14.24–27, which were moved to their present position at a later stage. This stratum can be traced through 17.12–14 as far as chs. 28–31; we may count 29.5–8; 30.27–33; 31.4f., 8f., as a part of it.

7. In the end I would prefer to leave open the question whether the historicizing insertions and alterations in 3.8f.; 5.13, 14* (15, 16); 7.1*, 4b, 5b, 8b, 16ba*β, 17b, 18aβ*, bβ, 20aβ*; 8.7 and aβ, 8aα*, 23b and 9, 8aβ, 20a (?) are connected with it or, as I have occasionally suggested in the commentary, give expression to a certain anti-eschatological approach. In principle, this tendency may be connected with the pseudepigraphical concern of the Assyrian revision.

8. Additions like those in 1.26, 27f. are overshadowed by the universal eschatological expectation without giving any indication of belonging to particular strata. The announcement of judgment against those who participate in nature cults in 1.28–31 is also overshadowed by the major revisions. Through 17.7f.; 31.6f. it is possible to trace links which go beyond the collection known as

[11] Cf. also O. Kaiser. 'Geschichtliche Erfahrung und eschatologische Erwartung', *NZST* 15, 1973, 272ff. = *Eschatologie im Alten Testament*, ed. H. D. Preuss, WdF 480, Darmstadt 1978, 444ff.

Proto-Isaiah and presuppose its combination with Trito-Isaiah (cf. 57.5; 65.3b–4, 11–12; 66.17). The insertion of 2.2–5 involved the addition of the heading in 2.1, which is meant to claim for the prophet Isaiah the promise which has also been handed down in the book of Micah.[12] This also, however, called for 2.6–9*, to form a bridge with 2.10–17*. Here once again we have a retrospect over the disastrous history of the nation. At the same time it provided the possibility of stressing clearly the eschatological character of 2.10ff.*, and in 2.18–21 of prophesying the end of the idols and the collapse of the idolaters. This polemic is clearly dependent on sayings like 40.19f.; 41.6f.; 42.17; 44.9–20; 45.16b, 20b; 46.5–8; 48.22, and this in turn demonstrates the connection of the book with the collection known as Deutero-Isaiah.

9. The man who exchanged the final strophe of the poem with its refrain about the outstretched hand of Yahweh (5.26–29) with the final woe in 10.1–3, composed 5.25 as a bridge, and thus gave the strophe a new eschatological significance, was similarly influenced by the universalist expectations which combine notions of judgment and salvation; that is, if we may also ascribe 5.30 to him. By this transposition he dissolved the connection between ch. 5 and the memorial and not only cut the first five chapters clearly away from what follows, but also gave them an appropriate conclusion. However, with its almost puzzling reticence, 5.30 at the same time raises the question how the enemy will meet his fate, and thus points beyond itself to what is to come. Presumably the same hand also transposed 14.24–27 to its present place. It would also be attractive to ascribe 6.13bβ to this editor, who is certainly also responsible for the final revision of the refrain poem, for which he provided a new conclusion in 10.4.

10. These alterations evidently provided the basis for reshaping 10.5–12.6, taking account of existing material, so that it formed a brief history of the end-time. The new additions can of course be recognized as late by their mosaic style and their borrowing of phrases from the book of Isaiah, the Psalter and finally the Song of the Sea (Ex. 15). Thus the message of the remnant can be noted once again in 10.20–23; 10.24–27 sums up ideas from 9.2ff. [1ff.]; 10.5ff. in a new light, and 11.10–16 draws a picture of the messianic age with its restoration of the Davidic kingdom and the return of the prisoners from captivity, whose thanksgiving (12.1–6) has a prophetic tone. The insertion of 10.24–27 at the same time sought a new understanding of 10.33–34, in that the verse is now interpreted in terms of the attacking Assyrians instead of the people of Jerusalem. Perhaps 10.16–19 were also added only as a consequence of these expansions

---

[12] Cf. also P. R. Ackroyd, ZAW 75, 1963, 320f., and SVT 29, 1978, 32f.

and reinterpretations. The notion of a universal peace embracing both men and animals, as expressed in 11.6–8(9), is strangely isolated in this context.

11. In all the exuberance of expectation, anxiety at what is to come and hope for the salvation which will dawn with it, we hear at the end the sober voice of a wisdom which is content with God's ever-active judgment; with barely concealed scepticism, resembling that of the Preacher, it considers the eschatological proclamations and expresses its own thoughts in 2.22; 3.10f.; 5.24. Alongside it, however, we find an expectation of the end which is as fantastic as it is realistic in its own interest; this has found expression in 4.2–6. In its contrast with the words of the wise it documents the antagonism between conservative theocratic Judaism and Judaism with an eschatological bent, which became more pronounced in the Hellenistic period, when the contemporaneous opening up of conservative circles to Greek ideas led to the crisis of the period of the Maccabees.

What is laboriously unearthed by the scholar and reader, bit by bit and step by step, in the end reflects the internal history of post-exilic Jerusalem Judaism, to which the book itself owes its present form. Consequently, the figure of the prophet Isaiah, the son of Amoz, the man whose name probably means 'Yahweh has given aid',[13] and whose father's name, in its full form, means 'Yahweh has proved himself strong',[14] seems to retreat into the shades of legend, in the splendour of which he has become the symbol of divine help for his people and his city. However, where the prophet's words ring out, they are not concerned with human affairs nor with the good fortune and misery of personal experience; they are concerned with the God who down the ages calls men to be his messengers, so that the light of faith, of the fear of God, and of hope is not quenched, and so that men remain human and entrust to God's hands the consummation of history which they themselves are constantly prevented from bringing to pass. Thus in the failure of even specific expectations about the future, God frees himself from human constraints; he encounters man in constantly new ways and at the same time draws him into a future of which he himself remains Lord, even where man can see nothing but death and finitude (25.8a).

Who were the men who make up this chain of witnesses in the tradition of the book of Isaiah? They seem likely to have been the levitical groups from whose numbers the Deuteronomic and Deuteronomistic movement arose. As guilds of singers, at the time of the second temple they entered into the heritage of the pre-exilic

[13] Cf. also M. Noth, *Die israelitischen Personennamen im Rahmen der gemeinsemitischen Namengebung*, BWANT III, 10, Stuttgart 1928 = Hildesheim 1966, no. 772 and p. 176.
[14] Cf. also Noth, *Personennamen*, no. 185 and p. 190.

cultic prophets, who perhaps similarly emerged from this context. So a clarification of the earliest history of the Deuteronomic movement may ultimately also lead to a sharper portrait of the prophet whose name the book bears.

I think that it is possible to recognize the various hopes and ideas of these guilds of singers in the history of the redactions of the collection we call Proto-Isaiah; there are similarities in the Asaph and Korah psalms.[15] Here we see the inheritors and dispensers of the sacral traditions of their people. It is not surprising that they also came to play this role in wisdom thinking, and that their sayings are not only indebted to the spirit of the Deuteronomistic movement, cultic poetry and a study of the prophetic heritage, but also, especially at the beginning and the end, to wisdom. They transmitted the book of Isaiah from one generation to another, and each generation, when its hour came, gave new emphasis and new form to the words which were being handed down. If we allow twenty years for the work of each generation as I have attempted to describe it in the commentary, we still keep essentially within the fifth century BC.[16] In the fourth century, in its new openness to wisdom and early science, eschatological thought seems to have approximated more closely to apocalyptic; at all events, apocalyptic began to develop in the third century.[17] Eschatological thought goes beyond the bounds of death, which up to that point had been strictly observed,[18] dethrones the king of the underworld, the king of terrors (Job 18.14), and makes it possible for the witnesses to the risen Christ to understand the appearances vouchsafed to them as the victory over human failure, despite man's sinfulness, finitude and limitations, ending in his death.

What I have said so far, and the commentary which follows, will certainly cause additional difficulties for the modern reader, who is accustomed to take the details about the authorship of a book literally. The reader might therefore be disposed to see the process of tradition sketched out here as the result of literary forgery.[19] This

[15] Compare Pss. 50; 73–83 with Pss. 42–49; 84–88*; cf. Kaiser, *Introduction*, 351f., and G. Wanke, *Die Zionstheologie der Korachiten*, BZAW 97, Berlin 1966.

[16] The dating of the so-called 'Book of the Watchers' (Enoch 1–36) by J. T. Milik, *The Book of Enoch. Aramaic Fragments of Qumrân Cave 4*, Oxford 1976, 22f., along with reflection on the place of the redactions of the prophetic books and those who carried them out, has led me to abandon the late datings which I put forward in my OTL commentary on Isa. 13–39 and the first edition of this book.

[17] Cf. Milik, op. cit.

[18] Cf. O. Kaiser and E. Lohse, *Tod und Leben*, Kohlhammer Taschenbücher, Biblische Konfrontationen 1001, Stuttgart 1977.

[19] Cf. also in this connection W. Speyer, *Die literarische Fälschung im heidnischen und christlichen Altertum. Ein Versuch ihrer Deutung*, Handbuch der Altertumswissenschaft I, 2, Munich 1971.

would go against his concept of holy scripture, because God's holiness and the truth of his testimony belong together. However, those who concern themselves with the Old Testament or with Near Eastern literature generally have to rid themselves of presuppositions which seem self-evident, and adopt a different approach. This other approach knows nothing of the Western concept of authorship, inherited from the Greeks; its sole concern is to write along the lines of the man who gives his name to a particular book: this is seen as adequate justification for presenting personal views in his name. This way of thinking is not oriented on the personal achievement of an individual, but on the matters with which he is concerned and the God to whom he testifies. When such thinking created new factors in history, as I believe to be the case with the memorial, it was only drawing conclusions from the information at its disposal. Thus, quite analogously to the modern historian, who works in a totally different way, it could believe that it had discovered what actually happened. In our eyes, of course, as the introduction of the sons of Isaiah seems to indicate, this brings it close to symbolic poetry. Here we can recognize that the historical concern of the writers involved in the development of the book of Isaiah was not with the past as such, but with its ideal, typical form and its significance for the time of each particular writer. Thus the prophetic sayings as they had been handed down were not thought to be unalterable; they needed continual reshaping and reinterpretation as history went on. The direct continuation of this process of rewriting, which had long continued from one generation to another, only came to an end when Judaism broke up into rival sects and its writings became known in the Hellenistic world. At that point translations intended primarily for Diaspora Judaism emerged alongside the basic texts, interpretation became detached from the text, and turned into commentary and preaching, as is the case even today.

In fact both forms of tradition, rewriting and exegesis, are concerned with the same task, that of keeping alive the divine testimony of the fathers of the faith for each new generation. And this process will continue so long as men are seized by the content of these scriptures and in the light of their conviction recognize the God who embraces the mystery of all human life at work among themselves and in their world. The only justification for the laborious business of tracing the various stages of the growth of this book, as a theological task, is in the fact that the historical clarification of the circumstances and intentions of the biblical sayings can clarify their connection with the God who is still at work today. To consider them within the horizon of the church, working out their strength and their weaknesses, involves our own Christian faith and our present understanding of the world; for today, as of old, God can only be witnessed and testified to through involvement in the contemporary situation. In this sense there is no such thing as a *theologia perennis*, a theology with particular propositions which are true once and for all, nor is there an exegesis which is valid for all times.

It may be that the witnesses who speak to us in the chapters discussed in the commentary which follows disturb us with their references to the degree to which our own forgetfulness of ourselves and God contributes to our share in responsibility for our own fate and for the future of God in our day. These witnesses may relativize our utopias in the light of their own, which never achieved historical realization, and make us ask once again what is the real content and consummation of human life. If so, they may bring us to an opening where once again we may be encountered by the figure of the man Jesus, crucified and risen. For perhaps what we lack is precisely that element the lack of which they saw as the cause of the downfall of their own people: trust in God.

Chapter 1.2–3

Prologue: Foolish Sons

2   Hear, O heavens, and give ear, O earth,
     for Yahweh is speaking:
     'Sons I reared and brought up,[1]
     but they rebelled against me.
3   The ox knows its owner
     and the ass its master's crib.[2]
     Israel has no knowledge,
     my people shows no insight.'

[2f.] Verses 2 and 3 are clearly divided from the heading in v. 1 and the woe which begins in v. 4; thus in form they are an independent small unit. The construction is simple. The appeal to heaven and earth in v. 2aα and the prophetic quotation formula in v. 2aβ are followed in vv. 2b, 3 by the word of Yahweh. In it, in clear metaphorical language, Yahweh compares his experience with Israel

---

[1] For the syntax of the verb cf. Davidson §58a.
[2] The *pluralis majestatis* may be redactional, so as to refer to Yahweh.

with that of a father whose sons have repaid all his care by breaking off relations with him. Verse 3 evocatively stresses the heedless folly of this reaction of the people towards their God by contrasting it with that of beasts of burden towards their owners.

[2a] Because the content of the word of Yahweh which has been entrusted to him is so unheard of that it cannot be allowed to go unheeded in a world in which the name of this God is known only in Israel, the poet begins by addressing what he has to say to heaven and earth, which for the Hebrew meant the whole world.[3] However, those really addressed are not of course heaven and earth but the members of the community which hears the message of the book of Isaiah. In view of the solemn invocation of heaven and earth, they are to pay heed, be disturbed at the assertions made by God about the conduct of his people, which fluctuate strangely between lament and accusation, and then, by comparing themselves with the animal world, recognize their own folly. Wherever that happens, a child comes to recognize clearly his divine father, and that means giving him the obedience that he is owed.

What this brief section is saying may be easy to understand, but that is not the case when it comes to defining its background in the history of the tradition. To become aware of this difficulty, we need only ask whether heaven and earth are called on as never-failing witnesses to the word of God, or so that they may give the assent expected of them to the verdict passed on the people in v. 3. There is support for both interpretations. According to Deut. 4.26; 30.19, Moses called upon heaven and earth to bear witness to the truth of his words. According to Ps. 50.4, Yahweh himself called upon them when he was judging his people. Accordingly it is possible to interpret v.2aα as an appeal to witnesses and vv. 2b, 3 as an accusation.[4] In the history of religions, the appeal to heaven and earth is a replacement for an appeal to other gods by a reference to the two elements which make up the habitable world (according to pre-scientific and early scientific thought). It took this form because of the exclusive character of the claims of Yahwistic belief. In that case, the history of the tradition underlying the simple structure of the section would have unfolded in many stages. It would have begun with the formulation to be found in the state treaties of the ancient Near East which included as guarantors, alongside others,

---

[3] Cf. e.g. Gen. 1.1.
[4] On this cf. e.g. L. Köhler, *Deuterojesaja (Jesaja 40–55) stilkritisch untersucht*, BZAW 37, Giessen 1923, 111f.; J. Begrich, *Studien zu Deuterojesaja*, BWANT 77, Stuttgart 1938, 19 = ThB 20, Munich 1963, 27; H. J. Boecker, *Redeformen des Rechtslebens im Alten Testament*, WMANT 14, Neukirchen 1964, 83f.

the gods of heaven and earth.[5] The parallel to this formulation in Israel would have been the covenant formula, which expressed in binding form the relationship between the people and Yahweh.[6] Against the background of this notion of this covenant, there would then have developed a cultic contestation and a pattern of procedure according to which Yahweh brought charges against his people through the mouth of his prophets.[7]

On the other hand, we should not fail to notice that the closest parallel to the appeal to heaven and earth as found in the present section appears in Deut. 32.1. Of course there it is subsequently interpreted as a call to witness by means of 31.28, but we may be certain that heaven and earth were originally summoned to hear so that in the end they could join in the praise of this God (cf. 32.3b).[8] From this perspective, then, it is a matter of making the basic powers of the world themselves hear the word of God and confirm his judgment.[9]

Only a moment's thought will show that in the end the actual difference between these two positions is small. The distinction lies above all in the background that is presupposed and in the further assessment of Yahweh's speech. If we begin by taking v. 2aα as a summons to witnesses, we shall necessarily understand the passage as an accusation. However, the defection of a son from his father was quite unheard-of in antiquity; as unheard-of as the summons

---

[5] Almost all the works mentioned in the following note give examples. Cf. e.g. the treaty of the Hittite king Muršilši II with Duppi-Tešup of Amurru from the fourteenth century BC in K. Baltzer, *The Covenant Formulary*, Oxford 1971, 182ff., the treaty between Bargaya of KTK and Mati'el of Arpad, *KAI* 222 A 7ff. from the eighth century, and the vassal treaty of the Assyrian sovereign Esarhaddon from the seventh century BC in D. J. Wiseman, *Vassal-Treaties of Esarhaddon*, London 1958, 31f.

[6] On this cf. above all G. E. Mendenhall, 'Ancient Oriental and Biblical Law', *BA* 17, 2, 1954, 26ff.; id., 'Covenant Forms in Israelite Tradition', *BA* 17, 3, 1954, 50ff. = *Recht und Bund in Israel und im Alten Orient*, ThSt(B) 64, Zurich 1960; K. Baltzer (n. 5); W. Beyerlin, *Origins and History of the Oldest Sinaitic Tradition*, ET Oxford 1961; also D. J. McCarthy, *Treaty and Covenant*, AnBib 21 A, Rome ²1978, especially 277ff., which is based on research carried out hitherto.

[7] For the discussion of the background of Isa. 1. in a *rīb* pattern, in which Yahweh makes a reckoning with his people, who are bound to him through the covenant, see most recently Vermeylen I, 50ff., and for the starting point still E. Würthwein, 'Der Ursprung der prophetischen Gerichtsrede', *ZTK* 49, 1952, 1ff. = *Wort und Existenz*, Göttingen 1970, 111ff., together with Wildberger's interpretation, ad loc.; Schedl. *Rufer des Heils*, ad loc., and Hoffman, *Intention*, 82f.

[8] For the evidence cf. C. Steuernagel, HK I, 3,1, Göttingen ²1923, ad loc., and for the 'summons to receive instruction', H. W. Wolff, *Hosea*, Hermeneia, Philadelphia 1974, 96, and the conclusions drawn from this by Ilse von Loewenclau, 'Zur Auslegung von Jesaja 1, 2–3', *EvTh* 26, 1966, 294ff. For criticism of the *rīb* pattern which is presupposed cf. Whedbee, *Isaiah and Wisdom*, 28ff.

[9] Cf. also Ilse von Loewenclau, 305, though she settles too one-sidedly for the lament.

issued to Abraham to leave his ancestral home and go abroad into the unknown (Gen. 12.1). If a father's attempts to educate his son by admonitions and corporal punishment were to no avail, he could ask the local assembly of elders to investigate the son's disobedience; if need be, the son could be punished by death (Deut. 21.18ff.). However, if a father speaks of the inconceivable behaviour of his sons, that need not necessarily be understood as a legal accusation; a father has paternal feelings and sorrows even in the case of a son who has gone astray. So there is an indefinite element in the remarks in these two verses: they can be understood as an accusation which at any time can be implemented at law. In the light of vv. 4ff., which follows, we may say that at any moment Yahweh can proceed to the next, and now final, annihilating blow against his people. In that case heaven and earth would bear witness to the justice of his action (cf. Ps. 50.6). But at the same time we can and should also understand the words as the lament of the father who sadly looks at the course his children are taking and describes what he sees, provided that in addition we do not forget the inexorable demand for obedience which underlies this.

[2b–3] Yahweh says that he has reared and brought up his sons. We should not divide this expression into two distinct successive acts of nurture: while the child is growing up and subsequent provision of an adequate and respectable position in life. The two terms should be taken as synonymous (cf. 23.4; also Ezek. 31.4). Of course the substance of the saying is that Yahweh, from small beginnings, made Israel his people and gave them the land (cf. Deut. 32.8ff.). In Israel, as in any society which has not gone out of its mind, it was taken for granted that the son would be obedient to his father and respect his mother (cf. Prov. 23.22); the chastising of the disobedient and foolish son is seen as a duty, indeed as a sign of love (Prov. 13.24; cf. 13.1).

It is striking that while Israel is expressly said to be made up of sons of Yahweh, he himself is not designated their father. The reason for this restraint, which is characteristic of the Old Testament, may be seen to be the concern to preserve the distinction between God and man, creator and creature, and thus keep distinct from the monophysitism of the surrounding world which ascribed to gods and men an infinite quantitative, but in no way qualitative difference. In the Old Testament, man does not share in God's nature, but is merely endowed with the divine breath of life (Gen. 2.7; Eccles. 12.7); he is not in any way distinguished from the animal world (Ps. 104.30; Eccles. 3.19ff.). In the view of the prophets, the sonship of Israel was grounded in Yahweh's calling of Israel out of Egypt (cf. Hos. 11.1; Jer. 3.19; Ex. 4.22). And if, according to the tradition that we now have, Yahweh is addressed for the first time as 'our father' in Isa. 63.16, the thought is of his intervention as an advocate for Israel, one who represents his enslaved people as though they were orphans. The notional connection between God as creator and God as father is the basis for the derivation of the appeal either to his fatherly mercy on his creatures (cf. Isa. 64.7), or to the obligation of these creatures to show solidarity among one another and towards their creator (cf. Mal. 2.10).[10]

To break with one's father remained unheard-of; going away was a criminal offence.[11] It is clear from the following verses that Yahweh has not yet made a decision to resort to a final expedient, though this is within the realm of possibility.[12] Thus in fact it is important not to be over-hasty in removing the situation from the ambiguity intended by the poet through an approach to its elements which is one-sidedly oriented on form criticism.

[3] This shows clear links with wisdom, which is the natural setting for comparisons with animals (cf. Prov. 6.66ff.; 30.24ff.). In terms of both form and content, the nearest parallel to v. 3 is in Jer. 8.7, where the failure of the people to discern the ordinance of Yahweh is similarly contrasted with the wisdom of animals.[13] Talk of knowledge and insight in all its different aspects is similarly originally a feature of wisdom,[14] and presupposes that it is possible for men to elucidate their position and calling in the world adequately by means of their reason. We do not find the modern contrast between a rational capacity limited to the sphere of experience of the world and a supernatural knowledge of God resting on a particular revelation, which is in any case very problematical. Rather, the one embraces the other and at the same time ensures an appropriate approach to the world (cf. Prov. 1.7; 9.10; 15.33).

A people which does not know and recognize its God and father is more irrational than the cattle who are well able to distinguish their owner and master from any other person, and can find the way back to their master's yard and manger from the fields or from a ride without getting lost.[15] Israel's lack of insight is unreal (cf. 29.9f.; 5.13; 6.9; 32.3f.), and puts its very existence at risk.

The purely literary character of the prologue emerges from the fact that no firm content is given to the accusations which it contains,

---

[10] On this see also H. Ringgren, *TWAT* I, cols. 16ff. (TDOT 1, 16ff.).
[11] Cf. Deut. 21.18ff. For the phrase here cf. also Hos. 7.13; Isa. 43.27; Jer. 2.8; 33.8; Ezek. 2.3, and also, on the same term, R. Knierim, *THAT* II, col. 490.
[12] Cf. below, p. 19.
[13] Cf. Vermeylen I, 63f., and also below, p. 45 n. 34.
[14] Cf. e.g. Prov. 19.25; 29.7; Job 38.4.
[15] From the Akkadian *abūsu, AHw* I, 9b; this need not necessarily be restricted to the manger, as it also includes the place for unharnessing or the stall.

so that to understand them the reader has to carry on reading, and therefore was originally pointed beyond 1.4–6*; 1.18f. to the basic stratum of chs. 28–31. The prologue shares this characteristic with 1.4ff.; 1.18f., and together with these units was intended to form the introduction to the original scroll of the book. An investigation of the cultural context of the author confirms this assumption: the conception of the Israelites as sons rebelling against Yahweh recurs in 30.1, and the charge of lack of insight, indeed blindness, in 29.9f. Furthermore, there is clear mention of the people as sons of the divine father in the hymn of Moses (Deut. 32). Because of the state of the text, a charge made against the people in v. 5 can no longer be elucidated properly.

In v. 6 they are said to be foolish because they are ungrateful to the father who created them, and a historical explanation of Yahweh's paternal care and the ingratitude of the people is given in vv. 8–18. The accusation that the sons are unfaithful is repeated in v. 20; this time it can clearly be discerned from the wording, and in v. 21 is explained in terms of idolatry. Finally, in vv. 28f. there is a further attack on the foolishness of the people, because they do not recognize the defeat inflicted on them, by an enemy who is in no way superior numerically, as the consequence of their being abandoned by Yahweh (cf. also Isa. 30.17). There is a parallel in the Song of Moses (v. 1), and in three further passages in Deuteronomy, to the striking way in which the address to heaven and earth in v. 2a of the prologue is bracketted off from the divine discourse and must therefore be regarded as a word of the prophet. Thus we can hardly avoid the conclusion that the author of the prologue is influenced by Deuteronomy, though we might hesitate to think in terms of any direct literary dependence.[16] If I was right earlier in my interpretation of chs. 28–31, finding in its basic material the traces of a revision made either in the late pre-exilic or the exilic period,[17] we are advised to date the present saying as late as the sixth, or perhaps even better in

---

[16] Earlier scholars like K. Budde, *Das Lied Mose's Deut 32*, Tübingen 1920, and E. Sellin, 'Wann wurde das Moselied Dtn 32 gedichtet?', *ZAW* 43, 1925, 161ff., who indicated the sixth or fifth centuries, may have been more correct than, for example O. Eissfeldt, *Das Lied Moses Deuteronomium 32, 1–43 und das Lehrgedicht des Asaph Psalm 78*, SSAW 104,5 Berlin 1958, and G. E. Wright, 'The Lawsuit of God: A Form-Critical Study of Deuteronomy 32', in *Israel's Prophetic Heritage*, Festschrift J. Muilenburg, London and New York 1962, 26ff. Cf. also the criticism by Vermeylen I, 68. The relationship between 1.3 and Jer. 8.7, along with other parallels between the two books, calls for a separate investigation. It has not been demonstrated that Jer. 3.8 is the model for the present passage.

[17] On this cf. *Isaiah 13–39*, 234, and, on 30.8ff., ibid., 292ff.

the early fifth century BC.[18] By dating it in this period I am in no way belittling the achievement of the man who by his own command of language and ability to develop sharp antitheses created a prelude which makes an unforgettable impression on the mind of the hearer and transcends time in making him ask about his relationship with God, on whom he may call as a father through his discipleship of Jesus, and in whom he may put his trust.

Perhaps it will contribute to restoring true biblical depth to the Christmas story if, in conclusion, I point out that the animals which are an indispensable part of our picture of the crib, the ox and the ass, have been inserted into the Christmas landscape by virtue of the understanding of v. 3a as a prophecy of Christ's birth.[19] Against the background of the prologue to Isaiah they warn men not to be more senseless than animals, and to recognize where their Lord encounters them and God discloses himself to them in the trustworthiness indicated by his name of Father.

CHAPTER 1.4–9

To the Survivors

4   **Woe, sinful nation,**
       a people laden with guilt,
       brood of criminals,
       band of evildoers.
       They have forsaken Yahweh,
       despised the Holy One of Israel,
       drawn themselves back.

5   **Where[1] will you still be smitten,**
       that you continue to rebel?

[18] Cf. also Vermeylen I, 63f., 70f. – L. Rignell, *Isaiah Chapter I*, ST 11, 1957, 141f., has already called attention to this dependence on the nucleus of Deuteronomy. As he did not question that this section of the chapter and the one which follows were composed by Isaiah, he came to the conclusion that Deuteronomy is older than Isaiah. For this cf. Kaiser, *Introduction*, 118ff.

[19] For this see the Gospel of Pseudo-Matthew 14,1ff., in Hennecke-Schneemelcher-Wilson, *New Testament Apocrypha* I, London 1963, 410, and e.g. the representation of the birth of Jesus in the small travel notebook from Palestine (end of the sixth century) preserved in the Vatican collections, in P. Hinz, *Deus Homo* I, Berlin/DDR 1973, plate 129.

[1] For the vocalization of the interrogative pronoun cf. G-K[28] § 37e.

The whole[2] head is sick,
and the whole[2] heart faint.

6   From the crown of the head
to the soul of the foot
there is no point in him whole,[3]
but bruising and boils,
and fresh wounds,
They are not pressed out,[4] nor bound up,
nor softened with oil.[5]

7   Your country – a desolation!
Your cities – burnt with fire![6]
Your land – in your very presence
aliens devour it <   >[7]!

8   And the daughter of Zion is left
like a booth in a vineyard,
like[8] a lodge in a cucumber field,
<like a refuge in the sheepfold>[9]!

9   If Yahweh Sebaoth
had not left us a remnant,[10]
we should almost have become like Sodom,
we should have been like Gomorrah!

[4–9] The initial 'Woe' indicates that a new unit begins in v. 4, and the fact that it ends in v. 9 is indicated by the new opening of v. 10. However, on closer investigation the section 1.4–9 proves to consist of a number of pieces. At first glance we might bring vv. 4–6 and 7–9 together, the first presenting the imagery and the second the content; however, it soon emerges that the two halves do not fit together at all; whereas vv. 5f. are concerned with the state of the people, the two following verses (vv. 7f.) are concerned with the

---

[2] Cf. G-K[28] § 127c.

[3] For $m^e t\bar{o}m$ cf. B-L 493d.

[4] For the passive form of the qal cf. G-K[28] §67m, 52e or B-L 287h.

[5] For the construction cf. G-K[28] § 144b.

[6] For the passive participle in the construct state before a causative genitive cf. G-K[28] § 1161.

[7] 'And the desert is like the conversion of aliens', or corrected to 'of Sodom', along the lines of v. 9, is the addition of a later reader, spurred on by w. 9f.

[8] But cf. BHS.

[9] M: 'Like a watched over/preserved city' does not fit in the context. Despite Duhm and Kaiser[1], it must be accepted that Dillmann-Kittel and Wildberger, ad loc., are right in arguing that the meaning 'watch' cannot be extracted from the Hebrew $\hat{\imath}r$ in the present text. Marti's reference to II Kings 17.9 does not change this at all. We should therefore perhaps read $k^e\hat{e}ser\ b^e s\bar{\imath}r\bar{a}$, cf, the Arabic $'aṣar^{un}$, 'refuge', and $ṣ\bar{\imath}r\bar{a}$, 'fold'.

[10] Cf. BHS. For the construction cf. Ps. 94.17.

state of the land and the city of Jerusalem. Over against this, v. 9 in
turn occupies a special position because it abandons the standpoint
taken up in vv. 4–8 of being set over against the people, and now
tends rather towards identification with them. Furthermore, the
first half draws on Ps. 94.17 and the second on v. 10. Therefore we
may immediately eliminate v. 9 as being redactional.[11] It is not so
certain whether from the fact that the perspective in v. 8 narrows
towards Jerusalem, in contrast to that of the preceding verses, we
may draw the conclusion that here we have another addition;
however, in view of the fact that the saying against Jerusalem in vv.
21ff.[12] evidently has the same specialization and, as will emerge
later, is similarly redactional, it is highly probable that this is the
case.[13] But if that is so, the transition from the people to the land in
v. 7 may also be an addition. Its dependence on Lev. 26.33 and the
way in which its content echoes Deut. 28.51 make it at least exilic. It
is almost universally conceded that in bβ the verse has been further
expanded under the influence of vv. 9, 10. It is difficult to know
what to make of v. 4b. In view of the evidence of the Septuagint, the
Greek Bible, which omits it, the last clause of the verse seems to be
a very late expansion.[14] There is some argument as to whether we
should also exclude the rest, because it represents a disruption
between v. 4a and v. 5 and has elements of prose style.[15] The
suspicion that a later editor did not find the charges raised in the first
half of the verse precise enough and expanded them with material
from the Deuteronomistic repertory[16] is so great that here too we
seem led to think in terms of a later interpretation. Consideration of
the origin of the nucleus which remains, in vv. 4a, 5, 6*, is likely to
remind us of 30.1, 9, and also 1.2b. We cannot rule out the possibility
that this once belonged in the context of chs. 28–31, though again
there is no proof. The fact that no firm basis is given for the charges
made, as in 1.2f., suggests that we should regard the small poem as
a saying which has also been created for its present position.[17] The
divine accusation is now answered by a prophetic voice uttering a

[11] Cf. also F. Crüsemann, *Studien zur Formgeschichte von Hymnus und Danklied in Israel*, WMANT 32 .Veukirchen 1969, 163f., and H. Barth, *Jesaja-Worte*, 190f.
[12] Cf. below,
[13] Cf. also V .meylen I, 52, though he attributes vv. 8 and 9 to the same stratum.
[14] Cf. 42.17; Ps. 35.4; 40.15; 44.19; 70.3; Ezek. 14.5.
[15] With Marti and Gray, ad loc., and Donner, *Israel unter den Völkern*, 120.
[16] Cf. e.g. I Kings 9.9 par. II Chron. 7.22; Hos. 4.10; Judg. 2.12f. or Num. 16.30; Deut. 31.20 and Ps. 74.18; also Isa. 5.24.
[17] Cf. above, 14f., and Vermeylen, I, 50ff., and 70.

cry of woe which again is strangely somewhere between a threat, a rebuke and a lament.[18]

[1.4–6] *The smitten and disobedient people.* With an outbreak of passion, the speaker lets fly at the people in order to break down the stubborness of those who survived the catastrophe of 587. In his view these survivors have still not drawn the right conclusion from their defeats and suffering. They have to acknowledge Yahweh as their lord and trust and obey him unconditionally (cf. 30.9ff.). In describing his people as sinful and guilt-laden, the poet is introducing two fundamental theological Old Testament concepts, those of sin and guilt. The basic meaning of the verb *ḥāṭā'*, which I have translated 'sin', is 'to fall short' (cf. Judg. 20.16). When it is transferred to human conduct, it produces a concept of order measuring deviation from an ideal order which really requires another way of life (cf. e.g. Prov. 19.2). In the world of religion, this deviation goes against the form of conduct expected and required by Yahweh; it therefore becomes objective failure or sin.[19] The development of the meaning of the word *'āwōn*, which I have translated 'guilt', followed a similar course. Here too the underlying verb *'iwwā* denotes a change of movement, in the sense of to 'diverge, run astray, deviate, bend'. The term can be used quite literally, in the statement that Yahweh 'bends' the surface of the earth (24.1). The metaphorical significance emerges almost automatically in a similar application, for example, to the distortion of justice (Job 33.27). In some circumstances the intended character of the action can be given particular emphasis by the context, because the word has certain intrinsically purposive connotations. The noun 'guilt' denotes both incurring guilt and the corresponding punishment (cf. Lev. 5.1). God does not fail to respond to the disruption of order brought about by men.[20] So here the threatening 'Woe' is directed against a people which has transgressed both objectively and subjectively against its God and thus has to bear its guilt. Calling the people a brood of criminals (cf. 14.20), sons who act corruptly, not only stresses their own responsibility but introduces the historical dimension: the sons are continuing their fathers' behaviour![21]

[18] Cf. Vermeylen I, 50ff., and above, 11. In its present form, 1.4–8 combines in a remarkable way, reminiscent of 1.2f., elements of threat, rebuke and lament, though on the whole the character of the rebuke is predominant. Cf. also G. Fohrer, 'Jesaja 1 als Zusammenfassung der Verkündigung Jesajas', in *Studien zur alttestamentlichen Prophetie*, BZAW 93, Berlin 1967, 153; Vollmer, *Geschichtliche Rückblicke*. 166, and W. Janzen, *Mourning Cry and Woe Oracle*, BZAW 125, Berlin and New York 1972, 56f.

[19] Cf. also R. Knierim, *THAT* I, col. 543.

[20] Cf. also R. Knierim, *THAT* II, cols. 243ff.; id., *Hauptbegriffe für Sünde im Alten Testament*, Gütersloh 1965, 235ff.

[21] For the *mᵉrē'îm*, the evildoers, cf. also Ps. 22.17 and also the analogous statements in Ps. 26.5; 64.3. For the *mašḥitîm*, the spoilers, cf. also Gen. 18.28.

[5–6] These verses compare the state of the people with that of a slave or a son who is flogged because of persistent rebelliousness (cf. 30.1, 9; also Deut. 21.18ff.).[22] Using the rod on a son was regarded as a necessary means of education (Prov. 23.13f.; 29.15; 13.24). If repeated chastisements did not induce submission in him, parents could bring the case before elders who in some circumstances could decide that the son should be stoned. And if flogging a freeman was thought to be legitimate, it was certainly legitimate to flog a slave. If the slave survived this ill-treatment for only a day, his master incurred no penalty (Ex. 21.20f.). According to rabbinic law, a master who had killed an Israelite slave was exiled in the same way as a father who had killed his son (cf. b. Makkoth III, 1 and fol. 8b).[23] Only a few comments are necessary on the medical aspect of the passage: the body of the person who has been flogged displays clear marks where the blood vessels have been ruptured under the surface (haematomata), fresh, suppurating weals, and open wounds. It is obvious that both the head and the heart of someone who has been flogged many times in short succession will both be affected: even if his wounds do not produce fever, his circulation is likely to be severely impaired. The sequence in the list of treatments not applied, which appears in the same form in Luke 10.34, is quite remarkable: here binding up precedes the softening of the scabs on the wounds with oil.[24] The divine father has already chastized the people over whom he laments (vv. 2f.) to the limits of what they can bear. There is no room for further visitations. So will God leave them to disaster, because even now they will not give up their disobedience?

If we are looking for a historical context for this saying, we might put it after the great catastrophe of 587, in which the body of the people really was smitten and the kingdom destroyed.

[7] *The land, devastated and occupied.* The editor breaks up the imagery and recalls the situation of the people still for the most part living in the land, even after some of them had been carried off to captivity in Babylon, the Golah, and others scattered, especially to Egypt, in the Diaspora.[25] They had to suffer the hardships of life under occupying forces, and conditions in their largely devastated homeland. Things may have seemed even worse than in 701, when

---

[22] In my view, and against Wildberger, the question in v. 5a excludes the interpretation of *makkāh*, blow, as sickness, though this is quite possible in itself (cf. e.g. Lev. 26.21; Deut. 28.59, 61; 29.21). In addition, there is a logical connection between the punishment of a rebel (cf. also 30.1; 31.1 with Deut. 21.18ff.) and flogging.

[23] Cf. also e.g. D. M. MacDowell, 'The Law in Classical Athens', *Aspects of Greek and Roman Life*, London 1978, 80f., 129ff.

[24] For this cf. also J. Jeremias, *The Parables of Jesus*, ET London ³1972, 204f.

[25] On this cf. E. Janssen, *Juda in der Exilszeit*, FRLANT 69, Göttingen 1956, 39ff.

the Assyrian king Sennacherib boasted that he had sacked forty-six fortified cities and numerous small places and had deported their inhabitants,[26] at the conclusion of the eighteen-months' siege of Jerusalem by the Babylonian king Nebuchadnezzar.[27] In 701, Isaiah could only have said with qualifications that the land had been devastated and its cities burnt down. An attempt has been made to connect the Assyrian reports about the defection of the conquered cities to the Philistine kings of Ashdod, Ekron and Gaza with the present verse to produce a reconstruction of a situation in which the whole of the kingdom of Judah was divided up, with the exception of its capital.[28] However, as there is no trace of these measures anywhere in the sources, this can be no more than a figment of the imagination. Quite apart from the fact that this view is undermined by the dating of the verse proposed here, there was already an earlier suggestion that the conquests and subsequent divisions of territory by Sennacherib were limited to the cities of the Shephelah, lying to. the west of the hill-country of Judah, and a number of other fortresses (cf. Micah 1.10ff.; II Kings 19.8 par. Isa. 37.8). In favour of this view it can be argued that thirty-nine places in the Shephelah of Judah are mentioned only in Josh. 15.33ff.[29] On the other hand, the destruction of the kingdom of Judah and its transformation first into a Babylonian and then into a Persian province provide the political presuppositions for the lament that foreigners are consuming the produce of the fields before the eyes of the people. Here, in addition to Bedouin forays, we should think of the claim on substantial parts of the harvest by the occupying forces and even of regular requisitions of houses and property (cf. Lam. 5.2, 4, 9; Isa. 62.8f.; 65.21f.).[30]

[8] *The lodge in the cucumber field*. Jerusalem, proud and thought to be impregnable (Lam. 4.12), the capital referred to as daughter by poets and named Zion after the temple mount (cf. 10.32; 16.1; II Kings 19.21 par. Isa. 37.22),[31] was caused bitter suffering by the destruction inflicted by its conquerors, the breaches made in its walls, and the burning of the gates and the homes of the nobility, not to mention the temple and the royal palace (cf. II Kings 25.8ff.; Neh. 2.11ff.).

[26] Cf. *TGI*², no. 39, 68; *AOT*², 353 or *ANET*²⁻³, 288a.
[27] Cf. also Janssen, op. cit., 42ff.
[28] Cf. also A. Alt, 'Die territorialgeschichtliche Bedeutung von Sanheribs Eingreifen in Palästina', *KS* II, 242ff.
[29] Cf. Y. Aharoni, *The Land of the Bible*, London 1967, 340; A. H. J. Gunneweg, *Geschichte Israels bis Bar Kochba*, TW 2, Stuttgart ²1979, 118; for his interpretation of II Kings 18.8 cf. also J. Gray, *I & II Kings*, OTL, London ²1970, ad loc.
[30] Cf. also Kaiser, ATD 16, 2, *Klagelieder*, and C. Westermann, *Isaiah 40–66*, OTL, London 1969, ad loc.
[31] Cf. also Micah 1.13; 4.8; 10, 13; Zeph. 3.14; Jer. 4.31; 6.2, 23; and e.g. Lam. 2.1.

As a result it became *de facto* an open city, given over to the attacks of any plunderers. This condition was only remedied when the walls were rebuilt in the second half of the fifth century BC by Nehemiah, a governor in the service of the Persians. Despite their limited extent, the excavations on the south-eastern hill of Jerusalem by Kathleen M. Kenyon have shown that the destruction of the city wall running along the foot of this hill produced such considerable erosion that the whole of the terraced part of the city on this side of the slope fell away.[32] On the other hand, we know nothing about any destruction of Jerusalem in 701.[33]

It is in accordance with the evidence that the editor interested in the fate of Jerusalem should compare the city in v. 8 with the temporary shelter afforded to farmers and shepherds against inclement weather by huts of the kind that travellers can still see even today in fields in the countries of Asia Minor (cf. also Jer. 10.5; Job 27.18; Isa. 24.20).[34] With the picture of the destruction of their city before their eyes, the inhabitants of Jerusalem are asked whether they want to experience the complete annihilation of their city or whether they will turn to Yahweh and see its restoration.

[4b] *Apostasy from Yahweh*. The vagueness of the charges made in v. 4a has led a later reader to supply the deficiency which he felt and to fill in the gap in the spirit of a Deuteronomistic theology oriented on the book of Deuteronomy; he reduces this to the formula of apostasy from Yahweh and a turning away towards other gods.[35] He stresses the danger of this conduct by taking up the designation of Yahweh as 'the Holy One of Israel', a term typical of the book of Isaiah.[36] To speak of God as the Holy One was presumably something which the Israelites took over from the Canaanites. The pre-Israelite cultic traditions of Jerusalem could have played a mediating role here.[37] As the Holy One of Israel, Yahweh lays claim to its possession and the obedience of his people (cf. also Josh. 24.18). The prophetic admonition to heed this demand is answered, according to 30.11; 5.19, with more or less sceptical mockery. The frivolity to be found

---

[32] On this cf. K. M. Kenyon, *Royal Cities of the Old Testament*, London 1971, 148ff., or id., *Digging up Jerusalem*, London 1974, and esp. 170f.; the best account is *PEQ* 94, 1962, 72ff.; 95, 1963, 7ff.

[33] Consequently what is evidently the provisional dating of 1.4-7abα in the eighth or even the seventh century by Vermeylen I, 55 is surprising.

[34] On this cf. also G. Dalman, *Arbeit und Sitte in Palästina* I, Gütersloh 1928, 161; II, 1932, 61.

[35] Cf. the evidence in n. 16, p. 18 above.

[36] Cf. 5.19; 30.11f., 15; 31.1; also 5.24; 10.20; 12.6; 17.7; 29.19, 23; 37.23 par. II Kings 9.22; 41.14, etc.; 58.13, etc.; also Jer. 50.29; 51.5; Ps. 71.22; 89.19.

[37] Cf. W. H. Schmidt, 'Wo hat die Aussage: Jahwe "der Heilige" ihren Ursprung?', *ZAW* 74, 1962, 62ff.

here is particularly clear in the light of the epiphany of the thrice-holy one as it is depicted in ch. 6.[38]

[9] *Survival as grace*. If the verses discussed hitherto all pointed to the danger in the situation, the wrath of God which still hung over the people, and thus indirectly to their penitence and conversion, a last hand added the comforting yet demanding notion that survival[39] itself is a sign of the grace of Yahweh (cf. Ps. 94.17). If everything happened only in terms of law and righteousness, there would be no escape from the divine judgment. This conclusion is drawn by the scribe from the story of the two cities of Sodom and Gomorrah (cf. Gen. 19.24f.),[40] which he knew, and the address to the authorities and the people which follows in v. 10.

CHAPTER 1.10–17

Obedience and Sacrifice

10 Hear the word of Yahweh,
  you rulers of Sodom!
  Give ear to the teaching of our God,
  you people of Gomorrah!
11 'What to me is the multitude of your sacrifices?'
  says Yahweh.
  'I have had enough of burnt offerings of rams
  and the fat of fed beasts;
  The blood of bulls <>[1] and of he-goats
  does not please me.
12 When you come <to see>[2] my face,
  ....[3]

[38] For this cf. below, 128, and H.-P. Müller, *THAT* II, cols. 597ff.
[39] For the phrase cf. also Num. 21.35; Deut. 2.34; Josh. 8.22; II Kings 10.11; Lam. 2.22; Jer. 31.2 etc.
[40] Cf. also Deut. 29.22; Isa. 13.19; Jer. 49.18; 50.40; Amos 4.11; also Isa. 1.10; 3.9; Lam. 4.6; Ezek. 16.46ff. and Zeph 2.9; Deut. 32.32.
[1] LXX omits 'and lambs', probably rightly. It disrupts the listing in order of the size of the animals and the two-membered parallelism to aβ, and is to be taken as a gloss.
[2] Read *lir'ōt* instead of the *niphal*. The Jewish tradition, which can also be detected in LXX and V, has altered the earlier cultic formula, which it now found offensive, to accord with its later conception of God which maintained a marked distinction between him and the world.
[3] Presumably half a line has been omitted here, cf. 25 below.

Who has required this of you,[4]
to trample my courts?
13   Do not continue to bring me vain offerings,
the smoke of sacrifices, which is an abomination to me.
New moon and sabbath and the calling of assemblies –
I cannot endure wickedness[5] and festivals.
14   Your new moons and your feast days,
my soul hates.[6]
They have become burdens to me;
I am weary of bearing them.
15   When you spread your hands out,
I will hide my eyes from you.
However much you pray,
I will not listen.
Your hands are full of blood.[7]
16   Wash yourselves; make yourselves clean;
remove the evil of your deeds
from my eyes.
Cease to do evil,
17   learn to do good.
Seek justice,
help <the oppressed>[8].
Defend the fatherless,
plead for the widow.

[10–17] The present text, a prophetic instruction on sacrifice or a sacrifice Torah, is one of the most significant texts in the book of Isaiah from a historical point of view, though at the same time it is one over which there is the most dispute. Fortunately, however, thanks to the drama of its poetry, it is also one of the most impressive sayings in the book, so that it transcends all scholarly arguments in capturing the mind of anyone who reads it with attention or listens to it carefully. The main problem in elucidating it, which has been discussed a great deal, is whether it is meant to reject sacrifice in principle or whether it is concerned with cultic regulations connected with a particular situation.[9] In addition, in connection with the

[4] Literally, by your hands.
[5] Instead of this, LXX reads, ṣōm, fasts.
[6] Cf. also Brockelmann, §35b.
[7] IQIs[a] adds: your fingers in guilt.
[8] Read ḥāmūṣ, with LXX A, Σ, Θ, V and T.
[9] For this see on the one hand e.g. Duhm, Marti, Gray and Eichrodt ad loc., and especially R. Hentschke, Die Stellung der vorexilischen Schriftpropheten zum Kultus, BZAW 75, Berlin 1957, 94ff., and on the other hand e.g. Feldmann, Procksch, Fischer, Kissane, Hertzberg, Steinmann, Herntrich, Penna, Fohrer, Kaiser[1], Wildberger and Auvray ad loc., and especially E. Würthwein, 'Kultpolemik oder Kultbescheid?', in Tradition und Situation, FS Artur Weiser, Göttingen 1963, 115ff. = Wort und Existenz, Göttingen 1970, 144ff.

present commentary the question arises whether critical scholarship
hitherto is right in its unanimous opinion that the passage goes back
to the prophet Isaiah, so that it can go on to discuss whether it is to
be assigned to an earlier or a later period of his activity; perhaps, like
the two preceding sayings in 1.2f., 1.4ff., it derives from an anonymous prophetic writer of the early post-exilic period working against
the background of the second temple.

The extent of the saying is evident. It begins with the summons to
receive instruction in v. 10.[10] In vv. 11–17 there follows the word of
God, manifested by its content and by the quotation formula in v.
11aα2, of which the prophet is the vehicle. The repeated prophetic
quotation formula in v. 18a shows that a new unit begins at that
point. Within the words of God contained in vv. 11–17 there are a
number of striking features. First of all, there is no parallel statement
to v. 12a. If we suppose that half a line has fallen out here, we find
that we have a poem of two strophes, each comprising nine lines,
the first of which ends after v. 13. Acceptance of this division reduces
the second problem, the fact that the same word appears at the
beginning of v. 13b and v. 14a. Finally, it is unusual that the
parallelism is abandoned in the sequence made up of v.15b and v.
16aα. In fact the great Isaiah manuscript from Qumran Cave 1 has
inserted 'Your fingers in guilt' after 'Your hands are full of blood.'[11]
However, this addition leads to further disruptions in the structure
and therefore does not commend itself.

A few general observations and comments are necessary if we are
to understand the remarkable form, the content and the situation
which is either presupposed or envisaged by the prophetic writer.
In Israel, we should not suppose that the work of the priests and the
prophets was completely distinct. With different degrees of exclu-
siveness, the work of both these groups was connected with the
temple, as the place of the presence of God, who approached the
community for sacrifices of intercession and thanksgiving. It was
here that the priest carried out his daily service in concern for the
temple as the house of God; here he offered sacrifice for the people
and each of its members in the daily acts of worship and those
provided for special occasions. In the temple forecourts he instructed
the people about correct sacrifice, as about purity and impurity,
decided the cases presented to him and gave rulings about sacrifices
and purity. In matters of the acceptance or rejection of a sacrifice and
thus of the hearing or rejection of the petition connected with it,
over the course of time the place of the technical priestly oracle seems
to have been taken by the inspired oracle of the cultic prophet,

[10] Cf. also 12 n. 8 above.
[11] Cf. also n. 7.

whose task it therefore was to make a cultic ruling. In a whole series of psalms of individual lamentation we find a remarkable change of mood from lament and petition to thanksgiving. The best way of explaining this is to assume that these psalms contain a form of prayer in which room is left between the lamentation and the thanksgiving for the cultic decision (cf. e.g. Pss. 6; 28; 54).[12] There are certainly historical reasons why in the post-exilic period the role of the cultic prophets was taken over by the levitical temple singers.[13] The headings to a whole series of psalms tell us that these were poets. We can hardly be wrong in concluding that theirs was the task of preserving liturgical material and safeguarding the spiritual legacy of their people.

If with this in mind we turn to the present section, we can explain the fact that a prophetic book makes a comment on sacrifice on the basis that it was the task of the prophet to make a decision on sacrifices. At the same time, however, the summons to receive instruction in v. 10 prevents us from using this explanation without further qualification. According to Jer. 18.18, the *tōrāh*, teaching or instruction, was as typical of the priest as counsel was typical of the wise and the word was typical of the prophet. Indeed we may begin from the fact that it was the special task of the priest to give answers to all questions connected with the practice of the cult and with the correct form of sacrifice, with purity and impurity (cf. Lev. 1–7; 11–15; Hag. 2.1ff.; Mal. 2.7).[14] Alongside this, however, there was the equally fundamental wisdom *tōrāh* based on critical examination of the tradition in the light of experience (cf. e.g. Prov. 3.1; 6.20; 13.14). This was to show a physical or spiritual 'son' the way to life which was blameless before God and man, long and happy by virtue of God's response to man's purity.[15] That this included concern for sacrifice followed from the traditionally fundamental significance of sacrifice in maintaining man's relationship with God.[16] Because in the present text the traditions of the priesthood, prophecy and wisdom (which is already expressed in the opening phrase) come together, we might first be tempted to explain it by the fact that the

[12] See Würthwein, 125f. = 154f.; A. R. Johnson, *The Cultic Prophet and Israel's Psalmody*, Cardiff 1979, 251ff., 359ff., and e.g. J. Begrich, 'Das priesterliche Heilsorakel', *ZAW* 52, 1934, 8ff. = *Gesammelte Studien zum Alten Testament*, ThB 21, Munich 1964, 217ff., and O. Plöger, 'Priester und Prophet', *ZAW* 63, 1951, 157ff., in *Aus der Spätzeit des Alten Testaments*, Göttingen 1970, 34f.

[13] Cf. A. R. Johnson, *The Cultic Prophet in Ancient Israel*, Cardiff²1962, 69ff.; A. Cody, *A History of Old Testament Priesthood*, AnBib 35, Rome 1969, 186f., is more restrained.

[14] Cf. J. Begrich, *Die priesterliche Tora*, BZAW 66, 1936, 63ff. = ThB 21, 232ff., and J. Jensen, *The Use of* torah *by Isaiah. His Debate with Wisdom Tradition*, CBQM 3, Washington 1973, 6ff., and 16f.

[15] For the concept of *tōrāh* cf. also G. Liedke and C. Petersen, *THAT* II, 1032ff.

[16] Cf. below, 31ff.

prophet Isaiah was educated in the school of wisdom; this course has been followed repeatedly over the last two decades.[17] One can point in this connection to the similar content in Amos. 5.21ff.; Hos. 6.6; 8.13; Jer. 6.19ff.; 14.14f.; Mal. 1.10; 2.13ff., and thus regard it as a genuine prophetic saying.[18] On the other hand, such a mixture of tradition forces us to put the question the other way round and ask whether what we have here is really a prophetic saying originally delivered by word of mouth, or whether it is not rather, like the two preceding texts, a piece of writing from a later period which was written specially for its present literary context.[19] One can hardly promise a contribution towards clarification solely on the basis of an investigation of sacrificial terminology, including possible references to cultic declarations about the acceptance or rejection of the sacrifice. The way in which the language is connected with the subject matter here rules that out. However, it is worth noting that the introduction of the question in v. 11 appears again in Jer. 6.20, which is also critical of sacrifice, and the declaration of displeasure which concludes the verse is paralleled not only in Hos. 6.6 but also, more exactly, in Ps. 40.7f., where there is even a repetition of the sequence of meal-offering and burnt-offering as found here.[20] It is perhaps more significant that the only parallel to the phrase 'seek something from someone's hand' which opens v. 12b is in I Sam. 20.16 and thus in a Deuteronomistic text.[21] If we follow up this clue we discover that the formula 'the evil of deeds' which we find in v. 16aβ hardly occurs at all in the eighth century, but is to be found rather in the later seventh and early sixth centuries; it is used frequently in the book of Jeremiah, including its Deuteronomistic strata.[22] It is striking to note that the double invitation in vv. 16b, 17a$_1$ is an exact reversal of the sayings handed down in Jer. 4.22; 13.23. We need to go on to note that the demand to give their rights to the widow and the fatherless is one of the prominent features of the thought of Deuteronomic and Deuter-

[17] Cf. J. Fichtner, 'Jesaja unter den Weisen', *TLZ* 76, 1951, cols 75ff. = *Gottes Weisheit. Gesammelte Studien zum Alten Testament*, AzT II, 3, Stuttgart 1965, 18ff.; W. McKane, *Prophets and Wise Men*, SBT 1,44, London 1965, 65ff., who sees the prophets involved in a controversy with earlier Wisdom, and J. Jensen (see n. 14 above), 68ff., 122f.

[18] Cf. Vermeylen I, 57, and also 109.

[19] Cf. 14f., 19 above.

[20] For the evidence in Ps. 40.7ff., cf. also J. Becker, *Israel deutet seine Psalmen*, SBS 18, Stuttgart 1966, 70ff.

[21] Cf. T. Veijola, *Die Ewige Dynastie*, AASF B 193, Helsinki 1975, 82ff.

[22] Cf. Deut. 28.20; Hos. 9.15; Jer. 4.4; 21.12; 23.2, 22; 24.2ff.; 25.5; 26.3; 29.17, and Ps. 28.4. For the difficulties in Hos. 9.10ff., cf. the attempt to remove them by Ina Willi-Plein, *Vorformen der Schriftexegese innerhalb des Alten Testaments*, BZAW 123, Berlin 1971, 178ff., though she does not succeed completely. For what is recognized as the Deuteronomistic part of the book of Jeremiah see the summary in Kaiser, *Introduction*, 240f.

onomistic theology,[23] though there we find the trio of the stranger, the fatherless and the widow. And finally, we should recollect that the principle that Yahweh loves obedience more than sacrifice belongs in the same tradition (cf. I Sam. 15.22).[24] Together with my earlier allusions to the influence of wisdom thinking and the further comments I shall make below, these references may justify the conclusion that in this section, too, we have a saying formulated under the shadow of Deuteronomistic theology. Furthermore, it is not difficult to demonstrate why the prologue should have been expanded in this way. At a time when Judaism had taken shape as a cultic community around the sanctuary in Jerusalem, with its ancestral country under alien control as a Persian province, it must have seemed natural to urge Yahweh to intervene on behalf of his people by increasing the number of sacrificial offerings. Texts like I Sam. 15 and Ps. 50 of themselves demonstrate that in this situation there was a temptation to neglect the duties of moral solidarity in favour of cultic duties.[25]

Who could work over the various traditions in the shadow of the Deuteronomistic heritage in so sovereign a way? Once again, we should probably recall the group of temple singers whom we should probably see, ultimately, as those who handed on and increased the spiritual possession of their people in the post-exilic period. Thus it was probably one of their number who gave specific expression in 1.10–17 to the accusations about the godlessness of the people which were made in such general terms in 1.2f., 4ff., 18ff., and in so doing availed himself of the possibility of protesting on behalf of all those who saw themselves as superfluous in the face of such a flourishing cult. This at the same time implies that the present section was incorporated into the prologue at a later stage than the sayings mentioned above.

[1.10–13] *Wickedness and festal assembly.* The unknown person introduces his rebuke and admonition, in the name of the God in whose worship he knows himself to be at one with the community, by using the same summons to receive instruction as in 1.2a. He asks for attention to the following instruction in the name of Yahweh

[23] The trio of stranger, fatherless and widow can be found in Deut. 10.18; 14.29; 16.11,14; 24.17ff.; 26.12f.; 27.19; Ps. 146.9; for the twofold formula cf. Jer. 7.6; 22.3; Ezek. 22.7 and plural, Ps. 68.6.

[24] Cf. Veijola (n. 21), 102, and id., *Das Königtum in der Beurteilung der deuteronomistischen Historiographie,* AASF B 198, Helsinki 1977. 88.

[25] As the Asaph psalm argues against the background of the concept of the covenant, there are two reasons for regarding it as post-exilic. For the Asaphites cf. n. 46 below; for the age of the idea of the covenant cf. L. Perlitt. *Bundestheologie im Alten Testament,* WMANT 36, Neukirchen 1969, 279ff., and for the dating of Ps. 50 see also A. Deissler, *Die Psalmen,* Düsseldorf ²1979, 204.

(cf. also 30.9; 8.16). He envisages someone from among the political leaders,[26] who are described as 'princes of Sodom', and the common people, who are addressed as 'people of Gomorrah', visiting the kind of sacrificial festival which used to be held in the inner courtyard of the temple.[27] As in 1.2f.; 1.4ff., it is maintained here that the *whole* people as constituted at that time has fallen under Yahweh's judgment of extermination, which was said once to have destroyed the legendary cities of Sodom and Gomorrah (cf. Gen. 18.20f.; 19.24f.).[28] As there is not only an accusation, but positive instruction at the end, this prelude gives the whole discourse the character of an emphatic call to repentance; it becomes a lesson in how the people doomed to destruction can still escape divine judgment.[29]

[11] The angry rhetorical question which, as is usual for its kind, expects a negative answer, and marks the beginning of Yahweh's discourse proper in v. 11, attacks an understanding of sacrifice which comes late in the history of religions and is to be regarded as both degenerate and atavistic. This contradictory characterization implies that where there is mention of sacrifice the history of belief in God and of the human soul emerges in a strange way, reminiscent of the upheaval of volcanic rocks. Thus the understanding of sacrifice put in question here is late because sacrifice is understood as a gift to the deity. The origin of sacrifice probably lies in the experience that life is maintained only through death. In this sense sacrifice repeated the death of the deity, from which life had sprung and from which it would continually spring.[30] At the same time it is degenerate because it regards the accumulation of sacrifices in itself as being an activity which is pleasing to God. Finally, it is atavistic because it fancies, taking an outdated concept of God, that God has the same needs as a human being. Nevertheless, it is original in that it requires that the blood in which life itself flows shall be sprinkled for atonement on the altar of God and in this way be restored to the giver of life (cf. e.g. Lev. 17.11; Gen. 9.4). In a changed world it could be justified only as a sign of grateful surrender and renunciation until it was transcended in a renewal of the primal understanding of sacrifice at a higher level and thus itself made superfluous (cf. also Heb. 7). Verse 11 mentions both the basic forms of Israelite sacrifice: the *zebah*, sacrifice, and the *'ōlāh*, the burnt offering. The former was shared between the deity, the priest and the person offering the

---

[26] For the Hebrew *qāṣīn* cf. also Arabic *qaḍā*, decide, and *qāḍī*, judge; also 3.6f.; Micah 3.1,9; Sir. 48.14; Judg. 11.6; Dan. 11.18.
[27] Cf. also H. P. Rüger, *BHH* III, col. 2119.
[28] Cf. also above, 23 n. 40.
[29] Cf. also H. W. Hoffmann, *Intention*, 95.
[30] Cf. e.g. A. E. Jensen, *Die getötete Gottheit*, UB 90, Stuttgart 1966, 125ff., and M. Eliade, *Patterns in Comparative Religion*, London 1958, 362ff.

sacrifice. Taking the form of a meal, it restored table-fellowship between God and man (cf. Lev. 3; 7.1ff.). With the exception of the hide, which was the priest's share, the burnt-offering or holocaust was burnt on the altar as a gift to God (cf. Lev. 3.1ff.). Animals offered were bulls, rams, he-goats or doves in the burnt-offering and cattle, sheep or goats in the meal-offering.[31] Fattened rams and oxen were probably used in both kinds of sacrifice, as the mention of the fat of the latter indicates (cf. also I Sam. 15.22), but in the meal-offering the fat was burnt as an offering to the deity along with the kidneys and entrails. The mention of blood refers to the manipulations which went with the burnt-offering (cf. e.g. Lev. 1.5; 3.13; etc.).[32] All this, Yahweh declares through his plenipotentiaries, 'does not please me'. This phrase may come from the declaration made by the priest as to whether or not the sacrifice was acceptable to Yahweh, and will have entered criticism of sacrifices from that source (cf. Hos. 6.6; Mal. 2.17; Ps. 40.7; 51.18).

[12] Verse 12a stresses how paradoxical the discourse will have sounded to Israelite ears: of course anyone could justify their pilgrimages and sacrifices from the fact that Yahweh himself required them to appear with hands full three times a year in the temple, at the feasts of Unleavened Bread, Weeks and Tabernacles.[33] The formula 'see the face of God' comes from pre-Israelite cultic language. It presupposes that in the sanctuary the pilgrim sees the face of God in his image. In Israel it was reduced to being merely a technical term for visiting the temple, because images of the deity were forbidden there. However, it need not necessarily have lost the overtones which it occasionally had in the terminology of Babylonian prayer, of asking for and finding help from the god being visited (cf. e.g. Ex. 23.15, 17; Deut. 16.16; Ps. 42.3; 84.8).[34] Given the state of the people, what is in fact required by Yahweh has become blasphemy (cf. v. 14): the visits of pilgrims high and low are undesirable and the crowds of them are disparagingly said to be trampling the courts.[35]

[13] The next verse therefore forbids the whole practice of the cult and gives the reason why. Verse 13aα is formulated in the style of a prohibition, an unconditional divine prohibition such as we find for example in the Decalogue, the Ten Commandments (cf. e.g. Ex. 20.13ff.). By contrast, v. 13aβ with its mention of abomination takes us into an area of terminology in which legal and wisdom thinking

---

[31] Cf. also F. Blome, *Die Opfermaterie in Babylonien und Israel*, Rome 1934, 415ff.

[32] Cf. also R. de Vaux, *Studies in Old Testament Sacrifice*, Cardiff 1964, 27ff.

[33] Cf. Ex. 23.17; 34.20b; Lev. 23; Deut. 16.16.

[34] Cf. F. Nötscher, *'Das Angesicht Gottes schauen'* in *biblischer und babylonischer Auffassung*, Darmstadt ²1969, 88ff., cf. also 72ff.

[35] Cf. also Ps. 84.11.

overlap;[36] in this way it stresses Yahweh's implacable opposition to meaningless cultic activity. Therefore any further offering[37] of sacrificial gifts[38] is vain and injurious.[39] The smoke of the sacrifices which was thought to be well-pleasing to Yahweh and able to assuage his wrath (cf. e.g. Gen. 8.21; Lev. 1.9; 3.5) is in fact an abomination to him.[40] The same goes for regularly recurring festivals like that of the new moon, the day on which the crescent of the moon was seen again for the first time (Sir. 43.8), the sabbath (cf. Ps. 81.4), and any days of penitence or thanksgiving that might be called.[41] Verse 13b gives the reason for this in an incisive and impressive way: Yahweh finds intolerable the juxtaposition and combination of conduct which injures the community (cf. also 10.1; Micah 2.1; Prov. 6.18)[42] with the festive assemblies which are consequently degraded so that they become pious affectation.[43]

This criticism of the cult is by no means to be attributed to a genuinely prophetic impulse; it has a long prehistory in the intellectual movement known as wisdom, which can be traced back to the third millennium in Egypt and Asia Minor. Such thinking was a reflection on the use and purpose of things in this world and brought enlightenment insofar as it was constantly stimulated by experience. Thus the principles reduced in I Sam. 15.22 to the pregnant formula that obedience is better than sacrifice, can already be found in Egyptian wisdom from the end of the third millennium BC in the so-called 'Teaching for Merikare'. In lines 127ff. of this 'Teaching', we find: 'Enrich your house of the West; embellish your place in the necropolis as an upright man and as one who executes the justice (*maat*) upon which men's hearts can rely. More acceptable is the character of one upright of heart than the ox of the evildoer.' However, this is balanced out in the next sentence, which shows that this 'better than' is not aimed at the abolition of sacrifice but at a basic attitude which makes its acceptance possible. The wise man

[36] Cf. e.g. Lev. 20.13ff.; Deut. 17.1; 22.5 with Prov. 6.16; 15.8; 11.1 and see J. Jensen (n. 14), 74ff., 76 n. 51.
[37] For the technical use of *hēbî'*, offer, in sacrificial language see e.g. Gen. 4.3f.; Lev. 4.4ff.; 5.6ff.
[38] The terms *minḥāh*, gift, and *qᵉṭōret*, smoke of sacrifice, may be understood in a general sense here and are not necessarily to be connected specifically with meal offerings and incense offerings. But cf. Feldmann ad loc.
[39] For *šāw'*, nothingness, cf. e.g. Jer. 2.30; Ps. 60.13; Hos. 10.4; Deut. 5.20 and, with care, J. F. A. Sawyer, THAT II, cols. 882ff.
[40] For Yahweh, a *tō'ēbā*, an abomination, is something which he rejects because it causes him revulsion, and marks out the person responsible for extermination: cf. e.g. Lev. 18.22, 26ff.; Deut. 12.31; Prov. 3.31f.; 6.16ff., and on this E. Gerstenberger, THAT II, cols. 1051ff.
[41] Cf. also Num. 10.2,7, and Wildberger ad loc.
[42] Cf. also K. H. Bernhardt, TWAT I, cols. 151ff.; TDOT I, 140ff.
[43] For *ᵃṣārā* cf. E. Kutsch, VT   1952, 65. It properly means rest from work.

continues: 'Act for the god, that he may act similarly for you, with oblations which make the offering-table flourish and with a carved inscription – that is what bears witness to your name. The god is aware of him who acts for him'.[44]

We find the same insight in Old Testament proverbial wisdom. This is already evident from the first passage which I cited, Prov. 15.8, with its parallel Prov. 21.3. We can see how close these are to the Egyptian work, though here it is said that the sacrifice of the godless is an abomination to Yahweh, whereas the prayer of the righteous is well-pleasing to him.[45] The remark in Prov. 21.3, that Yahweh prefers the practice of justice and righteousness to sacrifice, points in the same direction.

If we look forward in time to the end of Old Testament wisdom and beyond, the Preacher pointedly comments that listening in the temple is better than the sacrifice of the fool (Eccles. 4.17). Jesus Sirach balances out obedience and sacrifice by recognizing the true worship of God in obedience, gratitude and mercy (35.1ff.), while at the same time stressing that this does not remove the obligation to offer sacrifice as it is commanded (35.6ff.). The end of Psalm 50 indicates a similar position. It is ascribed to Asaph and therefore to a guild of temple singers who were probably already active at the time of the first temple; they seem to have had their hey-day in the post-exilic period, in the first century.[46] Verses 8ff. deny that Yahweh is in any way dependent on human sacrifices, but v. 14 is nevertheless an exhortation to offer sacrifices of thanksgiving and so to fulfil vows.[47]

It will probably do no harm if we look back not only to ancient Egypt but also to a rather later period, in Greece, where we can see that the best minds there held a similar view. Thus in the *Laws*, IV, 716d–717a, Plato makes his Athenians declare:

that to engage in sacrifice and communion with the gods contin-ually, by prayers and offerings and devotions of every kind, is a thing most noble and good and helpful towards the happy life, and superlatively fitting also, for the good man; but for the wicked the very opposite. For the wicked man is unclean of soul, whereas

[44] Quoted following *ANET*[2-3], 617b; cf. also A. Volten, *Zwei altägyptische politische Schriften*, AAeg 4, 1954, 3ff., in H. H. Schmid, *Wesen und Geschichte der Weisheit*, BZAW 101, Berlin 1966, 215; cf. also *AOT*[2], 35, and H. Brunner, *Grundzüge einer Geschichte der altägyptischen Literatur*, Darmstadt 1966, 37ff.

[45] Cf. also J. Jensen (n. 14), 74f.

[46] Cf. H. Gese, 'Zur Geschichte der Kultsänger am zweiten Tempel', in *Abraham unser Vater, Festschrift Otto Michel*, AGSU 5, Leiden 1963, 222f. = *Von Sinai zum Zion*, BEvTh 64, Munich 1974, 145ff.

[47] For the interpretation of Ps. 50.14, cf. C. A. Briggs, *The Book of Psalms* I, ICC, Edinburgh 1906 (1969), ad loc. Cf. also, on Ps. 51.18ff., ibid., II, 1907 (1969), ad loc.

the good man is clean; and from him that is defiled no good man, nor god, can ever rightly receive gifts. Therefore the great labour that impious men spend upon the gods is in vain, but that of the pious is most profitable to them all.[48]

According to Porphyry, *De abstinentia* II, 15, Theophrastus, the pupil of Aristotle, is said to have remarked: '. . . the deity looks more on the disposition of the person offering sacrifice than on the size of the sacrifice'. Wherever people have reflected independently about God, they have come to the conclusion that cultic offerings do not excuse men from moral obedience and that readiness to offer help on earth is more pleasing to God than an accumulation of sacrifices.

[1.14–17] *Right worship.* The first strophe was exclusively concerned with a negative aspect, the rejection of a piety which consists exclusively in external worship unaccompanied by action which benefits the community (cf. also 29.13f.). The second strophe moves through an extension of the rejection to include even prayer, and a heightening of the accusation (v. 15), to end in positive instructions as to how the people must behave if they are truly to please God in their actions. The inclusion of prayer in those things which God rejects shows more clearly than anything that this whole section is not concerned with a fundamental rejection of cultic piety but with a rejection which is bound up with a particular situation. For prayer is not just an optional extra to faith in God, which people can refrain from if they wish; it is the fundamental expression of that faith. The seriousness and constancy of prayer shows whether the believer really takes seriously God and his possibilities of intervening to bring about change in a world in the making, or whether his faith is only a systematic conclusion to a world which disturbs him by its infinite lack of any conclusion and therefore God is no more than a theoretical notion.[49]

However, so long as the community believes that it can draw a distinction between its direct duties towards God and its duties to those in its midst in need of help, or behaves as though this is what it is doing, the whole religious enterprise, including prayer in the Jerusalem temple, is hateful to Yahweh.

[14] The rejection of feast days and festivals (cf. Lev. 32.2), which moves from passive to active repudiation, describing these as burdens hateful to Yahweh (cf. Ps. 11.5; Amos 5.21; Deut. 1.12) which he is weary of bearing, shows that right relations between man and God amount to no more and no less than man's own life;

---

[48] Plato, *Laws*, LCL, Vol.I. London and New York 1926, 297.
[49] On this cf. also F. Heiler, *Prayer*, Oxford 1932, 1ff.

for the God who is tired of a person or thing has the power to rid himself of them and so put an end to them (cf. Jer. 15.6).

[15] Verse 11b rejected sacrifice; v. 15a takes the same attitude towards prayer. The poet's use of the language of prayer suggests that God is thus doing the opposite of what is expected by the suppliant[50] who comes before him with outstretched hands. Instead of seeing him and his need, he closes his eyes to him (Ps. 10.1); and instead of hearing his laments, he also closes his ears (Lam. 3.56).[51] Perhaps these words again echo the content of ritual sacrifice and prayer.[52]

We should also not fail to note the rejection of the superstition that the power of prayer depends on its length, and its effectiveness on the frequency of its repetition (cf. also Eccles. 5.1; Matt. 6.7). Verse 15b gives the cause of the rejection of sacrifice and prayer and in so doing is perhaps alluding to the situation of the community which is offering sacrifice, with the blood of the slaughtered animals on its hands, as also to the numerical saying in Prov. 6.16ff., according to which those who shed innocent blood are an abomination to Yahweh. At all events, this saying indicates the prevailing situation. A community whose hands are stained with blood[53] does not even fulfil the requirements for entering the sanctuary (Ps. 24.4). Objectively, it is not fit to offer worship and for two reasons deserves death: first, because Yahweh avenges the shedding of innocent blood (cf. Ps. 9.13; Gen. 4.1ff.); and secondly, because it has made the temple precinct unclean by entering the inner courtyard.

[16–17] As the continuation shows, the invitation to wash and be clean[54] does not relate to the blood of sacrifices but to hands stained with guilt, and is therefore metaphorical in character (cf. Ps. 51.12). The command explaining the instruction, to cease doing evil,[55] is now followed in sharp contrast by the twofold summons to stop doing harm and instead to learn to do good, i.e. to help. From a literary point of view it sounds like the conversion mentioned in Jer. 4.22; 13.22. The next double command, to seek justice (16.5) and to help the oppressed, shows that the thought here is not of general matters which might be taken for granted, like everyday help of

---

[50] Cf. e.g. Ex. 9.29; I Kings 8.22, and on the question whether the prayer was spoken standing or kneeling see R. Ap-Thomas, 'Notes on Some Terms relating to Prayer', VT 6, 1956, 225ff.

[51] Cf. Deut. 33.7; Ps. 17.1,6; 27.7; 28.2; 30.11; 39.13; 54.4; 61.2; 84.9; 102.2; 119.149; 130.2; 143.1, and Pss. 65.2; 69.34.

[52] Cf. Jer. 7.16; 11.14; 14.12; and on the passages, Würthwein (n. 9), 121 = 150.

[53] Cf. Ex. 22.1f.; Hos. 4.2; Micah 3.10; Hab. 2.12.

[54] Cf. also J. Jensen (n. 14), 78, and e.g. Ps. 58.11; Job 29.6 and Ex. 2.5 or Ps. 73.13; Prov. 20.9 and Ps. 119.9.

[55] See the examples given above, n. 22.

one's neighbour. Only the final instruction becomes specific, showing what the poet sees as standing between God and the sacrifices and prayers of his people: the exploitation of the situation of those who are helpless when it comes to the law and therefore need the honest support of an advocate, the widows and the fatherless, classic examples of the wretched of the ancient Near Eastern world.[56] They were thought to be in particular need of protection and therefore were specially entrusted to the keeping of the gods and the king. According to his own report, the sign of sure justice brought about by the reforms of the Sumerian king Urukagina of Lagash in the twenty-fourth century BC is that 'The mighty no longer wrong the fatherless and widow'.[57] And in the epilogue to the famous codex of the Babylonian king Hammurabi, from the eighteenth century BC, the monarch does not fail to mention that he has seen that the mighty do not oppress the weak and that fatherless and widow get their rights.[58] If we turn to Egypt, we also find references in the teaching for kings to protection at law for widows and fatherless,[59] and in Ugarit in Canaan the capacity of the king to rule had to be demonstrated by his concern for their rights.[60] Obviously the same thing held for Israel. Here too it was one of the duties of the king to have a ready ear for the concerns of widows and to see that the fatherless and widows were not oppressed (cf. II Sam. 14.1ff.; Jer. 22.3). Evidently the temptation to deprive widows of their rights and to exploit their situation, even to the point of seizing children as payment (cf. II Kings 4.1ff.), was so great that they were entrusted to the special protection of Yahweh (cf. Ps. 68.6; Ex. 22.21ff.). Similarly it was regarded as the special duty of the righteous man to help them secure their rights (cf. Deut. 10.18; Jer. 7.6; Isa. 1.23; 10.1f.; Ps. 82.3). The fact that there is a parallel to the prohibition against seizing the land of widows and the fatherless in Prov. 23.10,[61] in the Teaching of Amenemope 7.14f.,[62] again shows us that this idea also found a place in wisdom.[63] In the eyes of this matter-of-fact man

[56] On this see E. Hammershaimb, 'On the Ethics of the Old Testament Prophets', SVT 7, Leiden 1960, 75ff., and F. C. Fensham, 'Widow, Orphan and the Poor in Ancient Near Eastern Legal and Wisdom Literature', *JNES* 21, 1962, 129ff.; there are also general comments in H. Bolkstein, *Wohltätigkeit und Armenpflege im vorchristlichen Altertum*, Utrecht 1939. – For v. 17b cf. also Ps. 82.3.

[57] Quoted following H. Schmökel, *Das Land Sumer*, UB 13, Stuttgart 1955, 65.

[58] XXIV lines 53ff.; *AOT*² 402, and *ANET*²⁻³, 178a.

[59] See the Teaching for King Merikare and the Teaching of Amenemhet, *ANET*²⁻³, 415a, 418a.

[60] Cf. *CTA* 19, I, 20ff.; 17,V, 4ff.; 16, VI, 32ff., 39ff.

[61] For the text cf. also B. Gemser, HAT I, 16, Tübingen ²1963, ad loc,

[62] Cf. Irene Grumach, *Untersuchungen zur Lebenslehre des Amenope*, MÄS 23, Berlin 1972, 56; *AOT*², 40, or *ANET*²⁻³, 422b.

[63] Cf. also Jensen (n. 14), 82f.

from the fifth century, injustice, whether secret and hidden, or evidently tacitly tolerated by society, separates the people from their God and devalues their sacrifice and prayers. The witness of the books of Amos, Hosea, Jeremiah and Malachi comes to his support,[64] asking how the faithful of our own time respond. Here we may be sure that the evidence presented here would have ruled out a shift in the perspective of their questioning towards our contemporary contrast between faith in God and active help for the neighbour whose rights are threatened. They would have rejected this as inappropriate, because it was their conviction that taking God seriously gave man the strength for moral purity and thus for readiness for unselfish help.

CHAPTER 1.18–20

The Call to Decision

18   'Come now, let us judge together,'
        says Yahweh.
        'If your sins are like a glittering garment[1],
        are they at the same time[2] as white as the [3] snow?
        If they are red like crimson material,[4]
        are they at the same time[2] like the[3] wool?
19   If you are willing and hear,
        in so doing[2] you will eat the best of the land.
20   But if you refuse and rebel,
        in so doing[2] you shall be devoured <by the sword>.[5]
        Indeed the mouth of Yahweh has spoken.

[1.18–20] The decisive terms of this brief discourse of Yahweh,

[64] Cf. Amos 5.21ff.; Hos. 6.6; 8.13; Jer. 6.19ff.; 14.11ff.; Mal. 1.10; 2.13ff.

[1] The plural attested in M may have in mind dyed material, and should perhaps be preferred to the singular, now also attested by 1 QIs^a as the *lectio difficilior*.

[2] For the postponed 'imperfect' used to describe a concomitative action, cf. Bobzin §7, 1b. – Once we appreciate the syntactical structure of the verse, further discussion of its meaning is unnecessary. The remaining problem, whether the sentence is to be understood as statements or questions, is irrelevant for its content.

[3] For the use of the article in comparisons see G-K^{28} §126o.

[4] For the concrete use of the word cf. Lam. 4.5.

[5] Read *bahereb* with 1 QIs^a; but cf. also G-K^{28} §121c.

modelled on a legal process of investigation,[6] have a clear Deuteronomistic stamp, so it is in no way to be taken as a saying of the prophet Isaiah living in the eighth century BC,[7] since the Deuteronomic movement only seems to begin in the seventh century.[8] The obvious connection of the discourse with 28.7ff. (cf. v. 12) and 30.8ff. (cf. vv. 9, 15) comes out in v. 19a. The evidence as a whole suggests that it should be ascribed to the same hand as 1.2f. and 1.4ff. As in 1.10ff., 16f., the indirect admonition is now followed by a direct one which confronts the people with the need to decide between obedience towards Yahweh and life, and disobedience and downfall (cf. also Deut. 30.19f.). In the present context the appeal has its content supplied in 1.17 and indirectly also in 1.21ff.: obedience towards Yahweh would have to manifest itself in righteousness shown even to the weakest members of the people. As in 1.2f., 1.4ff., here too the poetic power of the prophet as a writer and preacher of repentance is shown in his ability to use evocative metaphorical language, to employ lively rhetorical questions and not least to compose sharp antitheses. As in the case of 1.2f., 4ff., 10ff., 21ff., the *Sitz im Leben* is to be seen as the setting of the passage in this book.

[18a] In this saying Yahweh emerges as an opponent of his hearers, with whom he is engaged in a dispute, requiring them to join him and submit themselves to a trial.[9] The fictitious character of the situation is already evident from the fact that in the last resort human beings would have no chance of forming their own valid assessment of the situation, differing from God's view (cf. Job 9.1ff.). Yahweh does not stand before any judge. So like Job, the only thing that they could do would be to appeal to God against God. However, the dispute supposed here is not a mere stylistic expedient. Rather, it takes up a lament circulating among the people that their misfortune is a matter of Yahweh's injustice towards them, and gives the one under attack an opportunity to reply, so that he can make the people realize the situation and thus repent.[10] In fact the lament of the

---

[6] Cf. H.-J. Boecker, *Redeformen des Rechtslebens im Alten Testament*, WMANT 14, Neukirchen 1964, 68f.

[7] Cf. also T. Lescow, 'Die dreistufige Tora', ZAW 82, 1970, 373, and J. Vermeylen, I, 58ff.

[8] Cf. e.g. Kaiser, *Introduction*, 120ff., 158ff.

[9] For the meaning of the verb *yākaḥ* cf. Boecker, 45ff., and for usage Isa. 2.4; 11.4; 29.21; 37.4, and also e.g. Ps. 50.8, 21; Hos. 4.4; Amos 5.17; Micah 4.8; Ezek. 3.26; Prov. 3.12; 9.8; Job. 6.25; 13.3; 19.5.

[10] Against G. Sauer, 'Die Umkehrforderung in der Verkündigung Jesajas', in *Wort-Gebot-Glaube*, Festschrift Walther Eichrodt, ATANT 59, Zurich 1970, 292f. Cf. also Hoffmann, *Intention*, 103.

people can only be over the consequences of the collapse of the Davidic kingdom in 587.

[18b] This double question[11] undeniably establishes that the people's sins,[12] compared to bright red material dyed with egg and the bodies of the kermes, a kind of insect,[13] cannot at the same time be as white as snow or as bright as natural wool (cf. also Ps. 51.9). A sinful people cannot be sinless at the same time, nor can a guilty people expect to be treated as though it were innocent. Some scholars have thought that they could discover the substantive background to the comparison in an account in the Talmud: according to b. Yoma VI, VIII, when the temple was still standing, on the great Day of Atonement a scarlet curtain was fastened to the doorway of the temple hall. It became white when the scapegoat had gone out into the wilderness and the sin of the people had thus been expiated (cf. Lev. 16.20ff.).[14] However, it is very questionable whether there ever was such a usage; it seems more likely that the account will be a conclusion drawn by the rabbis from the present passage.

[19–20] For the poet, the way to remove the guilt which stands between Yahweh and his people is not a matter of ritual manipulations but rather of concrete obedience. If the people accede to God's message in this book with all the resolution at their command,[15] the way is open for them to lead a free and happy life. We should understand v. 19b as a contrast to 1.7b: if the people are obedient, they will again be masters in their own land, and as a sign of this will be able to enjoy the best the land can offer.[16] But if they close their ears to Yahweh's message and continue to rebel against him,[17] in the further confusions of war they will be completely destroyed.[18] The preacher stresses the seriousness of this call to decision by ending with a relatively rare formula, which particularly stresses the divine authority of the message: 'The mouth of Yahweh has spoken' (cf. 40.5; 58.14).

---

[11] For a question without introduction cf. G-K[28] §150a.

[12] For *ḥēṭ*, sin, cf. 31.7; 38.17 and e.g. Deut. 15.9; 19.15; 21.22, 26; 23.22; 24. 15, 16; II Kings 10.29; 14.6.

[13] Cf. H. Gradwohl, *Die Farben im Alten Testament*, BZAW 83, Berlin 1963, 73ff., The insect in question is *Coccus ilicis L.*

[14] Cf. R. Press, 'Das Ordal im alten Israel', *ZAW* 51, 1933, 241ff.

[15] For the use of the phrase 'be willing and hear' as a formula cf. 28.12; 30.9, 15 and Lev. 26.21; Deut. 13.6; 13.9; Josh. 24.10; Judg. 19.25; 20.13; I Kings 20.8; Ezek. 3.7; 20.8.

[16] For the formula cf. Gen. 45.18; Deut. 6.11; II Kings 8.9; Ezra 9.12; Ps. 27.13.

[17] For 'refuse' cf. e.g. I Sam. 8.19; Hos. 11.5; Jer. 5.3; 8.5; 9.5; 11.10; Ex. 16.28; Neh. 9.17; for 'rebel' e.g. I Sam. 12.15; Num. 20.24; 27.14; Deut. 1.26, 43; 9.7, 24; 31.27; I Kings 13.26; Jer. 4.17; Hos. 14.4; Lam. 1.18, 20; 3.42; Ps. 5.11; 105. 28.

[18] For the formula in the active cf. e.g. Deut. 32.42; II Sam. 2.26; Jer. 2.30; Hos. 11.6; Neh. 2.14; Isa. 31.8; also Kaiser, *TWAT* II, col. 173.

CHAPTER 1.21–28

The Purification of Jerusalem

21 Ah, how the faithful city
has become a harlot.
She was full of [1] justice,
and righteousness lodged in her,[2] *but now murder.*[3]
22 Your silver has become dross,
your drink adulterated, *with water.*[3]
23 Your princes – rebels
and companions of thieves.
Everyone[4] loves a bribe
and runs after gifts of welcome.[5]

They do not defend the orphan,
and the widow's cause does not come to them.

24 Therefore the Lord says, Yahweh Sebaoth,
The Mighty One[6] of Israel:
'Ah, I will gain comfort from my oppressors,
and avenge myself on my enemies.
25 And I will turn my hand against you
....[7]
and will purify your dross <in the furnace>[8]
and remove all your lead.

26 Then I will restore your judges as at first,
and your counsellors as at the beginning.
Afterwards you shall be called,
'Citadel of righteousness,
faithful city.'

[1] For the poetic form of the feminine construct with the so-called *yōd compaginis* cf. B-L 526k.
[2] For the use of the so-called imperfect to denote a concomitative action, cf. Bobzin § 7,1b.
[3] That the words are a gloss is evident from their content and from the way in which they disrupt the metre. Verse 22b is evidently the explanation of a rare expression, and v. 21b represents a classification which distinguishes between the faithful and their enemies, cf. Ps. 94.6; 62.4 and on the issue Vermeylen I, 71f.
[4] For the construction cf. Davidson § 116 R.
[5] Cf. Akkadian *šulmānu*, greeting, gift (of office), *AHw* 1268a.
[6] *ᵃbīr* is a designation for God which is artificially dissimilated from *'abbīr*.
[7] Cf. p. 41 below.
[8] With Marti, instead of *kabbōr* ('like lye') read *bakkūr*.

27   Zion shall be redeemed by justice,[9]
        and those who return to her[10] by righteousness.[9]
28   But evildoers and sinners shall be <destroyed>[11] together,
        and[2] those who forsake Yahweh shall be consumed.

[21–28] These verses are held together by their concern with the
present and future fate of Jerusalem, but nevertheless hardly form
an original unit. In vv.21–23 we have a rebuke directed against the
leading circles in Jerusalem, derived from the secular lament over
the dead. The introductory lament, 'Ah, how',[12] the contrast between
the glorious past and the wretched present,[13] and the metre, in
which the double stress alternates with the triple stress, indicate the
qinah or lament over the dead. The more recent commentaries tend
to regard poems of this kind occuring within a prophetic book as
prophetic funeral dirges. The most famous examples outside the
present section are Amos 5.2f.; Isa. 14.4bff.

In content, vv. 21–23 have the character of a rebuke or accusation.
Verse 23b falls outside the metric structure of the poem. In content
it corresponds to the half-verse 17b. So it might have been inserted
later, to bring out the connection of the thought with 1.10ff.,[14] and
at the same time to give the poem, which in its present form
comprises vv. 21–26, two equal parts each with five lines, i.e. vv. 21–
23, 24–26.

Although even most recent scholarship sees vv. 24–26 as the
original continuation of the rebuke, it is at least questionable whether
that is the case. The section as a whole may have had a much more
complicated prehistory. Some further general considerations are
worth bearing in mind in clarifying this question. First of all, it is
striking that the transition to the threat or announcement of judgment in v. 24a breaks the metre, and that v. 26b has been inserted
only with some difficulty. Suspicions are not altogether removed by
regarding v. 24a as a later expansion of the designation for God (cf.
e.g. 3.1; 10.16), because in addition to the formal problems there are
more serious problems of content. In the light of 3.1ff., it is improbable that the idea of a purifying judgment imposed upon Jerusalem

---

[9] One might wonder whether, with Ex. 13.13, we are to see righteousness as the
prize, as the translation suggests, or whether, with Neh. 1.10, we are to see it as the
means. Cf. also Vermeylen I, 106f.

[10] LXX: her captivity. The Hebrew šābēhā can be referred both to the converted
and to those returning home. T reads both into the passage. The translation I have
chosen is probable in the light of 35.10; cf. also Vermeylen I, 106.

[11] Read $w^e šubb^e r\bar{u}$, cf. LXX and T.

[12] Cf. e.g. II Sam. 1.25; Lam. 1.1; 2.1; 4.1.

[13] On this cf. Hedwig Jahnow, Das hebräische Leichenlied im Rahmen der Völker-
dichtung, BZAW 36, Giessen 1923, 92ff.

[14] Cf. also Vermeylen I, 73.

belongs to the earliest stratum of the material concerned with the fate of the city. Proof is hardly needed that it is to be found in vv. 24, 25 and even more clearly in v. 26. Now it is striking that there are only three parallels to the use of the phrase 'oppressor and enemy' in v. 24b – four if we accept the conjecture in Nahum 1.8. One of these, Micah 5.7, clearly has only the nations in mind, while the others, Isa. 59.18; Nahum 1.2, 8, could additionally refer to enemies within the people.[15] If we take into account Deut. 32.41, a verse which evidently had some influence on the present passage, it is clear that the enemy are once again the nations. Accordingly it seems likely that the statement in v. 24b does not refer exclusively to the law-breaking upper class in Jerusalem, but at the same time, and above all, to the nations whose annihilation was expected in connection with their eschatological attack on Jerusalem (cf. Isa. 66.6; Joel 4.9ff.).[16] If we also note that in the original text vv. 25 and 26 each begin with the same word, we cannot conclude that v. 25aα is a later addition.[17] As in 1.12a, the missing half-line can be the result of an error in copying. Accordingly, the repetitions of words could indicate that v. 26 is itself secondary to vv. 24, 25. That vv. 27, 28 are even later is evident from the fact that the purificatory judgment which has been announced with increasing clarity in vv. 25, 26 has become a selective judgment, to which only sinners fall victim (cf. also Ezek. 9.3ff.). If this view is correct, then 1.21–28 came into being in four stages. The nucleus is vv. 21–23a. Verses 24 and 25 were then added to clarify the message of judgment contained there. To ensure that the purificatory judgment was in turn followed by a time of salvation, a later hand added v. 26, and then v. 23b to balance the lines in the strophe. Finally, a last editor formulated the declaration of principle in vv. 27–28.

[1.21–23] That the basic saying, comprising vv. 21–23a, is redactional and not a saying of the prophet Isaiah (despite the almost unanimous view of recent scholarship), follows in all probability not only from its context but also from its links with Deuteronomistic theology, which it shares with the texts in the prologue which precede it.[18] First of all we must challenge the view that Deut. 16.18ff. is the model for the ideal of the judge which underlies the rebuke,[19] because the demands made here seem all too obvious; however, it must be somewhat reluctantly conceded that the sequence of the

[15] Cf. C. Westermann, *Isaiah 40–66*, OTL, and K. Elliger, ATD 25, ad loc.
[16] Vermeylen I, 94, recognizes the connection of v. 24 with Deut. 32.41, but expressly identifies the enemies only with the ruling circles in Jerusalem.
[17] Against e.g. Duhm; Fohrer and Wildberger, ad loc.; Vollmer, *Geschichtliche Rückblicke*, 156; Vermeylen I, 74f.
[18] Cf. also above, 2.
[19] Cf. Vermeylen I, 95ff.

concepts of justice and righteousness which governs v. 21 reappears in Deut. 16.19f., and the prohibition against receiving gifts contained in v. 23a and Deut 16.19 may be seen as typically Deuteronomistic.[20] It may be thought superfluous to relate the key saying about rebellion in v. 23 to Deut. 21.18ff., in view of the fact that it occurs in 1.5, but here too we are advised to be cautious once we recognize that the rare word chosen for the alcoholic drink in the charge against the drunken son made there has a recognizable parallel in the Hebrew here (the root). So in the end we cannot rule out the possibility that the idea of whoring has been prompted here by the other charge of lasciviousness made in Deut 21.20. In this passage, as in the previous sections, we must marvel at the poetic power of the author, whom we would do best to put well into the fifth century.

[1.21–23] *The apostate city of Jerusalem.* The prophetic writer responsible for 1.21–23a begins a funeral dirge over the city of Jerusalem with an 'Ah, how', and thus announces her downfall: she has forgotten her initial faithfulness to Yahweh and has thus become a whore. In describing the city as a whore he goes back to a metaphor used since the days of Hosea to describe the apostasy of the people from Yahweh and then transferred to Jerusalem (cf. Hos. 3.1; 4.12ff.; Jer. 2.20ff.; 3.1ff. with Ezek. 16.15ff.). However, he gives the term a new twist by relating it to the doubtful justice which has found its way into the city. In v. 21b he sketches out an idealized picture of Jerusalem's past which the historian might find hard to verify. Presumably he is not thinking of the reign of a single king of Judah like, say, Solomon (cf. I Kings 3.5ff., 16ff.; Ps. 72; also I Kings 11.1ff.), but of the whole period of the monarchy of Judah down to Hezekiah, tacitly excluding the reigns of those monarchs who fared badly in the judgment of the Deuteronomistic history work.[21] However, it is possible that he had already come to judge things in the same way as the Chronicler and only laid the responsibility for the decline at the feet of the last three kings (cf. II Chron. 36.5ff., 9ff., 11ff.)

The Hebrew meaning of the two terms which we translate 'justice' and 'righteousness' really overlaps. 'Justice', *mišpāṭ*, is primarily the appropriate legal judgment given in a particular situation (cf. e.g. Deut. 16.18; Jer. 5.28; Zech 7.9), and then the appropriate pronunciation of judgment (cf. e.g. Ex. 23.6; Deut. 24.17; Isa. 10.2) and administration of justice (cf. e.g. Isa. 16.5; Hos. 2.21; Ps. 33.5;

---

[20] Ex. 23.8 sits loosely to its context. An investigation is needed as to whether this is because it was put there at a later date, as J. Halbe, *Das Privilegrecht Jahwes Ex 34, 10–26*, FRLANT 114, Göttingen 1975, 434f., assumes. – Cf. Deut 10.17; 16.19; 27.25; I Sam. 8.3. and the evidence mentioned in n. 25 below.

[21] Cf. I Kings 14.21ff.; 15.1ff.; II Kings 8.16ff., 25ff.; 16.1ff.; 21.1ff.; and with the last passage, II Chron. 33.9ff.

Gen. 18.19).[22] 'Righteousness', *ṣedeq*, is a condition which preserves the claims of the community (cf. e.g. Ps. 40.10f.; 72.1ff.; Hos. 2.21), and also conduct which upholds right in the community (cf. e.g. Isa. 26.9f.; 11.4; 32.1).[23]

[22] In the next verse the poet already drops the image he took up in v. 21a and replaces it with two other metaphors, the meaning of which is evident from their position behind v. 21: silver which has become dross, i.e. a waste product from the process of refining silver, and drink adulterated with water, stand for lost righteousness. The reader should not concern himself with the question how refined silver can later turn into dross, any more than the poet did.[24] He was content with this impressive and terrifying formula, which was appropriate for emphasizing the change from the splendid past to a wretched present.

[23] The denunciation of the 'princes' made in v. 23 is not an argument against the post-exilic dating of this section, for which I argued above, since this loanword, taken over from Akkadian, the language of the Babylonians and the Assyrians, could denote not only a royal official but anyone in charge of an institution or group. Thus Ezra 8.29 speaks of the 'princes' of the priests and fathers' houses, i.e. the oldest members of the clans, and Neh. 3.9ff. of the presidents of the city districts and Neh. 7.2 of the commandant of the Jerusalem citadel. This reflection of post-exilic terminology already shows that the reference is to the authorities of the city. Called to be guardians of law and order, in practice they consort with thieves (cf. Prov. 1.10ff.) by countenancing the primal evil of oriental and orientalized administrations, bribery, and making their decisions in accordance with the presents they have been given instead of with justice, behaviour which in the eyes of the poet is downright rebellion against Yahweh (cf. Hos. 9.15; Isa. 1.5; 30.1). Yahweh expects earthly judges to be as incorruptible as he is (cf. Deut. 10.17 with Deut. 16.19).[25] So with its decadent upper classes, the city can expect what is coming to it. Taking up verse 17, v. 23b adds that those who suffer from the corruption of justice will be the widows and fatherless, examples of the weakest members of the people who have no rights of their own.

[22] Cf. G. Liedke, *THAT* II, cols. 1004ff.
[23] Cf. K. Koch, *THAT* II, cols. 507ff.
[24] However, we should not overlook the fact that there is still considerable confusion over the process presupposed. Cf. the remarks in L. Köhler, '*Sîg, sîgîm* = Bleiglätte', *TZ* 3, 1947, 232ff. with those of R. J. Forbes, *Studies in Ancient Technology* VIII, Leiden 1964, 228, and the careful discussion by S. Abramski, ' "Slag" and "Tin" in the First Chapter of Isaiah', *Eretz-Israel* 5, 1958, 89*.
[25] Cf. also Prov. 17.23; Ps. 15.5; Micah 3.11; Isa. 5.23; 33.15; Ezek. 22.12; Ps. 26.10; I Kings 15.19; II Kings 16.8; Isa. 45.13; Prov. 6.34f.; Ezek. 16.33; Prov. 17.8; 21.14.

[1.24–25] *The purification of Jerusalem*. The man whose voice we hear in these verses is convinced that the inexorable judgment which is coming upon Jerusalem does not mean the final annihilation of the city but its liberation from the ruling circles which are sapping its strength and corrupting it.[26] With deliberate solemnity the poet introduces his announcement of judgment in v. 24 with the formula denoting a saying of God which, unusually, is put at the beginning. He makes it stronger by inserting 'the Lord'[27] before 'Yahweh', which usually appears on its own, and adding 'Sebaoth,[28] the Mighty One of Israel'. This additional designation for God is an archaizing transformation of the earlier designation 'the mighty one of Jacob' (cf. Gen. 49. 24; Isa. 49.26; 60.16; Ps. 132.2, 5).[29] The purpose of all these additions is to recall the power which stands behind Yahweh's words. If Yahweh takes vengeance on his enemies, even the faithless lords of Jerusalem will have to believe in him. However, to make them take notice he must turn against the whole city.[30] Prompted by the metaphors in v. 22a and the conception of the purificatory judgment common in the psalms of lamentation (cf. Ps. 17.3; 26.2; 66.10), and perhaps also by Prov. 25.4f.; 17.3,[31] he identifies the expected judgment with the process of purification in which the faulty results of the first smelting are put back in the furnace and the lead which goes with the silver is removed (cf. also Jer. 6.27ff.). The passage differs from Ezek. 22.17ff. in that the process of smelting is not related to the annihilation without qualification. However, the prophet nevertheless continues to proclaim the separation of the lead, i.e. the faithless upper class, without looking beyond the judgment to the time of salvation to come. So we may be reminded of 6.13abα and not least of 3.1ff.

[1.26] *Jerusalem, the city of justice*. In the conviction of the redactor, looking forward to the time of salvation, the expected judgment is only the necessary transition towards liberating the city from its self-seeking rulers and restoring just judges and counsellors as it had before. We may ask whether in this he is cherishing the anti-monarchical ideal to be found in some Deuteronomistic circles,[32] or

---

[26] E. Robertson, 'Isaiah Chapter I', *ZAW* 52, 1934, 234f., has also stressed that vv. 24ff. are independent of vv. 21ff.; he in fact includes v. 26 with vv. 24f.

[27] Cf. also 3.1; 10.16, 33; 19.4.

[28] Cf. below, 126f. on 6.3.

[29] Cf. also A. S. Kapelrud, *TWAT* I, cols. 43ff. (TDOT 1, 42ff.).

[30] For the negative significance of v. 25aα, cf. the parallels in Jer. 6.19; Ezek. 38.12; Amos 1.8; Zech. 13.7; Ps. 81.15.

[31] Cf. also Prov. 27.21.

[32] We find them in the additions made by the Deuteronomistic nomist, DtrN, cf. T. Veijola, *Das Königtum in der Beurteilung der Deuteronomistischen Historiographie*, AASF B 198, Helsinki 1977, 119ff.

does not rather have in mind the renewed kingdom announced in 9.1ff.; 11.1ff. In that case the judges and perhaps even the counsellors should be seen as members of the renewed dynasty.[33] At all events, the future masters of Jerusalem will rule so justly that they will gain a reputation for so doing, and in contrast to Jer. 6.30,[34] Jerusalem will acquire the epithet 'citadel of righteousness and faithful city' (cf. also 62.2, 4, 12; Zech. 8.3).

[1.27–28] *A rejection of false hopes*. The prospect of a time of salvation contained in v. 26 and the preceding words of judgment which exclusively have in mind the fate of the Jerusalem upper class have caused one anxious reader to guard against false expectations that consequently the remnant of the people at home and abroad would in principle be excluded from Yahweh's imminent vengeance. So in v. 26 he formulates the principle according to which Yahweh will act in the liberation of his people: he will act according to justice in both the redemption of the people of Jerusalem[35] and also that of those returning home from abroad[36] (cf. Ezek. 34.16; Ps. 112.5). Verse 28 develops what that means. Then all those who have broken with Yahweh (cf. 1.2b) and remained in their sins (cf. 1.4a), and those who have openly turned away from him (cf. 1.4b), will repent (cf. 8.15; 28.13). According to 33.14 we may imagine that Yahweh's presence on Zion will consume his enemies in the city like a devouring fire. Thus the pastor responsible for this addition requires his readers to examine themselves and see whether they will be able to stand in the coming Day of the Lord (cf. Mal. 3.2).

---

[33] Vermeylen I, 90, sees the ideal time mentioned in v. 21 as being that of the judges, failing to note that at that time Jerusalem was not part of Israelite territory.

[34] The remarkably numerous parallels between Isa. 1.2ff., and individual sayings in the book of Jeremiah disconcert the reader to the point of raising the question whether the poetical parts of the book of Jeremiah really are earlier than the Deuteronomistic sermons or are later additions, at least partially oriented on the book of Isaiah. A thorough investigation of the parallel texts might introduce some clarity here.

[35] Cf. Ps. 25.22; 44.27; 130.8; Jer. 31.11; Isa. 29.22.

[36] Cf. Isa. 35.10; 51.11; Ezra 2.1; 3.8; 8.35; Neh. 8.17; Ps. 126.1.

CHAPTER 1.29–31

The End of the Idolaters

29   Yes, they[1] shall be put to shame because of the oaks
     which you treasured,
     and you will be ashamed because of the gardens
     which you prefer.
30   For you shall be like a terebinth
     whose leaf withers;
     and like a garden
     without water.
31   Then the strong[2] shall become tow
     and his work[3] a spark,
     and both of them shall burn together
     with none to quench them.

[1.29–31] This small section is the final expansion of the discourse
beginning with 1.21 which in turn has arrived at its present form in
a process of several stages.[4] Its purpose is to give colour to the charge
of apostasy from Yahweh contained in v. 28b (cf. also v. 4b). In
content, with its polemic against the nature cult deriving from
Canaanite religion, it comes close to sayings like 57.5; 65.3b–4, 11–
12; 66.17.[5] Therefore we cannot rule out the possibility that it belongs
to the same stratum of revision.[6] Thus v. 29 is not concerned with
the attempt to appropriate the orchards of the weaker members of
society (cf. 5.8; I Kings 21.1ff.), but with the trend towards cultic
activity practised in groves and manifestly not connected with
Yahweh. According to Hos. 4.12ff.; Jer. 3.13, in the northern kingdom there was a widespread cult practised under green trees and

---

[1] LXX has the third person masculine plural throughout v. 29; V in 29a; T renders
it as though it were the second person masculine plural, and is followed by a number
of Hebrew MSS. The third person plural links up with 1.28 and so betrays the
redactional character of the saying. Cf. on this also Barth, *Jesaja-Worte*, 292 n. 44. For
the lengthening of the preformative vowel see G-K[28] §72h.
[2] As in v. 29aα, the textual evidence shows signs of an attempt to smooth things
out. 1 QIs[a] offers an interesting mixed reading, but, as the sequel shows, intends
hosn^ekēm, 'your strength', to be read. We might ask whether the poet had difficulty
in writing an ending or whether in v. 31 we have yet another hand.
[3] For the erroneous form see B-L 582u'.
[4] Cf. above, 40f.
[5] Cf. e.g. J. Becker, *Isaias*, 47.
[6] Thus Barth, op. cit.

connected with sexual rites. According to Jer. 2.27 trees were called
'my father' and stones 'my mother'. Isaiah 57.5 mentions idolatry
under green trees and child sacrifice in the same breath, so that we
are reminded of the groves in which the Carthaginians offered their
child sacrifices to the goddess Tannith.[7] If we are right to identify
this goddess with the consort of the father god of the Canaanite
pantheon El, the goddess Asherah,[8] we cannot rule out the possibility that worship dedicated to her underlies this polemic (cf. Deut.
16.21; and e.g. Isa. 27.9).[9] We should imagine that the failure of
Yahweh to provide help that would transform the destiny of Judaism
meant that, as the Persian period progressed, people were fascinated
with cults[10] the deities associated with which were thought to
intervene directly in the forces of life and thus seemed to guarantee
direct help in everyday affairs. However, faith in Yahweh allowed
no compromises with faith in other forces which were thought to
have equivalent authority to him. The God of Israel allows no other
gods beside him who might encroach on his claim to possess his
people and rule over them; he requires that the people shall serve
him alone (cf. Ex. 20.3 par. Deut. 5.7; 11.16f., 26ff.). And if the other
peoples turned their eyes in worship to the stars, this was surely by
virtue of a special ordinance of Yahweh, who had chosen Israel for
himself (cf. Deut. 4.19f.; 32.8f.).

Anyone who trusts in Yahweh should and can know that in the
end he has to do with this God in all that he experiences and
encounters. Accordingly, even apostasy from him will have its
consequences, so that it must become evident that the apostates will
objectively be put to shame because of their idolatry.[11] In metaphorical terms, those who expect an enhancement of their life from the
divine forces associated with the trees will in fact discover the
opposite. They are doomed to destruction like a tree whose leaves
wither because – this is probably the way in which we should
interpret the two halves of v. 30 together – the garden is no longer
watered (cf. Jer. 8.13; Isa. 64.5 and Ps. 1.3; Isa. 58.11). Thus the
strength which they feel that they gain in the end becomes a cause

---

[7] Tertullian, *Apologeticum* 9. Cf. also O. Kaiser, 'Salammbo, Moloch und das Tophet,
Erwägungen zum Kindopfer der Karthager', *Die Karawane* 19, 1978, 1/2, 3ff.

[8] Cf. F. M. Cross, *Canaanite Myth and Hebrew Ethic*, Cambridge/Mass 1973, 28ff.,
and also R. D. Barnett according to *PEQ* 111, 1979, 1f.

[9] Cf. also K. Galling, 'Aschera', *BRL*³, cols. 12f., and H. Gese, *Die Religionen
Altsyriens*, RM 10, 2, Stuttgart 1970, 151f. In this interpretation I presuppose that vv.
29a and b are to be understood as synonyms, which would rule out reading Adonis
gardens into the passage. For this see my commentary on *Isaiah 13–39*, 80ff., on Isa.
17.9–11.

[10] For the use of the verbs ḥāmad and bāḥar as terms for free choice of foreign gods,
cf. also 44.9; 41.24; 66.3.

[11] For this pair of concepts cf. Ps. 35.4, 26; 40.15; 70.3; 71.24; 83.18.

of weakness and even death; instead of experiencing a heightening of life, by participating in these cults the initiate brings death upon himself. Perhaps the poet, zealous for his God, was unconsciously stimulated by the conception of the fire which accompanies Yahweh (cf. e.g. Ps. 50.3),[12] to change the imagery and imagine the initiate, portrayed as the strong one, as tow in the hands of the hemp-dresser, which was used in making fire because it was so inflammable (cf. Judg. 16.9[13]), while his idolatry was the spark which set it on fire and disappeared along with it, in an inevitable end.[14]

CHAPTER 2.1

The Heading: A Word of Isaiah

1 The word which Isaiah the son of Amoz saw concerning Judah and Jerusalem.

The heading in 2.1 repeats the formulations in 1.1a, but instead of the 'vision' speaks of 'the word'. Were it in fact the heading of an earlier collection, as scholars widely assume, we would expect 'the words' instead of 'the word' (cf. e.g. Amos 1.1; Jer. 1.1). So quite apart from the fact that the evidence in the subsequent chapters, which in my view do not contain earlier sayings of Isaiah, is not sufficient to support this hypothesis, it is likely that we should see in this heading an express claim that the prophecy of the pilgrimage of the nations to Zion, which also appears with slight changes in the book of Micah, should be attributed to the prophet Isaiah.[1]

---

[12] Cf. also Lam. 2.4 and on it Kaiser, *Klagelieder*, ATD 16, 1980, ad loc.
[13] Cf. G. Dalman, *Arbeit und Sitte in Palästina* V, Gütersloh 1937, 28.
[14] For the formula cf. Amos 5.6; Jer. 4.4; 21.12; also Jer. 7.20.
[1] For this cf. P. R. Ackroyd, 'A Note on Isaiah 2,1', ZAW 75, 1963, 320f., and id., 'Isaiah I – XII: Presentation of a Prophet', SVT 29, 1978, 32f.

CHAPTER 2.2–5

The Pilgrimage of the Nations to Zion

2   And it will come about:
      in future days,
      the mountain of the house of Yahweh
      shall be established[1]
      on the summit[2] of the mountains
      and raised up as a hill.
      Then all nations will flow to it,
3   and many peoples shall come and say,
      'Come, let us make pilgrimage to the mountain of Yahweh,
      to the house of the God of Jacob,
      that he may teach us his ways
      and that we may walk in his paths.'
      For out of Zion shall go forth instruction
      and the word of Yahweh from Jerusalem.
4   Then he shall judge between the nations
      and decide for many peoples.
      Then they shall beat their swords into ploughshares,
      and their spears into pruning hooks.
      Nation shall not lift up sword against nation,
      and they shall not learn war any more.
5   O house of Jacob, come and let us walk
      in the light of Yahweh.

[2.2–5] Given that the present description of salvation has also been transmitted in Micah 4.1–4, it poses a literary problem. The chief difference between the two versions is that a number of words have been transposed. Furthermore, the Micah text is one line longer (or two, if we take into account the formula identifying it as a saying of God). Finally, the two prophecies of salvation have different liturgical additions, directed at the community (cf. Isa. 2.5 with Micah 4.5). On a more detailed comparison, the Micah text leaves the impression of being more coherent, though not in all details. The

---

[1] A comparison with the text of Micah 4.1–5 falls outside the scope of the textual criticism of this section.

[2] Cf. e.g. I Sam. 9.22; I Kings 21.9; Nah. 3.10 and also Dillmann-Kittel, ad loc.

metre is more balanced[3] and the content more rounded as a result of the positive description of the expected state of peace in v. 4a. However, there has long been disagreement among scholars precisely over the question whether this verse belongs to the prophecy.[4] Both texts end with an addition drawing the conclusion from the prophecy for their own community. Micah 4.5 culminates in the contrast between the Gentile way of life governed by polytheism and the eternal obedience of Israel, whereas in the light of the criticism of the people of God in ch. 1, Isa. 2.5 calls for like behaviour from the house of Jacob.

There are basically four possible ways of defining the relationship between the two texts. After brief consideration, the first two may be excluded. The reader unfamiliar with Old Testament scholarship might arrive at the idea that the two prophecies were given independently to both the prophet Isaiah and the prophet Micah. However, everything that we now know about the composition of the books of the Bible tells against this assumption, which is only tenable within the framework of a strict belief in inspiration. So this possibility is ruled out of scholarly discussion *a priori*. On the other hand, it would be quite conceivable that the promise came from either the prophet Isaiah or the prophet Micah and was later taken into the collection of the sayings of one prophet from that of the other. However, there are again serious objections to this hypothesis in view of the redaction-critical evidence from both books. Regardless of what we decide about the authorship of Isa. 1 and 2.6–4.1,[5] it is clear that 2.(1)2ff. interrupts the theme of the future judgment on Jerusalem and Judah which governs these chapters as a whole. Verse 5 discloses the purpose of the insertion, which is to stimulate the community to be obedient to Yahweh's will in the face of the coming judgment, by holding out a prospect of the future glorification of the city of God. On the basis of this observation it seems reasonable to suppose that this section was incorporated into the book of Isaiah purely on redactional grounds, and we cannot conclude from this that it was written by Isaiah. Of course the extremely complex question of the

---

[3] On this cf. the judgment of T. H. Robinson, HAT I, 14, Tübingen ²1954, 140, and Ina Willi-Plein, *Vorformen der Schriftexegese innerhalb des Alten Testaments*, BZAW 123, Berlin and New York 1971, 83 (with special reference to her text-critical comments, 84) with the view of A. S. van der Woude, *Micha*, De Prediking van het Oude Testament, Nijkerk 1976, 128 and 273 n. 3.

[4] Cf. the positive judgments of e.g. K. Marti, KHC XIII, Tübingen 1904; Robinson, HAT I, 14; and A. Weiser, *The Psalms*, OTL, London and Philadelphia 1962, ad loc., with the negative judgment of B. Duhm on Isa. 2.4; Wildberger, 77; S. Talmon, 'Typen der Messiaserwartung um die Zeitwende', in *Probleme biblischer Theologie*, Festschrift Gerhard von Rad, Munich 1971, 579, and v.d. Woude, *Micha*, 136, with the restraint of W. Rudolph, KAT² XII, 3, Gütersloh 1975, 81.

[5] On this cf. above, 2ff., and below, 63ff.

age of the Zion theology and its connection with the theme of the battle with the nations and the pilgrimage of the nations is also relevant to contemporary discussion of the age and derivation of the passage. In the end this can only finally be answered against the background of a more refined method of studying the psalms and a comprehensive history of the redaction of the prophetic books.[6] Nevertheless, even at this point it can be established that elsewhere we only find the kind of universalism of salvation which is represented here in the prophecy of Deutero-Isaiah (Isa. 40–55), that is, at the earliest at some time into the exilic period.[7]

Hesitations must also be expressed against attributing the saying to the prophet Micah of Moresheth, Isaiah's contemporary. In the light of Micah 3.12; Jer. 26.18, it is already improbable that the prophet who predicted the destruction of the Jerusalem temple could at the same time proclaim his future positive view of the world without trivializing his message of judgment.[8] In this connection we should note the difference between the original prophecy, in the mainstream of its time and of the historical response of the people, and the later written prophecy with an eschatological tendency, which was produced after the people ceased to be an active political factor in history.

The theological revision brought about by the exile, which provided the background to the expectation of a new divine act leading to salvation through a renewed judgment, was responsible for the incorporation of the prediction into the two prophetic books. In addition, the literary evidence of the book of Micah tells against the attribution of this passage to Micah: words which go back to this prophet can in fact be found only in the first three chapters and in 6.9ff.[9] This position is not altered by the observation that the connection between the content of Micah 3.9–12 and Micah 4.1–4 is much closer than that between Isa. 1.21ff., 27f.[10] and Isa. 2.2ff. However, it could well suggest that the prediction was first incor-

---

[6] Cf. e.g. W. Nowack, HK III, 4, Göttingen 1903, 223f.; E. Cannawurf, 'The Authenticity of Micah 4.1–4', VT 13, 1963, 26ff., and in contrast H. Wildberger, 'Die Völkerwallfahrt zum Zion, Jes 2,1–5', VT 7, 1957, 62ff., and BK X, 1, 76ff., and, so that this view too is grounded on at least two witnesses, G. von Rad, 'The City on the Hill', in The Problem of the Hexateuch and Other Essays, Edinburgh 1966, 232–42, and id., Old Testament Theology II, London 1975, 292ff.

[7] Cf. also Isaiah 13–39, 86, n.b. As a sign of the revival of literary-critical discussion of Isa. 40–55, which seemed to have come to an end, cf. now H. C. Schmitt, 'Prophetie und Schultheologie im Deuterojesajabuch. Beobachtungen zur Redaktionsgeschichte von Jes 40–55', ZAW 91, 1979, 43ff.

[8] Cf. also v.d. Woude, Micha, 128f.

[9] Cf. Ina Willi-Plein, op. cit., 70ff., 82ff., and B. Renaud, La formation du livre de Michée. Tradition et actualisation, EtB, Paris 1977, 383ff.

[10] For 1.29ff. cf. above, 46f.

porated in the book of Micah and was later transferred from memory into the book of Micah. Another point in favour of this hypothesis is that it is more likely that a text would be transferred from a less significant book into a more important one than vice versa.[11] A final consideration is that the brief description of salvation might first have been in circulation without any connection with either book and was subsequently incorporated into both.[12]

In my view, the proximity in content of this passage to the Songs of Zion composed by the levitical guild of temple singers known as the Korahites, whose rise seems to have begun at the end of the fifth and the beginning of the fourth century BC,[13] gives justification to the assumption that the present prophecy came into being under the influence of their thinking, even if it was not actually composed by members of the guild.[14] The insertion of 2.1–5 in turn resulted in the provision of a new framework for the message of world judgment in 2.10–17* by the addition of 2.6–9, 11, 19–21. So, too, in v. 6 the mention of the house of Jacob is taken up from 2.5, and the old text about judgment is now interpreted in terms of the people of God.

[11] Cf. Ina Willi-Plein, op. cit., 83.

[12] The question whether the description of salvation has been inserted into both books by the same redactor has been raised by J. Becker, *Isaias*, 47.

[13] Cf. H. Gese, 'Zur Geschichte der Kultsänger am zweiten Tempel', in *Abraham unser Vater*, Festschrift Otto Michel, Leiden 1963, 229ff. = *Vom Sinai zum Zion*, BEvTh 64, Munich 1974, 154ff., and G. Wanke, BZAW 97, 23ff.

[14] To give the reader some impression of the discussion of authorship, I would report that Isaiah's authorship has been supported e.g. by Duhm, Dillmann-Kittel, Hans Schmidt, Sellin, H. Gressmann (*Der Messias*, FRLANT 43, Göttingen 1929, 207), Feldmann, Procksch, Fischer, von Rad (cf. n. 7), Wildberger (*VT* 7, 1957, 62ff., and BK X, 1), R. Martin-Achard, *Israël et les nations* (CT 42, Neuchâtel and Paris 1959, 57f.), Eichrodt, H. Junker (TTS 15, Festschrift for Bishop Wehr, 4, 1962, 26ff.), R. Rehm (*Der Königliche Messias im Lichte der Immanuel-Weissagungen des Buches Jesaja*, Eichstätter Studien NF 1, Kevelaer 1968, 247f.), J. Jensen (*The Use of torah by Isaiah*, CBQM 3, Washington DC 1973, 84ff.), Rudolph and A. S. van der Woude, while a post-exilic dating is supported by e.g. B. Stade (*ZAW* 1, 1881, 161f.), Marti, Gray, Guthe, Nowack, Robinson, R. H. Pfeiffer (*Introduction to the Old Testament*, New York and London 1941 [1948], 439,593), A. Weiser (*Introduction to the Old Testament*, ET London 1961, 188, 254), Fohrer (ad loc.), J. Lindblom (*Prophecy in Ancient Israel*, Oxford 1962, 390), Cannawurf (*VT* 13, 1963, 31ff.), O. Eissfeldt (*The Old Testament. An Introduction*, Oxford 1965, 318), B. Renard (*Structure et attaches littéraires de Michée IV-V*, CRB 2, Paris 1964, 91), S. Herrmann (*Die prophetischen Heilserwartungen im Alten Testament*, BWANT 85, Stuttgart 1965, 141ff.), J. Becker (*Isaias*, 47), Auvray (ad loc.) and R. Smend (*Die Entstehung des Alten Testaments*, TW 1, Stuttgart 1978, 150). Vermeylen I, 121ff., has given an impressive demonstration of the difficulty of fitting the text even into the framework of a relatively traditional assessment of Isaiah's own contribution to chs. 1–39; of course, whether one accepts his view that the oracle came into being in connection with the centralization of the cult attributed to Josiah is another question. For the problems here cf. E. Würthwein, ZTK 73, 1976, 395ff., and, more briefly, Kaiser, *Einleitung in das Alte Testament*, Gütersloh ⁴1978, 123f. (not in the ET). For suggestions of other contexts cf. Rehm. *Königliche Messias*, 244; C. Schedl, *Rufer des Heils*, 51.

[2a] The depiction of salvation is introduced by an indication of time which since the translation in the Greek Bible, the Septuagint, and the Latin translation by Jerome, the Vulgate, has usually been rendered 'in the last days'.[15] Here we have an adaptation, alien to authentic Old Testament thought, to the late-Jewish conception of the end of the present world in space and time as it is to be found in the context of the doctrine of world ages, based on Babylonian astronomy and astrology, which spread forcefully westwards after the middle of the last millennium BC.[16] The Hebrew phrase translated above as 'in future days' should really be rendered 'on the backward side of days'. This expression reflects a temporal orientation which is opposite to our logic in such a matter. What has already happened is seen by the Hebrew as lying before him; what is to come is behind him.[17] Passages like Gen. 49.1; Num. 24.14; Deut. 31.29; Jer. 23.20 are sufficient evidence that the phrase 'in future days' can primarily denote any particular moment in a more or less indeterminate future. Accordingly, the unknown prophet whose words are to be found here agrees with the expectations of his predecessors up to Second Isaiah in looking not for the end but for the consummation of history.

The notion that the Jerusalem temple will stand firm and therefore not be shaken is an indication of associations with the notion of the nations surging up against Zion like the sea (cf. Ps. 46.4, 7; Isa. 17.12ff.; 5.30 with Ps. 93.1ff.; 24.1.; 96.10 par. I Chron. 16.30). If we look further, at Ps. 48.9, we could probably say that the temple mount has shown itself to be securely grounded in the storms of the last attack of the nations launched against it in history, and therefore to be impregnable. In the background of this eschatological myth is the old Canaanite conception of the mountain of God which is the abode of the weather god and against which the rising sea storms in vain.[18] In this self same psalm, Ps. 48, it is transferred from the mountain of God in the north, Mount Zaphon, with Baal's shimmering cloud palace, to Zion, whose limestone rocks, modest in comparison with other mountains in the land, are celebrated in v. 3 as the summit of Zaphon (cf. also Ps. 68.16f.).[19] Thanks to the temple

---

[15] Cf. also G. W. Buchanan, 'Eschatology and the "End of Days" ', *JNES* 20, 1961, 188ff.

[16] Cf. B. L. van der Waerden, 'Das grosse Jahr und die ewige Widerkehr', *Hermes* 80, 1952, 129ff., and especially 187ff.

[17] On this cf. also T. Boman, *Hebrew Thought compared with Greek*, London 1960, 149ff.

[18] Cf. H. Gese, *Die Religionen Altsyriens*, RM 10, 2, Stuttgart 1970, 59ff., or O. Kaiser, *Die mythische Bedeutung des Meeres in Ägypten, Ugarit und Israel*, BZAW 78, Berlin ²1962, 44ff.

[19] Cf. also R. Hillmann, *Wasser und Berg. Kosmische Verbindungslinien zwischen dem kanaanäischen Wettergott und Jahwe*, Diss. Halle 1965, 161ff.

standing on it, the place in which mysterious contact was made between the heavenly and the earthly palaces of God,[20] the whole city could participate in this property of being the earthly counterpart of the heavenly city of God. Consequently the prophet whose words appear here expected that the mythical saying would indeed come true, that the temple mount would indeed become the highest of all mountains, and that in this way it would become manifest to the whole world that here was the sanctuary of the true Lord of heaven and earth.

[2b–3] Because of the violent transformation of the whole earth which will be associated with these events, the Gentile world as a whole[21] will need no special summons and instruction. It understands the language of God in nature, with which he has manifested his deity, and has recognized his temple as the real centre of the world; now, in all instances of distress and dispute, instead of turning to their former gods, the people come to the mountain of Yahweh[22] and the God of Jacob who lives there[23] (cf. also Deut. 17.11; 24.8). In so doing they follow the old custom of going to a god to seek instruction in all the decisive questions of life.[24] The invitation to one another put on the lips of the nations, with its declaration of intent, corresponds to the petition with which the faithful in Israel approached Yahweh in their search for instruction (cf; Ps. 27.11; 86.11).[25] Sayings like Ex. 19.5f.; Isa. 61.5f., which appoint Israel a priesthood for the nations, will remind us of what this was thought to be in practice. However, in view of the connection between cultic impurity and disasters coming upon land and people, which was so much a matter of course for antiquity, we should understand *tōrāh*, instruction, and the word of Yahweh as not being exclusively the resolution and clarification of disputed or obscure issues by the decision of an oracle; it also comprised instruction on cult and ritual, and therefore, in view of the time when the prophecy may be supposed to have been composed, instruction on the basis of the

---

[20] Cf. M. Metzger, 'Himmlische und irdische Wohnstatt Jahwes', *UF* 2, 1970, 139ff.

[21] For the inclusive and non-inclusive sense of the Hebrew *rabbīm*, many, cf. Joachim Jeremias, *TDNT* 6, 536ff., esp. 537 10ff.

[22] Elsewhere only Micah 4.2; Ps. 24.3; Isa. 30.29.

[23] Elsewhere only II Sam. 23.1; Ps. 20.2; 46.8, 12; 75.10; 76.7; 82.2, 5; 84.9; 94.7; cf. also Ps. 114.7, and Wanke, BZAW 97, 54ff.

[24] Cf. also Wildberger, ad loc., with his references, and also e.g. H. W. Parke, *The Oracles of Zeus, Dodona. Olympia. Ammon*, Oxford 1967, 253ff.; G. Roux, *Delphi, Orakel und Kultstätten*, Munich 1971, 71ff., and O. Kaiser, 'Das Orakel als Mittel der Rechtsfindung im Alten Ägypten', *ZRGG* 10, 1958, 193ff.

[25] It should be noted that Ps. 86.9f. refers to the pilgrimage of the nations.

Law of Moses which had been put down in writing.[26] In practice this amounts to an incorporation of all the nations in the Jerusalem theocracy.

[4] The sequel shows that this assertion is no exaggeration. There is indeed to be above all a decision on and resolution of the points of dispute that arise between the nations (cf. Deut. 17.8ff.; Ps. 96.13; 98.9). In view of the universal recognition of the authority of Yahweh, it will be safe to have world-wide disarmament. The universal world peace presupposes a universal recognition of God and subjection to his judgment. Only when this has happened can humanity think of completely destroying all weapons without endangering themselves or, as is said here in the context of a pre-industrial peasant society, of turning their weapons into agricultural implements. Swords are to become ploughshares[27] and spears pruning hooks.[28]

In deliberate contrast to v. 4b, Joel 3 [4]. 10 says that the nations are to turn their ploughshares into swords and their pruning hooks into spears, to find a certain end in the valley of Jehoshaphat during the onslaught on Jerusalem.[29] In any further demonstration were still needed after this deadly irony, Joel 3[4].17 and 19 here show the exclusive character of the expectation in the book of Joel, which debars the nations from salvation. Precisely in the light of such a prophecy, prompted by hate of the nations as a consequence of the suffering they have caused, the one discussed here takes on a special significance, transcended in the book of Isaiah only by 19.19ff. and above all by 19.24f., as evidence of a hope that God will not act anxiously and selfishly for himself, but will wait until he is in fact Lord of all nations.

As I commented, there is only universal peace when God is universally recognized. Such peace is achieved in a living society of men and women, brought about by God himself, in which there are no more barriers of language, race and class. At this point, however, we have presumably left even this prophet behind us and put his message in the light of the gospel which is for all people, and which, while allowing Jerusalem its historical prominence as the place of

[26] For the *tôrāh* terminology, cf. Hos. 8.12; I Chron. 16.40; 22.12; Sir. 41.4; Hos. 4.6; Zeph. 3.4; Jer. 18.18; Isa. 1.10; 8.16, 20; 30.9f.; for the word of God in the sense of the written law cf. Ex. 20.1; 24.3; 34.1ff.

[27] Cf. also *BRL*[2], 59, and pl. 17; 255 and pl. 66.

[28] Cf. also *BRL*[2], 201, and pl. 47; K. Galling, 33a.

[29] Cf. H. W. Wolff., *Joel and Amos*, Hermeneia, Philadephia 1977, ad loc., taken up by Wildberger, BK X, 1, 87, and W. Rudolph, KAT[2] XIII, 2, Gütersloh 1971. 83. For the biblical understanding of peace cf. H. Gross, *Weltherrschaft als religiöse Idee im Alten Testament*, BBB 6, Bonn 1953, 118ff.; J. J. Stamm and H. Bietenhard, *Der Weltfriede im Alten und im Neuen Testament*, Zurich nd (1959); O. Kaiser, 'Krieg und Frieden in der Sicht des Alten Testaments', *Anstösse* 1964, 4, 155ff.; H. H. Schmid, šālōm, 'Frieden' in Alten Orient und im Alten Testament, SBS 51, Stuttgart 1971.

the revelation of Christ, no longer reveres it as a contemporary place of revelation, and does not expect its future glorification because God now wills to be worshipped in spirit and in truth (John 4.19ff.; Heb. 13.14). In the context of the gospel, suffering in the world as a follower of Jesus becomes suffering as a disciple on behalf of the world.

[5] Here the prophet, or perhaps rather the editor who inserted this prophecy into the Isaiah scroll, now turns directly to his community, whose situation and task he knows he shares. Because of the mention of the God of Jacob in v. 3, he addresses them solemnly as the house of Jacob, and thus reminds them of the modest beginnings of the people in the twelve sons of the patriarch, who himself could spend only part of his life in the promised land and had to live out the rest partly in Mesopotamia and partly in Egypt. It was thanks to God's faithfulness to his promise that God's people arose from Jacob's sons.[30] So now, although many of them may be living in exile in Babylon or in the Diaspora in Egypt, instead of in their homeland, they can still take comfort in the saving presence of their God and the power of his promises, as they were bestowed along with the temple and in his word (cf. Hab. 2.20; Ps. 119.105). Thus even now they can walk in the light of his countenance, that is, of his grace (Ps. 89.16),[31] although they are still in the power of alien masters (cf. Micah 7.8; Ps. 27.1). However, this also includes the obligation laid on them by God's secret presence, not only to wait until the nations and therefore others hearken to him, but to be obedient themselves this very day (Ps. 119.135).

CHAPTER 2.6–22

The Day of Yahweh

6   Surely you have rejected your people,
        O house of Jacob,
        because they were full of <diviners>[1] from the East

---

[30] For the formula 'house of Jacob' cf. 2.6; 8.17; 10.20; 14.1; 29, 22; 46.3; 48.1; 58.1; Jer. 2.4; 5.20; Ezek. 20.5; 39.25; Amos 3.13; 9.8; Obad. 17f.; Micah 2.7; 3.9; 4.2; Ex. 19.3.

[31] Cf. F. Nötscher, 'Das Angesicht Gottes schauen' in biblischer und babylonischer Auffassung, Darmstadt ²1969, 144.

[1] Insert a qos^emīn in front of miqqedem; this could have fallen out by haplography. But cf. also the radical remarks by D. W. Thomas, ZAW 75, 1963, 88ff., on what he thinks may have been the original form of v. 6b.

and of soothsayers like the Philistines
and thus[2] abounded with children of foreigners;

7 and his land was full of silver and gold
and there was no end to his treasures;
his land was filled with horses,
and there was no end to his chariots;

8 his land was filled with idols,
so that[2] men worshipped the work of their hands,[3]
what their own fingers had made.

9 So men have been humbled and man has been brought low.
Forgive them not![4]

10 **Enter into the rock**
and hide in the dust
before the terror of Yahweh
and his glorious majesty,
<when he rises so that the earth quakes>![5]

11 The proud eyes of men <shall be brought low>[6]
and the arrogance of men shall be humbled,
and Yahweh alone will be exalted
on that day.

12 **Indeed a day is coming for Yahweh Sebaoth**
against all that is proud and lofty
and against all that is lifted up and <high>,[7]

13 **and against all the cedars of Lebanon <   >[8]**
and against all the oaks of Bashan;

14 **and against all the high mountains**
and against all the lofty hills;

15 **and against every high tower**
and against every fortified wall;

16 **and against all the ships of Tarshish**
and against all ships with luxury goods.

17 **Then the haughtiness of man shall be humbled,**
and the pride of man shall be brought low.
And Yahweh alone shall be exalted
on that day.

18 But the idols shall perish[9] altogether.

---

[2] For the use of the so-called imperfect to denote a concomitative action cf. Bobzin §7, 1b.

[3] For the syntax cf. Davidson §116 R 1.

[4] Given 5.15b, there may originally have been a 'by which the eyes of the haughty were brought low' here.

[5] Expanded on the basis of LXX; cf. vv. 17, 21.

[6] Read *tišpalnā*, cf. 1 QIsᵃ.

[7] Follow LXX in reading *wᵉgābōᵃh* instead of the 'and lowly', not unjustifiably inserted by an aristocrat.

[8] Delete v. 13a as a gloss drawn in from v. 14.

[9] Read the plural *yaḥᵃlōpū* with IQ1sᵃ and the old translations.

19   Then they shall creep into the caves of the rocks
        and the holes of the dust
        from before the terror of Yahweh,
        and from his glorious majesty,
        when he rises to make the earth quake.

20   On that day man will throw away
        his silver idols[10] and his golden idols,[10]
        which each man[11] made to worship,
        <to the shrews>[12] and the bats,
21   to escape into the caverns of the rocks
        and the clefts of the cliffs
        from before the terror of Yahweh
        and from his glorious majesty,
        when he rises to make the earth quake.

22   *Turn, then, away from man*
        in whose nostrils is breath,
        for of what account is he?

[2.6–22] Bernard Duhm, the famous Old Testament scholar living at
the end of the last century, said of the present poem about the Day
of Yahweh that it was 'the worst preserved poem in the whole book'.
It does indeed pose numerous difficulties to the commentator: a text
which has sometimes been copied carelessly, traces of insertions to
provide a new interpretation and pointers to at least a systematic
revision, not to mention the ambiguous closing note provided by a
reader. However, in addition the interpretation of the song has also
suffered from the way in which commentators look round for words
of the prophet Isaiah contained in it before interpreting it in the form
which has come down to us, so as to divide it up into what are
supposed to be its different parts. Here in the end the linguistic force
of individual sections, and particularly what is obviously the heart
of the piece in vv. 12–17, seemed to tell in favour of assigning the
poem to the eighth-century prophet.

So as not to make the same mistake, I am beginning with an
interpretation of the song the divisions of which derive solely from
its content, without taking into account the lines which occur like a
refrain. Once we have understood the poem in the form in which it
has been handed down to us, final considerations of the way in

---

[10] Cf. Davidson §24 R 2.
[11] Cf. Davidson § 116 R 1.
[12] Read *laḥ⁼parpārōt*. Whether this is really a reference to the shrew, which shuns
the light, or not rather, as Liebermann, *HAL* 327b conjectures to a certain kind of bat,
is a matter for observation.

which it came into being, which necessarily remain hypothetical, can at any rate avoid doing too much damage.

[2.6–9] *The abandonment of the people.* The poem begins distinctively enough with a short lament addressed to Yahweh. He has abandoned his people, chosen in the patriarch Jacob-Israel,[13] and thus acted in precisely the opposite way to what one might have expected from I Sam. 12.22; Ps. 94.14. If we consider the passages in the Old Testament which speak of the abandonment of the people by Yahweh, it becomes clear that this is brought about in the victory and rule of their enemies (cf. Judg. 6.13; II Kings 21.14).[14] **[9a]** Thus we should not pass over v.9a too rapidly; we need to recall that it is taken up again in 5.15 to indicate the fulfilment of the threats in 5.13, 14 in the destruction of Jerusalem in the year 587 and during the exile.[15] Brief and terse though the reference to this downfall may be in v. 9, with its parallelism using two terms for 'man', characteristic of wisdom,[16] it is important for our understanding not only of the first four verses but also of the whole poem. Evidently it looks back to a great catastrophe and at the same time expects, as the next verses (10ff.) already show, an even more comprehensive and greater one which will evidently not be limited to the people of God and therefore justifies talk of mankind generally.

[6b–8] The reason for the earlier catastrophe given in the next verses is presumably intended to assure the reader that the expected judgment of the world will also take place if he sees similar circumstances in the land in his own time. At all events, whether or not our reconstruction of v. 6aβ is correct,[17] the passage is headed by a reference to mantic practices. While such practices certainly once existed in Israel, as elsewhere (cf. e.g. I Sam. 28),[18] according to Deut. 18.9ff., in the post-exilic period they were certainly thought to be incompatible with belief in Yahweh[19] and, as a look at II Kings 21.1ff. (cf. v. 6) shows, they were thought to be one of the causes for the collapse of the kingdom of Judah. We may already infer from the polemic against the nature cults in 1.29ff.; 57.5ff.; 65.3f. that all kinds of mantic practices from neighbouring countries had found their way into the province of Judah. We can only guess why the Philistines are associated with conjuring up the dead:[20] here Egyptian

[13] References for the term 'house of Jacob' are given above, 56 n. 30.
[14] Cf. also Jer. 23.33, 39.
[15] Cf. 108f. below.
[16] Cf. e.g. Prov. 12.14; 19.22; 24.30; 30.2; Ps. 49.3; and 62.10; also Wildberger, ad loc.
[17] Cf. 56 n. 1 above.
[18] The present text has been worked over in the light of Deut. 18.
[19] Cf. also 8.19f.
[20] Cf. *KBL* 721, s.v. 'nn.

influence and that of the world of the Aegean could have been combined. In view of the inevitable generalizations in poetry, it is hard to decide whether v.6b is a reference to the increased presence of foreigners or denotes mixing of races. It is evident from Neh. 13.23ff. (cf. Ezra 10) that for a while mixed marriages with non-Jews caused problems. And certainly there were more than Phoenician merchants in the country (cf. Neh. 13.16ff.; Joel 4.4ff.; Gen. 37.25).

[7] There is an amazing parallel to v. 7a in Nahum 2.10, even if the meaning is not the same. There is a parallel to wealth consisting in precious metals and horses and chariots, which are here perhaps looked on critically against the background of Deut. 17.16, only in the ideal picture of Solomon's kingdom (cf. I Kings 9.28; 10.7, 10f., 14ff., 26ff.), unless we want to go on as far as the period of the Ptolemies. When we read the description of Solomon's riches, of course our attention is also drawn to the following chapter, I Kings 11.1f., which mentions Solomon's numerous wives and the idolatry which they introduced. International contacts and riches lead to idolatry – this association can hardly be intended to be no more than a comment on history; it will also have in mind the dangers and perils of the time in which it was made.

[8] Thus v. 8 with its reference to the increase of the number of gods in the land follows naturally, though it is surprising that the theme is not treated along with manticism. The characterization of the 'no-things' as the work of men's hands is a traditional description, common in the Deuteronomic and Deuteronomistic traditions, and meant as an 'enlightened' comment.[21] It presupposes a simple identification of the image with the god and is therefore at best applicable only to popular superstition. In their idols people worship their own creations instead of their creator. That is the burden of the charge. And again, the increase in polemic against idolatry in the post-exilic period shows that this was a particular evil of the time (cf. Ps. 105.4; 135.15; Isa. 40.19f.; 41.6f.; 42.17; 44.9–20; 45.16f., 20b; 46.5–8; 48.22, and 17.8; 31.7).

[9a] The result of this internal alienation of the people had been its apostasy from Yahweh, and a consequence of this apostasy was abandonment to its enemies, naturally resulting in the profound humiliation[22] of all those who had previously been proud of their riches and their idols. [9b] This half-verse, which commentators usually treat as an addition,[22a] shows that the interpretation which brings out the double perspective of the poem cannot have been

---

[21] Cf. Lev. 26.1; Ps. 96.5; 97.7; Isa. 10.10f.; 19.13; 31.7 and Micah 5.12; Deut. 4.28; 27.15; II Kings 19.18 par. Isa. 37.19; II Kings 22.17 and Jer. 25.6f., 32.30, 34; 44.8.

[22] Cf. also Prov. 14.19; 29.23; and I Sam. 2.7; Ps. 147.6; 29.4; 10.33; 25.11f.

[22a] Cf. also 57 n. 4 above. It should be noted that 1QIs[a] has omitted the clause.

completely wrong. Criticism of the present is concealed within criticism of the past. For the invitation directed to Yahweh not to forgive them, and therefore those who act in the way described, presupposes that the reader responsible for the addition found the malpractices thus attacked in the circumstances of his own time.

[2.10–19] *The future Day of Yahweh*. In accordance with the use of the generic term 'man', characteristic of the interest of wisdom literature in the individual, the invitation, which is concerned with the poet's time, is addressed to an individual and through him to everyman. All are summoned to seek security in rocks and caves (cf. Jer. 4.29; Isa. 29.4), in view of the imminence of the terrifying appearance of the powerful majesty of God,[23] the moment when he rises to judge the peoples of the earth,[24] so that the earth recoils in horror (cf. Ps. 76.9f.; 10.12, 18; Zeph. 3.8). Then the pride of man is finally broken (Ps. 18.28; Isa. 13.11), and it becomes manifest that Yahweh alone is exalted (33.5; 12.4; Ps. 148.13). The additional 'on that day' forms a powerful conclusion and at the same time points forward to v. 12a. [12a] This verse is the beginning of the real announcement of the Day of Yahweh. It is the day on which he has planned to intervene, on which he will reveal his power to the whole world (cf. 34.8; 13.6, 9; Ezek. 30.3).[25]

[12b–16] In the subsequent verses, in ten couplets the poet describes the annihilation of everything that can impress man by its size. Without explicitly mentioning it, he shows us the force of a violent hurricane which tears through the land from north to south, spreading terror before it and devastation in its wake. The background to this is the description of a storm theophany like that depicted in Ps. 29. Verse 12b gives a general picture which is then evoked in more specific terms in vv. 13–16: the coming Day of Yahweh will affect all earthly pride and all earthly things (cf. also Ezek. 21.32). First to experience it are the mighty cedars of Lebanon (cf. Ps. 29.5); then come the oaks of Bashan, somewhere in the region of the present-day Golan heights[26] (cf. Ps. 29.9; Nahum 1.4; Zech. 11.1f.). But even the mountains and hills are not spared, so that the catastrophe takes on cosmic dimensions (cf. Jer. 4.24ff.; Nahum 1.5; Hab.3.6; Ezek. 38.20). Whatever promises people sure refuge, high towers and fortified walls (cf. 30.25; Ezek. 38.20; Isa. 25.12), is torn

[23] For the formula 'fear of Yahweh' cf. I Sam. 11.7; II Chron. 14.13; 17.10; 19.7; 20.29; Ps. 36.2 and also Isa. 24.17.
[24] Cf. also Ps. 44.27; 82.8 and, in the context of the individual lament, Ps. 3.8; 7.7; 35.2; 17.15.
[25] Cf. also Jonah 1.15; 4.14; Zeph. 1.7, 14; also Amos 5.18, 20; Jonah 2.1, 2, 11; 3.4; Zech. 14.7; Mal. 3.23; and also Zeph. 2.2. For discussion of the derivation of the concept of the day of Yahweh see *Isaiah 13–39*, 15f.
[26] Cf. also B. Reicke, *BHH* I, cols. 203f.

down. And of course the trading ships with their precious cargo, returning from distant parts, are not spared (cf. also Ps. 48.8). They are described as ships of Tarshish, after the ancient destination of Phoenician sea trade, situated on the Iberian peninsula. Kings of Judah are said to have engaged in such seafaring, partly with Tyre (I Kings 10.22),[27] and partly from Elath on their own territory (I Kings 22.49; II Kings 14.22).

At the end the reader wonders whether the storm which tears down and annihilates all that is mighty does not conceal the enemies coming from the north, to advance against Zion (cf. Jer. 4.15ff.; Isa. 10.28ff.; 13.2ff.; Zeph. 1.2ff.), and whether the cosmic colours of the phenomena accompanying the theophany of Yahweh do not represent an event in earthly history. [17] However, the generalizations in v. 12b and v. 17 show that the person who wrote these verses is still a long way from such specific ideas, and is only thinking in quite general terms of that moment when all earthly greatness, including of course all the power of the nations, will be brought to nothing before the God who makes his appearance. Where human beings have to deal directly with God, their pride and their self-assurance collapse. It is only after this collapse that God reveals himself in his solitary splendour.

[18–19] So in v. 18 a reader makes the obvious comment that this means the end of the idols.[28] In that case only one thing is left for men, to creep into caves in the rocks and clefts in the cliffs, so that they are not destroyed by the majesty of the presence of God. In contrast to 33.14ff., the poet draws no distinction between sinners and righteous. And again we may ask whether he took the redemption of the righteous so much for granted that he did not find it necessary to mention it, or whether he did not want to teach all his people to be terrified before God and thus bring them to repentance. Or did he go against the views of his time while standing on God's side, and was he so convinced of the cosmic necessity of the approaching crisis that expectation of it formed the sole centre of his thought? The generalizations are in favour of this understanding, so we are justified in discovering here the message of the coming judgment of the world as it has been described in 24.1ff.; 13.9ff., in the shadow of which there also grew up an expectation of the judgment of the world that would take place before the gates of Jerusalem (cf. also 5.14, 17; 6.12–13abα and 7.23–25*).

[27] Cf. also *Isaiah 13–39*, 163f.; E. Würthwein, *Die Bücher der Könige I*, ATD, 126, and K. Galling, *ZDPV* 88, 1973, 1ff., 140ff.; now also W. Helck, *Die Beziehungen Ägyptens und Vorderasiens zur Ägäis bis ins 7. Jahrhundert v. Chr.*, Erträge der Forschung 120, Darmstadt 1979, 158f.

[28] Cf. also below, 65.

[2.20–21] The present-day reader may well pass over the elaboration of what will happen 'on that day' to the valuable statuettes of gods made of gold and silver, the idols. However, there must have been a reason why the theme begun in vv. 8,9a and repeated and really concluded in v. 18 should be taken up again and brought to an end by a revision of vv. 10, 19. If we are to understand the content of v. 20 we need to know that the animals mentioned here, especially the bat, mentioned in second place, were thought to be unclean, and therefore were looked on with repugnance (cf. Lev. 11.19; Deut. 14.18).[29] In an attempt to hide as quickly as possible from the consuming majesty of Yahweh at his appearance, seeking the caves and clefts in the rock, people will throw away the idols before whom they have hitherto prostrated themselves, valuable because of the precious metal of which they are made, into the darkness in which unclean animals have their lair, and thus desecrate them. Not only does the presence of God correct perspectives in the human sphere; it also teaches men to pass a right judgment on the things of the world and thus destroys their religious or pseudo-religious idolatry.

[22] We may take it as certain that this verse is the addition of a later reader. There is dispute as to what it means to say. Some see it as a closing admonition not to trust in man either, an admonition which rounds off the poem.[30] In that case it would be along the lines of 7.9; 28.1; 30.15. Thus in view of the imminent Day of Yahweh it would be vital to trust neither in idols nor in man, but to rely only on God and in that way to avoid judgment. However, perhaps we should prefer the view of the other commentators, supported by the echoes of the individual lament, in which reference to man's transitoriness is one of the themes which should cause God to be merciful (cf. e.g. Ps. 39.13f.; Amos 7,5; Job 7.16).[31] They see the verse as a pious ejaculation, directed to the eschatological teacher by a reader who thinks little of eschatology and its expectations of the Day of Yahweh, and who expressed his displeasure at the poem by asking that the short life allotted to transitory humankind should not be made more difficult by such day-dreams. In that case the theology of this addition comes close to that of Ecclesiastes, who regarded the expectation of a transformation of the world and a future life with indomitable scepticism (cf. Eccles. 1.9f.; 3.19f.; also Ps. 22.30b M).

[2.6–22] *The literary problem.* Now that we have commented on the prophecy in its present form it is appropriate to consider how it came into being. The following pointers indicate that it is not all of a piece.

1. The direct address to Yahweh in v. 6aα, like a lament, is

[29] Cf. also above 58 n. 12.
[30] Cf. e.g. Marti; Fohrer; Kaiser[1]; Eichrodt; and Schedl, *Rufer des Heils*, ad loc.
[31] Cf. e.g. Duhm and Wildberger, ad loc.

surprising: it leads us to expect a prayer, but is followed instead first in vv.6aβ–9 by a retrospect on previous disasters and in vv.10–21 by a prophecy.

2. The adoption of a direct address to Yahweh in v. 9b, and furthermore in the form of a so-called vetitive, an admonition characteristic of wisdom, is surely an addition.

3. Verse 22 is also certainly not original, however we may now understand it.

4. Verse 11, along with v. 17, looks like a refrain, but the way in which the thoughts in vv. 10f., 17 + 19 reflect one another rules out this assumption, at first glance giving the impression that the composition is circular.

5. It is striking that despite some variations there are correspondences between vv. 9a, 11a, 17a, 5.15; again between vv. 11b, 17b and 5.16; and finally also between vv. 10, 19 and 21. Here 5.16 at any rate must be seen as a redactional change, intended for its present context.[32]

6. Verse 18 makes a break between vv. 17 and 19, and in addition the verse clashes with vv. 20, 21, which are to be seen as an addition because of the introduction with the formula 'on that day'. However, even if we exclude v. 18, v. 19 really seems lame after v. 17b, because the announcement that the glory of Yahweh will be all that is left at the end cannot be followed by anything else.

7. We may note that v. 6a$\beta\gamma$ and v. 8, both concerned with religious offences, should have been set side by side had they originally belonged together. All this is sufficient illustration of the complexity of the evidence. It is not surprising, therefore, that as a result there have been largely mutually exclusive attempts in modern scholarship to illuminate the formation of the section.[33] In the end they only agree – here confirming the following investigation – that vv. 12–17 at any rate belong together; they conflict with the considerations I advance here in supposing that the verses may be attributed to

---

[32] Cf. below 109.

[33] In this note I shall give a selection of analyses made in this century. Duhm found three fragments of 'boisterous youthful discourses' by the prophet in 2.6–10, 18–21; 2.11–17; 5.15–16. Marti reconstructed for himself a refrain poem with verses 2,10, 6–8, 9* (=11a), 11b, 10, 19bβ 12–18, in that order, Fohrer put together 6aα, 7,8,11, 12–17, 19–21. Wildberger found four fragments of Isaiah in 2.6; 2.7–9a(18); 2.12–17; 2.19. Fey, *Amos und Jesaja*, 77ff., singled out 6–7, 11, 12–17, 19 as a nucleus. Hoffmann, *Intention*, 107ff., rightly recognized that there is a historical retrospect in 7,8a, 9a – between 8a and 9a he posited a lacuna – and put them together with 12–17, 19. Vermeylen I, 133f., distinguished between 2.12–17 as the basic material from Isaiah and 6a–7, 9a + Micah 6.9b–11,13 as a poem the parts of which have now been broken up among the remaining redactional material. Barth, *Jesaja-Worte*, 222f., recognized the connection between 10 and 12–17 and found in 7–8a, 9a a fragment, despite his usual disinclination to reckon with such things.

Isaiah. On the other hand, they come to differing conclusions as to the question of the demarcation of the poem at its beginning and end. Evidently the picture presented by the poem is so perplexing that there can be no definitive explanation of the evidence; at best we can only attempt in all modesty to clarify the way in which the section presumably came into being.

I shall begin with my own comments on the end of the text. The exegesis has shown that v. 22 may certainly be put on one side, so we may turn directly to vv. 20, 21. Here it is evident that the verses form an independent expansion of what has gone before. This is clear formally from the new beginning with the prophetic formula 'on that day', and in content from their dependence on the announcement of the Day of Yahweh. It is impossible to resolve whether they have taken over the theme of idolatry from v. 8 or rather have prefigured this verse. However, we may assume that the former is more likely and that the nucleus of the poem in vv. 10, 12–17 had already been expanded by the retrospect on previous disasters in vv. 6–8. That this in turn is not of a piece is already evident from the fact that the reason for the abandonment of the people by Yahweh in v. 6aβγb anticipates that in v. 8. As vv. 7, 8 are a self-contained unit, v. 6aβγb is to be seen as a subsequent expansion of the retrospect on disaster, which serves as a bridge text between 2.2–5 and 2.10ff.* It is evident that v. 9a looks back to v. 17a. As the thought of the half-verse, in view of v.6aα, is not necessarily part of the retrospect, we must reckon with the possibility that it too was added later to provide a conclusion to the bridge text similar to the nucleus of the poem and perhaps also the additional strophe. In turn, v. 9b has the task of providing a link between the retrospect, rounded off in this way, and the following threat of judgment. Perhaps this half-verse owes its existence to the same hand as that which also inserted v. 18. In view of its bombastic version of the first line compared with 5.15b, v. 11 remains suspiciously like an addition presupposing both v. 9a and v. 17. In turn, v. 21 may imitate v. 19.

In my view, we then arrive at the following literary stratification. At a first stage of editing, the nucleus of the poem about the coming Day of Yahweh in vv. 10, 12–17 was expanded by vv. 6aα, 7–8 as a text linking it with 2.2–5, which had just been taken into the Isaiah scroll. At a next stage the prophecy about the attitude of the idolaters in the eschatological judgment (vv. 20, 21) was added. To give the retrospect on disaster more weight to balance it with the following proclamation, v. 9a was added in the same way as v. 17a. Verse 9b seeks to remove the tension between retrospect and prophecy which clearly emerges as a result. Perhaps we also owe the insertion of v. 18 to the hand which inserted this half-verse. Both are brief insertions

taking Yahweh's part. Verse 6aβγb could already have been added
to the retrospect before the addition of v. 9a without this amounting
to a clear stage in the process of redaction, as in the case of vv. 11, 19.
However, we cannot rule out the possibility that v. 19 was added to
the nucleus of the poem even before v. 18, as otherwise we would
have to assume that the person responsible for the addition failed to
notice that grammatically the idols mentioned in v. 18 are the subject
of v. 19. I have already indicated the special position of v. 22.

As to the origin of the poem about the great Day of Yahweh in vv.
10, 12–17, which forms the nucleus of this section, it must be asserted
from the start that there is nothing within the context of the results
of the preceding investigation to suggest that this is a fragment from
Isaiah. Historically speaking, the expectation of a future world
judgment which is contained in it belongs not in the eighth century
BC but rather in the Persian period. That already implies that the
verses presumably derive from a redactor of the Isaiah scroll. His
work can be traced through as far as ch. 32.[34] The retrospect on past
disaster is intended to support the expectation of judgment by a
reference back to the catastrophe of 587. The reason given for it in
turn prompted the expansion of the announcement of judgment by
the threat against the idolaters.

CHAPTER 3.1–11

Collapse and Anarchy

1   For behold, the Lord,
        Yahweh Sebaoth,
        is taking away from Jerusalem and from Judah
        stay and staff,[1]
        the whole stay of bread and the whole stay of water.[2]

---

[34] See above, 3f., and *Isaiah 13–39* on 32.9ff.
[1] For the juxtaposition of a masculine and a feminine word to denote universality
cf. Davidson §17 R 5.
[2] For the editorial additions see the commentary.

2   Mercenary and warrior,
      judge and *prophet and diviner* elder,

3   Captain of fifty and man of influence,
      counsellor and wise man *in magic arts and expert in charms.*[2]

4   Then I will make boys their princes,
      and caprice[3] will rule over them.[4]

5   And the people shall be oppressed, one man by another
      and everyone by his neighbour,
      so that the young is insolent to the old
      and the base to the honourable.

6   (Then) when a man takes hold of his brother
      in the house of his father:[5]
      'You have[6] a mantle;
      you shall be our leader,
      and this heap of ruins
      shall be under your hand.'

7   On that day he will rise and say,
      'I will not be ruler,[7]
      and in my house there is no *bread nor*[2] mantle,
      You cannot make me
      leader of the people.'

8   *Yes, Jerusalem stumbled*
      and Judah fell;[8]
      because their speech and their deeds were against Yahweh,
      defying the eyes of his glory.

9   *Their respect of person*[9] *testified against them*
      and they proclaimed their sins like Sodom: they did not hide them.
      Woe to them,
      for they brought down disaster upon themselves.

10   <Blessed>[10] is the righteous man for it is well with him,
      because he enjoys the fruit of his deeds.

11   Woe to the evil man, it goes ill with him,
      because he is recompensed according to the deeds of his hands.

[2] For the editorial additions see the commentary.

[3] Abstract for concrete, the property for the one who has it.

[4] For the use of the so-called imperfect to denote a concomitative action cf. Bobzin §7,1b.

[5] Marti and Kissane take the word *śimlā*, 'garment', into the previous clause and interpret *lᵉkā* as 'well, then', i.e. as an extended imperative of *hālak*.

[6] For the writing of a pronominal suffix *plene* cf. G-K[28] §103 g.

[7] LXX translates *archēgos*, V *medicus*. Cf. HAT 278a s.v. *ḥābaš*, and Job 34.17.

[8] Judah is treated as masculine, thinking of its inhabitants; cf. also G-K[28] §122 and Joüon §134g. For the possibility of understanding the present 'perfect forms' as a *perfectum confidentiae*, cf. G-K[28] §106n; Meyer[3] §101,4a, and W. Fischer, *Grammatik des klassischen Arabisch*, Wiesbaden 1977, § 182. However, it is quite possible to understand vv. 8a, 9a as a retrospect. Cf. also Wildberger, ad loc.

[9] *pᵉnēhem* is a subjective genitive.

[10] Read *'aśrē*.

[3.1–4.1] These verses contain a series of sayings concerned with a future judgment of Yahweh on Jerusalem and Judah. It is hard to see where one ends and another begins, because although the content of the verses is connected, they have strange breaks in style or seem fragmentary. **[3.1–11]** That is immediately evident here: vv. 9b, 10 and 11 evidently mark a break, though in theme there is a connection between vv. 8 and 9a on the one hand and v. 12 on the other. However, the section 3.1–9a which remains is not without a problem: not only does a divine discourse begin quite abruptly in v. 4, but vv. 8, 9a are formulated in such a way that we are not sure whether they are a note of the fulfilment of 5.15f. or a prophecy expressing the utmost certainty. The manifest addition in v. 1b shows that we must expect further additions. If we assume that the metre is the *qīnah* or funeral dirge, then 2b and 3b, which do not fit it, must be seen as disruptions. And although from v. 6 on the metre becomes broader and more disturbed, v. 1b helps us to recognize the addition in v. 7a. The editor here was on the one hand thinking of the famine leading to capitulation and on the other hand following 2.6a in stressing the presence of questionable religious practices in the land.

As vv. 6, 7, like 4, 5, represent an extension of what has gone before, we may ask whether the section 3.1–9a did not already come into being in four stages: the prophecy of the removal of all the men needed for defending and governing the country in 3.1–3 will have been supplemented in 4–5 by a saying about the anarchy which would result, and in 6–7 by one about the impossibility of finding anyone able and ready to take over government; 8–9a would be a reference to the cause of the collapse. However, in view of the material in this chapter generally, it is quite possible that 3.1–9a comes from a single hand, that of an author who was uncertain of form.[11]

[1] The very fact that the introductory *kī*, 'for', has been inserted into the metre indicates that in 3.1ff. and, as will later emerge, also in the other units which make up the chapter, we have literary constructions. There are further weighty reasons to support this judgment in the case of 3.1ff. First of all in this connection it should be noted that vv. 1–3 evidently imitate 2.12–16 by listing those affected by the future judgment of Yahweh in five pairs; in each case the list is headed by a generalizing pair which incorporates the other four. Secondly, we might note a relatively colourful terminology,

---

[11] Vermeylen I, 145, has argued that vv. 4–7 should be understood as an insertion. – For the make-up of the other sections, 3.12ff., 16ff., 25ff., cf. 75ff., 79ff., 82ff. below.

which is not, however, very original, despite the originality of the description in vv. 6,7. From the evidence given in the note, two word-usages deserve special consideration: the probability that the verb of 1.25b is taken up again in v. 1a, and that v. 8b, which seems stilted, is dependent on 1.16, 20; 6.3. If the 'Sodom' in v. 9a is original, then this would be a further reference to 1.10.[12]

Now the mention of the *gibbōr*, the 'hero' or, as we might translate it in a less pretentious way, the mercenary, and the '*īš milḥāmā*, the warrior or the member of the people's army,[13] seems to tell against the assumption that 3.1–9a is a post-exilic redactional work standing in the shadow of 1.10–17; 1.21–25, and also partly dependent for its construction on 2.12ff., though that is what the assessment of these texts proposed above would in fact require.[14] However, this argument is not as telling as it might appear at first sight, since the governors of the Persian province of Judah, who were evidently almost all descended from Jewish families,[15] necessarily had their own soldiers, however many or however few they may have been: there was a commandant for the citadel which defended the city, and unless in the case of Nehemiah we have an emergency measure which was later dropped, a city guard provided by the inhabitants (cf. Neh. 4.10; 7.1ff.). In complete contrast to the picture that we

[12] For the use of *hinnē*, 'behold', and a participle governed by Yahweh as subject as the introduction to a prophecy cf. 10.33; 17.1; 19.1; 24.1; 26.1; 30.27. We find the practice of speaking of Jerusalem and Judah in that order, a usage generally taken to be pre-exilic, in e.g. Isa. 5.3; 22.21; 44.26; Jer. 25.18; 34.19; 40.1; Lam. 1.7; 2.4f., while mention of Judah and Jerusalem occurs e.g. in Micah 1.5, 8; Jer. 7.17; 11.6; 17.26, etc. There is no support for the assumption that in the time of the monarchy Jerusalem was constitutionally superior to Judah in the fact that the Books of Kings speak of the kings of the southern kingdom as kings of Judah who reigned in Jerusalem; cf. e.g. I Kings 14.21; II Kings 16.1f.; 23.1. For the phrase 'mercenary and warrior', cf. Ezek. 39.20 and I Sam. 16.18; Neh. 11.14. Mention of 'judge and elder' occurs elsewhere only in Deut. 21.2, and there it is in reverse order and in the plural. For the term *n'śū pānīm*, translated 'man of influence' above, cf. 9.14; Job. 22.8; II Kings 5.1; Deut. 28.50. There is a striking parallel to v. 4b in Ps. 19.14; it is worth comparing v. 5aα with Deut. 15.2. Verse 5aβ is a formula, cf. Judg. 7.22; I Sam. 14.20; Isa. 19.2; Zech. 8.10. With v. 5b cf. Prov. 6.3; Jer. 16.14; 23.9. There is a parallel to v. 7b in Judg. 11.11. It is doubtful whether we should look for a literary model for the formula 'stumble and fall' in v. 8a, but compare 8.15; 31.3 and Ps. 72.2; Jer. 46.6, 12, 16; 50.32; Dan. 11.19; Prov. 24.16f.; also Jer. 6.15; 8.12. Verse 8b is illuminated by 1.16, 20; 6.3; but should also be compared with Ps. 78.36, 17. Verse 9aα takes up the reproach in Deut. 1.17; 16.19; Prov. 24.23; 28.21, and certainly has 1.17, 23 in view. For *'ānā b'*, cf. Deut. 19.16; II Sam. 1.16; Isa. 59.12; Hos. 5.5. Verse 9aβ is worth comparing with Ps. 38.19 and, for the formal juxtaposition of the verbs, also with I Sam. 3.18; Job. 15.18; Josh. 7.19.

[13] Cf. R. Knierim, *ZAW* 73, 1961, 169.

[14] Cf. above, 28, 40f., 65f.

[15] Cf. N. Avigad, 'Bullae and Seals from a Post-Exilic Judean Archive', *Qedem* 4, Jerusalem 1976, 32bff.

might form of the post-exilic period, according to Neh. 4.7 Nehemiah could even call upon an armed people's army, organized in groups according to clan, to defend the city. This might almost be seen as a successor of the former levy of Judah. That also explains how in a later text the *śar ḥᵃmiššīm*, the prince or leader of fift[16], can emerge, whether he has now retained his old miltary functions or given them up entirely in favour of the duties of a judge which he took up later in the context of the clan (cf. Ex. 18.21b, 25b with e.g. II Kings 1.9ff.).[17] The purpose of the present text can easily be explained from its references: by virtue of its formal imitation of 2.12ff. it proves to be an attempt at a specific interpretation of this announcement of the destruction of all the lofty and proud in the coming judgment. Here the concentration on the fate of Jerusalem and Judah[18] is completely in line with 1.10ff.; 1.21ff.: both texts bring into prominence the collapse of the leading class. Accordingly 3.1ff. and the additions which extend as far as 4.1 deal with the fate of Jerusalem and Judah in the final judgment.

[**3.1–3**] *The people is stripped of its leaders.* Underlining the power of the God of Israel quite emphatically with its use of the designations 'the Lord'[19] and 'Yahweh Sebaoth'[20], the announcement of the fate of Jerusalem and Judah in the last judgment begins by showing that although the God of Israel might seem long ago to have disappeared from the stage of world history, he is still, as before, Lord of all lords (cf. Deut. 10.17), and has the power to set in motion all the forces of earth and heaven. He will use them to remove all the men among the people who could give them support and stay (cf. also Ps. 18.19; II Kings 18.21 par. Isa. 36.6). It emerges from the fact that this general statement first becomes more specific with a mention of mercenaries and the people's army that the impending judgment will again take the form of a complete military defeat, including the conquest of Jerusalem (cf. vv. 25f.). Here we have a transformation of the expectation of world judgment which reduces it from its cosmic dimensions to the pseudo-historical dimension of the onslaught of the nations upon Jerusalem, which had found particularly clear expression in the Assyrian stratum of Isaiah (1–39),[21] and which in my view can already be found to underlie 1.24.[22]

---

[16] Cf. Ex. 18.21, 25; Deut. 1.15; II Kings 1.9, 11; II Chron. 8.10.
[17] Cf. also Knierim, *ZAW* 73, 1961, 160ff.; G. C. Macholz, *ZAW* 84, 1972, 323; and also CD XII.19 – XIII.2.
[18] For the evidence of their being mentioned in this order cf. above, 69 n. 12.
[19] Cf. 1.24; 10.16, 33; 19.4; Mal. 3.1; Ex. 23.17; 34.23; and also O. Eissfeldt, *TWAT* I, 62ff., *TDOT* 1, 59ff.
[20] Cf. below, 126f.
[21] Cf. 14.24ff.; 17.12ff.; 29.1ff.; 30.27ff.
[22] Cf. above, 40f.

[2-3] With their mention of judges and elders, captains of fifties and nobles, counsellors and wise men, the next three pairs show that the expected catastrophe, like that of 587, will also affect the whole civil administration and all those men who by virtue of their birth might exercise special influence,[23] or by virtue of their knowledge might be able to provide practical help. The reader is left to imagine whether this might come about by executions (cf. II Kings 25.18ff.; Lam. 5.12) or deportations (cf. II Kings 24.12ff.; 25.11ff.; Jer. 52.28ff.; Zech 11.4ff.). We may take the fact that in this context there is no mention of the king as a further decisive indication to be added to the arguments advanced above for a late dating. [1b] The redactor whose comment can be heard here envisages that in agreement with II Kings 25.3 (cf. also II Kings 18.27 par. Isa. 36.12; Isa. 22.9ff.) the city was starved into submission. At least the first part of his comment, which seems to us somewhat artificial, could be meant quite realistically, having in mind the baker's wooden batons on which the circular loaves were arranged. This kind of structure can still be seen even today in the alleyways of cities in the Near East.[24] If it did not see the prophecy fulfilled along the lines of vv. 8f. in the catastrophe of the year 587, this addition reflects the confidence in the impregnability of the city regained as a result of Nehemiah's wall-building.

[3.4-5] *The rule of caprice.* As a consequence of the stripping of the capital and the country of its leading class, which he expects, the poet foresees the anarchy which usually comes about in history, far from all utopian conceptions, as a *bellum omnium contra omnes*, a free-for-all war, and therefore a state of utter lawlessness. All natural and social ties and concerns disappear: the young do not, as in a healthy society, respect the old (cf. Lev. 19.32; Prov. 16.31; 20.29), nor do the common people respect those whom they have made responsible for their society. Instead of this, caprice holds sway, the caprice of those who claim to themselves the right of the strong. In these circumstances those who claim to be self-appointed authorities are simply bands of young men who act as they want in the cities. However, if vv. 6, 7 are later additions, v. 4 could have in mind an emergency government composed of young men which, because of its inexperience, puts into effect whatever majority decisions are made at any time and thus does the people more harm than good (cf. Eccles. 10.16; Sir. 10.3; CD XIV. 6ff.; Plato, *Laws* VI, 785b).

[23] Cf. 9.14; Job 22.8; II Kings 5.1.
[24] Cf. Köhler, *Kleine Lichter*, Zurich 1945, 25ff., who refers in particular to the batons stuck on flat wicker baskets, with circular loaves piled up on them, which are used by bread-sellers as far west as Italy.

[3.6–7] *The hopelessness of the situation.* The general situation of the country and its capital is reflected in the fact that in contrast to normal times, no one is prepared to lead the people. No one will even allow himself to be forced to take office under pressure from his clan or his fellows (cf. II Sam. 19.13; Lev. 19.17). At that time possession of a mantle, i.e. sufficiently representative clothing, will be regarded as adequate qualification. However, anyone who has this qualification will reject the doubtful honour of the ruler's insignia and deny outright that he has a mantle in order to evade the thankless task, so despoiled is the land (cf. 33.1f.; Zech. 14.2) and so hopeless the situation.[25]

[3.8–9a] *The collapse and its causes.* I have already indicated that it is uncertain whether these verses are to be understood as prophecy or as a note of prophecy fulfilled. It is clear from v. 1b that the later additions to vv. 1–3, 7 can well be understood as preparation for an addition which suggests that the announcement was already fulfilled in the collapse of the kingdom of Judah in 587. We might wonder whether the mention of the prophet alongside the diviner in vv. 2f. is an indication of a decline in his reputation, which finally emerges in Zech. 13.3ff. Such a note of fulfilment could demonstrate a strange tendency to neutralize the eschatological message such as we seem to find elsewhere in the wisdom additions in 2.22; 3.9b–12. However, it could also be interpreted as a consequence of the view that this was a prophecy of Isaiah from the eighth century; and finally, we cannot even rule out a deliberate historicization in the interest of concealing the announcement from Persian observers of the religious life of the Jews.

Whereas the retrospect on disaster in 2.6–9 gives the following prophecy greater weight by stressing the analogous situation then and now, the note of fulfilment makes it peripheral (cf. also Lam. 4.22a.). Whether it is in fact a note of fulfilment, as I have conjectured, or the opposite, a quite self-confident prophecy to be confirmed in the future, it is at all events clear that the cause of the catastrophe is to be sought in open rebellion to Yahweh which expresses itself in word and deed (cf. also 5.18f.; 30.9f.). In accord with 1.17; 1.21ff. (cf. also 10.1f.), disobedience to Yahweh's will is manifested in the partisan nature of the legal decisions which are guided by respect for persons (cf. e.g. Deut. 16.19; Prov. 24.23) instead of by the content of the claims, thus putting at a disadvantage the common people and all those who rely on the help of others in law, and doing

---

[25] Plato, *Republic* VII, 520d, has rightly observed that hesitating to take office can also be the special virtue of a ruler.

violence to them.[26] The man whose voice is to be heard here sees the disruptive element in this conduct in the fact that it happens quite publicly and that no one even tries to hide it. Consequently it has been compared, either by him or by a later writer, with the sin of the Sodomites, who did not hesitate to give unbridled expression to their desires in despising the rights of aliens (cf. Gen. 19.4ff.).

If this were in fact a reason for a disaster which was still to come, in religious terms we would here have a reference to the social conflict in the later Persian period and the crisis in belief in Yahweh which went hand in hand with it (cf. also Neh. 5.1ff.). At all events, even now it is worth noting that crisis in a society at the same time reflects a crisis in its relationship with God. It follows from this that the one cannot be resolved without the other, however much a materialistic philosophy of history may protest against this and see spiritual upheavals as no more than a reflection of economic crises. In reality, however, both times it is a matter of the man who understands himself, of his self-understanding and the work which results from this. However, we must recognize that human reality cannot be grasped within the framework of the artificially reduced horizon of a mere individual, but is rather always caught up in constellations of destiny which transcend the subjective and the individual.

[3.9b–11] *The teaching of wisdom.* These verses express the certainty that every man forges his own destiny. Thus they are in the wisdom tradition, and are part of an affirmation which can be traced into the post-exilic period and which finally led to the objections of the Job poetry and the Preacher.[27] Verse 9b is as ambiguous as vv. 8, 9a which precede it. It can therefore be understood either as retrospective, applying to the victims of the catastrophe of 587, or prospective, and therefore an admonitory lamentation. If one prefers the former interpretation, the possibility cannot be ruled out that the author of v. 9b is to be identified with the author of vv. 8, 9a. In that case he would already have come across the two following verses, 10 and 11, and applied their teaching to history in such a way as to see the collapse of the kingdom of Judah and its consequences as a disaster which the people brought upon themselves. Accordingly, the form of the lament would have been given him by v. 11, whereas for content he could go back to tradition (cf. Prov. 11.17a).

[10–11] These verses take up the idea of the differing fortunes of the righteous and the godless, as that is to be found in the terminology

---

[26] Delitzsch and Kaiser[1] misunderstood the formal terminology and so applied it to a rejection written on the face of the godless.

[27] Cf. e.g. H. H. Schmid, *Wesen und Geschichte der Weisheit*, BZAW 101, Berlin 1966, 155f., 173f.

of wisdom and the individual lament which is partly influenced by its thought.[28] Rooted in it, the speaker congratulates[29] the righteous because he can count on having a long and happy life in accordance with his deeds (cf. Prov. 11.30f.). By contrast, the life of the godless is lamentable because his own actions similarly come home to him, and he can be sure of a short unhappy life with a terrible end (cf. Prov. 11.31). We may well ask whether these two verses, coming after the eschatological prophecy of 3.1-7, are meant to stress that the connection between action and outcome will not be removed even in the judgment to come. In that case they would have the role of interpreting it as a selective event which merely destroyed the evil. The other possibility would be that in them a man indebted to wisdom thinking countered the eschatological expectations in order to direct attention to the ever-present active judgment of Yahweh, who gives every man his due at all times. Here the redactor would be close to those theocratically inclined circles which had found in Yahweh's ever-prevailing presence and his special concern for Israel in providing for atonement through the cult, a compensation for the nation's loss of independence.

CHAPTER 3.12-15

Yahweh's Dispute

12   'My people – every one of their governors[1] is a plunderer,[2]
        and <usurers>[3] rule them!

---

[28] Cf. e.g. Prov. 10.7, 11, 16; 11.30; Ps. 7.10; 11.2f., 5f.; 37.25, 28f.
[29] Cf. e.g. Prov. 3.13; 8.34; 28.14; Isa. 30.18; 56.2; Ps. 1.1; 2.12.
[1] Cf. G-K[28] §1451, but also §124 f. IQIs[a] reads *ngśw*.
[2] For the meaning cf. Zorell, 602, s.v. *ᶜll* poel. For the discussion cf. Wildberger, ad. loc.; Vermeylen I, 147.
[3] MT *nāšīm*, women. Read *wᵉnōšīm* as is required by the subsequent predicate of the third-person masculine plural. Cf. also T and LXX.

My people, your leaders are seducers,
who confuse the path on which you should walk.'[4]

13 Yahweh stands ready to contend,
he comes forward to judge <for his people>.[5]

14 Yahweh comes to the judgment
with the elders of his people and his princes:
'And you,[6] you have devoured the vineyard;[7]
the spoil of the poor is in your houses.

15 What do you mean by crushing my people
and grinding down the face of the poor?'[8]
is the oracle of the Lord[9] Yahweh Sebaoth.

[3.12–15] This small section has the same literary character as the other parts of this chapter: it is a redactional unit with a relatively loose structure. It begins with a lament of Yahweh over his people in v. 12, the second half of which is directly addressed to them. In a continuation of the thought, v. 13 proclaims that Yahweh will intervene in judgment in favour of his people. With v. 14 the scene changes from before the judgment to the situation at the judgment. Verse 14a gives the elders and princes of the people as opponents in the trial. Then, in vv. 14b, 15a, a short accusation follows. It is brought to an end by the oracle formula in v. 15b. The restless change of forms and addresses should not tempt us to sub-divide the section or to assume that fragments have been worked over here. First of all, despite the playful change in form, the content is connected; secondly, an investigation of the terminology shows the redactional character of the saying. Its role is to give a subsequent justification for the announcement of the removal of the upper classes made in 3.1ff.[10] The increased liveliness provided at the end of the section by

[4] For the break-up of the expression 'way of your path', cf. also Wildberger, ad loc.

[5] LXX has preserved the right reading, *'ammō*, in accordance with the context, over against M and the tradition which follows it, which reads *'ammīm*, peoples. At a later stage M is concerned to establish that the judgment on the leaders of the people will take place in connection with the judgment on the nations.

[6] Cf. G-K[28] §154b.

[7] Uncertainty whether to translate *b'r* as I, 'set on fire', or II, 'remove', is already reflected in the translations: cf. LXX with Σ and V. The decision is made in the light of 5.5.

[8] For the use of the so-called imperfect to denote a concomitative action, cf. Bobzin §7,1b.

[9] IQIs[a] adds *'dōnāy*; it is absent from LXX, whereas Σ, V, and T support MT. It may be a subsequent assimilation to v. 1.

[10] This may not be said of v. 12a without taking into account v. 4b, or of v. 12b without taking into account 9.15. Job. 6.18 should also be compared with v. 12bβ. There are parallels to v. 13a in Ps. 82.1; 74.22; Isa. 51.22; Jer. 50.34; 51.36, and to v. 13b in Deut. 32.36; Ps. 135.14; the wording is echoed in Ps. 50.4; Micah 6.2. With v. 14aα

the reference back to the judgment discourse is one of the stylistic means used by the author responsible for the basic material in the composition of 3.1–4.1 (cf. 3.6f.; 4.1).

[12] *Yahweh's lament.* The God whose inexorable resolve to judge is directed against his people is nevertheless not a God who loves to punish and who looks on his creation without mercy. So the poet makes him utter a lament over his people, probably prompted by 1.2, because he sees that they are led into disaster by their leaders, who simply seek their own advantage and suck the people dry. They respond to calls to seek the best for the land like directors of forced labour who force the aliens inexorably to continue with their work (cf. Ex. 3.7; 5.5ff.). Their exploitation is so harsh that people cannot even pick the grapes from their own vineyards, the leavings from which belong to the poor and the aliens (cf. v. 14b; Lev. 19.10; Deut. 24.12).[11] To practise usury among one's own people and to lend out against interest was prohibited according to Ex. 22.24; Deut. 23.20f. However, such practices had advanced to such a degree in the province of Judah in the fifth century that the governor Nehemiah felt obliged to intervene by enacting a general remission of debts in order to prevent the collapse of the people (cf. Neh. 5.1ff.). At that time the rich and the officials so shamelessly exploited the distress of the poor that heavy indebtedness had arisen, leading to the loss of houses and land, the pledging of children and finally even the selling of them into slavery.

As a rule such rapacity is not limited to the ruling class but also extends to the people who look up to them and imitate them, because selfish covetousness is the characteristic of those who think that they have to live out a transitory life in their own strength, and so employ every possible means to serve their self-preservation and self-assurance. The lament of Yahweh over his people, misled by their leaders, includes both criticism of a people which allows itself to be led astray, although it could have made a better choice (cf. Micah 6.8; Rom. 2.1, 12ff.), and criticism of those who bear the greater responsibility as leaders because of their greater power.

[3.13–15] *The judgment.* Against the background of confused humanity, among the nations as in the case of the individual, God always stands as the power who makes the guilty fall by their

---

compare Job 22.4, with v. 14b Isa. 5.1ff., 5, with 6.13a and 10.2; cf. Lev. 5.23; Ezek. 18.16; 33.15; Ps. 35.10. A parallel to the address in the form of a question can be found, as this form demands, in Ps. 50.16; Micah 6.6; Ps. 82.2.

[11] This lament echoes down the ages, though patterns of rule change and one empire gives way to another. Cf. e.g. Gregory of Nazianzen's complaints in the fourth century AD about conditions in the Eastern half of the Roman empire in K. Christ, *Die Römer. Eine Einführung in ihre Geschichte und Zivilisation*, Munich 1979, 200.

reciprocally rising guilt and in so doing demonstrates his divinity. Verses 13 and 14f. show that God's judgment is a struggle for and against man: the advocate for his people must call the rulers to account as those who bear the utmost responsibility, but if he inflicts punishment, all will be affected by it. The notion that Yahweh is disputing with the leaders of the people in a legal process is based on the idea that Israel is in a special way his possession,[12] but at the same time it might also have been encouraged by the Deuteronomistic conception of the relationship of covenant or alliance existing between Yahweh and his people (cf. Ps. 50.4).[13] With its opening, which seems to have been torn from a larger context, the accusation reflects how Yahweh has long been concerned with the state of his people and has now finally lost his patience because he has come to recognize that the rulers have selfishly stripped bare the people who were entrusted to them like a vineyard (cf. 5.1ff. and especially 5.5). Along the lines of the explanation of v. 12 given above, in concrete terms this means that they have exploited the distress of the peasant farmers, pledged their possessions and finally bought them up as well. The angry question in v. 15 shows the thoughtlessness of such conduct, which does not take God's response into account and so provokes the catastrophe.

The violation of human solidarity is in any form and in any circumstances a sign of the forgetfulness of a humanity whose existence is meant to be co-existence; of one who receives himself not only physically, but also spiritually, from others; and is reminded of the fact that others accept him, work with him and for him, and support him.[14] Anyone who refuses to accept others as human beings devalues them so that they become mere objects and thus violates their very persons. This rebounds on those who act in this way in solitude and as hatred. Thus movements are set in train the violence of which ultimately destroys the whole of society. Man is not left to choose whether to respond to the call of his being or to withhold himself. Therefore he comes to grief in his self-forgetfulness and thus in the God who addresses him (Rom. 7.23f.). Life in the redemption given in Jesus Christ consists in the strength to forgive one another even this, to accept one another, and thus to give everyone the chance of being what he or she really is. In this way a new path is continually opened up to life together. Taking

---

[12] Cf. Ex. 19.5; Deut. 7.6; 14.2; 32.9; Ps. 135.4.
[13] Cf. the literature mentioned above, 12 nn. 6, 7, and H. Huffmon, 'The Covenant Lawsuit in the Prophets', *JBL* 78, 1959, 285ff.; J. Harvey, 'Le "Rib-Pattern"', requisitoire prophétique sur la rupture de l'Alliance', *Bib* 43, 1963, 172ff. It should be noted that v. 13b can also be translated 'to judge his people', cf. Ps. 50.4.
[14] On this cf. M. Heidegger, *Being and Time*, London 1962, 153ff.

God seriously at the same time means taking ourselves and our neighbours seriously. It opens up the possibility of overcoming failure in the power of the hope of God's never-ending presence.

CHAPTER 3.16–24

The End of the Proud Women of Jerusalem

16   And Yahweh said:
      Because the daughters of Zion are haughty[1]
      <and><walk>[2] with outstretched necks
      and ogle[3] with their eyes,
      mincing along[4] as they go,
      and thus[5] tinkling with their[6] feet,
17   the Lord will bind up[7] the crown of the daughters of Zion
      and Yahweh will lay bare[8] their[6] forehead.
18   On that day the Lord will take away the finery of the anklets, the headbands and the crescents, 19 the pendants, the bracelets and the veils; 20 the headdresses, the pacing chains, the sashes, the perfume boxes and the amulets; 21 the signet rings and nose rings; 22 the festal garments, the mantles, the cloaks and the handbags, 23 the garments of gauze[9] and the chemises,[10] the turbans and the shawls.
24   And thus it shall be:
      Instead of perfume there shall be rottenness,

---

[1] For the stative significance cf. also Bobzin §6, 3.

[2] Read *wᵉtēlaknā*. This form is governed by the *kī*, cf. Bobzin §9, 4b, 2.

[3] Cf. LXX and V. In principle the translation 'and paint their eyes' is also possible. Cf. Jastrow II, 1021a, s.v. *śāqar* II pi. also R. Payne Smith, *Compendious Syriac Dictionary*, Oxford 1903 (1957), 389a, s.v. *sqr* (b); but also on the *pa'el*. The parallelism supports the tradition.

[4] Literally: 'a going and tripping'.

[5] For the use of the so-called imperfect to denote a concomitative action, cf. Bobzin 7, §1b.

[6] For the replacement of the feminine suffix by a masculine one, characteristic of everyday speech, cf. G-K²⁸ §135o. For the parallel phenomenon in vulgar Arabic, cf. also A. Wahrmund, *Praktisches Handbuch der neu-arabischen Sprache*, Giessen 1898, 225. But cf. IQIsᵃ.

[7] For the meaning of *śāpaḥ* cf. G. R. Driver, *VT* 1, 1951, 241f., and V and T. It is usually connected with *mispaḥat*, 'scab', and translated 'make scabby', cf. KBL 928b, s.v. *śāpaḥ*.

[8] For the form cf.Meyer³ §74, 1b.

[9] Cf. also Jastrow I, 248f. s.v.

[10] Cf. also Jastrow II, 957a s.v.

and instead of a girdle, a rope,
and instead of well-set[11] plaits, baldness
and instead of a rich robe, a girding of sackcloth;
<shame>[12] instead of beauty.

[3.16–24] Beginning 'and Yahweh said . . .' this passage, with its
announcement of judgment against the proud women of Jerusalem,
claims to be a continuation of the scene which begins with v. (12) 13.
The charge against the men of the ruling classes is now followed by
a reckoning with the women. If the former proved to be part of the
redactional composition which begins with 3.1ff. and ends with 4.1,
the same can also be said of the present prophetic composition. In its
loose construction it is similar to 3.1ff., 12ff., 25ff. Already in v. 17
not only is the limping qīnah metre, or funeral dirge, abandoned; it
is even forgotten that the prophecy had begun as a discourse of
Yahweh (cf. also 3.1ff. with 3.4).

It is widely recognized today that the prose in vv. 18–23 beginning
with the prophetic formula 'on that day' is an addition made by a
man who looks with especial disfavour on feminine desire for
adornment. However, given the general nature of the composition
made up of 3.1–4.1, the remaining verses, 16f., 24, can hardly be
claimed as a composition by the prophet Isaiah.[13]

The theme of the humiliation of the haughty by Yahweh, which
underlies the saying, had been presented quite generally in 2.10ff.
Its roots are to be found in the notion that Yahweh helps the poor
while he brings down the eyes of the proud, a notion that has found
classic formulation in Ps. 18.28, and also was common in Wisdom
(cf. Prov. 21.4; Job 22.19). In v. 16 it is applied to the women of
Jerusalem who deliberately held their heads high and also cast
enticing or derogatory glances around them, tripping along with
their feet restrained by pacing chains (cf. v. 20), and tinkling with
their anklets (cf. v. 18). The social background is not further developed as it is in Amos 4.1ff. So it is not clear that the prophetic critic
has anything but feminine vanity and delight in jewellery in mind;
this, along with an exaggerated self-consciousness, causes him
offence.

[17 + 24] In accordance with its basic ideas, the announcement of

[11] For the appositional construction cf. G-K[28] §131b.
[12] Add bōšet, with I QIsᵃ; cf. also Wildberger, ad loc.
[13] An investigation of the terminology in the context of biblical literature which is
male dominated must remain barren unless the countless hapax legomena can be
interpreted with some degree of confidence. At all events, it should be noted that the
'daughters' of Zion are mentioned outside 3.16f. only in 4.4 and in Song of Songs 3,
11, and that the nearest parallel to the clause beginning ya'an kī, 'because', is in Ezek.
28.2; 31.10; for the use of the verb cf. also Ezek. 28.5, 17; II Chron. 17.6; 26.16; 32.25.

judgment holds in prospect the reversal of present circumstances: Yahweh himself will bind up the hair of these proud women, who would be ashamed and be thought shameless to show themselves in public without veil and head-covering. That means that they will be degraded to the status of slaves, taken prisoner in war.[14] As no one keeps stinking slave-girls in the house,[15] v. 24 might suggest the march of the women into captivity, on which they go to meet an unknown fate unwashed, stripped of their proud clothing, with shorn hair to mark their change of owner (cf. Deut. 21.12), and at the mercy of all the attentions of their captors.

[18–23] Puzzling though the meaning of some words still are,[16] the catalogue inserted into vv. 18–23 of everything that would make the heart of Hebrew woman beat faster is important evidence for cultural history. We see Hebrew women tripping through the street wearing rings round their ankles, joined together and often one on top of the other;[17] sewn and woven headbands, at their simplest made of wool, and at their most ornate, precious gold plates held on with bands.[18] In addition, there are amulets, crescents, worn on valuable necklaces or as individual items, which may have been hoped to provide protection from evil spirits as well as external adornment.[19] Earrings dangle from their ear-lobes, hanging on a chain, shaped like droplets or with several elements (cf. also Judg. 8.26).[20] Bronze bracelets shine on their arms, the open ends of which often had the shape of an animal head; some are even made of pure, heavy gold.[21] Veils, supported by a turban, conceal their faces (cf. also Isa. 61.10; Isa. 24.17).[22] Small chains restrict their walk and help the women to trip along in a flirtatious way (cf. also Judith 10.4).[23] A girdle worn over the hips (Prov. 31.17), and here perhaps even a breast-band (cf. also Jer. 2.32), offer further opportunity for fashion.[24] In addition, they may even carry flasks of perfume made of fine pottery or glass in

[14] Along with G. R. Driver, *VT* 1, 242, compare the Middle Assyrian Law Code §40, in G. R. Driver and J. Miles, *The Assyrian Laws*, Oxford 1935, 127ff., or R. Haase, *Die keilschriftlichen Rechtssammlungen in deutscher Übersetzung*, Wiesbaden 1963, 104; or *AOT*², 418; *ANET*²⁻³, 183b.

[15] But see the report of Johann Wild, captured by the Turks, in his *Reysebeschreibung eines Gefangenen Christen Anno 1604*, Bibliothek Klassischer Reiseberichte, Stuttgart 1964, 48f., 53.

[16] For a detailed account see H. W. Hönig, *Die Bekleidung des Hebräers*, Zurich dissertation 1957, esp. 116ff.

[17] Cf. Helga Weippert, *BRL*², 280a;

[18] Ibid., 287b.

[19] Cf. K. Galling, *BRL*², 11a; Helga Weippert, op. cit., 287a.

[20] Cf. Helga Weippert, op. cit., 285b f., and plate 75.

[21] Ibid., 284f.

[22] Cf. G. Fohrer, *BHH* III, col. 1702.

[23] Cf. also F. Nötscher, *Biblische Altertumskunde*, HSAT.E III, Bonn 1940, 67f.

[24] Cf. also KBL s.v. and Nötscher, 59.

their handbags, though it is highly uncertain how we are to translate the word interpreted in this way, and in some instances what is meant in an amulet described as a 'soul house'.[25] Israelite women were as fond as modern women of wearing rings on their fingers. In some instances a signet ring with a cylinder or stamp as a seal, or perhaps a scarab, would testify to the exalted status of the woman and her own personal rights at law.[26] Even the nose might be adorned with an open ring, which might also be put in the ear (cf. Ex. 31.2).[27] In addition, there would be a great variety of garments, from the cloak to the under-garment like a chemise, and also the various veils in bright colours.

Only a misogynist can take any delight in seeing young girls and mature women going around in clogs, coarse stockings and dull-coloured sacklike garments devoid of all charm. On the other hand, the New Testament admonition to women that modesty and discipline and good works are their finest adornment (I Tim. 2.9ff.) is worth remembering when excessive slavery to fashion blinds the reason and enslaves people. Here too, the Greek *mēden agan*, nothing in excess, indicates the happy medium. It gives the senses what they need and the understanding what it needs. But taste is also required. In addition, it remains true that all finery and all baubles are transitory, and that they vanish in times of distress and in military defeats. And if on the basis of the idea of judgment we discover man's responsibility for what he does with his actions, in this sphere we must also reflect on the social consequences of his own action – and his own transitoriness. To be adorned before God – what would that mean?

CHAPTER 3.25–4.1

Jerusalem Forsaken

25   Your[1] men fall by the sword
       and your mighty men in battle.

[25] Cf. Wildberger, ad loc.
[26] Cf. Helga Weippert, *BRL²*, 285a; P. Welten, op. cit., 299b, 303a.
[27] Cf. Helga Weippert, *BRL²*, 285b.
[1] The second person singular pronominal suffix relates to personified Jerusalem, the virgin Zion.

26   Then her[2] gates lament and mourn,
        abandoned, she[3] sits on the ground.
4.1   Then seven women take hold
        of one man on that day[4],
        and say, 'We will eat our own bread and wear our own clothes,
        only let us be called by your name;
        take away our reproach.'

[3.25–4.1] These verses are formally held together by the limping
qīnāh metre, the lament for the dead, while in content they are all
connected by the announcement of a military defeat (v. 25) and its
consequences (v. 26; 4.1). Here it is striking that v. 25 is addressed
quite directly to a woman, who by context and content is Jerusalem,
while v. 26 speaks equally directly in the third person of the fate of
the city, and 4.1 concentrates on the fate of those women who
survive the defeat. Investigation of the terminology of vv. 25, 26
clearly indicates that here we have a unit which is entirely the
product of redactors rather than a collection of fragments.[5] The vivid
illustration of the fate of the surviving women given in 4.1 recalls
3.7f., and may be as redactional as that verse. We now have express
confirmation of something which was echoed in 3.2a: Jerusalem is
again on her way to a military defeat. Thus this brief announcement
of judgment brings to an end the redactional composition of which
ch. 3 consists with the prospect of an eschatological visitation on
Jerusalem and Judah, at the same time forming a conclusion to the
whole of the first three chapters, which at the time it was composed
still lacked the additions promising eschatological salvation (1.25,
27, 28; 2.1–5).

[25] That the brief threat in ch. 3, made without any reason being
given, should be interpreted as a whole emerges from the fact that
v. 25 as it were contains the commentary on 3.1ff.; 3.16ff., by
expressly declaring that the men of Jerusalem are falling in battle.[6] In
contrast to 3.1, 8, but in agreement with 3.16ff., the perspective is
narrowed down on Jerusalem, in accordance with the significance of
the city in the Persian period as the centre of religious life and the
eschatological expectations of Judaism.[7] [26] This verse sketches a

---

[2] The third person singular pronominal suffix again refers to Jerusalem.
[3] One could also translate this 'you sit', and see this as the second rather than the
third person singular feminine.
[4] The absence of the prophetic formula of rebuke in LXX, together with the way in
which it disrupts the metre, strongly suggests that this is a gloss.
[5] For the mētîm, men, in v. 25, cf., with Vermeylen I, 152, Deut. 2.34; 3.6; 4.27;
28.62; Jer. 44.28, and for v. 26a also Jer. 14.2.
[6] For the numerous examples of the phrase 'fall by the sword', cf. O. Kaiser, TWAT
III, 167.
[7] Cf. also below, 86f., on 4.3.

picture of the depopulated city and thus, like the closing verse, 4.1, has in mind the consequences of the catastrophe. The proximity of the short poem to Lamentations is unmistakable:[8] as there, the lament is over the abandoned city, robbed of her sons (cf. Lam. 1.1, 15). Echoing Lam. 1.1; 2.10, Jerusalem is said to sit abandoned on the ground, and as in an echo not only of Jer. 14.2 but also of Lam. 1.4; 2.8, we are told that the gates[9] lament and mourn (cf. also 19.8). [4.1] Here the arrogance of the women who survive the downfall of the people, censured in 3.16, is turned into its opposite; now without protection or rights at law because they have lost their husbands and all their male relatives, they will forget all their pride and try to be married to someone, even seven to the same man,[10] at any price, including the renunication of the right to support which was taken for granted as the duty of any husband.[11] The main thing is that he should be prepared to bestow his name on them and by this legal act, which ended the marriage proceedings, recognize them publicly as his possession and therefore as standing under his protection,[12] thus removing the reproach which lay upon them. In Israel, child-lessness was regarded as a special shame and reproach for a woman (cf. Gen. 30.26; I Sam 1.6; cf. also II Sam. 13.13), as also was remaining single or being abandoned, along with the barrenness which went with such a fate (cf. 54.1, 4.). Being abandoned without any rights in a time of anarchy (cf. 3.4ff.), and being prevented from becoming a mother, were probably disasters which women could escape after the catastrophe expected by the poet only by overcoming their natural modesty and restraint. We may conclude from the fact that polygamy to this degree could be regarded as a sign of extreme need that it was no longer regarded as the normal form of marriage for the Judaism of the Persian period, though it need not therefore have been thought offensive (cf. Deut. 21.15).[13]

In conclusion, it may be worth recalling that 3.16ff.; 3.25–4.1

---

[8] Cf. also D. Jones, 'The Tradition of the Oracles of Isaiah of Jerusalem', ZAW 67, 1955, 242f.

[9] For the use of petaḥ, opening, to denote the gate of the city, cf. e.g. Gen. 38.14 with Josh. 8.29.

[10] Cf. also Prov. 7.13; Zech. 8.23, and on the last mentioned passage K. Elliger, Das Buch der zwölf Kleinen Propheten II, ATD, ad loc.

[11] On the question how far there was a written marriage contract in Judaism cf. F. Nötscher, Biblische Altertumskunde, HSAT. E. III, Bonn 1940, 79. For the use of the phrase 'bread and clothes' to denote economic provision, cf. Deut. 10.18.

[12] For the legal usage cf. also H. J. Boecker, Redeformen des Rechtslebens im Alten Testament, WMANT 14, Neukirchen 1964, 167f.

[13] On this question cf. also W. Plautz, 'Monogamie und Polygynie im Alten Testament', ZAW 75, 1963, 3ff., and R. de Vaux, Ancient Israel, London 1961, 24–26. For the historical reasons for the encouragment of polygamy in Mohammed's preaching cf. W. M. Watt, Muhammad at Medina, Oxford 1956 (1962), 274ff.

occupy a similar position to 32.9ff. with its saying similarly addressed to women with a prospect of eschatological distress.[14] We get the impression that the divine judgment, annihilating all wickedness and all arrogance among both the people of God and the world of the nations, obsessed the thought of the prophetic writer like a dark, inexorable fate, and distracted his attention from the prospect of a happier future.

CHAPTER 4.2–6

The New Jerusalem

2   On that day,
       what Yahweh causes to shoot up
       shall be beauty and glory,
       and the fruit of the land
       shall be pride and adornment
       for the escaped of Israel.

3 And it shall be that he who is left in Zion and remains in Jerusalem will be called holy, everyone who has been recorded for life in Jerusalem. 4 When the Lord has washed away the filth of the daughters of Zion and thus[1] cleansed the blood-guilt from its midst by a spirit of judgment and a spirit of devastation,[2] 5 then Yahweh will create over every site on Mount Zion and over her assemblies a cloud by day, and smoke and the shining of a flaming fire by night; for over all glory is a cover. 6 And it will be a booth for a shadow by day from the heat and for a refuge and a shelter from the storm and rain.

[4.2–6] It is probably because of the liturgical use of the Isaiah scroll in Jewish worship that the announcements in 2.6–4.1 of the divine judgment to come are now followed by a prophecy of salvation. This is intended to give the hearers courage, strengthened by hope, to obey God's will (cf. 2.5 with 4.3). Yahweh's last word to his people is not judgment, but his saving will; indeed, judgment is the means of realizing his saving will, because salvation can only be complete

---

[14] Cf. *Isaiah 13–39*, 326ff.

[1] For the use of the imperfect to denote a concomitative action cf. Bobzin, *Tempora*, §6, 1b.

[2] For the reading in 1 QIs[a], 'spirit of the storm', cf. Wildberger, ad loc.; he refers to the frequent use of the phrase in Ezek. 1.4, etc.; Ps. 107.25.

where human beings have a firm foundation in their humanity. So Yahweh brings his saving work to completion through his purifying judgment.

Both form and content suggest that this section is not all of a piece, but came into being in at least three stages. Whereas v. 2 is clearly poetry by virtue of its metric structure, consisting of two lines each with two sets of three stresses,[3] vv. 3ff., are prose. And whereas v. 2 speaks of the fertility of the land, vv. 3ff. are concerned with the glorious future of Jerusalem. However, these too seem to be less than coherent. The explanation of v. 5a given in v. 5b is taken up and developed in v. 6. As a result, the picture of Yahweh's presence over Zion, protective and at the same time concealed, is expanded and at the same time coarsened by the announcement of permanent protection from the weather.

With its 'on that day', v. 2 goes back via 4.1; 3.18, 7, to 2.12ff. and 2.2, and thus already suggests its own redactional character and therefore that of the whole section. We can only make a relative judgment on the age of the prophecy: at all events it is later than 2.6–4.1; 2.(1)2–5. It obviously forms a loose antithesis in v. 2 and a closer one in v. 4 to 3.16ff. (cf. 3.17, 24). Furthermore, v. 4 seems to suggest 1.15f. The transformation of the theme of the cloud indicating Yahweh's presence, from which by night lightning flashes forth, into a means of giving shade and light to Jerusalem, points to a developed stage of the tradition. Thus we may be justified in seeing here an indication that the section was composed well into the Persian period or even as late as the early Hellenistic period. The changes show that this is scribal work.

[2] The poet of the description of salvation in v. 2 regards Yahweh's great day of judgment as being at the same time the decisive turning-point in the destiny of Israel. It puts an end to the time of injustice amd thus the time of disaster. So Yahweh can reveal his full grace upon those Israelites who have escaped the last catastrophe.[4] Then they will no longer boast of their own vain works and deeds, nor even of their empty pomp, but of the great works which God does in his creation and with which he visibly glorifies his name before all the world by testifying to his presence in Israel through the fertility of his land. For in contrast to the messianic interpretation,[5] which occurs for the first time in the Targum (the Aramaic translation of the Old Testament which at the same time brings it up to date),

[3] Cf. also Kaiser, *Introduction*, 319ff.
[4] For the expression 'deliverance of Israel', cf. 10.20f.; 37.31f. = II Kings 19.30f.; Ezek. 14.22; Obad. 17; Ezra 9.8, 13ff.; Neh. 1.2; Jonah 3.5
[5] T: 'In that time the anointed of the Lord will be for joy and praise and those who keep the law shall be for glory and praise for those of Israel who have escaped.'

the 'shoot of Yahweh' is not to be understood here as in Jer. 23.5; 33.15; Zech. 3.8; 6.12, as the king of the time of salvation from the house of David,[6] nor even as the holy remnant of Israel,[7] but in accordance with the parallel mention of the fruit of the land as quite simply whatever Yahweh makes to grow in the land.[8] So here we find the expectation of the inexhaustible fertility of the land in the time of salvation which is also suggested in other eschatological prophecies.[9] For Old Testament thought it is indissoluble from the moral and religious perfection of the people. We need only go on to read how Ps. 72 connects just rule over the land with the fertility of people and land (cf. Ps. 72.3, 16), or how the Deuteronomist promises Israel blessings which will extend to the kitchen and the cellar if it is obedient to the will of God (cf. Deut. 28.1ff.), in order to recognize the firmness of this association. Correspondingly, the fertility of the land in the time of salvation reflects the new righteousness of Israel. The natural presupposition for these expectations is the understanding of the world as a unity which embraces both nature and history. In it, heaven and earth respond in accordance with God's command to what men and women do, whether good or evil, with salvation or disaster.[10] If the world in man is whole, it too will become whole.

[3] Without recognizing this presupposition, the modern reader cannot follow the logic which makes the writer who added this verse promise holiness to the people of Jerusalem who survive the catastrophe. Verse 4 goes on to interpret this as freedom from all impurity and all injustice (cf. also 29.23). As a matter of course the prophet-poet looks to Jerusalem alone for the remanant which has escaped the judgment. This reflects the significance which the city acquired as the religious centre of Judaism under the Persian kings after the loss of political independence.[11] It was here that the glorification of Yahweh before all the peoples of the earth was expected to take place; he would frustrate their onslaught on his city by annihilating them.[12] At the same time this onslaught of the nations would accomplish his judgment on his people. The prophet knows that only those whose names stand written in the heavenly book of life

---

[6] Against Herntrich et al.

[7] Against Reuss.

[8] Thus the majority of recent commentators, e.g. Duhm, Marti, Gray and most recently Fohrer, Wildberger, Auvray, ad loc.

[9] Cf. 29.17; 30.23ff., Jer. 31.12; Ezek. 24.29; 47.1ff.; Hos. 2.23f.; Jonah 4.18; Amos 9.13f.; Zech 14.8; Mal. 3.11f.

[10] Cf. also O. Kaiser, 'Dlke und Sedaqa', NZST 7, 1965, 251ff.

[11] Cf. Wildberger, ad loc.

[12] Cf. also O. Kaiser, 'Geschichtliche Erfahrung und eschatologische Erwartung', NZST 15, 1973, 281ff. = Eschatologie im Alten Testament, ed. H. D. Preuss, WdF 480, Darmstadt 1978, 456ff.

will escape it. We do best to leave open the question whether the statement is to be understood in predestinarian terms, along the lines of Ps. 139.16, or juridically, as in Ps. 69.29; Ex. 32.32ff.; Jub. 30.22; 36.10. In the former instance the idea would be that God has predestined a definite number of people to righteousness and to life in the time of salvation.[13] The ultimate religious background to this would then be the astrological belief in destiny held by the Babylonians, who were convinced that the gods determined men's fates every year on New Year's Day and inscribed them on tablets of destiny.[14] In the second instance the author would have expressed his conviction that at this judgment Yahweh would destroy the evil ones on the grounds of their actions, for which they themselves were responsible.[15] In that case, underlying the conception of the heavenly book we might have the memorials kept by rulers in the ancient Near East which recorded news brought into the kingdom by messengers, and events of special importance.[16] It is striking that there is evidence in the second half of the last millennium before the Christian era, from Iran to Greece, of a book associated with the judgment of the dead which recorded men's acts, though we should not necessarily assume that these conceptions were originally dependent on one another.[17] The idea of the heavenly book to be found here would fit into the framework of a kind of thinking which had still not got as far as belief in a world to come.

[4] The mention of the spirit of judgment or of righteousness in 28.6 suggests that here, too, the underlying Hebrew expression should be translated in the same way and not as 'storm of judgment',[18] which would be possible purely on the basis of the meaning of the world. If we may take it that the thought of the verse is connected with v. 3, v. 4 probably conveys that Yahweh himself will bring about the decisive repentance, here described as cultic purifi-

[13] Cf. also e.g. Phil. 4.3; Luke 10.20; Rev. 13.8. For the concept of the heavenly book cf. the thorough study by H. Bietenhard, *Die himmlische Welt im Urchristentum und Spätjudentum*, WUNT 2, Tübingen 1951, 231ff.

[14] Cf. B. Meissner, *Babylonien und Assyrien* II, Heidelberg 1925, 124f.

[15] Cf. e.g. Enoch 98.7f.; 104.7; 108.7; Rev. 3.5. Again the place of Dan. 12.1 is questionable.

[16] Cf. Esther 6.1ff.; Letter of Aristeas 298f.; K. Elliger, *Das Buch der zwölf Kleinen Propheten* II, ATD, on Mal. 3.16. For the attempt to derive the conception from the list of inhabitants of cities, cf. Wildberger, ad loc.

[17] From the world of Zoroastrian religion see Yasna 31.14: 'This then I will ask Thee, O Ahura Mazda! . . . What events are coming now, and what events shall come in the future; and what prayers with debt-confessions are offered with the offerings of the holy? And what (are the awards) for the wicked? And how shall they be in the (final) state of completion?' (*The Zend-Avesta* III, Sacred Books of the East, ed. F. Max Müller, Vol. 31, Clarendon Press 1887, 48). For evidence from the Greek world cf. Euripides fr. 506 and A. Dieterich, *Nekyia*, Leipzig and Berlin [2]1913 = Darmstadt [3]1969, 126 n.l.

[18] Against Kaiser[1]; cf. also Wildberger, ad loc.

cation, in the final danger through his spirit.[19] Of course we should not picture the women of Jerusalem, who are here mentioned explicitly in the wake of 3.16ff., as being really smeared with their own excrement; the vivid phrase is to be understood as a colourful expression of extreme religious, ritual and moral offence (cf. e.g. Lam. 1.8f.; Ezek. 23.36ff.). Similarly, we are not to relate the blood guilt which is certainly no longer laid at the door of the daughters of Zion in particular, but of all the people of Jerusalem, to actual murder (cf. e.g. Ex. 22.2), but to any transgression in the ritual or the legal sphere which goes against Yahweh's will and merits death (cf. Lev. 17.4; Isa. 1.15f.; Micah 3.10), and no less in the primarily religious sphere extending as far as idolatry (cf. Ezek. 22.3ff).[20]

[5] The meaning of v. 5a is obscure. In the light of the tradition we would expect that the cloud by day and the fire by night indicate Yahweh's presence over his holy city, as they are said to have represented his presence over the tent in the wilderness (cf. Num. 9.15ff.; also Ex. 13.21). Similarly, we find in Isa. 60.19f.; 24.23 the expectation that Yahweh will illuminate the city by his presence. However, in this passage a clear distinction is made between Yahweh and the cloud and the fire veiled in smoke, which are his creation. So we may ask whether v. 5b and v. 6 have not ultimately continued v. 5a as its author intended. In that case the cloud would be for protection from the heat, and the fire for illuminating the night. Verse 5b might understand the brilliance from which protection was needed, not as the glory of Yahweh concealed behind the cloud (cf. Ex. 16.10 etc.), but as the splendour of liberated Jerusalem and its richly adorned temple, which is elaborated in anticipation of the future in Isa. 60.6ff.

[6] The booth or tabernacle needed by anyone who wants to be quite certain of being protected from any kind of bad weather in liberated Jerusalem is in turn really only a slight transformation of the hope of the Psalmist of finding protection in evil times in Yahweh's tabernacle, i.e. his sanctuary. But anyone who has experienced the heat of a summer's day or the violence of a rainstorm in the streets of one of the cities of the Near East will ultimately understand how the person responsible for the addition wanted to see the city of God protected in the airy shade of a booth.

A life in a fertile land, life without guilt in sure protection, afforded and prepared by God himself, in the community of the city of God

---

[19] In addition to 1.16, cf. also Prov. 30.12, and for the ritual language Ex. 29.4; 40.12; Lev. 8.6; and Ezek. 40.38; II Chron. 4.6.

[20] Cf. Wildberger, ad loc., and H. Christ, *Blutvergiessen im Alten Testament*, Basel dissertation, Theologische Dissertationen, ed. B. Reicke, 12, Basel 1977, 40f.

– that is the expectation expressed here; it is something that might
still be able to express our own hidden longings (cf. Rev. 21.3ff.).[21]

CHAPTER 5.1–7

The Song of Yahweh's Vineyard

1   I will sing for my friend
    a song of my love for his vineyard:
    My friend had a vineyard
    on a fertile hill.

2   He digged it and cleared it of stones
    and planted it with choice vines;
    he built a watchtower in the midst of it,
    and hewed out a wine vat in it;
    and he looked for it to yield grapes,
    but it yielded wild grapes.

3   And now, inhabitant of Jerusalem
    and man of Judah,
    judge between me
    and my vineyard.

4   What more was there to do for my vineyard,
    that I have not done in it?
    Why did I look for it to yield grapes,
    and it yielded wild grapes?

5   And now I will tell you
    what I will do for my vineyard.
    Remove[1] its hedge, so that it becomes pasturage.
    Break down[1] its wall, so that it is trampled,

6   I will deliver it to plunder;[2]
    it shall not be pruned and shall not be hoed,
    so that thorns and thistles grow up.
    And I will command the clouds
    that they rain no rain upon it!

[21] For the symbolic transformation of the city in the language of the Bible cf. also J.
Hempel, *Wissenschaftliche Zeitschrift der E. M. Arndt Universität Greifswald* 5, 1955/56,
123ff.
[1] For the use of the infinitive absolute instead of a finite form in excited language cf.
G-K[28] § 113z.
[2] For the meaning cf. HAL 159b, s.v. *bātā*.

7   Yes, the vineyard of Yahweh Sebaoth
     is the house of Israel,
     and the man of Judah
     is the planting in which he delights.

     He looked for justice
     but behold injustice;
     for righteousness,[3]
     but behold, a cry!

[5.1–7] The so-called 'Song of the Vineyard' is one of the poetic masterpieces of the Old Testament. It asks the reader to imagine himself in a square or a street in Jerusalem, among a tumultuous throng in the midst of which a singer suddenly gains a hearing by announcing his song, so that the loud hubbub of voices ebbs away around him, and the crowd silently composes itself with rapt attention. This is certainly not going to be any old peasant story. That would be unsuitable for a song. The vineyard could be an image for a young girl, so that it could be about the tragic love of the friend for his fiancée (cf. Song of Songs 8.12). The reader may ask whether the friend is Yahweh and the people of God is the faithless bride and the vineyard, in accordance with the serious context of a prophetic book.[4] But he too should put himself in the place of the hearer who has no time for such considerations and for answering the question where he had once heard 'My friend had a vineyard' (cf. Song of Songs 8.11a), because to begin with all his attention is occupied with his practical knowledge as a peasant-farmer or vineyard owner. Only from the sound of the tragic, limping rhythm derived from the funeral dirge can he recognize that the song is not being sung here in jest, but in earnest. He cannot even satisfy his curiosity as to who is represented by the singer's friend. He has to wait and listen to the story being told until it solves the mystery by itself.

[1–2] So, then, the singer's friend had a vineyard in a good position on a hillside, with the added advantage of fertile soil,[5] thus providing the basic conditions for good growth and ripening by the sun. And of course before putting in the young vines he did the necessary work of digging the top soil, removing the weeds and gathering up the stones exposed by the rain and the cultivation, and building

---

[3] With the connotation of reliability.

[4] Cf. Jer. 2.2, 32; 3.6ff., Hos. 2.4ff., and Jer. 2.21; 5.10; 8.13; 12.10; Hos. 10.1f., Ezek. 15.1ff.; 17.6ff., 19.10ff.; Isa. 3.14; 27.2ff., and not least Ps. 80.9ff., on which also Vermeylen I, 162f.

[5] Σ interprets this as *in cornu in medio olivarum*. In connection with *qeren*, since this is the only evidence for this usage, reference should perhaps also be made to the Arabic *qurnat*[un], 'outward corner', Wehr 678a.

them into a stone wall round the edge of the vineyard (cf. v. 5).[6] 'Bright reds', a type of large grape still valued in the Near East today, were then planted in the ground which had been prepared (cf. also Jer. 2.21).[7] The further work shows that the owner of the vineyard envisaged using the field as a vineyard on a permanent basis and counted on a good harvest, for instead of the temporary booths which otherwise would be put up specially for the harvest (cf. 1.8), he built a permanent watch-tower, Furthermore, he excavated a wine vat in the rocky ground, in which grapes were usually trodden by foot (cf. 63.3), so that the juice ran out through channels, also made in the rock, into containers for clarification and fermentation.[8]

But now, with the harvest, came the great disappointment: all the labour of preparation proved vain, because instead of the large, sweet and juicy ones which had been expected the vines[9] only produced small, hard and sour grapes – so sour that one's teeth were set on edge when biting them (cf. Jer. 31.29; Ezek. 18.2).

[3] The song now takes a new turn. The story-teller fades into the background, and instead the owner of the vineyard himself begins to speak. The solemn and official-sounding designation of the audience as inhabitants of Jerusalem and men of Judah, the sequence of which attests the pre-eminence of Jerusalem as the centre of post-exilic Judaism,[10] and the call to decide between the claims of the vineyard, which are evidently not mentioned, and those of its owner, which are known, goes beyond the situation of a mere game. The peasant-farmer would have asked the other peasant-farmers, the vineyard-owner the other vineyard-owners, for advice, not for a decision. So it begins to dawn on the audience that what is going on here is something different from the failure of a vineyard-owner. At the same time the scene of judgment, which governs the construction of the song from the beginning to the end, begins to take shape:[11] verses 1b and 2 contain the accusation, and the reasons given for it. In vv. 3, 4 there follows the calling of witnesses to confirm the innocence of the accuser. Then in vv. 5, 6 the vineyard-owner himself pronounces judgment, revealing his secret step by step.

[6] A. Giglioni, 'Nuova versione di "SQL" in Is. 5.2; 61.10', RivBib 15, 1967, 385ff., in Vermeylen I, 164, also argues for the concrete meaning 'a wall built of stones'. But cf. also Jastrow II, 1020b, s.v.

[7] For kinds of grapes see also R. Gradwohl, Die Farben im Alten Testament, BZAW 83, Berlin 1963, 21 n. 146.

[8] Cf. J. B. Pritchard, Gibeon where the Sun Stood Still, Princeton 1962, 69ff., and K. Galling, BRL², 362f.

[9] The reader familiar with central European vineyards should not imagine these to be trained up on stakes. They were either ranged between olive and fig trees or grew as bushes. Cf. also G. Dalman, Arbeit und Sitte in Palästina I, Gütersloh 1928, 69.

[10] See 69 n 12 above.

[11] Cf. also Vermeylen I, 160f.

Finally, v. 7 discloses the parabolic, metaphorical character of the song.[12] Perhaps one hearer or another would note even now, before he thought again about the whole of the song after it had come to an end, how the question of the vineyard-owner as to what measures he had failed to take in his vineyard and why his expectations had been so bitterly disappointed, raised a quite different question, namely why an ungrateful people had faithlessly refused to obey its God (cf. Jer. 2.4ff.; Micah 6.2ff.).[13]

[5] The silent witnesses, who are beginning to suspect that they themselves are the accused, hear the judgment of the master who is going to give his property over to be pasturage, to be trampled on by cattle and wild animals,[14] by tearing down the protective hedge which keeps off the wind and removing the wall which deters the wild animals.[15] This is an obvious metaphor for surrendering his people to the enemy (cf. Jer. 12.9ff.). It is as obvious that he will stop caring for the abandoned vineyard, that he will no longer hoe[16] it and prune it, as it is that it will now be overrun and stifled by wild thorns and thistles. Weeds and bushes grow up on land plundered by the enemy and stripped of its inhabitants, making it impossible for people to go on to the uncultivated fields.[17] The telling of the parable does not culminate in the one idea of disappointed hope and subsequent abandonment, but also contains throughout allegorical features which are capable of individual interpretation. If everything that the owner says in vv. 5,6a remains in the sphere of earthly reality, determined by the point of comparison, in v. 6b he shows himself in all his divine majesty and power as the lord of clouds and rain (cf. Job 37.12f.; Ps. 147.8; 104.3). [7] In this way it is clear to all, as v. 7 finally discloses, that the owner of the vineyard is none other

[12] According to R. Bultmann, *History of the Synoptic Tradition*. Oxford 1963, 174, the character of the parable is that it 'transposes the facts which serve for a similitude into a story'. W. Schottroff, 'Das Weinberglied Jesajas', *ZAW* 82, 1970, 68ff., has come out against claims that the song is a parable and is in favour of seeing it as a fable. A fable is a narrative which transposes human situations into the world of animals or plants. The following arguments may be advanced against such a categorization of the song: 1. that different interpretations from this are quite possible; 2. that this does not deal with a happening in the world of animals or plants, but with a situation involving both human beings and plants. Schottroff recalls the content of fables which can be traced back to Sumerian times in which a dispute between animals and plants is finally decided by a god. Cf. also W. G. Lambert, *Babylonian Wisdom Literature*, Oxford 1960, 150f.
[13] Cf. also Vermeylen I, 163.
[14] Cf. 3.14; 6.13 and 7.25; 28.18; 10.6; Micah 7.15; Ps. 80.14.
[15] Cf. also Ps. 80.13.
[16] Cf. also 18.5. According to Dalman, *Arbeit und Sitte* I, 164, vineyards were hoed in January and February and pruned in March.
[17] Cf. 7.23–25, 9.17; 27.14; also 32.13.

than the almighty Yahweh Sebaoth[18] himself, and that the vineyard is his people Israel[19] and in particular the people of the south, Judah. His hope that it would repay him for its decisive advantage over the brother kingdom in the north, realized in history (cf. Ps. 78.67ff.), by especial faithfulness and thus especial delight in him,[20] has come to nothing. At the end, with a repeated *Stabreim* and final rhyme, the preacher impresses on his hearer and reader that the people of Judah has not fulfilled the expectations of its God that it would be a people which judged rightly and therefore enjoyed peace: instead of just judgment there has been unjust bloodshed,[21] and instead of impartial justice, ensuring the well-being of the land,[22] the cry of the oppressed has rung out – whose avenger is Yahweh (cf. Ex. 22.2; Ps. 9.18; Job 34.28).

[5.1–7] Despite its brief and pregnant form, this generalized accusation needs to be backed up with some specific content. That can be found in the seven woes which begin in 5.8. Accordingly, we may assume that the song provides their literary introduction. Given the fictitious situation of the song, the question provoking it is not what Yahweh *will do* to the people of the southern kingdom of the Davidic dynasty, but why he *had done* what he here proclaims as his judgment. Or, to put it another way: contrary to the general view of scholars, the Song of the Vineyard in 5.1–7 is not a *prophecy* of Isaiah; Vermeylen, rather, is to be followed in seeing it as a retrospective *theology of history* standing in the shadow of the Deuteronomistic movement.[23] The preacher puts on the prophet's mantle and in this way answers the questions of his fellow-countrymen in Jerusalem and Judah about the causes of the loss of freedom and the collapse

[18] For these epithets cf. 126f. below on 6.3.

[19] 'House of Israel' also occurs in Isa. 14.2; 46.3; generally speaking, the phrase is much rarer than one might expect. In the Pentateuch it occurs only in P (cf. Ex. 40.38; Lev. 10.6; Num. 20.29; cf. also Josh. 21.43). In the Deuteronomistic history work it appears in I Sam. 7.3; II Sam. 1.12; 6.5, 15; 12.8; 16.3; I Kings 12.21; 20.31; also Amos 5.1; 6.14; 7.9; Hosea 1.4, 6; 5.1; 8.1; 9.4; 12.1; Micah 3.1, 9 and often in the books of Jeremiah and Ezekiel. Cf. also the late Ps. 115.1. The *'îš y^ehûdā*, man of Judah, occurs in Isaiah only here; also in Jer. 32.32; 11.2; 16.12; 18.11; 44.26f.; II Kings 23.2; II Chron. 13.15; 20.27; 34.30. For the terminology of the song cf. also Vermeylen I, 163ff.

[20] Cf. also Jer. 31.20.

[21] Here I am following the traditional derivation of the word *miśpaḥ* given by Gesenius-Buhl and Zorell s.v.; KBL 571 a s.v. differs. Cf. also Wildberger, ad loc.

[22] For the phrase 'justice and righteousness' cf. Amos 5.7, 24; 6.12; Isa. 1.27; 5.16; 28.17; 32.16; 33.5. On this question see also above, 42f.

[23] I, 163. For the literary evaluation of the song, in addition to the article by Schottroff mentioned in n. 12 above, cf. also H. Junker, 'Die literarische Art von Is 5, 1–7', *Bib* 40, 1959, 259ff., and D. Lys, 'La vigne et le double je. Exercise de style sur Esa'ie V 1–7', *SVT* 26, Leiden 1974, 1ff.

of the Davidic kingdom. The guilt of the people, and not Yahweh's impotence, is responsible for the exile of the nation.

CHAPTER 5.8–24

The Great Woe

8   Woe to those who join house to house,
       who add field to field,
       until there is no more room,
       and you settle alone in the land.
9   In my ears,
       Yahweh Sebaoth:[1]
       'Surely,[2] the many houses
       shall become a wilderness,
       the great and good,
       without inhabitants.
10   For ten acres[3] of vineyard
       shall only yield one bucket-full.[4]
       and an ass's load of seed
       shall yield only a bushel.[5]
11   Woe to those who rise early in the morning
       and run after strong drink,
       who tarry late in the evening;
       wine inflames them.
12   There is lyre and harp, timbrel and flute
       and wine at their feasts.
       But they do not regard the deeds of Yahweh,
       and they do not see the work of his hands.
13   *Therefore my people goes away*[6]
       without knowledge,
       their nobles <weak>[7] *from hunger,*
       their multitude parched with thirst.

---

[1] Cf. 22.14 and 105 below.
[2] Cf. G-K^{28} §149e.
[3] Cf; G-K^{28} §93m.
[4] Literally: a bath.
[5] Literally: an ephah.
[6] Cf. 108 below and 67 n. 8 above.
[7] Because of the parallelism read $m^e z\bar{e}$ with many commentators from Hitzig to Wildberger (cf. Deut. 32.24).

14   Therefore the underworld *made* wide[8] its maw
      and opened its jaws beyond bounds,
      so that its[9] nobles and its[9] multitudes go down,
      and her throng and whatever exulted in it.[10]
15   *Then man was humbled and men brought low,*
      and the eyes of the haughty were lowered.
16   *But Yahweh Sebaoth was exalted in judgment,*
      and the holy God showed himself holy in righteousness.
17   Then shall lambs graze in their pasture;[11]
      in the ruins of the destroyed sheep <>[12] shall feed.
18   **Woe to those who draw guilt <with cattle ropes>[13]**
      and sin with cart-ropes,[14]
19   who say: 'Let his work
      make haste,
      that we may see it.
      Let the purpose of the Holy One of Israel
      draw near and come,
      that we may know it.'
20   **Woe to those who call evil good**
      and good evil,
      who make darkness light
      and light darkness,
      who make bitter sweet
      and sweet bitter;
23   **who acquit the guilty for a bribe**
      and take away[15] thus the right[16] of the righteous.
21   **Woe to those who are wise in their own eyes,**
      and understanding in their own sight.
22   **Woe to those who are heroes at drinking wine,**
      and to men who are valiant at mixing drink.

24   Therefore as a flame consumes straw,

---

[8] The *hirhība* replaces an original *tarhīb*. Cf. 97 below.

[9] Namely of Jerusalem.

[10] For the proposed emendation by J. A. Emerton, *VT* 17, 1967, 134ff., to read *we'ōz libbāh*, 'and the strength of their heart', i.e. their stubbornness, cf. Wildberger, ad loc.

[11] Or understand the form as a suffixed infinitive of *dābar*, 'as they want'.

[12] H. W. Hertzberg, BZAW 46, Berlin 1936, 112, proposed understanding *gārīm*, 'aliens', as a later interpretation designating the alien masters of the land; cf. also 1.7. This interpretation, extracted from Vermeylen I, 173, is perhaps to be preferred to that suggested by G. R. Driver, *JTS* 38, 1937, according to which *gārīm* is a miswriting of a gloss *ge'dīm*, 'little goat'.

[13] For *haššāw'*, 'of wickedness', read *haššōr*.

[14] As the oxen were harnessed to a cart, an alteration here is superfluous.

[15] For the use of the so-called imperfect to denote a comitative action, cf. Bobzin §7, 1b.

[16] For the use of a singular suffix to refer back to a plural, cf. Davidson § 116 R 1.

and as hay[17] sinks down into the flame,[18]
so their root will be as rottenness,
and their blossom fly up[18] like dust.
For they despised the law of Yahweh
and rejected the word of the Holy One of Israel.

[5.8–24 + 10.1–4] These verses contain a composition consisting of seven woes. As a result of redactional activity the last woe has been detached from its original context and inserted into a new one.[19] Its place has been taken by the last strophe of the refrain poem which begins in 9.7, about the outstretched hand of Yahweh (cf. 5.25ff.), and the woe itself replaces this. We shall have to think about the reasons behind this exchange in connection with the interpretation of 5.25ff.[20] A look at the second woe with vv. 11–19 shows most quickly that the remaining six woes, too, are no longer in their original form: some of them have later been expanded and reinterpreted. In order to trace this process, it is worth beginning with a form-critical examination of the origin and basic form of the prophetic woe. It seems to have arisen from the cries of woe in the lament for the dead. Depending on the age and status of the dead person, people would lament, 'Woe, my brother', 'Woe, my sister', or 'Woe, master' (cf. Jer. 22.18f.; 34.4f.; I Kings 13.30).[21] In an extended funeral lament the woe could presumably also introduce a malediction on a murderer.[22] Thus when applied to a living person, the woe includes the threat of death. As such, it requires neither a special accusation nor an enumeration of grounds for guilt: the accusation is contained in the designation of the agent, the grounds in the woe which announces his death. If with this in mind we turn to the present woes, we note that this basic form has been lost in the first, second and seventh (cf. vv. 9f., 13ff.; 10.3). The question therefore arises whether all these expansions which, moreover, do not treat all the sayings in the same way, are original; indeed we can even go further and ask whether the different lengths in the descriptions of the agents do not indicate later activity. Such a suspicion will be further supported by the observation that the present situation conceals an

---

[17] The Hebrew *hašaš* corresponds to our loan word hashish.

[18] For the use of the so-called imperfect to denote a comitative action, cf. Bobzin §7, 1b.

[19] Cf. 111 below. A different view is held by Donner, *Israel unter den Völkern*, 66ff.; Fey, *Amos und Jesaja*, 83ff., and W. Janzen, *Mourning Cry and Woe Oracle*, BZAW 125, Berlin and New York 1972, 50 n. 23.

[20] Cf. 111 below.

[21] Cf. H.-J. Krause, *'hôj als prophetische Leichenklage über das eigene Volk'*, ZAW 85, 1973, 19ff.

[22] Cf. Janzen (n. 19), 27ff.

originally clear arrangement. This strikes us as soon as we move away from the specific form and consider only the thematic outline of the individual woes. It then emerges that they form a circular composition: the first, fourth and seventh woes are concerned with transgressors of the law; the second and sixth with drunkards and the third and fifth with frivolity which is forgetful of God.

[23] A recognition of this ordering already justifies a first literary-critical intervention, the moving of v. 23 behind v. 20.[23] The transposition evidently came about because of the removal of the seventh woe (10.1ff.), so as to make the mutilated series end with a clear and weighty accusation. [11–17] In the form in which it has been handed down, the outline of the composition is concealed by the unequally distributed expansions and additions, which in the second woe even go so far as to contradict the original. Here careful analysis produces the following result. [14 + 17] These verses really belong together, and announce a future complete destruction of an unnamed city. As in 3.25f., we are evidently to understand this as Jerusalem. The parallel suggests that the two verses, like 3.1–4.1; 6.12–13abα; 8.21–23a, are an eschatological announcement of disaster, in view of a last annihilating judgment. A characteristic of this editor, as is shown especially by 3.25f.; 8.21ff., is that he takes insufficient notice of the context. In this commentary we can leave on one side the question whether this is because he is wrapped up in his own ideas and expectations or is quoting directly from another source. His work shows that he was convinced that the reproaches contained in the woes still applied to his own time. However, the futuristic aspect and the understanding of the two verses emerges clearly only in v. 17. [13] In the light of this verse, v. 14aα can be understood as a retrospect: deportation and mass deaths were the consequence of the conduct attacked in vv. 11, 12. The woe was fulfilled in the catastrophe of the kingdom of Judah and in particular in the conquest of Jerusalem by the Babylonians in 587. Fortunately, however, the man who later put v. 13 in front of vv. 14, 17 intervened only very superficially in v. 14. Against the basic rule of the syntax of the Hebrew verb, in v. 14a he introduced a historic perfect, but allowed the so-called consecutive perfect, which denotes a future action, to stand. Presumably he is also the editor responsible for the insertion of 5.25ff.[24] [15–16] In addition, his transformation of the threat into a historical statement made possible the insertion of vv. 15 and 16,

---

[23] Cf. also Fey, *Amos und Jesaja*, 57ff.; Wildberger, ad loc.
[24] Cf. also below 111.

oriented on 2.9, 11, 17, which break the connection between vv. 14 and 17.[25]

[9 + 10] The fact of the later eschatological interpretation by means of vv. 14, 17 necessarily raises the question whether the same hand is also responsible for further additions, or whether its intervention was limited solely to the second woe. If we look at the first woe from this perspective, further investigation soon shows that there is a more complete parallel to v. 9a in 22.14, which at that point similarly serves as the introduction to a divine oath.[26] Furthermore, the train of thought in vv. 9 and 10 is striking: presumably we may connect the desolation of the land with its devastation by enemies (cf. 7.17, 18f.; 8.7f.; and for the formula also 6.11).[27] But how does the author arrive at the idea of connecting it in v. 10 with the diminishing fertility of the land, whether as a cause or more probably as a further visitation? Surprisingly, a look at 5.6 provides the answer: v. 10 is an interpretation of 5.6b which takes the comment literally (cf. also 24.6f.). This is sufficient justification for the assumption that in vv. 9, 10, too, we have a later elaboration of the woe.

[12 + 19] Although the earliest stratum of the book of Isaiah is already familiar with the form of the elaborated cry of woe (cf. 30.1ff.; 31.1ff.), we can hardly go wrong if we extend the result gained from the investigation so far to the elaboration of the accusations made in vv. 12, 19; 10.3. Here, at any rate, one might refer to the bare form of the fifth and the sixth woes in vv. 21, 22. In v. 12 the form utilizing a $w^eh\bar{a}y\bar{a}h$, 'and there is', can be taken as an argument demonstrating that this is a subsequent extension.[28] In this connection it is also worth noting that in terms of content we should observe a passing reference to Amos 6.5–6,[29] and a similar one to Ps. 28.5. There are variations here on the themes of hardening the heart in 6.10 and blinding in 29.9f., both in view of the impending last judgment.

There is no disputing the fact that v. 19, with its mention of the work and plan of Yahweh, the content of which is supplied by its context in the text (cf. Ps. 106.13), can be connected with the

---

[25] The fact that the editor responsible for the insertion, whom one can perhaps identify with the editor of 2.6–9, changed the consecutive perfect at the beginning of v. 17, shows that his feel for Hebrew had already been weakened by Aramaic; cf. e.g. H. Bauer and P. Leander, *Grammatik des Biblisch-Aramäischen*, Halle 1927 = Hildesheim and New York 1969, 77a and 79n, and R. Degen, *Altaramäische Grammatik*, Abhandlungen für die Kunde des Morgenlandes 38, 3, Wiesbaden 1969, 74.

[26] For the use of *'im lō'*, 'if not', to introduce a divine oath, cf. Jer. 15.11; 49.20; 50.45; Ezek. 36.5, 7; Mal. 3.10, and by contrast e.g. Ezek. 17.19; 20.33.

[27] Cf. also 1.7.

[28] In 30.3 things are clearly different.

[29] Cf. also Fey, *Amos und Jesaja*, 7ff., and for the evidence in Amos 6.1ff., H. W. Wolff., *Joel and Amos*, Hermeneia, Philadephia 1977, ad loc., but cf. also Whedbee, *Isaiah and Wisdom*, 90ff.

scepticism of the upper class in Jerusalem towards the eschatological proclamation (cf. also 28.21f.). However, one must concede that the real decision is made on the basis of the evidence discussed earlier. In view of the terminological parallel in Micah 7.4, and the parallel to the content in 2.12ff., an eschatological interpretation of 10.3 can be justified.

Thus the basis of the circular composition proves to be 5.8, 11, 18, 20, 23, 21, 22 and 10.1–2. It consists of simple woes which preserve the basic form. By turning to address the audience in v. 8b, it provides a link with 5.1–7 (cf. v. 3). Its function is to justify the charge of corrupting justice made in v. 7. It is hard to decide clearly whether the series of seven woes had a previous history of its own, or whether it was brought together for its present position. Perhaps the affinity of vv. 20, 23 to Amos 5.7, 10, 12,[30] and finally also the sequence maintained in the mention of widows before the fatherless in 10.2, which is not normal in the Old Testament,[31] tells in favour of the second possibility. Along with 5.1ff., these woes had the function of supplementing the reason for the catastrophe which befell the kingdom of Judah given in the memorial[32] and in the earliest stratum of the book of Isaiah (which can be detected in chs. 29–31), in terms of a failure to trust in God along the lines of the prophetic procla-mation of justice in the book of Amos and the theology of history put forward by the Deuteronomistic school, by reference to law-break-ing, thus at the same time helping the present generation towards a more specific self-examination.

[24] The insertion of v. 24 is a consequence of the exchange of the last woe (10.1ff.) and the closing strophe of the refrain poem (5.26ff.).[33] Since by means of the insertion of v. 13 and the interpo-lation of v. 25 the meaning of the woes was changed, against the eschatological redaction, so that they again served their original function of giving the reason for the judgment in 587, the editor whose voice we find here felt it appropriate to stress their permanent validity. Thus the history of the woes reflects in microcosm not only the history of the Isaianic collection but also that of the spiritual trends and controversies in Jerusalem Judaism during the Persian period.

[5.8, 11, 17, 20–23 + 10.1–2] *The sevenfold woe.* The seven woes

---

[30] Cf. Fey, *Amos und Jesaja*, 57ff., and for the evidence in Amos 5.1ff., H. W. Wolff, *Joel and Amos*, ad loc.

[31] The order widow-fatherless occurs elsewhere only in Ex. 22.21; Zech. 7.10 and Mal. 3.5; the reverse order can be found not only in Isa. 1.17, 23 but also in Deut. 10.18; 14.29; 16.11, 14; 24.19, 20, 21; 26.12, 13; 27.19; Jer. 7.6; 22.3; Ezek. 22.7; Ps. 68.6; 109.9; 146.8.

[32] Cf. 114ff. below.

[33] Cf. 111 below.

which form the basis of the composition 5.8–24 + 10.1–4* show up
an upper class who, in a frivolity which is heedless of God and an
arrogance which has forgotten him, combine boundless covetousness and sensuality, and in so doing live at the expense of the
common people, whose law they destroy by corrupt judgment and
whose basis of life they shatter in apparently legal ways.

[5.8] The very first woe envisages the practice of increasing one's
own house and land by exploiting economic strength, taking advantage of the distress of small farmers and craftsmen which may have
been caused by sickness, crop-failure, inflation or excessive taxation.
Such people would be offered a loan; and if they were unable to pay
it back at a later date, their movable possessions would be pawned,
their children would be taken in payment and thus be made slaves,
and finally their house and land would be seized (cf. Neh. 5.1ff.,
and, for an illustration, II Kings 4.1ff.). Such a procedure first
offended against the conviction that Yahweh is the real owner of the
land and that its inhabitants have received it from him on loan, like
tenants (Lev. 25.23),[34] and secondly against the ideal preserved from
the earliest days of the people that the land was to remain in the
possession of the clan and thus sustain its economic strength and
provide the basis for life. Both notions were combined in the late
theory that the tribes had received their land from Yahweh by lot (cf.
Num. 26.55ff.; 36.2ff.; Josh. 14.2).[35] At all events it is worth considering whether in the early days of Israel the land belonging to a
community identical with a confederation of clans was divided
among kinsfolk by lot (cf. Ps. 16.6).[36] Be this at it may, underlying
the legal usage that in the case of over-indebtedness or other such
reasons the male relatives, who originally were the only ones with
hereditary rights, were given prior right of purchase, was the intent
to preserve the basis of a clan's life (cf. Ruth 4.1ff.; Jer. 32.6ff.; Lev.
25.25ff.).[37] Obviously reality was very different from the ideal:
differences in competence and differing fortunes did away with any
equality of possessions, and this process would be accelerated by
the monarchy with its feudal system and later by the interests of

[34] In addition to K. Elliger, HAT 1, 4, Tübingen 1968, 354, cf. also F. Horst, 'Das
Eigentum nach dem Alten Testament', in Gottes Recht, ThB 12, Munich 1961, 215ff.
For the narrative in I Kings 21, much quoted in this connection, cf. E. Würthwein,
'Naboth-novelle und Elia Wort', ZTK 75, 1978, 375ff., esp. 384f.
[35] Cf. M. Wüst, Untersuchungen zu den siedlungsgeographischen Texten des Alten
Testaments I, Ostjordanland, Beihefte zum Tübinger Atlas des Vorderen Orients B 9,
Wiesbaden 1975, 210ff.
[36] Cf. also A. Weiser, Psalms, OTL, ad loc.
[37] Cf. also K. Elliger, HAT I, 4, 354ff.

provincial administration.[38] The extension of the right of inheritance to daughters in the post-exilic period created further problems (cf. Num. 27.8ff. with Num. 36). The attempt of religious legislation to prevent the decimation of free peasant families by means of a remission of debts to be effective every seven years (Deut. 15.1ff.), or a year of remission to take place every fifty years, in which all property pledged or sold would return to its original owner (Lev. 25.13ff.), has left behind no trace in the Old Testament period[39] and must therefore be regarded as utopian.[40] According to this woe, what is regarded in economic practice as an unavoidable development and as a necessary consequence of human inequality nevertheless does not fall out of the hand of God, who loves justice and by that understands the right of even the weakest member of the community to live and sustain that life. To preserve their independence and to guard against an economic concentration of power extending to an unlimited degree, whether this was in the name of private, political or state alliances and unions, would be in accord with the concern of the first woe, which recognizes the roots of the former collapse in the social misuses of the past and sees the prospect of a further collapse as a result of their continuation in the present. For the saying which interprets the past in faith is at the same time most profoundly directed towards the present.

[5.11] *The second woe.* The second woe in this verse is concerned with the drunkards who are at their wine from morning to night. From the point of view of tradition, this verse is indebted to wisdom thinking (cf. Prov. 23.30).[41] In the circles of the wise it was natural to paint a deterrent picture of the dangers of drunkenness and excessive wine-drinking: wine clouds the senses and involves the alcoholic in trouble and suffering, makes him an object of contempt (Prov. 23.29ff.; cf. also 28.7), destroys his well-being (Prov. 23.20f.) and hinders success (Prov. 21.17). If the ruler is in his cups early in the morning, things bode ill for his subjects (Eccles 10.16b). Separated from the later interpretation in v. 12, the woe is primarily independent: all those who can live such a life and who have confined

[38] Cf. A. Alt, 'Der Anteil des Königtums an der sozialen Entwicklung in den Reichen Israel und Juda', KS III, 348ff.; H. Donner, 'Die soziale Botschaft der Propheten im Lichte der Gesellschaftsordnung in Israel', OrAnt 2, 1963, 229ff.

[39] Nehemiah 10.29ff. at best shows that in the fourth century attempts were made to give validity to these regulations. For the evidence cf. S. Mowinckel, Studien zum Buche Ezra-Nehemiah III, SNVAO II, 2, Oslo 1965, 142ff., and esp. 152ff.. For the implementation of the regulation that Israelite slaves were to be freed after seven years cf. Ex. 21.2ff. with Deut. 15.12ff. and Lev. 25.39ff., 44f., and also Jer. 34.8ff.; Neh. 5.1ff.

[40] Cf. R. de Vaux, Ancient Israel, London 1961, 164ff., 176.

[41] Cf. H. Fichtner, 'Jesaja unter den Weisen' (1951), in Gottes Weisheit, AzT II, 3, Stuttgart 1965, 21ff., and Whedbee, Isaiah and Wisdom, 93ff., and esp. 98ff.

themselves to satisfying their desires come to a bad end. In the past they have shared in responsibility for the fall of the kingdom of Judah, and in the present too they will be punished; they no longer see the obligation which they all bear towards the people as a whole and will hardly act better than the prophets and priests depicted in 28.7ff. unless they are touched by the call to repent. Against the background of the first woe which precedes it, this second one at the same time raises the question at whose expense such a life of luxury or dissoluteness is being lived (cf. also Amos 6.6 and 2.8; 4.1).

[5.18] *The third woe.* This is directed to those who as inevitably call down Yahweh's punishment with their conduct as the waggon follows the ropes with which it is fastened to the draught oxen.[42] It concerns all those who blatantly and frivolously violate the will of God. In connection with the two previous woes, and those which are to come, we have to think of the property speculators with their dispossession of the peasantry; the drunkards who are heedless of the fate of their people; and not least the corrupt judges (cf. also 3.9).

[5.20, 23] *The fourth woe.* The fourth woe, like the first, is directed against unprincipled covetousness.[43] Its external extent already shows that the author was particularly concerned with the corruptibility of the judges, which is the misuse which he attacks. And we have to agree with him here, because this is a cancer which gnaws away at any state. As its foundation, a state needs the security of law. Instead of doing their duty by discovering the truth with their hearings and judgments, finding out the guilty and acquitting the innocent, venal judges in a partisan way twist the truth in their own interest (cf. v. 20 with Amos 5.7; 6.12). The judge who allows his freedom in coming to a decision to be affected by a gift, or has any other kind of personal advantage in view, has himself become a party in the case (cf. 1.23). Observations and assessments characteristic of wisdom are also to be found in the background to this woe: the wise men regarded it as established that Yahweh abhors those who acquit the guilty and convict the innocent (Prov. 17.15). Thus the acceptance of bribes is a sign of godlessness (Prov. 17.23). If even a ruler succumbs to this partisanship which goes against his calling, he is met with the execrations and curses of the peoples (Prov. 24.24). So underlying the fourth woe is the basic conviction that Yahweh punishes those who misuse their office or their calling for their own advantage and to the detriment of those who have no protection and no help.

Nothing shakes confidence in state and society more deeply than

---

[42] For putting under the yoke see the evidence in 209 n. 37 below.
[43] For the connection cf. above, 97.

the public corruption of justice and the removal of the certainty of fair treatment.[44] Therefore anyone who wants to bring about both seeks to spread the feeling that government is dominated by class interests, instead of by the notion of justice which gives each man his due. It is the supreme duty of every judge and every politician to refute this charge. The one is called to increase the certainty of justice by his judgments; the other to prepare for a continuation of legislation as a result of which the principle of giving to each in accordance with his contribution to the whole can be realized in constantly new circumstances. Where in a secularized age we would diagnose the undermining of a sense of togetherness and the collapse of state and society in terms of a disappearing sense of justice and a disappearing sense of security in justice which goes hand in hand with that, the Old Testament sees God himself secretly at work; there is a conviction here that those who enrich themselves unjustly will come to no good, as will the society which does not guard against injustice. That implies that we can really only find wholeness, salvation, in a community which is whole, since we are made for community and receive our nature from it. It follows from that that we must struggle to make a world which is more whole. If we are not to grow weary of doing that, in a world without wholeness we need that eschatological faith which knows that it cannot ask God for good fortune on its own account, yet nevertheless remains secure in him and through him in the circle of those who also believe in his rule and hope in his coming kingdom.

[5.21] *The fifth woe.* The words of the fifth woe of themselves indicate that they come from wisdom circles. For those who know that the fear of Yahweh is the beginning of wisdom (Prov. 3.7; 1.7), to regard oneself as wise is a sign of folly (cf. Prov. 26.12, 16; 28.11).[45] That is why the arrogant have met their downfall (Prov. 16.18); and that is also the meaning of the present woe. Read in conjunction with the other woes, it summons those who seek their own advantage to see whether they would not find it in obedience to God's will and wisdom, and in knowledge of his judgment to remember the rights and the well-being of all, in concern for the weak.

[5.22] *The sixth woe.* This woe focusses on men who boast of their capacity for drink and their skill in mixing alcoholic drinks. Anyone who is a hero only at drinking merely shows a regrettable lack of insight and self-control rather than his courage. And anyone who can boast only of knowing how to mix an intoxicating drink from

---

[44] Cf. also G. Radbruch, *Rechtsphilosophie*, ed. Erik Wolf, Stuttgart ⁶1963, 168ff., 196ff.
[45] Cf. also Whedbee, op. cit. 105ff.

honey and concentrated beer extract,[46] without being concerned for the well-being and salvation of his people, is a prime example of the fool who thinks himself wise and necessarily falls under the woe that is pronounced on such men.

[10.1–2] *The seventh woe.* In conclusion, the seventh woe takes up once again the theme of lawbreaking. There is some dispute as to whether by the 'regulations' of suffering it envisages an alteration of the current law in the direction of a release in trading in houses and property which sets itself above the interests of clan community, or rather of individual judgments, set down in writing, which trample down the rights of widows and the fatherless, who are dependent on others to act as advocates (cf. 1.7; 1.23).[47] In addition, we cannot exclude the possibility that the author, evidently well skilled in wisdom thinking, had in mind the excessive taxation demands of his own time, which widows and orphans could meet only by selling their inheritance (cf. Neh. 5.4). It is possible to argue either way, but underlying this woe is the conviction that the deity is the advocate of all those who cannot plead their own cause and carry it through (cf. Prov. 22.22f.; Ex. 23.6).[48]

Happy the people among whom belief in the working of divine righteousness has not yet died out, and among whom the powerful know that one even more powerful is over them. Happy, too, a people among whom the more insignificant do not allow themselves to be blinded by jealousy, recognize the success and achievement of others, and understand that a tyranny from below can have as corrupting an effect on the community as a tyranny from above. The prevalence of righteousness shows itself in the fact that we must all live up to its claim or fail by it, and therefore are all called to exercise moderation amd to preserve a happy medium.

[5.9–10, 12, 14, 17, 19; 10.3] *The later eschatological interpretation.* The seven woes originally served as an explanation of the catastrophe which had already befallen the people. The author put himself in Isaiah's position, but had in mind the outcome of the story. Thus in the end the woes are *vaticinia ex eventu*, prophecies in the light of what actually happened, which interpret the collapse as Yahweh's punishment of his people and at the same time hold up a mirror to the present. Their position between the Song of the Vineyard in 5.1ff. and the memorial which begins in 6.1 is in accordance with this.

Be this as it may, in the fifth century they were still being

---

[46] Cf. E. Huber, *RAL* II, 25ff.; K. Galling, *BRL*[1], col. 111, and D. Kellermann, *BRL*[2], 48f.

[47] Cf. also below, 226f.

[48] Cf. also Whedbee, op. cit., 107ff.

interpreted eschatologically, i.e. in terms of a last judgment by
Yahweh which would determine in a decisive way the further course
of the history of the nations. In so far as it is actually mentioned, the
expected punishment for the offences mentioned in the woes, which
in fact prove to be current ones, will consist in a reversal of
circumstances. **[5.9–10]** In the final judgment on Jerusalem which is
expected (cf. vv. 14; 10.3), the houses and land which have been
concentrated in a few hands, but which are not of course empty and
fallow, being partly occupied by members of the clan and partly let
out at a profit or worked by day-labourers, will lose their significance.
What Isaiah is supposed to have envisaged according to 6.11, a
hardening of the people's heart to the point of the evacuation of the
cities and the desolation of the fields, seemed still in force: the
hardness of heart had not been softened and the announcement of
judgment therefore still applied. However, its implementation
would now result in the same situation as that brought about by the
conquest of Jerusalem by the Babylonians. This time the proud new
buildings would really be left behind and present the eerie picture of
a dead city (cf. also Deut. 28.30). If we add v. 10 as an explanation of
the situation, as the old versions did, the ultimate emptiness is the
consequence of a great famine (cf. Joel 1.10ff.; Deut. 28.23f.; 24.6ff.).
What we must imagine is that the conquest envisaged in 3.25ff.; 10.3
was followed by substantial crop failures which finished off the
survivors who remained behind in the city and in the country. The
diminution in the fertility of the land imagined by this proto-
apocalyptist follows a pattern of reduction to a tenth, which is
evident in 6.13a and even more clearly in Amos 5.3. If a yoke of
vineyard, i.e. the amount of ground which a team of oxen could
plough in a day, and which on the basis of the information given in
the Talmud we can put at about 2,000 square metres, produces only
a *bath* (about 32 litres); and if an ass's load, 218 litres of seed, produces
only an *ephah* (21.8 litres) as a crop,[49] the result will be a quite
devastating famine. What will men and animals live on if the seed is
reduced to a tenth its quantity, instead of increasing between thirty
and a hundredfold (Mark 4.8))? The proto-apocalyptist seeks to
ground the inescapability, indeed the inexorable doom, in this
expectation on a revelation to him imparted in the form of a divine
oath (cf. also 22.14). As the oath includes the self-execration of the
omnipotent Yahweh Sebaoth,[50] who has power over heaven and
earth, and delivers the creation over to chaos, there can be no
stronger assurance behind a prophecy than this.

[49] For these measures, which are partly problematical, cf. Götz Schmitt, *BRL*[2],
204ff.
[50] For this divine epithet, cf. 126f. below on 6.3.

I mentioned above that the notion was suggested by 5.6b. Evidently there is an essential difference between the origin of an idea and the certainty with which it is held, as the realm of fact and the sphere of what can be grasped in the detached act of seeing are left behind and the level of personal relationships is reached. This consideration also includes the relationship with God and the relationship of God to the world as an answer to the nature of its perception by man. Of course, this certainty inescapably bears within itself the risk of a false assessment, because for the living person there is no final assurance apart from promising to stand by the other and one's own word. Therefore a man can swear by his future conduct only if he is prepared to limit his freedom and in some instances to act against his insight and conviction. The presumption of believing that one has heard God's oath is manifest in the indifference of history towards its content, in so far as one keeps to the specific expectation expressed in it. One can trust in God's never-ending presence and know that he makes the mistrust directed towards him fail in the collapse of human society and the struggle over the natural resources for life. As the one who discloses life in a whole world, he is of course also in control of nature, which has an ambivalence overcome only in an eschatological belief in salvation.

[5.12] Here the editor, without any knowledge of Amos 6.5f. (cf. also Isa. 22.12ff.) has perhaps pilloried the way in which people who simply surrender to their enjoyment are chained to vanity with their senses and their desires. In that case, with his mere enumeration he falls short of his model. Banquets at that time had to have lyres and harps (or lutes?),[51] timbrels and flutes,[52] which, to judge from the Eastern music that has been preserved, made people forget the everyday world by their monotones and sharp rhythms which captivated the senses. In a dream-world the earnestness of everyday life and the divine call which it contains do not take meaningful form. Thus it escapes the notice of those who are caught up in this world that God is at work in the history which is made up simply of everyday moments.[53] However, anyone who does not heed his hidden working is godless, guilty and subject to his judgment (Ps. 28.5; 64.10).

---

[51] Cf. F. Ellermeier, 'Beiträge zur Frühgeschichte altorientalischer Saiteninstrumente', in Archäologie und Altes Testament, Kurt Galling Festschrift, Tübingen 1970, 75ff.

[52] Cf. also H. P. Rüger, BRL¹, 234ff.

[53] For mention of the action of Yahweh cf. Ps. 28.5; 64.10; Ps. 95.9; Hab. 3.2; Ps. 44.2; 77.13; 111.3 and esp. Hab. 1.5; for the work of his hands cf. Ps. 28.5; 64.10; 111.7; 118.17; 107.22; Isa. 28.21; 10.12; 29.23; 60.21; Jer. 51.10, and on this also G. von Rad, 'Das Werk Jahwes', in Studia biblica et semitica Th. Ch. Vriezen . . . dedicata, Wageningen 1966, 290ff. = Gesammelte Studien zum Alten Testament II, ThB 48, Munich 1973, 236ff.

[5.14 + 17] The consequence of this forgetfulness of self and God is inescapable downfall. The proto-apocalyptist becomes a poet in depicting how the underworld,[54] like a violent animal, opens its jaws so wide that their limits cannot be seen, so as to be able to swallow up all the pomp and tumult which fills Jerusalem, with its uproar and its unrestrained noise, when all that 'descends'[55] to it. At all events, the roots of the conception are to be found in Canaanite mythology. In the Baal epic from Ras Shamra-Ugarit we are told that the God Mot, whose form strangely fluctuates between that of the lord of the underworld and the underworld itself,[56] opens one lip towards earth and the other towards heaven and stretches as far as the stars (CTA 5, Gordon 67, II, 1ff.). What is a certainty for all men, that one day they will be added to the domain of the powerful and constantly growing lord of the dead, will become the ultimate fate of Jerusalem (cf. vv. 9f.): to be left bereft of inhabitants.[57]

[5.19] Of course, at the time at which he writes, the proto-apocalyptist, with his sombre expectations, finds nothing but sceptical mockery among those who in his view are responsible for the fate of the city as a result of their behaviour (v. 18). Ironically they invite him to let the Holy One of Israel,[58] who is called upon so much, at last to implement the work that he has announced (cf. v. 12), and to bring in the plan which he is supposed to have made. The sceptic looks for proof. But this proof always follows as the unwanted demonstration of the power of God in judgment.

Underlying the conception of Yahweh's plan lies the experience that in the end man does not have control over the success or failure of his plans; it is borne in on him that he is confronted with a situation which cannot be perceived and in the end cannot be anticipated. In the fact that begins to become evident here, as in its ethical connection with self and society, the believer recognizes the power and the plan of God (cf. Prov. 19.21), no matter how dark this may sometimes

---

[54] For the derivation of the word, cf. also N. J. Tromp, 'Primitive Conceptions of Death and the Nether World in the Old Testament', BibOr 21, Rome 1969, 21ff., and L. I. J. Stadelmann, The Hebrew Conception of the World, AnBib 39, Rome 1970, 165ff. For conceptions bound up with the underworld cf. also O. Kaiser in O. Kaiser and E. Lohse, Tod und Leben, Biblische Konfrontationen, Stuttgart 1977, 25ff.

[55] For yārad, descend, as an expression of descent into the world of the dead, cf. Job 7.9; Ezek. 31.15; Ps. 22.30; 28.1; 88.5; Isa. 38.18; Ezek. 26.20; 31.14ff.; 32.18ff.; Ps. 115.17.

[56] Cf. CTA 4 (Gordon 67) VIII, 1ff. with CTA 5 (Gordon 51) II, 1ff. For the character of the god Mot as Lord of the ripe corn cf. H. Gese, Die Religion Altsyriens, RM 10, 2, Stuttgart 1970, 136.

[57] Cf. the exaggeration in 13.20f.

[58] For this designation for God cf. p. 22 above on 1.4.

seem to him to be (Job 38.2).[59] Only in confident surrender to God can man become certain that in the end God means well towards him (Ps. 73.24). The other side of the matter is that self-glorification which forgets God falls under judgment, because it offends against his will and plan which are manifest in the commandment (Ps. 10.7, 11; 106.13). Accordingly, the proto-apocalyptist is convinced that the downfall of those who despise God lies in Yahweh's plan; Yahweh shows himself as the Holy One, as the later editor whose words we hear in v. 16 has put it. The notion that salvation waits beyond judgment, and that Yahweh uses judgment finally to restore salvation, once again only belongs to the next stage of eschatological thought (cf. 14.26; Micah 4.12; Isa. 19.17; 25.1; 28.29).[60] We should not overlook the heightening which is to be found in v. 19 in contrast to v. 12: there is a difference between not heeding God because one is caught up by the senses, and the rejection of him in mockery, which reverences the principle that anything pleasurable is allowed. However, this difference does not accentuate or diminish the failing: for the proto-apocalyptist, both groups equally come to grief. Incurring guilt before God is not a subjective, but an objective event. And anyone who is not with him is already against him.

[10.3] The question to those who violate the rights of the weak, namely what they will do on the day of the divine visitation to save themselves, when the nations attack Jerusalem from afar (cf. 5.26; 13.4f.), like a storm (cf. 2.12ff.), in order to inflict Yahweh's judgment, rounds off the picture of the proto-apocalyptist's expectation. With its address to reader and hearer, it recalls all that is coming to them. There is no appeal to the possibility of repentance and return. In the eyes of this man judgment stands over the people like an inexorable fate, whose ruler and influential people are caught up in a blindness which makes them think only of themselves and forget God.

[5.13, 15, 16] *The later historicizing interpretations.* A sudden searchlight is thrown on the inner controversies and perhaps also the groups in post-exilic Judaism which intervened in the continuation of the writing of the book of Isaiah by the fact that it has a strange tendency to force back words with an eschatological bent either to the lifetime of the prophet, as in chs. 7 and 8, or to the fall of Jerusalem in 587, as we can see in 3.8f. and in the present passage. It is difficult to know whether here we have simply the beginnings of a historicizing interpretation of the prophet, or an intention to rob

---

[59] For the heightening of the sense of mystery in God's ways with the world cf. also O. Kaiser, 'Die Sinn(es)krise bei Kohelet', in *Rechtfertigung, Realismus, Universalismus in biblischer Sicht*, Festschrift Adolf Köberle, Darmstadt 1978, 3ff.

[60] Cf. also J. Fichtner, 'Jahwes Plan in der Botschaft des Jesaja', *ZAW* 63, 1951, 16ff. = *Gottes Weisheit*, AzT II, 3, Stuttgart 1965, 27ff.

the fearful threats of their effect by taking them back into the past. [13] So this verse, which was perhaps only twisted to have this meaning at a later stage, affirms that the threat contained in vv. 14, 17 has already been fulfilled in the exiling of the people of Jerusalem and that the deportation took place because the people did not come to see Yahweh's rule. Thus the editor maintains the theory of hardening the people's heart which is expressed in 6.9ff. Forced to their knees by hunger and thirst (cf. II Kings 25.3; Lam. 2.11f., 19f.; 4.5, 7ff.; 5.10 and Lev. 26.27ff.), nobility and people went into exile (cf. also Amos 6.7). [15 + 16] Probably a further hand saw in the fate of Jerusalem, as expressed in 2.9 and applied in 2.11, 17, the humiliation of the proud by Yahweh and at the same time the revelation of his exclusive loftiness and power, though he also showed himself as the Holy One before whom nothing unholy can stand (cf. Lev. 19.2; Isa. 6.3, 5) by punishing the guilty in accordance with his righteousness.

[5.24] *Interpretation in terms of a contemporary situation.* It is evidence of the living antagonism in the history of faith that the historicizing editors found their counterpart in another man who was convinced by looking at his own time and the will of Yahweh as contained in the law and the book of the prophet that the woes continued to be applicable as long as they related to people. As a comparison for the speed of the annihilation which was awaiting them, where he did not rely on his own observations, he took up the Song of the Sea from Ex. 15.7.[61] As such, the notion of the punishment suddenly coming upon the godless is part of the material of wisdom (cf. Prov. 6.15; 29.1; Job 22.10; Ps. 73.19; 6.11). The writer has also taken from wisdom the second comparison, which he uses the first to explain, namely that root and blossom and therefore the whole plant disappear without trace (cf. Job 18.16). What he means to say is that the godless who have set themselves above the will of the Holy One of Israel[62] manifested in the law and the word of the prophet perish suddenly and without leaving a trace (cf. 1.4; 30.9 and above all Amos 2.4).[63]

---

[61] Cf. also Isa. 47.14; Nahum 1.10; Obad, 18; Joel 2.5; Mal. 3.19 and the résumé in Isa. 33.11.

[62] For this divine epithet see above, 22 on 1.4.

[63] Cf. also Vermeylen I, 174f., against J. Jensen, *The Use of* tora *by Isaiah*, CBQM 3, Washington DC 1975, 95ff., and for v. 24b also Barth, *Jesaja-Worte*, 115f.

CHAPTER 5.25–30

The People from Afar

25   Therefore the anger of Yahweh was kindled against his people,
and he stretched out his hand against them and smote them.
And the mountains quaked and their corpses remained
like refuse in the midst of the streets.
For all this his anger was not turned away,
and his hand was stretched out still.

26   **But he is raising a banner** for the people from afar[1]
and is whistling for them from the ends of the earth –
and see, swiftly, speedily, they will come.

27   **None is weary and none stumbles among them.**
They do not slumber and do not rest,[2]
there is no one who loosens his waist-cloth,
and no one whose sandal-thongs are broken.

28   **Their arrows are sharp,**
and all their bows are strung.[3]
Their horses' hooves are <like flint>[4],
and their chariot wheels like the whirlwind.[5]

29   **Their roaring is like a lion.**
When they <roar>[6] **like young lions**
and growl and seize their prey
and carry it off – there is none to rescue.

30   And it thunders[7] over them on that day
like the roaring of the sea,
And if one looks at the land, thick darkness prevails,[8]
for the light is darkened in its[9] clouds.

[5.25–30] Two external features show that the section 5.26–29 is a continuation of the refrain poem about the outstretched hand of

---

[1] Read *leḡoy mimmerḥāq*, cf. Jer. 5.15 and v. aβ.

[2] A single redactional gloss following Ps. 121.4.

[3] I.e. taut.

[4] Read *kaṣṣōr* instead of *kaṣṣar* = 'like the enemy', and move the *zāqûp qāṭōn* after it.

[5] Follow Procksch by putting the verb at the end of the verse.

[6] Read *weyiš'aḡ*, and cf. Bobzin §9, 5.

[7] The tense can be explained by the way in which the redactor imitates and takes up the *weyinhōm* of the previous line.

[8] Shift the *zaqep qaton* to read *ṣār reʿōr*.

[9] The suffix refers back to *neḥāmā*.

Yahweh in 9.8[7]ff.: first, the preliminary insertion of the refrain in v. 25 (cf. 9.12 [11], 17 [16], 21[20]; 10.4), and secondly, the number of lines which correspond to its strophe construction.[10] These indications are matched by the intrinsic necessity that the refrain poem, intended as a retrospect on a history of disaster, should end in a strophe which reports a further blow by Yahweh against his people, going beyond the previous visitations and bringing them to an end. As what is now its last strophe, 10.1–4, in essence consists of a woe, and the series of woes beginning with 5.8 precedes the present section, it clearly follows that at a later stage the last strophe of the refrain poem was exchanged with the last woe. This happened after the woe had already been extended in terms of eschatological disaster, and before it had again been made contemporaneous by the addition of 5.24.[11] **[25]** There is some dispute as to whether this verse is in turn a fragment of a strophe of the refrain poem or was composed on the occasion of the transposition to make it the redactional transition from the woes to the judgment announced in 5.26ff. In view of the general state of the refrain poem, it is hard to arrive at any clear solution. However, the suspicion that the verse comes from the redactor is at least probable: the formula that Yahweh's anger is kindled against his people has a firm place at any rate in the Deuteronomistic history work.[12] That Yahweh stretched out his hand and smote is perhaps a phrase which has simply been derived from the refrain poem. It is a common feature of accounts of theophanies to say that the mountains shake (cf. Ps. 18.8).[13] In fact this passage hardly thinks of a real earthquake;[14] rather, it is a description of the power of Yahweh's action in judgment. In an earthquake the ruins of the houses would have buried the people under them.[15] So we should think of those slain by the enemy when they entered the cities of Judah and the capital, Jerusalem, whose bodies lay unheeded in the streets (cf. Jer. 16.4; Ps. 18.43; Lam. 2.21). The editor means it to be understood that the woes have found their fulfilment in the catastrophe of the year 587, and the wrath of Yahweh has still not come to an end. Rather, he will unburden himself in a last blow, the attack of the army of the nations against Jerusalem and Judah.

[10] Cf. 220f. below.
[11] Cf. 6 above.
[12] Cf. Num. 11.33; II Kings 23.26; Ex. 32.11; Num. 25.3; 32.13; Deut. 6.15; 7.4; 11.17; 31.17; Josh. 7.1; 23.16; Judg. 2.14, 20; 3.8; 10.7; Hos. 8.5 and e.g. Marti, ad loc.; but also Barth, *Jesaja-Worte*, 110 n. 39.
[13] Cf. further e.g. Ps. 77.19; Ex. 18.18; Judg. 5.4; Isa. 13.13; 63.19; Joel 4.16, and also Jörg Jeremias, *Theophanie*, WMANT 10, Neukirchen ²1977, 7ff.
[14] Cf. e.g. Amos 8.8; Joel 2.10f.
[15] With Marti, ad loc. cf. also Wildberger, ad loc.

[26] Whereas here there was originally mention of only one people from afar, the editor brings about his transformation by the slight change of making this plural. The theologian of history who wrapped himself in the mantle of the prophet Isaiah had understood the people to be the Babylonians; we are now to understand *the peoples* as the host of nations at the last judgment (cf. Zech 14.2; Joel 4.1ff.). [30] Of course the addition of this verse, which with its repetition of 'and it thunders' from v. 29 indicates the counter-stroke, makes this section end with prospect of the deliverance of the people of God: the onslaught of the nations upon Jerusalem really is the last visitation of Yahweh on his people. At the height of the danger, when everything already seems lost (cf. v. 29b; 17.14; 29.5ff.), he comes to the rescue: though the assailants may be in tumult like the sea (17.12), he will now engulf them, and in cosmic darkness they will feel Yahweh's annihilating blow (cf. 8.22; Job 18.6; Joel 4.15f.). From this perspective we can see what has moved the editor to make the transposition of the last woe with the closing strophe of the refrain poem: in this way he gave the first five chapters of the book of Isaiah a definite conclusion by bringing the eschatological drama, to which there has been constant allusion since 1.24, to its climax and its end.[16]

[26–29] In their original context, these verses prophesy the attack of *one* people: according to the traditional and agreed view this is the prophet Isaiah speaking of the onslaught of the Assyrians, and in my own view it is a theologian of history from the fifth century, in the guise of the prophet, speaking of the annihilating blow of the Babylonians against the kingdom of Judah.[17] In contrast to the numerous obscure features which are characteristic of the refrain poem,[18] the last strophe attains poetic pregnancy and clarity: Yahweh is presented to us as the Lord who holds mysterious sway over the nations. He gives the signal for the attack to the enemy (cf. 13.2), who is deliberately left mysterious, since in the poet's view he remains outside the knowledge of the prophet and is therefore designated merely as the enemy from afar (cf. Jer. 5.15; Deut 28.49).[19] He whistles for him as a bee-keeper whistles for his bees, according to 7.18, from the ends of the earth (Deut. 28.49).[20] His command is irresistible, so that immediately they set off at a quick march[21] and reach their goal with uncanny perseverance and resolution. No men

---

[16] Cf. also Becker, *Isaias*, 51.
[17] Cf. also above, 2f.
[18] Cf. also below, 221f.
[19] Cf. also *Isaiah 13–39*, 94, on 18.3.
[20] Cf. also below, 175 n. 12.
[21] Cf. also Deut, 28.20; Joel 4.4 for the formula 'swiftly, speedily'.

or material are left by the wayside. None of the enemy soldiers grows weary,[22] and none lags behind.[23] Their aprons do not ride up,[24] nor are the thongs of their shoes torn.[25] The bronze points of their arrows are sharpened (cf. Prov. 25.18);[26] their bows taut and therefore ready for action.[27] Nor are there any accidents among the chariots: the hooves of the horses are so hard that they are not hurt by the long and rapid march.[28] So the chariots hurtle towards their goal like the storm-wind. And the hostile army falls upon Jerusalem as its prey (Amos 3.4; Prov. 28.15),[29] like a lion at whose roar people are afraid (Amos 3.8); it carries the people off into exile and there is no one to save them.[30]

This is an uncanny vision, underlying which is another no less uncanny event: the annihilation of the kingdom of Judah and the deportation of its upper classes by the king of Babylon, Nebuchadnezzar (cf. II Kings 25). It sought to impress upon the survivors and those suffering under slavery and dispersion that here was a demonstration not of the helplessness but of the power of Yahweh, and along the lines of the message of the memorial also invited them in their apparently hopeless situation to trust and to hearken, because the God who controls the nations also has the power to save his people.

[22] Cf. also Deut. 25.18; Judg. 8.4f.

[23] Cf. also Ps. 105.37 or Isa. 28.13; 8.15; 3.8.

[24] Cf. also p. 258 n.44 below and Helga Weippert, *BRL²*, 186b.

[25] For this formula, which is presumably one from everyday language, cf. also Gen. 14.23; Mark. 1.7 and on the content G. Fohrer, *BHH* III, col. 1739, and *BHH* II, cols. 671f. plate 3.

[26] Cf. also Helga Weippert, *BRL²*, 249f.

[27] Cf. also e.g. Ps. 7.13; 11.2; 37.14; Lam. 2.4; 3.12 and Helga Weippert, *BRL²*, 49f.

[28] Cf. also Jer. 47.3; Ezek. 26.11; and Marie-Louise Henry, *BHH* III, cols 1438f., or Helga Weippert, *BRL²*, 250ff.

[29] Cf. also Hos. 5.14; Jer. 2.15; 51.38; Judg. 14.5; Ps. 22.14; Ezek. 22.25; Prov. 19.12; 20.2.

[30] Cf. Ps. 7.3; 50.22; 71.11; Job 5.4; Judg. 18.28; II Sam. 14.6; Isa. 42.22 and Deut 32.29; Isa. 42.13; Hos. 5.14; Job 10.7.

CHAPTER 6.1–9.6

The So-called Memorial of the Prophet Isaiah from the Time of the Syro-Ephraimite War

It may be said now to be a commonplace of Old Testament scholar-ship that 6.1–9.6 is a collection in its own right. However, it is similarly agreed that originally it extended only from 6.1 to 8.18. On the other hand, there is dispute as to whether 8.19–22 (or 23a) and 8.23b (or 9.1)–6 were added by the prophet himself or should be seen as redactional expansions. The beginning, with the prophet's account of himself in ch. 6 and the resumption of the first-person language in 8.1–18, seems to offer sufficient guarantee for the assumption that the prophet Isaiah himself is talking here in retro-spect about his completed and outwardly unsuccessful activity in the years of the Syro-Ephraimite war (734/33–733/32).

The fact that there is an alien account in ch. 7 is usually challenged to such a degree that it is supposed that here we have the transpo-sition into the third person of an account which was originally in the first person as well. However, it is obvious that there is a problem with this assumption, and that there is real tension between the theology of decision in 7.1–9 and that of hardening the heart in 6.1–11. The usual solution, which is of course necessary within the context of the hypothesis that Isaiah is the author of the narratives, is to assume that the prophet formulated the account of his call in ch. 6 in retrospect and hinted at his later insights in the account of his beginnings. This in fact seems to be the only possible way of preserving the unity of the prophet's person and making the change of theological position credible, as long as one continues to reckon with the presence of a first-person account.

In the four basic questions raised by the collection, the present commentary adopts different courses; though without having deli-berately sought to do so. Rather, these courses suggested themselves as the more probable solutions as the work itself progressed. Thus, still in agreement with scholars like Cheyne, Marti, Fohrer and Vermeylen, I see 8.19–9.6 as a redactional extension of the nucleus consisting of 6.1–8.18. I do not regard the change of person in the speaker between chs. 6–8 on the one hand and ch. 7 on the other as insignificant, but see 7.1–9* as the nucleus of the whole collection, a theological narrative which in the shade of Deuteronomistic theology answers the question why the Davidic dynasty has withdrawn and the people have been decimated, by referring to the wrong decision made by the royal house because of its lack of trust in God. It thus confronts its own community with the decision whether to believe or to go under (cf. 7.9b). At a second stage, this narrative has been extended by 7.10–17*, whether by the same hand or another, in order to demonstrate the king's lack of faith through his rejection of a sign that is offered to him, and at the same time to make specific the threat of downfall contained in 7.9b. In 7.18–25*, this itself was originally developed in three sayings. The connection of its content with 6.11 raises the possibility that in literary terms, too, it has a special connection with this chapter.

Once we have recognized the retrospective character of 7.1–17* and the fact that it is really aimed at the questions of the generations which survived the catastrophe of 587, ch. 6 also surrenders its secret; here, as also in ch. 8, the first-person account serves to transpose the narrative fictitiously into the time of Isaiah, using his ministry to reflect the fact that Yahweh was also present beforehand in the history of disaster which ended with the complete collapse of the people of God, and therefore to make clear and credible his abiding power over the future of this people. The explanation of the mystery of the sending of the prophet to harden the people's hearts is to be explained in theological rather than in psychological terms. Chapter 8 puts the failure of the people alongside that of the dynasty. Here the inscription (8.1–4), a sign given publicly and before witnesses, surpasses the sign which was rejected (7.10ff.*) and to which it corresponds. The people refuse its promise, so that they too succumb to the judgment (8.5–8, 11–15). At the same time, in 8.11–15 there is a delineation of the community of the disciples which is a witness to the sealing and thus the authenticity and truth of the prophetic message, for the fulfilment of which Isaiah and his children stand as a sign and a token (8.16–18). Thus a great arc stretches from the prophet's question about the length of the hardening of hearts in 6.11 to the confession of hope in 8.17, and reveals the real concern of the author of chs. 6; 8; to restore trust in Yahweh's power and thus hope for his help and for their own future to the people of the remnant who have been handed over to the world power. The separation between God and 'this people' contained in 6.9f., in which the prophet shares by virtue of being overwhelmed by the Holy One, is explained in (ch. 7 and above all in) 8.1–15. Thus ch. 6, which is strangely formulated in terms of a mission to harden the people's heart, proves to be framed with an eye to the continuation, especially in ch. 8. Accordingly, the dovetailing with ch. 7 is relatively loose, and if I am right, limited to the development of the message of judgment in 7.18ff.

We can immediately understand that the restrained but clear prospect of a shift towards salvation after the catastrophe (8.17) called for development. The people suffering in exile wanted to know what they might hope for. Hence the messianic revision with an eschatology of salvation to which we owe in the first place the Immanuel prophecy in 7.14b–16abα* and, by no means inferior to it in quality, at least the incorporation of 9.1–6. The Immanuel prophecy clearly presupposes another catastrophe coming upon the land (cf. 7.16abα), which is announced in 6.13abα and 8.21f. (23a). We must reckon with the possibility that the two sayings come from the same hand.

In addition to the insertion of 7.14b–16abα*, we presumably also owe to the messianic revision the insertion of 7.21–22, a passage which is at all events formulated in its spirit. As in 8.8* and 8.9–10, a saying framed with an eye to the catastrophe of 587 is here changed to refer to the eschatological devastation of the land. If we also assign 9.1–6 to the same redaction, we start from the fact that the Immanuel of 7.14ff. and the king of the time of salvation in 9.4f. are identical. We may leave open the question whether 6.13bβ is to be assigned to the same hand, or whether the forced addition is to be regarded as an independent addition.

It is strange that the memorial in chs. 7 and 8 was subsequently subjected in 7.1*, 4b, 5b, 8b, 16baα*β, 17b, 18aβ*bβ, 20aβ*; 8.6b, 7aβ, 8aα* (?) and 23b to a historicizing revision. This revision seeks to bring out more strongly the connections between the prophecies and the time of Isaiah, thus missing the way in which the sayings relate to the collapse of the state of Judah in the catastrophe of 587, and, apart from 8.23b, also have an eschatological character. We owe the unending riddle about Immanuel to its author, because he misunderstands the eschatological and messianic character of the prophecy, and has completely concealed it with his expansions. His work is a remarkable testimony to the beginning of an interpretation of scripture resting on the comparison of texts which are in apparent or actual connection with one another. In the light of what we have also learned from chs. 3 and 5,[1] if we leave aside 8.23b, in this revision we might also conjecture an anti-eschatological tendency. However, we cannot exclude the possibility that it is connected with the Assyria revision and so in the last resort with the announcement of the annihilation of that world power.[2]

[1] See above, 4ff.
[2] See above, 5f.

Thus the memorial proves to have four layers. The nucleus is in 7.1–9*, 10–17*. Around this the real creator of the memorial has placed the framework of 6.1–11; 7.18–25*; 8.1–4, 5–8*, 11–15 and 16–18. The development of the eschatology led to the incorporation of references to a new judgment in 6.13abα and 8.19–23a. Perhaps we may also include 6.12; 7.23b, 24b, 25b in this revision with its eschatology of disaster. At a later stage it was followed by the redaction in 7.14b–16b*, 21–22; 8.8b*, 9–10 and 9.1–6, with its eschatology of salvation. Again it is possible to add 6.13bβ to this stratum. I dealt with this historicizing revision in the last paragraph, so there is no need to repeat what I said there. The cross-references in the commentary indicate how the strata detected here relate to the other sections in the proto-Isaianic collection. It must be left to another place to discuss how they are to be evaluated.[3]

CHAPTER 6.1–13

The Call to Harden Hearts

1 In the year that King Uzziah died I saw the Lord sitting upon a throne, high and lifted up; and the hem of his garment filled the temple hall.[1] 2 Seraphim stood above him; each had six wings. With two he covered his face, with two he covered his feet, and with two he did fly. 3 And one called to the other and said:

'Holy, holy, holy is Yahweh Sebaoth,
his glory is the fullness of the whole earth.'[2]

4 Then the pivots of the doors in the foundation stones shook at the voice of him who called, and the house was filled with smoke. 5 And I said:

'Woe is me, for I must be silent;
for I am a man of unclean lips
and I dwell in the midst of a people of unclean lips.
For my eyes have seen the King Yahweh Sebaoth!'[3]

6 Then one of the seraphim flew to me, a burning coal in his hand,

---

[3] See above, 2ff.
[1] Literally: the palace (of heavenly and earthly gods).
[2] But cf. Wildberger, ad loc., and against him the commentary below.
[3] For the threefold grounding of the woe cf. C. Schedl, *Rufer des Heils*, 176.

which he had taken with tongs from the altar. 7 And he touched[4] my
mouth with it and said:
'If this touches your lips,[5]
your guilt is taken away, and your sin covered.'[6]
8 And I heard the voice of the Lord saying:
'Whom shall I send,
and who will go for us?'[7]
And I said:
'Here am I! Send me!'
9 And he said:
'Go and say to this people:
Only hear,[8] but do not understand;
only see,[8] but do not perceive.
10 Make the heart of this people fat
and make their ears heavy and shut their eyes,
so that they do not see with their eyes
or hear with their ears,
or their heart[9] understand,
and they are healed once again.'[10]
11 And I said, 'How long, O Lord?'
And he said,

'Until the cities are waste and without inhabitant,
and the houses without men,
and the field lies fallow like the wilderness!'
12   *Then Yahweh will remove men far away,*
       and the desolation will be great in the midst of the land.
13   *And though a tenth still remain in it,*
       it will be a pasture again,
       like an oak and a terebinth,
       whose stumps remain <after they have been felled>.[11]
       Holy seeds are the shoots thereof.

[6.1–13] *Date and origin.* There is a whole series of narratives in the
Bible which make a deep impression on the reader by the force of
their language and imagery, while at the same time leaving him

---

[4] Literally: 'made to touch'.

[5] For the construction cf. Brockelmann § 164a, and Josh. 2.18.

[6] For the use of the so-called imperfect to denote a concomitative action cf. Bobzin § 7, 1b.

[7] For the use of *l* to introduce a *dativus commodi* cf. Davidson § 101 R.1b.

[8] A form strengthened by the infinitive absolute.

[9] The continuation suggests that we should read *ūlᵉbābō* with MT instead of the *ūbᵉlᵉbābō* which is attested by 1QIsᵃ, many Hebrew MSS, S and V.

[10] It would also be possible to translate ' . . . and turn again'. However the context tells rather in favour of the reversive significance of *šūb*.

[11] Read *miššalleket*.

puzzled as to their content, because he finds it difficult, humanly speaking, to put himself in the situation that is being reported. These narratives include the story of the sacrifice of Isaac in Gen 22 and also Isaiah 6. The reader is seized by its large-scale sequence of imagery and scenery which presents itself to his inner eye and fills him with reverence before the holiness of God, and wonder at the man who appeared before the highest throne as God's messenger without hesitation or faint-heartedness. Yet in the end he tries in vain to understand a narrative which, instead of speaking about the content of the mission, the task of carrying it out and its aim, talks of sending the prophet to harden men's hearts.

How did the prophet whose voice the first-person narrative suggests that we should hear, arrive at this insight? Is there here an expression of the heroism of a man who despises his people because they have lost the foundation of their faith, and who nevertheless feels indissoluble ties to them? Or do we have here the voice of a man who has left his own time and gone wholly over to the side of his God, because he has arrived at the profoundest recognition that his people has fallen victim incurably to the vanity and nothingness of human existence? Or is there here, as has usually been suggested in most modern scholarship, a retrospect of one who has failed in his prophetic ministry, seeing commission and consequence together, believing that at a later time he can recognize God's real purpose in his failure, and thus understanding himself as an instrument of hardening men's hearts?

But is it credible that a man would interpret his own task from its end in such a way that he presents his subsequent insight as the word of God which he received right at the beginning? Does not the force of the moment and its solemnity tell against such a reinterpretation, so that the prophet would have struggled with his God, in the way in which Jeremiah in a comparable situation is said to have lamented to his God,[12] rather than alter a single word that he had heard in that memorable hour? And is it enough to explain the difference in terms of the stature of the two prophets, one of whom shrank back in terror before the divine call which came to him (Jer. 1.6), while the other of his own accord offered to be the messenger (Isa. 6.8)? Are we in any way on the right course if we are concerned to interpret this story in psychological and biographical terms; in the end is it not meant to be understood theologically? If we understand the so-called memorial of the prophet Isaiah in 6.1–8.18 as a literary

12 Cf. Jer. 11.18ff.; 12.1ff.; 15.10ff.; 17.12ff.; 18.19ff.; 20.7ff.; and Kaiser, *Introduction*, 244f.; R. Smend, *Die Enstehung des Alten Testaments* TW 1, Stuttgart 1978, 163f.

unity,[13] then it begins with a reference to the inescapability of the catastrophe that will befall the people of God. It is inescapable because Yahweh himself has resolved upon it and has used his prophet to harden the people's heart and thus drive them to their downfall. But at the end there is a saying about a hope based on Yahweh which goes beyond this downfall (8.17). Thus the memorial leads up to the moment in which judgment takes place and the survivors are confronted with the question whether the people of God as such still has a future, and whether their God has the power to transform a fate which in human terms is hopeless.

It has been rightly thought that underlying the saying about the hardening of people's hearts in Isa. 6 is a 'comprehensive understanding of the prophet's task which has been meditated upon intensively', an understanding which has here been changed into its opposite.[14] We come upon traces of it by noting the way in which, in the judgment of the memorial, king and people have incurred guilt. Both have forfeited permanence because they have failed to trust in their God, who promised them through his prophets rescue from the danger which threatened, and have taken the course of securing their existence by political means (cf. 7.9b, 11f.; 8.6f., 12f.). So the prophet here has been understood only to a limited degree as the man who presents God's resolve about the future; at the same time he is seen as the one who calls to decision, who confronts his people with the choice between life and death, existence or downfall. It is certain that this second way of understanding the prophet's ministry as his call to preach repentance and a change of behaviour is in essential correspondence with the Deuteronomistic picture of the prophet which was developed after the collapse of the state of Judah, and is probably separated from the time of Isaiah's activity by two whole centuries.[15] It has the twofold task of placing responsibility for the catastrophe which has happened meanwhile and for the further future on the people themselves. It reflects the effects which the pre-exilic prophecy of judgment had on the survivors. In view of the announcement of judgment which had long stood over the

---

[13] Cf. e.g. Duhm, 64; Budde, *Jesaja's Erleben*, 1ff.; E. Jenni, 'Jesajas Berufung in der neueren Forschung', *TZ* 15, 1959, 329; G. Fohrer, 'Entstehung, Komposition und Überlieferung von Jesaja 1–39', in *Studien zur alttestamentlichen Prophetie*, BZAW 99, Berlin 1967, 125, and not least O. H. Steck, 'Bemerkungen zu Jesaja 6', *BZ* NF 16, 1972, 188ff., and esp. 198ff., who has given an impressive demonstration that ch. 6 is open in a forward direction by very reason of its genre.

[14] J. M. Schmidt, 'Gedanken zum Verstockungsauftrag Jesaja (Is. 6)', *VT* 21, 1971, 75.

[15] Cf. Deut. 18.18f.; II Kings 17.13f.; Jer. 7.25ff.; 17.17ff.; 18.5ff.; Isa. 30.8ff. and E. W. Nicholson, *Preaching to the Exiles*, Oxford 1970, 55ff.; Kaiser, *Isaiah 13–39*, 292f.; and id., *Introduction*, 171f., 241ff.; or Smend, *Entstehung*, 124,159.

people, the survivors asked why it had not led the people to repent and thus to avert the disaster resolved upon by God. The notion of the call to harden men's hearts presupposes this understanding of prophecy while at the same time going beyond it by assessing the catastrophe, on this interpretation, primarily as a failure of the prophet and then making God himself responsible for it. Only in this way is there an end to the suspicion that Yahweh could in the last resort simply have proved impotent in the catastrophe which happened to his people, and a demonstration that without any doubt Yahweh has power over the history of his people in the present as in the past. That comment at the same time introduces the real concern of this narrative: it does not conjure up the past for its own sake, but proves to be the work of narrators concerned with the past of Israel as a mirror[16] in which the survivors are to recognize the catastrophe of their own time and the call which it contains to trust in Yahweh Sebaoth. At the same time this means that the narrator stands the other side of the catastrophe which his writing apparently has in prospect, to summon up the past in a vivid way in the garb of the prophet Isaiah. Thus the form of the first-person report here is no more a guarantee that the person introduced to speak is identical with the author than it is anywhere else, and we must give up the notion, still prevalent today, that in this chapter we can hear directly the voice of the prophet Isaiah.[17]

Genre. Having recognized that the narrative does not stand by itself but was written as an introduction to chs. 7 and 8, we still have to evaluate its genre. It is usually described as a call narrative. Here the difference from other call narratives handed down in the Old Testament is unmistakable. The most striking thing is probably that the prophet, instead of at first refusing a call and commissioning, both given to him directly by Yahweh,[18] volunteers that he himself will undertake the task. It has been noted time and again that the episode has clearer contacts with the story of the heavenly scene eavesdropped on by the prophet Micaiah ben Imlah (I Kings 22.19ff.) than with the call narratives: in both instances God asks the question who is willing to carry out his task, and then accepts the spontaneous

[16] Cf. e.g. Kaiser, *Introduction*, 85ff., 100ff., 109ff., and 169ff.
[17] One exception to this trend is C. F. Whitley, 'The Call and Mission of Isaiah', *JNES* 18, 1959, 38ff., but he neglects the perspective of tendency criticism and thus has not given the necessary grounding for his observations.
[18] Cf. Ex. 3.11; 4.10ff.; Judg. 6.15; I Sam. 10.22; and above all Jer. 1.6; also W. Richter, *Die sogenannten vorprophetischen Berufungsberichte*, FRLANT 101, Göttingen 1970, 136ff.; N. Habel, 'The Form and Significance of the Call Narratives', *ZAW* 77, 1965, 297ff., and not least W. Zimmerli, *Ezekiel* I, Hermeneia, Philadelphia 1979, 97ff.

declaration of readiness.[19] In contrast to I Kings 22, however, the scene is transferred from heaven to the Jerusalem temple as the place in which heaven and earth come into contact; the numberless host of Yahweh's heavenly servants is limited to the seraphim,[20] who for their part are not even allowed to look upon Yahweh;[21] and above all the question addressed by Yahweh to his council is limited to who is to be sent: there is no hint of the content of the mission. Here the prophet takes over the role which in I Kings 22 is played by a 'spirit'. It is further striking that Isa. 6 on the one hand stresses Yahweh's separation even from heavenly beings (cf. Job 15.15; 25.5; 4.17f.), and yet on the other at the same time changes the prophet from being a witness to being a participant in the heavenly council.[22] In this way it succeeds in elevating the status of the prophet without violating the transcendence of the divine sphere.

If we do not want to explain the affinity between I Kings 22.19ff. and Isa. 6 as common dependence on the conceptuality of the pre-exilic New Year Festival and the ceremony of the enthronment of Yahweh which formed part of it,[23] we might see Isa. 6 as a reflection of the later narrative.[24]

As I Kings 22.19ff. in fact belongs among the narratives of 'bestowing an extraordinary commission in the heavenly Council' such as are to be found e.g. in Zech. 1.7ff.; Job. 1.6ff.,[25] rather than among the call narratives, it has recently again been questioned whether Isa. 6 is a call narrative at all.[26] However, against this argument it must be objected that with its assumption of the prophet's activity before the outbreak of the Syro-Ephraimite war it presents a very shaky case, and in the end arises only from what is

[19] Cf. e.g. E. C. Kingsbury, 'The Prophets and the Council of Yahweh', *JBL* 83, 1964, 282; Habel, *ZAW* 77, 309f.; Zimmerli, *Ezekiel* 1, 99; Wildberger, 236; and R. N. Whybray, *The Heavenly Counsellor in Isaiah XL 13–14*, MSSOTS 1, Cambridge 1971, 50f., who evocatively stresses the difference between the council of Yahweh and the council of the gods (47).

[20] In view of its function, however, it is questionable whether the author thought that the heavenly assembly was in fact limited to this, cf. Zimmerli, *Ezekiel*, 99, and Whybray, op. cit., 79, also below, 131 n. 70.

[21] Zimmerli, *Ezekiel*, 99.

[22] Cf. also Isa. 40.1ff., and K. Elliger, BK XI, 1, 1978, 12; Whybray, op. cit; 82.

[23] Thus Kingsbury, *JBL* 83, 281, and J. Gray, *I & II Kings*, OTL, London ²1970, 451; cf. also I. Engnell, *The Call of Isaiah*, UUÅ 1949, 4.

[24] O. H. Steck, *BZ* NF 16, 1972, 192 n. 15, excludes any literary relationship between the two texts. As he rightly follows the literary-critical assessment of I Kings 22.19ff., made by E. Würthwein, 'Zur Komposition von I Reg 22, 1–38,' in *Das ferne und nahe Wort*, Festschrift Leonhard Rost, BZAW 105, Berlin 1967, 245ff., and regards Isa. 6 as Isaianic, he cannot arrive at any other result.

[25] O. H. Steck, op. cit., 191.

[26] K. Koch, *The Prophets*, I, London 1982, 111f. Details of earlier criticism in Wildberger, op. cit., 239f. If I understand Steck rightly, while he rejects the designation of the genre, he does not reject the fact that a call is narrated here.

thought to be the need to resolve the tension between the call and the Syro-Ephraimite war.[27] We could avoid this whole question by pointing out that on the whole the Old Testament narrators are not interested in biographical facts as such, but in their significance for the message. So these take on the character of a theology in narrative form, based on supposed or actual events. However, the twofold fact that with its act of purification Isa. 6 has the character of an initiation and that the call of the prophet Ezekiel is similarly narrated in connection with a throne scene, seems to justify our claiming the chapter as a call scene. It remains to note that it does not stand by itself, but has been composed as the introduction to the so-called memorial, which extends as far as 8.18.

Structure and unity. The account divides easily into three scenes, each arising out of another and so with an inner connection. The vision of the one holy King Yahweh Sebaoth and the praise of the seraphim which he hears in it (vv. 1–4) makes Isaiah aware of his impurity and his unworthiness to join in the praise of God. However, purified by one of the seraphim (vv. 5–7), he can venture to speak in Yahweh's council, and as a result is entrusted with the commission to harden men's hearts (vv. 8–11). Verse 12 marks the beginning of the additions. It is obviously an addition itself by virtue of its mention of Yahweh's action, in contrast to the speech of Yahweh in v. 11b. In content it supplements v. 11b by connecting the lack of people in the country with the deportation. In v. 13 abα there follows a second addition, looking towards the eschatological judgment. In turn, v. 13bβ is to be detached from it as an addition concerned with an eschatology of salvation.[28] It transforms the comparison related to annihilation in v. 13b into the rescue of a holy remnant as the nucleus of a new people of God.

[6.1–4] *The vision of the King Yahweh Sebaoth.* The narrator knew from the narrative available to him (7.1–9)[29] that the prophet had made an appearance at the beginning of the Syro-Ephraimite war without succeeding in gaining the ear of king Ahaz in his call to trust in Yahweh. In order to establish God's priority to all human history, he transfers the prophet's call aimed at hardening men's hearts into

---

[27] Cf. e.g. Duhm, 16, and Koch, *The Prophets* I, 106f.; also Kaiser, *Introduction*, 222, and Smend, *Entstehung*, 148f.; cf. also Steck, op. cit., 205f. It should be noted that Koch places Isaiah's criticism of society before the vision in ch. 6 and, against the claim of the chapter to be an account of the prophet's call, draws attention to its position in the book. However, it is questionable whether the book has an underlying biographical theme.

[28] Cf. also 7.15, 21f., and above all 8.21–23a.

[29] Cf. 142ff. below.

the year in which the king's grandfather, Azariah-Uzziah, died.[30] However the historian manages to calculate the dates of the kings of Judah in the second half of the eighth century, which have evidently been displaced through misunderstandings in the course of time, and accordingly reckons the year in which king Uzziah died,[31] and however the narrator himself may have dealt with the figures handed on to him, there can be no doubt that this author was convinced that Yahweh had taken the prophet into his service before the beginning of the complications leading to the Syro-Ephraimite war, as an instrument to harden men's hearts and to inflict judgment upon his people.

With impressive brevity he makes the prophet describe the vision of God, which was extraordinary and tremendous in the true sense of the word, even for Israelite sensibility: '. . . I saw the Lord'. In contrast to Ezek 1.26ff., no attempt is made to specify the form of the enthroned deity. All we have is the assertion that Isaiah saw him enthroned and thus exercising his authority.[32] In this restraint we may recognize both a reflection of the prohibition against images and a shrinking from looking on the one whose countenance brings death to human beings,[33] and before whose majesty even his heavenly watchers must cover their faces.[34] By stressing the height of his throne[35] and the enormous size of the hem of his garment, which is enough to fill the temple,[36] Isaiah paints an indirect picture

---

[30] The year of a king's death is the last calendar year officially counted as his reign (cf. also 14.28).

[31] Cf. J. Begrich, *Die Chronologie der Könige von Israel und Juda*, Tübingen 1929, 155: 747/46; K. T. Andersen, *ST* 23, 1969, 11f.: 741/40; C. Schedl, *VT* 12, 1962, 100; V. Pavlovský and E. Vogt, *Bib* 45, 1964, 347: 740/39; A Jepsen, in A. Jepsen and R. Hanhart, *Untersuchungen zur israelitisch-jüdischen Chronologie*, BZAW 88, Berlin 1964, 38f.: 736/35.

[32] Cf. also Amos 1.5,8; Isa. 40.22.

[33] Cf. Ex. 33.20; 19.21; Judg. 6.22f.; 13.22; Enoch 14.20ff.; also Gen. 32.31.

[34] Cf. also W. H. Schmidt, 'Ausprägungen des Bildverbots? Zur Sichtbarkeit und Vorstellbarkeit Gottes im Alten Testament', in *Das Wort und die Wörter*, Festschrift Gerhard Friedrich, Stuttgart 1973, 25ff., and O. Keel, *Jahwe-Visionen und Siegelkunst*, SBS 84/85, Stuttgart 1977, 58.

[35] In Isa. 57.15 the same phrase denotes the greatness of Yahweh.

[36] That the garments of gods and rulers in the Ancient Near East and in Egypt did not have flowing trains has been recalled by G. R. Driver, 'Isaiah 6:1 "His train filled the temple" ', in *Near Eastern Studies in Honor of W. F. Albright*, Baltimore and London 1971, 87, and Keel, SBS 84/85, 62ff. Accordingly it is impossible to envisage Yahweh sitting in the Holy of Holies with the train of his garment filling the temple hall before him, as I too assumed in the earlier edition of this commentary. We may ask whether the poet referred the word *hēkāl*, temple, evocatively to the temple building as a whole (cf. I Kings 6.3, 5), or naturally assumed that God was enthroned in the Holy of Holies. At all events, he is present in it only with his feet (which are not mentioned) and with the hem of his garment.

of the powerful figure who transcends all earthly dimensions. Verses 4 and 5 probably suggest that we should image the scene as taking place in an earthly context, i.e. specifically in the Jerusalem temple. However, as it is a vision, the prophet need not necessarily be thought actually to have been there, though the assumption that this is the way in which the narrator wanted the situation to be understood is still the most likely.[37]

Evidently we should direct our attention neither to the psychological question of the nature of such a vision nor to the question of its location nor that of the architectural characteristics and furnishing of the Jerusalem temple and its holy of holies.[38] We should be impressed by the tremendous magnitude of this deity whose holiness is celebrated by those who keep watch round his throne and whose figure is too great for any earthly house.[39]

[2] The fact that seraphim hover over him makes it quite clear how the heavenly and the earthly are conjoined in this vision.[40] In accordance with 14.29 and 30.6 we must imagine the seraphim themselves as winged serpents. But as one of them can handle a burning coal with tongs (v. 6f.), the poet evidently imagined them as mixed beings. They presumably took their name not from their appearance in the form of light (so that they could be addressed as personified lightning),[41] but from their painful, burning bite.[42] According to an attractive conjecture, in the last resort they are derived from the winged Uraei, the serpents who in Egypt protected God, the king and his throne, and who according to the discovery of countless seals were also known in Palestine as being with four wings.[43] Their real model is presumably the Egyptian cobra, *Naja*

---

[37] But cf. I Sam. 3.3ff.

[38] For the various reconstructions of the Holy of Holies cf. T. A. Busink, *Der Tempel von Jerusalem von Salomo bis Herodes*, I, Leiden 1970, 197ff., and A. Kuschke, *BRL*[2] 239f. While in pre-exilic times it housed cherubim and the ark, cf. I Kings 6.23ff.; 8.6ff., and was separated from the hall by a wooden wall and doorway (I Kings 6.16), in post-exilic times it was empty except for a stone which extended three fingers above the ground (b. Yoma V, II), and separated from the temple hall only by a curtain (b. Yoma fol. 52b), II Chron. 3.14; I Macc. 1.23; Pausanias V, 12, 4; I Macc. 4.51; Aristeas 86 and Matt. 27.51.

[39] Cf. Ps. 9.5; 132.7; Lam. 2.1 with I Kings 8.27; Isa. 66.1.

[40] Cf. M. Metzger, 'Himmlische und irdische Wohnstatt Jahwes', *UF* 2, 1970, 139ff., and esp. 145.

[41] Against Budde, *Jesaja's Erleben*, 10: Procksch and Kaiser[1], ad loc.

[42] Cf. Num. 21.6 and with Keel, SBS 84/85, 72 n. 105, also *AOT*[2], 385; *ANET*[2-3], 292b and Herodotus II, 75; III, 107ff.

[43] Cf. K. R. Joines, 'Winged Serpents in Isaiah's Inaugural Vision', *JBL* 86, 1967, 410ff., and Keel, SBS 84/85, 70ff. For the Uraeus see the article 'Uräus' by H. Bonnet, *Reallexikon der ägyptischen Religionsgeschichte*, Berlin and New York [2]1971, 844f.

nigricollis.[44] The poet feels free to adapt these figures to his understanding of the divine world, and by attributing three pairs of wings to them gives them not only the possibility of flying but also of covering their faces and what is euphemistically described as their feet, as a sign of the distance there is between them and God (cf. Ex. 3.6; Isa. 7.20). By concealing the pudenda, in which every human being is completely himself in the most intimate corporeality, these primal beings show that in our feeling of shame we know ourselves to be guilty.

[3] What the reader felt in the description of the attitude of the heavenly beings is confirmed for him by their song of praise which celebrates the king Yahweh Sebaoth as the one holy one. The threefold repetition of the 'holy' characterizes him as the all-holy and sole-holy one. The refrain in Ps. 99.3, 5, 9 seems to be almost in concentrated form here.[45] From the holiness of God there goes out to mankind the call to be holy themselves (Lev. 19.2). Because God is other than all the world, those who belong to him are also to correspond to him in their purity and righteousness.[46] This God, who is designated 'the Holy One of Israel' especially in the book of Isaiah,[47] is here given his cult-name Yahweh Sebaoth, which at the latest arose in the Jerusalem temple.[48] At all events, this name stresses the unlimited power of Yahweh over all heavenly and earthly authorities. Whether Sebaoth, to be translated 'of hosts', originally designated him the leader of the Israelite and Judaean armies, the earthly hosts (cf. I Sam. 17.45; I Kings 2.5),[49] or of the heavenly hosts (cf. Deut. 4.19; Judg. 5.20; Isa. 40.26; I Kings 22.19; Dan. 8.10),[50] or is not rather an abstract plural which indicates his

[44] M. A. Murray, 'The Serpent Hieroglyph', *JEA* 34, 1948, 117f., in Keel, SBS 84/85, 73f. Gray, ad loc., has pointed out that the insertion of seraphim in v. 2 without the article seems to suggest that there were an indeterminate number of them, cf. also G-K[28] §126 i, but the 'one to another' in v. 3a seems to indicate that there are two. Cf. also Keel, SBS 84/85, 114ff.

[45] The threefold repetition surpasses the twofold repetition which can be found in exilic and post-exilic poetry. Cf. H. Gese, 'Ps. 22 and the New Testament', *ZTK* 65, 1968, 6 = *Vom Sinai zum Zion*, BEvTh 64, Munich 1974, 185, and Isa. 40.1; 43.11; 48.11, 15; 51.9, 17; 52.1; Ps. 22.2. It seems to me to be questionable whether we should follow Keel, SBS 84/85, 118ff., in deriving this from magic and even associated it with an apotropaic seraph cult.

[46] Cf. K. Elliger, HAT 1, 4, Tübingen 1966, 255.

[47] Cf. above, 22, on 1.4. For the significance of the holy and the pure which so far resist any further derivation and are inherent in the root, cf. H. P. Müller, *THAT* II, cols. 589ff.

[48] Cf. e.g. I Sam. 4.4; II Sam. 6.2 par I Chron. 13.6, and F. Stolz, *Jahwes und Israels Kriege*, ATANT 60, Zurich 1972; 53; Ps. 80.2; 99.1; Isa. 37.16; Ps. 24.10.

[49] Cf. J. Maier, *Das altisraelitische Ladeheiligtum*, BZAW 93, Berlin 1965, 50ff.

[50] Maier, BZAW 93, 50, has of course pointed out that the singular *ṣābā'* is used here; in Ps. 103.21; 148.2 Qere the masculine plural is used.

power,[51] is still a matter of dispute. Opinions similarly differ as to whether the Israelites took over the divine epithet from the Canaanites in the time of the judges,[52] or only developed it in Jerusalem.[53]

If the first half of the heavenly song of praise celebrates God's innermost, hidden being, which nevertheless stands powerfully above all creation, the second half looks towards his presence in the world in his *kābōd*. This word designates that which gives a human being or God importance and respect, and accordingly his honour and glory (cf. e.g. Ps. 8.6; 29.2). In Priestly theology, Yahweh's *kābōd* was understood as his presence in the splendour hidden behind the cloud (cf. Ex. 16.10; 24.16f.; I Kings 8.10f.; Ezek. 11.22f.; 43.1ff.). The parallel with the word *tᵉhillāh*, praise (Isa. 42.8; cf. 48.11), shows that the meaning of *kābōd* is closely similar to that (cf. Ps. 19.2; 57.6; 96.3). The nearest parallel to v. 3b is the wish expressed in the prayer in Ps. 72.19 that the whole earth may be full of his, i.e. Yahweh's glory. Here the preceding mention of the honour of his name shows that it is a matter of Yahweh's praise in the world. And precisely that, too, may be the significance of the second half of the seraphim's song of praise (cf. also Hab. 3.3; his praise fills the whole world). What the heavenly beings praise in the immediate presence of the God whose glory and might are there before them, still needs to be seen on earth (Ps. 96.7f.). Here we can say with Volkmar Herntrich, 'In heaven there is no mention of how the world is, but the world is addressed in terms of its consummation.'[54] For when the recognition and acknowledgment of God's power and honour have become universal on earth, every will will be subject to him, the time will be fulfilled, and he will be all in all (I Cor. 15.28).

As the Christian is alive to the never-ending presence of God in his terrible might and his goodness in the reflection of the man Jesus of Nazareth and his career as the Christ, it makes good sense for the Christian community in the eucharist to take up the seraphim's song of praise to celebrate the arrival of the one to whom all honour and lordship are due (Rev. 4.9ff.), even if they differ from their ancestors in knowing that the trisagion did not originally envisage the mystery of the divine Trinity. In the division of this song into two, with its praise of the holiness and the honour of God, we encounter the mystery of revelation which consists in the fact that it always at the same time both unveils and increases the mystery of God. For God 'can be glorified aright only when he is known as the Holy One,

---

[51] O. Eissfeldt, *Jahwe Zebaoth*, Miscell. Acad. Berolin., Berlin, 1950, II, 2, 128ff. = *Kl. Schriften* III, 103ff., and most recently A. S. v. d. Woude, *THAT* II, 505f.

[52] Thus Eissfeldt, op. cit., 146f. = 119f., with some approval.

[53] Thus Maier, 51, who has made some impression.

[54] *Jesaja 1–12*, ATD, 1950, ad loc.

when he, the mysterious One, proclaims his mystery'.[55] If God discloses himself to us as trustworthy, at the same time he reveals to us his power and his holiness. He always waits on the basis of the anxiety which is part of our human existence, as Heidegger puts it, fallen towards death.

[4] The heavenly song of praise is too much for this earth: it makes the temple shake on its foundations, so that the doors, with their pivots set in corner-stones, shake (cf. I Kings 6.31, 33f.; also Amos 9.1).[56] The effect is that which Yahweh's appearance is traditionally supposed to produce.[57] By means of this transference of themes the poet stresses the infinite distance which separates man not only from God but even from the heavenly beings, who for their part may not even look upon his countenance. At the same time the hall of the temple is filled with smoke, which conceals God from human eyes so that the prophet will not be destroyed, but put in a position to experience what is to come. So the two features taken from the theophany tradition, the tradition of Yahweh's appearing, are not there for their own sake, to make the description as vivid as possible, but are rather strictly subordinate to the theological concern of the narrator.[58]

[6.5–7] *The purification.* The poet makes the prophet, overcome by the sight, burst out into a dismayed cry of 'Woe' rather than into joyful adoration. This cry betrays anxiety at the approach of an inexorable disaster.[59] As a man of unclean lips, who belongs to a people of unclean lips, he cannot join in the heavenly song of praise.[60] That which is unclean is of itself cut off from any contact

---

[55] E. Brunner, *Revelation and Reason.* London 1945, 45.

[56] For the architectural details cf. Busink, *Tempel* I, 186ff., with plates 57, 58; 204ff., and above 125, n. 38; or K. Galling and H. Rösel, *BRL²*, 348f., with pl. 88.

[57] Cf. Ex. 19.18; Judg. 5.4; Ps. 68.9; cf. also Ps. 18.8; 77.19; 104.32.

[58] Cf. also Gen. 15.17; Ex. 19.18; 20.18; and in addition above 124 n. 33. Here the smoke takes over the function otherwise fulfilled by the cloud, cf. Ex. 13.21; 16.10; 19.16; 24.15f.; 40.34; Deut. 9.15ff.; I Kings 8.10f., 12; Ezek 1.4; 10.3f.; Nah. 1.3; Ps. 97.2 and Isa. 4.5. There is some dispute as to whether the smoke is to be derived from a volcanic primal theophany or from a cultic theophany. For the former see most recently J. Jeremias, *Theophanie*, WMANT 10, Neukirchen ²1977, 207ff., and for the latter W. Beyerlin, *The Origin and History of the Oldest Sinaitic Traditions*, Oxford 1961, 156f. Obviously we have to connect the cloud with the cloud-chariot and cloud-palace of the Canaanite storm god, whose functions Yahweh has taken over (cf. Ps. 48.3). Cf. also R. Hillmann, *Wasser und Berg. Kosmische Verbindungslinien zwischen dem kanaanäischen Wettergolt und Jahwe*, Diss. Halle 1965, 127ff., 171ff., 175ff.

[59] Cf. (with G. Wanke, *'hōj* und *'ōj'*, ZAW 78, 1966, 216f.) Deut. 24.23; I Sam. 4.7f.; Isa. 24.16; Jer. 4.13, 31; 6.4.

[60] The word rendered 'I must be silent' is usually translated 'I am lost', or something similar. Cf. E. Jenni, *TZ* 15, 1959, 322, but also *HAL* 216b, s.v. *dmh* III, and e.g. R. Knierim, 'The Vocation of Isaiah', *VT* 18, 1968, 56.

with the holy; an unclean man and an unclean people are an abomination to Yahweh (Lev. 11.43f.). The concept of uncleanness certainly covers *a priori* defilement through contact; in the later period, however, it also includes the moral and religious sphere (cf. Ezek. 22.4; Job 14.4; 4.17; 25.4; Hag. 2.10ff.; Isa. 1.15f.). Unclean lips stand for the uncleanness of the whole person, whose condition and disposition they express (Matt. 15.18ff.). If a person or people comes to stand in their impurity before the holy God who is set apart by an infinite distance from the angels and even more from all mortal creatures, it becomes evident that they have spoiled their lives. This recognition on the part of the prophet already includes the realization that this task must be aimed at implementing Yahweh's pronunciation of guilt among his people.[61] For the sinful creature, the vision of the almighty, heavenly king[62] is not an occasion for joyful certainty, but evokes the feeling of guilt which is fallen towards death (cf. Job 41.5). However, God is free to make the fallen, guilty one an instrument nevertheless. The purification which is really brought about by the experience of the majestic superiority and purity of the Holy One and the recognition of his own fallibility[63] is embodied, in accordance with the narrator's understanding of the relationship between God and the world, conceived of in cultic and ritual terms, in an act of purification performed by one of the seraphim. It goes without saying that he does not act in his own right, but as the agent of a higher authority. With tongs he takes a glowing coal from the altar of incense in the temple on which the high priest of the second temple burned the incense offering morning and evening (Ex. 30.1ff., 7f.; cf. also Lev. 16.12f.),[64] to assuage and soothe Yahweh and put him in a friendly state of mind.[65] The coal, like the fire itself,

---

[61] In contrast to the interpretation by R. Knierim, *VT* 18, 1968, 47ff., the view is expressed here that the character of judgment does not lie in the theophany as such but in the condition of the person to whom it is given, as in that of the people to whom he is sent.

[62] Cf. e.g. Ps. 24.7; 29.10; 47.3, 7, 9, and for the twofold religious root of the kingship of Yahweh in that of the Creator god El and the storm god Baal, W. H. Schmidt, *Königtum Gottes in Ugarit und Israel*, BZAW 80, Berlin ²1966, 66ff., 80ff., or id., *Alttestamentlicher Glaube in seiner Umwelt*, Neukirchen ³1979, 142ff.

[63] Cf. also Plotinus VI, 9(9), 27f.

[64] The thesis first put forward by J. Wellhausen, *Prolegomena to the History of Ancient Israel*, reprinted Cleveland, Ohio 1957, 66, that there was no incense altar in the *hēkal*, the temple hall, in the pre-exilic temple, has been taken up again by Busink, *Tempel* I, 288f. A different view is held by V. Fritz, *Tempel und Zelt*, WMANT 47, Neukirchen 1977, 53f. For the special incense-offering in the temple cf. M. Haran, *Temples and Temple–Services in Ancient Israel*, Oxford 1978, 241ff.

[65] Cf. Fritz, op. cit., 54.

has purifying force (Num. 31.22f.).⁶⁶ [7] The action itself is interpreted by the seraphim's promise of forgiveness: guilt (ʿāwōn) is removed and sin (ḥaṭṭāʾt) covered by the touching of the lips with the coal. The language and conceptuality are cultic: what the priest does at each sin-offering and the high priest does for himself, his house and Israel on the great Day of Atonement (cf. Lev. 4.26, 35; 16.17), is accomplished by the heavenly being with his extraordinary act of atonement.⁶⁷ Here 'cover', kippēr, does not mean that in this way sin is hidden from God's eyes, but that the guilty one is to be preserved from the otherwise inescapable consequences of his failings.⁶⁸ Thus Isaiah is removed from the complex of guilt in which his people is involved, so that he can dare to speak in the heavenly council, and show how God can use him as his instrument.

[6.8–11] *The commissioning.* When the poet makes his prophet take the initiative in intervening in the heavenly council and without hesitation declaring himself ready to take on the task which has been announced, it sounds as though we have a step beyond the theme of refusal rooted in the call narratives.⁶⁹ Thus Isaiah appears as the man who, instructed by means of the theophany about the true power-relationships in this world (cf. also 8.11), resolutely takes God's side without enquiring into the consequences which will follow for his own person. The imaginary scene of purification on the other hand secures him against the suspicion of meddlesomeness, as its only purpose is to remove the sin which excludes him from converse with God. To this degree it is natural that Isaiah should now clearly respond to the question of his God, which, while apparently formulated in quite general terms, is, in the light of what has gone before, obviously directed towards him. In the dialogue the prophet on each occasion limits his words to what is absolutely necessary. In the eyes of the poet, talkativeness is the last thing appropriate for human beings in their converse with God (Matt. 6.7). The poet makes the prophet preserve the same restraint in the brief dialogue with Yahweh, which makes him avoid the divine name in vv. 1.8 and speak literally of 'my Lord'. In fact Yahweh's double

---

⁶⁶ For the rites of purification cf. also W. Robertson Smith, *The Religion of the Semites*, London 1927, 388ff.

⁶⁷ As we have no accounts of such a rite in Israel, it seems to me questionable to suppose, as Wildberger does, ad loc., that such an altar was in the background. That does not mean that I would take it to be physiologically impossible. Here one need only compare what E. Graf, *Das Rechtswesen der heutigen Beduinen*, Beiträge zur Sprach–und Kulturgeschichte des Orients 5, Walldorf – Hessen n.d., 56ff., says about the ordeal of licking a piece of red-hot iron.

⁶⁸ K. Elliger, HAT I, 4, 71. On this cf. also the tables in R. Knierim, *Die Hauptbegriffe der Sünde im Alten Testament*, Gütersloh 1965, 44ff.

⁶⁹ Cf. the evidence given above, 121f and in n. 18.

question[70] in v. 8a is a transformation of the formula 'Go, I send you', typical of call and commissioning, since it appears in Ex. 3.10, and in an altered form in Jer. 1.7; Judg. 6, 14 (cf. also Josh. 1.15; Ezek. 2.3f.).[71] Genesis 37.13 shows that it is rooted in the earthly sphere. With its intimation of his presence, 'Here am I', Isaiah's answer leaves open the question whether the prophet believes that he is addressed directly or indirectly (cf. Gen. 27.1, 18).[72] The decisive thing is that he declares himself ready to carry out God's task.

[9–10] With the commissioning formula 'Go and say',[73] in v. 9a Yahweh directs the prophet towards his task 'to this people'. In all the instances in which this designation is used for the people in the book of Isaiah, we cannot mistake its detached tone, with disparaging connotations.[74] As I have already stressed,[75] the real commissioning in vv. 9b, 10 does not envisage the content of the prophet's activity, but its effect. The style of the passage, as instructions to a messenger, shows that in particular it is concerned with the result of his speaking. But for all the pressure put on the people to hear, they are not to see or to arrive at any insight. The consequences of true insight and knowledge would be that its heart, now dulled, would be made whole again. Only from the divine commission and the prospect given in 8.11f. can we conclude that the people's sickness consists of a lack of fear of God and an inappropriate fear of men, and all the consequences which in practice arise from that (cf. also 1.5f.). What finds its clear fulfilment in Jer. 5.21 in the framework of a rebuke and in Deut. 29.3 in a retrospect on the history of the people, both in a natural context, here needs to be explained by a reference back, and thus opens itself to the suspicion of being parasitical on these sayings.[76] The blindness of the people, which according to v. 10b is already their state, is not to be removed by the appearance of the prophet, but rather to be heightened. Instead of opening[77] the heart,

[70] There is some dispute as to whether the *lānū* should be translated 'for us' or 'by us' and how the plural is to be interpreted. As there is not a mention of the heavenly court as such, and only the seraphim are mentioned, this is rather to be thought of as an allusion to it by a so-called *plural deliberationis*, a plural of consideration; cf. G-K[28] § 124g n. 3. From this perspective we may also doubt the justification of speaking of the prophet taking part in Yahweh's privy council.

[71] Cf. W. H. Schmidt, BK II, fascicle 2, Neukirchen 1977, 125.

[72] Cf. also Gen. 22.1, 11; 31.11; 46.2; Ex. 3.4, and also I Sam. 3.4ff., 16.

[73] Cf. Ex. 3.16; 7.15f.; II Sam. 7.5 par. I Chron. 17.4 and II Sam. 18.21; I Kings 18.8, 11, 14.

[74] Cf. 6.10; 8.6, 11, 12; 9.15; 28.11, 14; 29.13f.; Micah 2.11; Hag. 2.14; Zech 8.6 and J. Boehmer, 'Dieses Volk', *JBL* 45, 1926, 134ff. The phrase occurs strikingly often in the book of Jeremiah, with predominantly, but not exclusively, negative connotations.

[75] Cf. p. 118f. above.

[76] But cf. F. Hesse, *Das Verstockungsproblem im Alten Testament*, BZAW 74, Berlin 1955, 60ff.

[77] But cf. Ps. 13.6; 28.7; 33.21; 51.12.

directing[78] the eyes and the ears of the people towards God, he is to make their heart fat, so that it beats in the same old way even more sluggishly,[79] and to make them hard of hearing (Zech. 7.11) and stopped up (32.3). The understanding and senses of the people are to be incapable of perceiving God's call in his work and his words, so – and this is the unexpressed consequence of v. 10b – they will pine away and ultimately die.

If anyone hardens his heart, God will complete the hardening. Anyone whose heart is hardened has his condition made even worse by the call to repent. By this truth the poet is clearly interpreting the fate of his people; he makes God lead the people to disaster through the prophet in order to redeem God's power and freedom for his people in the present. We must keep this ultimate pastoral intent in mind[80] if we are not to lose ourselves in brooding before the mysteries of God, a process in which thought itself falls apart and which if the voice of human freedom rebels, makes it clear that the statement that the praise of this God fills the earth is not completely innocuous. It seems to offer praise of his power in collapse and failure, in which even the curses and screams of the dying still bear witness. However, at this point the theologian of today must guard against blasphemy, and instead of going on asking questions here, point to the cross, from which the call for God's help, and the question why such a terrible thing can happen, receives an answer in the Easter message.[81]

[11] As the answer shows, the prophet's question, 'How long, O Lord?',[82] in v. 11a, which has its parallel in the lament, relates not so much to the duration of his activity, which is to advance the hardening of people's hearts, as to the duration of that hardening. Here it is again clear that the narrator is looking beyond the lifetime of Isaiah to the catastrophe of 587.[83] Because the so-called memorial introduced by ch. 6 ends in a word of hope (cf. 8.17), God's answer envisages the end of the hardening and the possibility given with it of a new beginning to his history.[84] Both are to be expected only

---

[78] Cf. Ps. 40.7; Isa. 50.4f.; Prov. 20.12; Ps. 119.18.

[79] Cf. Hesse, op. cit., 21ff.

[80] Cf. 121 above.

[81] For allusions to this passage in the NT: Matt. 13.14f.; Mark 4.12; Luke 8.10; John 12.40; Acts 28.26f., and echoes in Mark 8.18; John 9.38; Rom. 11.8, cf. Hesse, op. cit., 64ff.

[82] Cf. Ps. 13.2; 74.10; 79.5; 80.5; 89.47; 90.13; Hab. 1.2.

[83] My earlier suggestion (in the first edition of this commentary), that the prophet's question involved him in the prophetic ministry of the intercessor, rested on a psychologizing interpretation arising out of a misunderstanding of the literary character of the narrative.

[84] As Delitzsch has stressed, ad loc., this understanding is required by the 'ad 'ašer 'im, in which the 'im has retained its conditional force. Cf. also Gen. 28.15; Num. 32.17.

beyond the utter collapse which will devastate cities[85] and deprive houses[86] of their inhabitants (cf. 5.9), turning farmland into a wilderness[87] (cf. 1.7;7.23ff.).[88] For the community to whom this story is told, that means that if it trusts in the almighty and holy Yahweh Sebaoth, it can hope in the change in salvation that he has brought about.

[6.12–13] *Additions.* The hand which added v. 12 felt the lack in v. 11 of a clear reference to the deportation of the people.[89] It may be that this person is to be identified with the one responsible for the continuation in v. 13abα, but we cannot be certain of this. In view of the failure of post-exilic Judaism to repent, and under the impact of the message of the coming judgment on the world, the editor whose voice we hear at this point thought it appropriate to remind the survivors that they were on their way towards a new divine judgment which would decimate their numbers.[90] This tenth, which is perhaps proverbial in Hebrew (cf. Amos 5.3; 6.9),[91] is compared to the stump of a great tree that has been felled, perhaps an oak or a terebinth,[92] and begins to send out fresh shoots or branches (cf. Job. 14.7ff.). These are then eaten by sheep or, more particularly, by goats and thus destroyed (cf. 5.5).[93] In the light of v. 11; 8.17, it is understandable that the prospect of eschatological judgment must attract the prospect of subsequent salvation. So the last editor who had a hand in this chapter has changed the comparison of v. 13bα into v. 13bβ: the stump which grows again is not gnawed completely away. It forms the holy seed of the new Israel, and replaces the old seed of the evildoers who have perished in the divine judgment (1.4). And because it is itself holy (cf. 4.3), and hallows the name of the Holy One of Israel (cf. 29.23), it will remain and grow into a new tree.

---

[85] Cf. Jer. 4.7; 26.9; 34.22; 44.22; also Deut. 28.21, 63.

[86] Cf. Jer. 32.43; 33.10, 12.

[87] Perhaps the narrator imagined the land as being completely void of people, on the basis of II Kings 25.11, 26. For the extent of the destruction and devastation in the conquest of the land by the Babylonians in 587, cf. K. M. Kenyon, *Archaeology in the Holy Land*, London ³1970, 219ff., and id., *Digging Up Jerusalem*, London 1974, 169ff.

[88] Cf. Lev. 26.33; Jer. 4.27; 12.10f.; 32.43; Ezek 6.14; 12.20 and 33.28f.; also Jer. 6.8; 9.10; 34.22; Isa. 17.9 and finally 7.16.

[89] For this meaning of *rihaq* cf. the use of the hiphil in Jer. 27.10; Ezek 11.16 and Joel 4.6; also the instances of the piel in Isa. 26.15; 29.13.

[90] Cf. also 8.21f.

[91] For the view that Amos 6.9 was composed after Amos, cf. H. W. Wolff., *Joel and Amos*, ad loc.

[92] The trees appear in reverse order in Hos. 4.13; cf. also Isa. 1.30; 2.13.

[93] For this, as for the possible identifications, see J. Feliks, in *Israel. Geography.* Israel Pocket Library, Jerusalem 1973, 139f. For the discussions sparked off by the readings in 1 QIsᵃ cf. the references in HAL 587b s.v. *maṣṣebet*, and Wildberger, ad loc.

CHAPTER 7.1–9

The Hour of Faith

1 **And it happened in the days of Ahaz** *the son of Jotham, son of Uzziah,* **king of Judah,** *that Rezin the king of Israel went up to Jerusalem to wage war against it, but could not conquer it;*[1] 2 **and the house of David was told, 'Aram has marched up**[2] **against Ephraim'. Then his heart and the heart of his people shook**[3] **as the trees of the forest shake**[3] **before the storm.** 3 **Then Yahweh said to Isaiah:**[4] **'Go out to meet Ahaz, you and your son Shear-jashub, to the end of the conduit of the upper pool, to the highway to the Fuller's Field,** 4 **and say to him: Take heed, be still, do not fear, and do not let your heart be faint because of these two smouldering stumps of firebrands,** *<before the fierce anger>*[5] *of Rezin and Aram and the son of Remaliah.* 5 **Because Aram**[6] **planned evil against you,** *Ephraim and the son or Remaliah:* 6 **Let us go up against Judah to tear it apart**[7]

[1] For the problems of the historicizing interpretation cf. below, 136f., 170f.

[2] The verb-form *nāḥā* can be analysed either as the third singular feminine of the so-called perfect of *nūᵃḥ* with Aram as feminine subject (as e.g. in II Sam. 8.5f.), or as the third person singular masculine of *nāḥā*, 'direct', with Aram as masculine subject as e.g. in II Sam. 10.18. As the verb *nāḥā* is attested elsewhere in the OT only in conjunction with an object, and in view of the *'el* in v. 3 the following *'al* cannot be regarded as a replacement for it, it is best to derive the verb from *nūᵃḥ*, settle; cf. also Gen. 8.4; II Sam. 21.10. The translation presupposes a technical military expression of which there is no evidence elsewhere.

[3] For the forms of *nūᵃᶜ*, cf. G-K²⁸ § 72t or q.

[4] The proposal put forward by e.g. Duhm and Donner, *Israel unter den Völkern*, 7, that instead of 'Isaiah', *'ēlay*, to me, should be read, is based on a misunderstanding of the literary character of the narrative.

[5] With S, read *mēḥari – 'ap* and cf. also Jer. 51.45.

[6] There is dispute as to whether v. 5f. is to be read with v. 4 as an explanation (so M. Saebø, 'Formgeschichtliche Erwägungen zu Jes. 7,3–9', *ST* 14, 1960, 56ff.), or with v. 7 as the ground for it, which is the usual interpretation. The Hebrew *ya'an kī* 'therefore, that; because', can in principle be connected to a preceding clause (cf. Isa. 61.1; 65.12 or 66.4), or to a subsequent one (cf. Isa. 8.6; 3.16; 29.13; 30.12; 37.29). The parallels in Isa. 1–39 and the form-critical argument that a reason should precede the threat in v. 7 suggest that H. W. Wolff, *Friede ohne Ende*, BS 35, Neukirchen 1962, 21; R. Kilian, *Die Verheissung Immanuels*, SBS 35, Stuttgart 1968, 23; Wildberger, ad loc.; Huber, *Völker* 14, are right in suggesting the usual connection of vv. 5f. with v. 7.

[7] As there are difficulties in deriving *ūnᵉqīsennā* from a verb *qūṣ* of which there is no evidence elsewhere, in view of the meaning to be given to the following verb in the light of II Kings 3.26, it seems better to follow Wildberger in explaining the form as hiphil of the verb *qūṣ*. 'quake, be afraid', for which there is evidence. If one has hesitations about that, it is better to return to the conjecture *nᵉṣīqennā*, 'and oppress it', suggested by Gesenius and e.g. Duhm and Huber, *Völker*, 12 n. 11.

and break it up for ourselves and set up the son of Tabeel[8] as king in
it.
7   Thus says the Lord Yahweh:
'It shall not stand and it shall not last longer,[9]

[8] The Massoretic vocalization as *Ṭāb⁽ᵉ⁾'al* is tendentious and is probably meant to
interpret the name as meaning 'worthless'. For the primary pronunciation as *Ṭāb⁽ᵉ⁾ēl*
cf. LXX and V, and not least Ezra 4.7.
[9] Following the tradition most clearly attested by LXX, v.7 is usually understood as
an independent clause relating to vv. 5, 6 and translated 'it will not come about and
will not happen'. Verses 8a and 9a then give the reason. To support this understanding
reference can be made to the corresponding use of *qūm* in 8.10; 14.24; 46.10; Jer.
44.28; 51.29; Prov. 19.21. But there are two difficulties about this interpretation. 1. In
that case the reason in vv. 5, 6 does not correspond to any threat, though the form of
the prophetic saying leads that to be expected; cf. in connection with this O.H. Steck,
'Rettung und Verstockung. Exegetische Bemerkungen zu Jesaja 7,3–9', *EvTh* 33, 1973,
81; 2. there are difficulties over the content, because vv. 8a, 9a would either envisage
the maintenance of the political status quo of the two confederate hostile kingdoms,
which was certainly not the intention of the narrator, who knows the outcome, or
have to be seen as an elliptical statement which does not actually express the decisive
notion. Among those who have argued to the latter effect are e.g. Procksch, ad loc.,
and E. Würthwein, 'Jesaja 7,1–9. Ein Beitrag zum Thema Prophetie und Politik',
Festschrift Karl Heim, Hamburg 1954, 60f. = *Wort und Existenz*, Göttingen 1970, 140:
thus the idea in vv. 8a, 9a would have to be extended to the king from David's house,
Jerusalem and Judah. W. Vischer, *Die Immanuel-Botschaft im Rahmen des königlichen
Zionsfestes*, TS (B) 45, Zollikon –Zurich 166, 18, has understood vv. 8a, 9a similarly
and has gone beyond the two authors mentioned above in conjecturing that a clause
to this effect has fallen out. Wildberger assumed, rather, that here there was
announcement of a limitation of the power of the enemy by Yahweh, against the
background of the Zion theology. Kilian has also explained things in similar terms.
However, he argues in the light of 31.3, instead of the Zion ideology. Duhm, Marti,
Feldmann and Fohrer, ad loc., explained vv. 8a, 9a by assuming that the prophet was
trying to calm down the king by referring to the enemies as well-known peoples and
capitals once ruled over by the house of David. Donner, *Israel unter den Völkern*, 13f.,
and more briefly J. Lindblom, *A Study on the Immanuel Section in Isaiah. Isa. 7.1–9.6*,
SMHVL 1957/58, 4, Lund 1958, 11, by contrast supposed that the passage envisaged
the collapse of the order to be found in the enemy camp. However, we may follow W.
Dietrich, *Jesaja und die Politik*, 83ff., by arguing against these attempts at interpretation
that the prophet or, as I would prefer to say for reasons which will soon become clear,
the author of the narrative, was unable to express himself clearly. The concessive
interpretation of the *kî* at the beginning of v. 8a, intended to mean, 'May also the
head', put forward by T. O. Vriezen in *Von Ugarit nach Qumran*, Festschrift Otto
Eissfeldt, BZAW 77, Berlin 1958, 269, comes to grief on the irresolvable tension which
in this way arises between v. 4a on the one side and vv. 8a, 9a on the other. Vriezen's
attempt to solve this by assuming a change from the divine perspective in v. 4 to the
human in vv. 8a, 9a, is to be adjudged a failure (so Huber, *Völker*, 15), because in that
case we would have to assume no human view and evaluation behind v. 7a with its
messenger formula. The experiment of avoiding the difficulties of the two groups of
interpretation by the assumption that here is a secondary entity formed by the
prophetic sayings 7.5a, 6, 7; 17.1–2; 7.8a, 9a, 20, 9b, suggested by Dietrich, op. cit.,
62ff., cf. 87ff., cuts the Gordian knot. So it still seems better to endorse the solution
accepted by Saebø, *ST* 14, 1960, 54ff., and by H. W. Wolff, *BS* 35, 1962, 21; Kaiser[1], ad
loc., O. H. Steck, *EvTh* 53, 1973, 78ff.; and Huber, *Völker*, 16ff., to translate the *kî* at
the beginning of v. 8a as 'that' and to interpret vv. 8a, 9a as subject clauses to v. 7a.
Here both verbs in v. 7b must be given durative significance. For *qūm* in the sense of

8   that Damascus is the head of Aram
     and Rezin the head of Damascus.
     Within sixty-five years
     Ephraim will be broken in pieces, without a people.
9   And Samaria the head of Ephraim
     and the son of Remaliah the head of Samaria.
     If you do not believe, you will not endure.'

[7.1–9] The section 7.1–17 is clearly marked off from ch. 6 by the new beginning in v. 1 and the transition from a first-person to a third-person narrative which is connected with it. The prophetic formula standing at the beginning of v. 18 and then repeated in vv. 20, 21, 23, partly in full and partly in abbreviated form, shows that with v. 18 a series of sayings begins which in form, at any rate, are independent of v. 17. In the narrative which remains, 7.1–17, there is an unmistakable break after v. 9. The account of the commissioning of the prophet Isaiah to give a particular divine message to king Ahaz, which begins with v. 1, ends with that verse. As it goes without saying that a prophet will carry out a commission of this kind, in Hebrew style an account of the way in which it is carried out is not absolutely necessary. 7.10–17 has a narrative about the offer of a sign which is rejected. If it came from the same hand as 7.1–9, we would expect a sentence providing a transition from one narrative to the other. In fact it would have had to deal with the reaction of the king to the word of God communicated to him by the prophet.[10] The account in 7.1–9 with its conclusion in v. 9b is directed towards the reader. Thus it seems to leave unanswered the question how king Ahaz reacted to the divine message. The narrator of 7.10–17 sought to supply this lack by using the instance of the rejection of the sign as an example of the failure of the house of David and drew the consequences of this along the lines of v. 9b.

If these considerations confirm that 7.1–9 is primary and independent, we still need to establish the original extent of the narrative, since even the reader without any training in literary criticism will see from v. 8b that in its traditional form it is not all of a piece. It breaks the connection between v.8a and v.9a, and would have made more sense if it had been inserted behind v.9a. We should not exclude out of hand the possibility that this half-verse is a subsequent

---

'stand', cf. I Sam. 13.14; Isa. 28.18; Amos 7.2; for *hāyāh* in the sense of 'continue' cf. Isa. 51.6, following C. H. Ratschow, *Werden und Wirken*, BZAW 70, Berlin 1941, 22, and Ruth 1.2; Dan. 1.21, with Huber, *Völker* 17. This interpretation fulfils the form-critical requirement that the reason or rebuke in vv. 5, 6 should be followed by a clear threat contained in vv. 7, 8a, 9a.

[10] Instead of this, the style of v. 10 has probably been assimilated to vv. 11ff., at a secondary stage. See also below, 151 n. 1.

historicization along the lines of a *vaticinium ex eventu*, a prophecy after the event.[11] Therefore the commentator faces the question whether the narrative has yet other editorial additions. Chronologically it belongs to the beginning of the so-called Syro-Ephraimite war of the years 734–732 BC, about which we are informed by Assyrian accounts and above all by II Kings 16.5ff.; II Chron. 28.5ff.[12] As the narrative in II Chron. 28 has very marked theological tendencies, even extending to the creation of new historical facts, which is a characteristic of the Chronicler's history,[13] it is best for us primarily to use the information contained in II Kings as a comparison. Chronicles took its essential historical information from the Deuteronomistic history, to which Kings also belonged.[14] The deliberate portrayal of king Jehoshaphat as the antitype, the counterpart of Ahaz, in II Chron. 20 shows that the author also knew the present account in the book of Isaiah; here in v. 20b the king is made to say something which not only goes back clearly to Isa. 7.9b, but at the same time draws a lesson from the whole story. If we read II Kings 16.5; Isa. 7.1 side by side, we immediately recognize that the wording of v. 1 partly coincides with that of II Kings 16.5, and that here, as I shall explain in more detail below, we have a not untendentious elaboration with the information taken from there.[15] We may also attribute to the same historicizing editor the factual explanation of the burnt stump mentioned in v. 4a by v. 4b, and with a high degree of probability also the lame mention of the Israelite war party in v. 5b, oriented on v. 9a. Here we find a hand which can be demonstrated to have been at work not only in the rest of ch. 7 and ch. 8, but also elsewhere in the book of Isaiah.[16]

Before we can consider the basic problem of the structure, the literary character and origin of the present narrative, we must attempt a systematic answer to the preliminary question of the

[11] In fact there could be a recollection here of an exchange of population of the kind that may have been carried out by the Assyrian kings Esarhaddon and Assurbanipal in connection with their intervention on the occasion of the rebellion of king Baal of Tyre or the Egyptian expedition of the year 671; cf. Ezra 4.2, 10 and H. Hirschberg, *Studien zur Geschichte Esarhaddons*, Diss. Berlin 1932, 61ff., reprinted in W. Rudolph, HAT I 20, Tübingen 1949, 33; cf. also A. Alt, *Kleine Schriften* II, 321, and for the historical connections e.g. H. R. Hall, *CAH* III, 1929 (1960), 280ff.

[12] Cf. below, 148f.

[13] Cf. e.g. II Kings 16.4f. with II Chron. 28.4f.; 16.7f. with 28.20f.; and 16.10ff. with 28.22f.

[14] Cf. e.g. Kaiser, *Introduction*, 179f., 186, and R. Smend, *Die Entstehung des Alten Testaments*, TW 1, Stuttgart 1978, 229.

[15] Cf. below, 170f. The assumption that II Kings 16.5 is derived from Isa. 7.1, as put forward, e.g. by Delitzsch, ad loc, may be taken, following Cheyne, *Introduction*, 301, to have been refuted.

[16] Cf. above, 5f.

attribution of individual verses and groups of verses. There has been a dispute in more recent exegetical literature as to whether vv. 5, 6 belong to v. 4 as their explanation, or to v. 7 as its motivation, and how the relationship between v. 7 and vv. 8a, 9a is to be defined. Verse 7b can be understood in turn either as an independent clause, the motivation of which is to be found in vv. 8a, 9a, or as a predicate of the subject clauses vv. 8a, 9a.[17] In addition, there are difficult technical problems, the detailed discussion of which cannot be undertaken in this context. Instead, I shall simply give a brief explanation of the decisions underlying my translation. As the necessary explanation of v. 4 can already be found in the details of the situation contained in vv. 1, 2, the form-critical consideration that vv. 5 and 6 should be seen as the anticipatory motivation or reasoning for the threat which follows should be regarded as decisive.[18] If we were now to understand v. 7b as the real threat and vv. 8a, 9a as its grounding in fact, we would be compelled to take vv. 8a, 9a as elliptical statements, the third member in which, comprising Jerusalem and the house of David, is not mentioned. So it is better to make the assumption that already follows logically from a decision about the character of vv. 5, 6 that v. 7b is the predicate and vv. 8a, 9a are the subject clauses that go with it.[19]

Formally, the narrative consists of the two basic elements of the exposition, comprising vv. 1, 2 and the report of the commissioning of a prophet to communicate a message from God in vv. 3–9. If we look more closely at the second part, which makes up the real body of the narrative, we can see the complexity of both its genre and content. In v. 3 there is an unusually exact reference to the implementation of the commission, which specifies in addition to the person to receive the message the place where it is to be given and who is to accompany the prophet. The way in which the name of the person accompanying the prophet is interpreted as a sign at the same time gives the report the underlying character of an instruction to perform a symbolic action when passing on the message. The centre and at the same time the most extensive part of the message from God which begins in v. 4 is formed by the threat against the enemies of the recipient of the message, consisting of vv. 5–9a. In content, therefore, it has the significance of a promise. However, it is put within the framework of the two admonitions vv. 4, 9b, which in turn prove to be rooted in the Deuteronomic-Deuteronomistic preaching of war.[20] Contrary to the expectation that the combination

[17] Cf. above, 135 n. 9.
[18] Cf. above, 134 n. 6.
[19] Cf. above, 135 n. 9.
[20] Cf. below, 140ff.

of a promise with an admonition leads to a conditional promise, the wording especially of the closing admonition decides the character of the whole divine message as a conditional threat. The present danger to the recipient of the message, judged by the first admonition and the following threat to be ultimately insignificant, will lead to his downfall if he disregards the second admonition.

The internal structure of the narrative proves to be as complex as its external form. On the surface it is concerned with the decision whether the Davidic dynasty will survive or go under. The narrator already indicates this theme in the exposition of vv. 1aα₁ and 2 by speaking of the house of David rather than of the king as the recipient of the message of disaster. To heighten the tension, we are only told in v. 6, in a retrospect which at the same time points forward to v. 9b that the military advance of the Aramaeans into the neighbouring territory of Israel is really aimed at the dynasty represented by king Ahaz. Thus the account of the plan to overthrow the dynasty and appoint a prominent Aramaean as puppet king for the alliance in v. 6, whether it is historical or projects back into the past problems in post-exilic Jerusalem, indicates the theme which stands in the foreground.[21] The narrator had, however, already referred indirectly in v. 2b to the fundamental character of the threat by means of his description of the reaction of the royal house to the news, which takes the form of a nature-simile of the kind to be found in Wisdom; the trees of the forest seem to quake before the storm because of the danger that they will be uprooted and blown down. In the light of the brief description of the situation in v. 2a, v. 2b would at the same time have the function of making the reader or hearer of the story ask the reason for this fear and therefore arouse his interest in the further course of events. The anxiety of the dynasty represented by Ahaz is contrasted by the narrator in v. 4 with the divine admonition to remain absolutely passive and fearless despite the approaching dangers, which will apparently shake the dynasty to its foundations.[22] What could make this attitude possible is not shown by the way in which the prophet discounts the apparently more powerful foes as smoking brands (v. 4b) which are really about to be quenched altogether and give the impression of being particularly dangerous now only because they have flared up for a second, but by the closing admonition in v. 9b. Thus an analysis of the inner structure shows that v. 9b is the climax of the narrative. The reason given for the prophecy of the downfall of the enemy inserted between v. 4 and v. 9b is clearly in vv. 5, 6a a development of the theme of the threat to

[21] Cf. below, 144ff.
[22] Cf. below, 141f.

the dynasty. The threat itself points in deliberately obscure but nevertheless comprehensible oracular style to the downfall of the hostile capitals and their kings and thus of the kingdoms they represent. The reason why the narrative avoids using the name 'Israel' for the brother kingdom and speaks of Ephraim instead is presumably that it contains a polemical claim to the kingdom for its own people. The fact that the purpose of the enemies to deprive the Davidic dynasty of its throne is enough to cause Yahweh to annihilate the hostile kingdoms shows that the house of David is under his special protection. It is his chosen dynasty.[23] However, the narrator is convinced that for its earthly fulfilment in the long run the divine election requires that the elect should be preserved and that the answer to the promise given to them should take the form of a trust in which they place themselves completely in the hand of God.[24]

An underlying concern in the narrative is of course the fate of the people. Therefore v. 2b reports that not only the house of David but also the people become afraid because of the approaching danger. Only in this way can we understand the introduction of Isaiah's son with the ominous name Shear-jashub, 'only a remnant will return'. His presence indicates that the decision called for in v. 9b is concerned not only with the continuance of the dynasty but also with the survival of the people. And as a symbolic action really does not have any significance as an admonition, but rather anticipates what is to come as a primal image and helps to bring it to pass,[25] the name of the son points beyond the apparently open situation in which a decision is to be made, presupposed by v. 9b, to a time in which only a remnant of the people remains.

Once we have recognized the two themes running through the narrative, which on the surface is concerned with the continuance or downfall of the dynasty, and underneath that with the survival of the people, we should not rush too quickly to explain it in terms of the situation presupposed, going beyond its character as an outside report and claiming it for the prophet Isaiah, as has happened almost universally in more recent scholarship.[26] Instead, we should begin

---

[23] Cf; below, 146f.

[24] Cf. also the comment made by Martin Luther, WA 31, 2, p. 58, 3f.: 'Sola ergo fides certificat et habet solidum fundamentum. Frustra autem fit promissio, nisi accedat fides '(Only faith authenticates and has a solid foundation. The promise happens in vain if not accompanied by faith.)

[25] Cf. G. Fohrer, Die symbolischen Handlungen der Propheten, ATANT 54, Zurich ²1968, 17. It should be expressly noted that Fohrer understands the present passage merely as a reference to the possibility 'that Judah can continue as the remnant of the whole people' (29f.).

[26] E. G. Kraeling has drawn attention to its character as an alien report, 'The Immanuel Prophecy', JBL 50, 1931, 277ff., without so far finding acceptance.

by taking it seriously as a narrative and asking the significance of the fact that with v. 9b it opens up towards the reader or hearer. Does this mean perhaps that its transposition to the time of the Syro-Ephraimite war has the purpose of interpreting the present situation of the narrator and his community in terms of the theology of history and ultimately confronting him with the very decision which faced the king at the time of the narrative? If we go on to investigate what situation the narrator might presuppose, the theme in the foreground suggests that in fact the dynasty had already fallen; in turn that would mean that the narrative is concerned with answering the twofold question why the chosen dynasty left the stage of history, involving the people in a catastrophe from which only a remnant escaped as the sole basis for the future and what was the hope of the survivors. If it is permissible to understand the narrative in this way, the background to the striking admonition to be passive in v. 4 is immediately clarified. The people who had been conquered and robbed of their statehood had had the weapons taken out of their hand. In themselves they had no possibility of protecting themselves against the supremacy of the world-empire to whom they had fallen prey. They could not but be still, externally remain passive and inwardly trust in the help of the God who in the defeat of the people had proved to be the one taking vengeance on unbelief.

Such considerations may well be accepted because of their internal consistency; however, further arguments are needed in support of a late date for this passage. They are not difficult to find. We need only investigate the history of the concepts used in vv. 4, 9, which are theologically central. Certainly v. 4 echoes Isaiah 30.15, with its

> 'In return and rest lies your salvation,
> in stillness (*hašqēṭ*) and trust
> your strength consists' (cf. also 32.17).

I have demonstrated elsewhere that this is at best a late pre-exilic reflection, even if it is not a saying which looks back on the catastrophe of 587.[27] Furthermore, v. 4 is an unmistakable parallel to the Deuteronomic-Deuteronomistic preaching of war with its invitation not to fear and its promise that Yahweh himself will lead his people in battle (cf. e.g. Deut. 1.29f.; 20.3f.). Transposed into a narrative context, the instruction on preaching war contained in Deut. 20.3f. occurs in the secondary Yahwistic saying Ex. 14.14, with its well-known 'Yahweh will fight for you, so you may be tranquil'.[28] Despite the difference which even he saw, Gerhard von Rad here

---

[27] Cf. *Isaiah 13–39*, 292f.
[28] Cf. F. Stolz, *Jahwes und Israels Kriege*, ATANT 60, Zurich 1972, 94ff.

presupposed a direct continuation of the Holy War tradition from the period before the state.[29] In fact, however, this might be an incorporation into literary form and an elaboration of the elements of those calls to war which are recognizable as such in the Deuteronomic-Deuteronomistic texts.[30] Here the divine cooperation which manifests itself as such in the outcome of the battle has become the sole working of God which man has to go along with passively, by trusting him (cf. Deut. 1.29f.; II Chron. 20.15, 20,22ff.). So Isa. 7.4, like 1 QM X, 3f. at a later date, might go back to Deut. 20.3. The 'Fear not' could perhaps have been put before the invitation not to tremble at heart under the influence of old oracular practice.[31]

Turning to the central concept of faith in v. 9b, we are again taken into the realm of Deuteronomic-Deuteronomistic theology: the people who fear Yahweh because of the demonstrations of his power at the Sea at the same time trust him and 'believe' in him (Ex. 14.21). In Deut. 1.32 the people is blamed because it did not continue to trust in Yahweh during the wanderings in the wilderness (cf. also Deut. 9.23). The prime example of this unbelief is the behaviour of the people on receiving the news from the spies about the strength of the inhabitants of the promised land (Num. 14.11).[32] The reader should note that there is a contrast in this verse between the unbelief of the people and the signs done by Yahweh, and in v. 22 of the same chapter between these signs and the tempting of God by the people. This is relevant to reflections on the next narrative, Isa. 7.10–17*. The people who had seen Yahweh's 'sign of faith' without responding with faith had in so doing tempted God. On the other hand, to have a perverse concern for such a sign is similarly to tempt God (cf. Deut. 6.16; Ex. 17.2). Thus the following narrative, too, seems to stand under the influence of Deuteronomistic theology.

In favour of the assumption that the central theological conceptuality of vv. 4, 9b represents a continuation of Deuteronomic and Deuteronomistic terminology, it should also be pointed out that in this narrative, in contrast to alleged parallels, the verbs 'guard against', 'fear' and 'trust' are used without an object. This is an indication of the development of the terminology. As long as Isa. 7 was seen as a narrative which originally, at any rate, had been set down by the prophet Isaiah himself and had been edited only more

[29] *Der Heilige Krieg im Alten Israel*, Göttingen ²1952, 56ff.

[30] Cf. J. Becker, *Gottesfurcht im Alten Testament*. AnBib 25, Rome 1965, 54, and Stolz, op. cit., 205.

[31] Cf. Becker, op. cit., 54, and e.g. Lam. 3.55ff.

[32] For the influence of Deuteronomic theology on the redactional stratum of the chapter involved here, cf. M. Noth, *Numbers*, OTL, London 1968, 108f.

or less superficially,[33] the encounter between Ahaz and Isaiah by the fuller's field had to be seen as the moment of birth for the Old Testament concept of faith.[34] This produced the strange situation, noted by Gerhard Ebeling, that the creation of the word was said to have come about in connection with a word-play, whereas one would really expect the formation of the concept to precede the word-play.[35] Although no less a scholar than Rudolf Smend supported the view that both processes took place simultaneously, and therefore maintained that the theological concept of faith was shaped by the prophet Isaiah,[36] the observations and considerations noted above seem to tell decisively in the other direction. As in another context I have shown that the corner-stone saying (Isa. 28.16) is already exilic,[37] we can now draw the conclusion that the absolute use of the concept of faith throughout the book of Isaiah is a continuation of the theological concept of faith which has its home in the language of the Deuteronomistic school. The argument may be finally established by noting further that Ernst Würthwein recognized in v. 9b an allusion to the 'abiding house', the bēt neʾmen of the Nathan prophecy (cf. II Sam. 7.16; I Sam. 25.28; I Kings 11.38),[38] but in the meantime this idea in the prophecy has also been demonstrated to be Deuteronomistic and therefore later.[39] So we can now say with some degree of certainty that the present narrative does not come from the prophet Isaiah but is heavily influenced by Deuteronomistic theology, and presumably belongs only to the late sixth or early fifth century BC.

The conjecture that the narrator of Isa. 7.1–9, like the narrator of the following story in 7.10–17*, felt that the Isaiah narratives as they have been handed down in ch. 20; 36–39 par. II Kings 18.17–20.19 justified him in telling his story gains in probability when we note that the two accounts represent Ahaz *de facto* as the antitype of the Hezekiah of the legend. Whereas the latter in his distress sent for the prophet Isaiah and received a promise which was immediately fulfilled (cf. II Kings 18.17ff. par. Isa. 36.1ff.), Ahaz refused to credit the promise, although Yahweh had sent the prophet to him before

---

[33] For this view cf. e.g. Budde, *Jesaja's Erleben*, 1. Wildberger, op. cit., 270, suggests that Isaiah or his pupils could have incorporated an outside account into the so-called memorial.
[34] In this sense see e.g. also A. Weiser, *TDNT* 6, 189.
[35] *Word and Faith*, London and Philadelphia 1963, 211 n. 2.
[36] 'Zur Geschichte von *h'mjn'*, in *Hebräische Wortforschung*, Festschrift Walter Baumgartner, SVT 16, Leiden 1967, 288f.
[37] *Isiah 13–39*, 292 ff.
[38] *Festschrift Karl Heim*, Hamburg 1954, 58ff. = *Wort und Existenz*, Göttingen 1970, 138ff.
[39] Cf. T. Veijola, *Die ewige Dynastie*, AASF B 193, Helsinki 1975, 68ff., 74ff.

the city was put in danger. By transferring the encounter between prophet and king in 7.3 to the very place at which later the Rabshakeh of the Assyrian king Sennacherib presented his demand for capitulation to Hezekiah, a location which is perhaps to be sought in the north or north-west rather than in the south of the city,[40] the narrator had in mind less the concern of the king to provide water for the city (which in his eyes was a lack of faith) than to produce an antitypical situation: one day the Assyrian general will stand on the very place where king Ahaz refused to accede to the demand of faith. However, that would mean that there is no original recollection behind this mention of place and that it is taken either from II Kings 18.17 or from Isa. 36.2. The same antitype also underlies 7.10–17*. Whereas Hezekiah in his sickness responds with a request for a sign to the prophetic promise that he will be healed and continue to live for a number of years, and this sign is given him by the prophet and fulfilled by Yahweh (II Kings 20.8ff.), Ahaz rejected the sign offered to him by the prophet, apparently as Yahweh's plenipotentiary, and so opened up the way to a policy which ended in the annihilation of the kingdom of Judah. As Isa. 38.7ff. has excluded Hezekiah's demand for a sign, probably under the influence of Deut. 6.16, the contrast between Ahaz' and Hezekiah's demands for a sign emerges only if we bring in II Kings 20.8ff.[41] Therefore we may rightly assume that the version of the narrative in Isa. 38 is later than 7.10ff.*, and the whole complex of chs. 36–39 was taken up into the Isaiah scroll only at a later date.

Is it too bold to suggest that the call to conversion contained in 30.15 and the reference to the pitiful remnant which survives the catastrophe in 30.17.[42] are concentrated in the name and figure of the prophet's son Shear-jashub, 'only a remnant will return'? And perhaps it is even possible that a contemporary controversy underlies the narrative about the son of Tabeel, to be set up as a puppet king (v. 6), rather than it being a historical reference. Albrecht Alt regarded the figure, whose name shows him to be an Aramaean, as

---

[40] This has been argued by J. Simons, *Jerusalem in the Old Testament*, Leiden 1953, 334ff., and Donner, *Israel unter den Völkern*, 10f. G. Dalman, *Jerusalem und sein Gelände*, Gütersloh 1930, 163ff., 202ff.; id, *Arbeit und Sitte* V, 1937, 152f.; L. H. Vincent, *Jerusalem de l'Ancien Testament* I, Paris 1954, 284ff., have argued for a location in the south of the city. Cf. also the detailed discussion of the problem in M. Burrows, 'The Conduit of the Upper Pool', *ZAW* 70, 1958, 221ff. For the activity of the fullers, who beat the cloth and then bleached it, cf. also R. J. Forbes, *Studies in Ancient Technology* IV, Leiden ²1964, 82f., 87ff.

[41] For Isa. 38.7ff., cf. also *Isaiah 13–39*, 400f.

[42] For literary-critical comments cf. *Isaiah 13–39*, 292f., and Vermeylen I, 411ff., and esp. 414ff.

a 'man of non-royal descent, but in an exalted position'.[43] However, it is not impossible that underlying this otherwise obscure character with all the aspirations ascribed to him we should find the Tobiads from Transjordan, of whose attempts to involve themselves in the futute of Jerusalem Nehemiah had to complain in the second half of the fifth century (cf. Neh. 2.19; 3.35, etc., and especially 13.4ff.).[44] Anyone who thinks this conjecture too bold may suppose that here we have a stray report from an unknown source about the Syro-Ephraimite war. In that case, however, they must be clear that in view of the investigations mentioned above, this one datum cannot bear the burden of proof for the historicity of the scene any more than can the name of the prophet's son.

[7.1–9] *Trusting and enduring*. The narrative presupposes that its audience has some knowledge of the Syro-Ephraimite war as it is depicted, with extraordinary brevity, in II Kings 16.5–9 and the previous notes in II Kings 15.29f., 37, the chronology of which is partly obscure. The reader would know that because Jerusalem was encircled by the combined armies of king Rezin of Aram-Damascus[45] and king Pekah of Israel, and had lost Judah's only port at Elath on the Gulf of Akabah, king Ahaz resolved to offer his submission to the Assyrian king Tiglath-pileser and to purchase his intervention in the war by a large amount of tribute. The narrator rightly recognized that this action contained within it the germ of the downfall of the kingdom of Judah, since in future the house of David was no longer able to escape permanent vassalship, and paid for the attempt to shake off the yoke of the neo-Babylonian empire, imposed on it instead of that of Assyria, with the loss of the throne and the downfall of the kingdom, thus bringing disaster to the people. Had the kings of the house of David trusted only in their God instead of involving themselves in political activity, the dynasty would have endured, in accordance with the promise given to it by the prophet Nathan (cf. II Sam. 7.16). Had Yahweh used the prophet Isaiah to tell king Hezekiah, who had hoped for his help, not to fear, and

[43] 'Menschen ohne Namen', *ArOr* 18, 1950, 23f. = *KS* III, 213. Against the attempt by W. F. Albright, 'The Son of Tabeel (Isaiah 7.6)', *BASOR* 140, 1955, 34f., cf. S. Mittmann, *ZDPV* 89, 1973. 16f. In view of the analysis of the name as Thobaal proposed by M. Weippert, 'Menahem von Israel und seine Zeitgenossen in einer Steleninschrift Tiglat-pilesers III aus dem Iran', *ZDPV* 89, 1973, 29, cf. 30 and 47, the brilliant attempt by A. Vanel, 'Tabeel en Is 7, 6, et le roi Tubail de Tyr', *Studies on Prophecy*, SVT 26, Leiden 1974, 17ff., to identify the son of Tabeel with a son of the king of Tyre (Tubail = Ṭôb'ēl), cf. the stele of Tiglath-pileser III from Toronto, published by Levine, line 6, may be a failure.

[44] On the other hand B. Mazar, 'The Tobiads', *IEJ* 1957, 236f., assumed that the Tobiads could have been descendants of the son of Tabeel.

[45] For what is presumably the more correct Hebrew form of the name, *Raṣyôn*, cf. Weippert, *ZDPV* 89, 1973, 46.

prophesied that the Assyrian army would go away (II Kings 19.6f.), he would certainly also have made use of Isaiah to warn Ahaz against what was to prove such a disastrous step, namely of submitting to the king of Assyria. So the unknown narrator told his story in complete confidence that he was telling his people the truth about the real background to the downfall of the kingdom.

[1–3] As the house of David and the people lost heart at the news of the advance of the Aramaean army into the neighbouring hills of Ephraim, and feared for their existence like trees shaking before the storm, Yahweh sent the prophet with his ominously named son Shear-jashub, 'only a remnant will return', to meet the king.[46] He was to meet him at the very place where a good thirty years later the Assyrian general presented his demands for capitulation. Along the lines of Isa. 22.11, we might imagine that in view of the imminent siege the king was visiting the reservoir in the city to take the necessary precautionary measures. However, it is not certain that the narrator was thinking of anything other than II Kings 18.17 and thus the generally antitypical situation of 701.[47] By contrast, he was necessarily aware that Ahaz's wrong decision led to the threat to the kingdom in the time of Hezekiah, because it was in line with his argument. The request directed by Yahweh to the prophet that he should bring his son Shear-jashub with him, which is not explained further, suggested to the reader that Yahweh can see the outcome of the encounter, and is aware of the consequences for the people and the dynasty: only a remnant will escape the final catastrophe to the kingdom (cf. also 30.16f.). Thus the sign of the son is directed more, and in any case ultimately, to the reader than to the king, whom it seeks to make aware of the seriousness of the decision required of him. We can understand how the theology of hardening the heart could arise out of reflection on this situation, because the name of the prophet's son anticipates the outcome and goes beyond the call to decision addressed to the king.

[4] The admonition at the beginning of the divine message corresponds to the reflection on the inexorable character of the end to be found in 30.15: the deliverance of the dynasty would have been found in a passiveness grounded in trust in God, of the sort

---

[46] For the two possible ways of translating the name: 'Only a remnant returns (from battle or war)', or 'Only a remnant is converted', cf. J. Lindblom, SMHVL 1957, 358, 4,8f.; M. Rehm, *Messias*, 35 n. 14, or Wildberger, op. cit., 277f. For this question cf. also U. Stegemann, 'Der Restgedanke bei Isaias', *BZ* NF 13, 1969, 161ff., and for the discussion of it, the survey by H. D. Preuss in W. E. Miller and H. D. Preuss, *Die Vorstellung vom Rest im Alten Testament*, Neukirchen 1973, 96ff., and esp. 119ff.

[47] Cf. also O. Kaiser, 'Geschichtliche Erfahrung und eschatologische Erwartung', *NZST* 15, 1973, 272ff. = *Eschatologie im Alten Testament*, ed. H. D. Preuss, WdF 480, Darmstadt 1978, 444ff.

developed by the Deuteronomistic preaching and theology of war with a view to the situation of the people, who had been deprived of all means of securing freedom by themselves as a result of the collapse.[48] There was no reason to fear the two hostile kingdoms, which were in fact already doomed to destruction!

The historian may indeed agree with this and recall that the Assyrian king could hardly have stood by idly and watched the extension of the rebellion in the south-west of his empire. However, such considerations will hardly have been decisive for the narrator. The important thing for him was that here was an attack on the dynasty chosen by Yahweh. Thus the attempt to put an Aramaean of mixed blood[49] on the throne was enough to cause Yahweh to intervene and destroy the two hostile kingdoms. From the news of their downfall in II Kings 15.29f.; 16.9, he drew the conclusion that here was Yahweh's answer to the attack on the house of David. And so, just as II Kings 16.5ff. saw Aram as the chief enemy, he did also. For him Pekah, king of the northern kingdom, who was descended from a non-royal line and is referred to contemptuously as Remaliah's son, was evidently a collaborator in the war rather than its instigator. So king Ahaz had needed only to trust the words of God's messenger to experience that the efforts made by the enemy were the last blossoming of its power before its decline; or, to put it metaphorically, that the smoke they caused was only the last blazing up from the embers of a dying fire.

[9b] The promise of the enduring house in II Sam. 7.16 gave the narrator the right to make the prophet announce to his king in the name of the God of promise the conditions on which it would endure and so demonstrate to him that the existence of his house was at stake in the political decision that he was making. If the dynasty then came to an end, it was only because it did not show the trust that was required of it,[50] but involved itself in political ploys and thus forfeited the support of the God in whose promise it was rooted (cf. also 30.1ff.; 31.1ff.). The 'if you do not believe, you will not endure' changes the lesson of the history of the downfall of the dynasty, interpreted in faith, into an admonition to the king who had led his house down a political road which ended in its downfall and the decimation of the people. But whereas the history of the kingdom of David seemed to have been completed and its kingdom

---

[48] Cf. above, 141f.

[49] We must presuppose an origin of this kind because a complete foreigner to the country in the eyes of a narrator would hardly have seemed to have been a likely claimant to the throne in Jerusalem.

[50] For the concept cf. above, 142f., and now also A. Jepsen, *TWAT* I, 313ff.; *TDOT* I, 292ff.

finally gone, the narrator leaves his story open at the end with an admonition to the reader. The reader is asked whether he is willing to trust God and endure or whether he will refuse to have faith in God's gracious future as is asked of him and similarly fail. Thus the narrator shows his people that it is up to them to decide for or against faith, whether God will open up his history with the remnant of his people, which seems to have come to an end, or whether they will be those with whom it comes completely to an end.

Strongly as the narrative comes home to a modern reader, and down the ages shows its power as the divine word which seeks to gain man's trust in God as the master of the future which stands darkly before him,[51] it does need a final reference to its not unchallengeable interpretation of trust in God as pure passivity. Certainly God is the last ground and the last goal of the trust put in him. But as basic trust, this has the task of protecting men from the threat of nothingness which rises up from within them, as well as from that which comes upon them from the outside. However, that does not relieve them of the need to act carefully in this world, nor does it relieve politicians who hold political responsibility of the necessity of making political decisions. Freed from anxiety, the action of the believer should be both more human and at the same time more appropriate to the situation than that of the unbeliever. Only where people are deprived of all possibilities and where destiny reduces them to inevitable passivity, as in the house of death, may he comfort himself with the thought that his trust in God's never-ending present is what is required of him, and that that is enough.

Excursus: The Syro-Ephraimite war. Given the sparseness of the Old Testament sources and the fragmentary character of Assyrian reports, we can obtain only a rough historical sketch of the course and consequences of the so-called Syro-Ephraimite war. As a firm chronological basis we have the information that in the year 734, Tiglath-pileser took to the field against Philistia, and in the two following years, 733 and 732, against the Aramaean kingdom of Damascus.[52] It has been assumed that there was a military encounter between Tiglath-pileser and king Pekah of Israel in connection with the campaign of 734, and that Pekah was deprived of the Israelite coastal strip, which was turned into the Assyrian province of Dur'u/ Dor. However, this is based on the hypothetical reconstruction of a

---

[51] Cf. also F. Gogarten, *Der Mensch zwischen Gott und Welt*, Heidelberg 1952, 424ff.
[52] Cf. the Assyrian canon of eponymi, C^b, lines 40ff. in A. Ungnad, 'Eponymen', *RLA* II, 431f.

fragmentary tablet which at least so far has not been confirmed.[53] As, according to II Kings 15.37, the beginnings of the Syro-Ephraimite war fell still in the reign of king Jotham of Judah, who according to the calculations of the chronology of the kings of Judah by Schedl and Andersen, both of whom agree on this point, died in the year 734/733,[54] his son and successor Ahaz at all events entered upon a difficult heritage.

The campaign of king Raṣyon/Rezin of Damascus and his ally Pekah of Israel was evidently aimed at forcing the kingdom of Judah to join its anti-Assyrian confederation, which at the latest came about under the pressure of the Assyrian campaign of 734. There is still dispute as to whether here they could refer back to the involvement of Uzziah king of Judah in perhaps a leading role in a similar coalition against Assyria, which of course did not come to anything.[55] The narrator of Isa. 7 has certainly concluded rightly that the campaign was specifically aimed at the deposition of Ahaz and the installation of a puppet king who would be open to their plans. In view of the danger which threatened Jerusalem, Ahaz at any rate bought Assyrian help by means of a recognition of their supremacy over his country and the payment of a substantial amount of tribute. The historian cannot exclude the possibility that Tiglath-pileser let things come to this and allowed the war to go on without apparently being interested because a weakening of both the Syrian states was obviously to his advantage. The situation drove the kingdom of Judah into his arms, and the war as a whole simplified the military intervention on his part that was ultimately unavoidable.[56]

[53] For this hypothesis cf. A. Alt, 'Tiglatpilesers III. erster Feldzug nach Palästina', *KS* II, 156f.; id., 'Das System der assyrischen Provinzen auf dem Boden des Reiches Israel', *KS* II, 200f., and against him H. Barth, *Jesaja-Worte*, 164, and S. Herrmann, *A History of Israel in Old Testament Times*, London ²1981, 246f, nn. 13–15; B. Obed, 'The Historical Background of the Syro-Ephraimite War Reconsidered', *CBQ* 34, 1972, 153ff., in his reconstruction of the historical cause of the war stressing a conflict of interest in Transjordan, overestimates the value of I Kings 22.5ff.; II Chron. 26.6ff.; 27.5f. as sources. Cf. E. Würthwein, in *Das ferne und nahe Wort*, Festschrift L. Rost, BZAW 105, Berlin 1967, 245ff., and P. Welten, *Geschichte und Geschichtsdarstellung in den Chronikbüchern*, WMANT 42, Neukirchen 1973, 153ff., 163ff.,

[54] Cf. *VT* 12, 1962, 90f., adopted by Pavlovský and Vogt, *Bib* 45, 1964, 337f., and K. T. A. Andersen, *ST* 23, 1969, 111f.

[55] See *TGI*² 23, 54f., and S. Herrmann, *History of Israel*, 247, who rejects it; M. Weippert, *ZDPV* 89, 1973, 32, agrees.

[56] There is dispute as to how the cultic measures of king Ahaz reported in II Kings 16.10ff. are to be interpreted. In the context of the general verdict passed on the king by the Deuteronomist, they are certainly to be understood in negative terms. What II Chron. 28.22 has made of them is late distortion. Presumably the new altar of burnt offering set up by Ahaz in the temple in Jerusalem was a copy of the altar on which he had sworn an oath to be vassal of the king of Assyria in Damascus. That does not mean that this altar had been dedicated to an Assyrian god; had the Deuteronomist heard anything to this effect he would hardly have refrained from adding this dark

The reports that have been preserved suggest that Tiglath-pileser first turned against Israel in 733, which avoided complete annihilation immediately through the murder of its king and the presentation of his murderer, Hoshea, as the next ruler. However, it paid for its rebellion from Assyria by the limitation of its territory to the heartland of Ephraim. The Assyrian provinces of Dor, Megiddo and Gilead which arose as a result hemmed in the rump state to the west, north and east,[57] while in the south the newly-gained vassal state of Judah seemed to provide sufficient guarantee for the protection of Assyrian rights in Palestine.

After clearing up things in Israel, the Assyrian king evidently marched on Damascus from the south; he succeeded in conquering it in the following year, 732, and similarly included the kingdom in the number of Assyrian provinces.[58] However, Ahaz had thus become the vassal of the great king.[59] That the state of Judah never again managed to escape the rule of Assyria or Babylon, which was then coming into its own, can be seen from the way in which all the attempts to win back its lost freedom ultimately came to nothing and the two last attempts undertaken by the kings Jehoiakim and Zedekiah resulted in the downfall of the kingdom.

---

feature to his picture of the king. J. McKay, *Religion in Judah under the Assyrians*, SBT II, 26, London 1963, 5ff. argues to this effect.

[57] Cf. II Kings, 15.29f., *AOT*[2], 347ff.; Luckenbill, *Ancient Records* I, §815ff.; *ANET*[2-3], 283, fragment from annals lines 1ff.; *TGI*[2] no. 26, 57ff.

[58] Cf. *AOT*[2], 346f.; Luckenbill, *Ancient Records* I, §777, and *ANET*[2-3], 283, Annals lines 205ff.

[59] Cf. *AOT*[2], 348; Luckenbill, *Ancient Records* I, §801; *TGI*[2] no. 28, 59, and Weippert, *ZDPV* 84, 1973, 52f.

CHAPTER 7.10–17

The Immanuel Sign

10 Then Yahweh[1] had the following conversation[2] with Ahaz: 11 'Ask a sign of Yahweh your God. As you do,[3] go deep into the underworld[4] or high[3] into the heavens.'
12 And Ahaz replied, 'I will not ask and tempt Yahweh.' 13 And he said,[5] 'Hear then, you of the house of David! Is it too little for you to weary men, that you weary my God also? 14 Therefore the Lord himself[6] will give you a sign: Behold, a young woman[7] will become pregnant and bear a son and give him the name Immanuel.[8] 15 Cream and honey will he eat, when[9] he knows how to refuse evil and choose good. 16 Indeed, before the child knows how to choose between evil and good, the land *before whose two kings you are in dread*[10] will be forsaken. 17 Yahweh will bring *upon you and*[11] upon your people and your father's house days such as have not come since the days when Ephraim rebelled from Judah, *the king of Assyria*.[11a]

[7.10–17] This narrative has a special significance for the Christian

---

[1] T's reading of 'Yahweh' instead of 'the prophet of Yahweh' is an attempt to harmonize the text of vv. 10, 11. However, at this point 'Yahweh' might have the task of guarding the prophet's offer of a sign in these two verses against the charge contained in v. 22, and therefore might simply be an old dogmatic correction. To support this assumption we need only refer to v. 13, which of course is not to be detached from its context and connected with 7.17–25, as it is by S. H. Blank, *Prophetic Faith in Isaiah*, London 1958, 16.
[2] For this meaning of *dibber* with a following *l'ēmōr*, cf. W. H. Schmidt, TWAT II, col. 106, TDOT 3, 102.
[3] For the continuation of finite verb-forms with the infinite absolute to indicate concomitant circumstances, cf. Joüon § 123r.
[4] For the Massoretic way of writing *š'ālā* instead of *š'ōlā*, which might be expected, cf. B-L, 535f.
[5] The proposal, introduced by Duhm and most recently taken up by Donner, *Israel unter den Völkern*, 9, to change the third person singular masculine to the first person singular common, rests on a misunderstanding of the literary character of the narrative. Cf. above, 141 and below, 152f., 165f.
[6] For the added strength given by the absolute personal pronoun cf. G-K[28] §32b.
[7] The reason for this translation is given below, 154.
[8] For the archaizing form of the third person singular feminine cf. G-K[28] §44f. and 74g and also B-L 376r; for an assessment see the commentary, below 169.
[9] For the use of *l'* to denote the time of an action, cf. Brockelmann § 107b.
[10] For the basis of these literary-critical decisions, see below, 158 and 171.
[11] For the basis of this literary-critical decision, see below, 171.
[11a] For the basis of this literary-critical decision, see below, 152, 171.

Church, so that the section is one of the most important not just of the book of Isaiah but of the whole of the Old Testament. The confessions formulated by the early church still keep echoing the saying about the Virgin Birth of Jesus, recorded in Matt. 1.18–25 as the fulfilment of Isa. 7.14.[12] However, anyone who expects there to be any agreement as to this meaning for the story in academic interpretation will be immediately disappointed at the quite incalculable and constantly growing mass of literature, with its different and mutually exclusive attempts at interpretation. This is a result not so much of the understandable prejudice or embarrassment of interpreters over a text which has so much significance for the history of theology, as of the literary character of the narrative itself.

Thus there is already a dispute as to whether 7.10–17 originally went with 7.1–9 or whether it is a secondary unit. Whereas vv. 1–9 contain a report about instructions given to the prophet Isaiah by Yahweh,[13] the present narrative about the offer and the prophecy of a God-given sign only superficially has the style of what has gone before.[14] So some scholars refer to the different genres and the loose link between the narrative and what has gone before, provided only by v. 10, thereby denying the primary connection, whereas others point out that it remains incomprehensible without the background of vv. 1ff., and accordingly claim that to be primary. In addition, there is the problem of the literary unity of the narrative itself. In view of the lame character of v. 17b with its mention of the king of Assyria, it is clear that the historicizing editor active in 7.1–9 has also had a hand in things here.[15] If we also ascribe to him the identification of the abandoned farmland in v. 16b with the lands of the kings of Israel and Damascus, we necessarily come to understand the whole verse in quite a different way from an approach which sees the explanation as being original. And as, in the threats which follow in vv. 18–25, vv. 21 and 22 seem to look forward to an age of extra fertility for the land after the time of disaster, and can therefore be regarded as an insertion made by a revision concerned with an eschatology of salvation,[16] the question arises whether v. 15, the content of which corresponds to these verses, or more radically the whole section 14b–16, which prophesies the birth of Immanuel, belongs to a comparable redaction, even if not to the selfsame one.

---

[12] For the understanding of scripture in the Gospel of Matthew cf. H. Freiherr von Campenhausen, *The Formation of the Christian Bible*, Philadelphia and London 1972, 10–17. For the reception of the Virgin Birth of Jesus in the early church cf. e.g. A. Grillmeier, *Christ in Christian Tradition* I, Oxford, ²1975, index s. v. Virgin birth.
[13] Cf. above 138f.
[14] Cf. n. 1 above.
[15] Cf. above 137 and below, 170ff.
[16] Cf. below, 177.

In addition, there is the dispute over the meaning of the Hebrew word ʿalmā, marriageable girl, young woman, which the Septuagint, the Greek Bible, translates *parthenos*, and which in Matt. 1.23 is related to the actual virginity of the woman who gives birth to the child Immanuel. Of course, in addition to this there are also the questions who the ʿalmā is and who the Immanuel is and what the sign in fact consists of. Finally, in the literature on the passage the same questions keep recurring as in the case of 7.1ff., whether the character of the narrative as an outside report is original or is only the result of a revision in this direction. As I have given above what I consider to be compelling reasons why the former alternative is to be accepted, and the present narrative certainly does not seem to be comprehensible without the background of the situation outlined in 7.1ff., we may regard this problem as resolved, and maintain the position that 7.10–17 too are a post-Deuteronomistic narrative which was in no way written by the prophet Isaiah himself.[17]

The new beginning with the prophetic formula in v. 18 shows that the passage comes to an end with v. 17. That vv. 18ff. provide so to speak a commentary on v. 17 is not affected by this assertion. The preceding narrative, with v. 9b, deliberately remains open to the reader, but is not in itself directed towards a continuation. That the prophet will carry out the commission given to him is a matter of course, and its consequences are illuminated partly by the report in II Kings 16.5ff., knowledge of which is evidently presupposed, and partly from the situation of the narrator in the time after the fall of the dynasty. The transition from 7.1ff. to 7.9ff. is a strikingly direct one from a narrative point of view.[18] In terms of content, 7.10ff. seems to be about the failure of the king in an hour which is fateful for the further history of his house and of his people, in a situation that goes beyond that of 7.1ff., and seems to draw the consequences of this, along the lines of v. 9b, in an explicit announcement of disaster. With v. 17 we have the negative result of the task imposed on the prophet and its consequences, a catastrophe going beyond the rebellion of the ten tribes of the northern kingdom of Israel from the house of David (cf. I Kings 11.29ff.). That this is the right understanding of v. 17a is confirmed by the development provided in the following verses, 18ff.* This therefore suggests that the narrative in vv. 10–17, while being clearly attached to what has gone before, is a continuation which, in literary terms at any rate, is independent.

[7.14–16] As vv. 21f. correspond to v. 15 and look to a time of

---

[17] Cf. above, 141.
[18] Cf. also above, 146f.

salvation lying beyond the catastrophe announced in v. 17 and in vv. 18ff.,* but are evidently secondary in their context,[19] the commentator must ask whether a similar revision, with a perspective directed towards final salvation, can also be demonstrated in vv. 10–17. However, this question can be answered only in connection with an investigation of the difficult collection of problems contained in the Immanuel prophecy. It is therefore worth beginning by investigating the significance of the central concepts of the story: 'ōt, sign; 'almā, marriageable girl; and the name Immanuel.

Gunkel gave a classic definition of the sign as 'a thing, a process, an event in which one is to recognize, learn or keep something in mind or consider the credibility of a matter'.[20] In the context of the narrative, v. 11 shows that the sign is authentication for the prophecy contained in vv. 5–9. Such a sign can consist in what we would consider to be a normal event (cf. I Sam. 2.31–34; 10.1–12; Jer. 44.27–30; Luke 2.11f.). II Kings 20.8ff. (cf. Isa. 38.7f.) shows that in the realm of legend it can take on miraculous features. Finally, it should be noted that the word sign in an inauthentic sense can denote simply that a certain event announced for the future will definitely happen, rather than authenticate another statement. This is the case in Ex. 3.12; Isa. 37.30.[21]

In the interests of a more coherent account, we need to consider the investigation of the name Immanuel, God with us. Extra-biblical parallels, 'immānū-yāh (Yahweh with us) and 'immādī-yāhū (Yahweh with me),[22] together with the confession of trust in Ps. 46. 8, 12, 'Yahweh Sebaoth is with us', show that this is primarily to be regarded as an expression of trust.[23] However, with its request, 'Yahweh, our God, be with us', I Kings 8.57 suggests that we cannot rule out the possibility of interpreting it as a wish in a suitable narrative context.

The Hebrew 'almā cannot be translated 'maid', because the term now has unavoidable associations with servants, so one can only resort to a bland periphrasis. The Septuagint translated it parthenos and Jerome in the so-called Vulgate translated it virgo. By contrast, the other translations into Greek made in Jewish circles chose the word neānis, perhaps with the intention of thus preventing the church from giving a christological interpretation of the passage. According to the lexica, the words parthenos and virgo do not

[19] Cf. also below, 173f.
[20] Genesis, HK 1,1, Göttingen ³1910 (=⁹1977), 150.
[21] Cf. also Rehm, Messias, 117f.
[22] Cf. J. J. Stamm, 'La prophétie d'Immanuel', RTP 32, 1944, 120, or id., 'Neuere Arbeiten zum Immanuel-Problem', ZAW 68, 1956, 53 n. 18, and M. Noth, Israelitische Personennamen, no. 1077.
[23] Cf. also Noth, op. cit., 160.

necessarily have the connotation of virginity in the strict sense.[24] The use of the Hebrew ʿalmā accords with this: in Gen. 24.43 it refers to a young girl who is nevertheless of marriageable age; in Prov. 30.19 it is already doubtful that virginity is meant;[25] that is certainly ruled out in Song of Songs 6.8.[26] The word seems to denote a marriageable girl up to the birth of her first child.

The fact that one has one view or another about the exegesis of Prov. 30.19; Song of Songs 6.8,[27] does not alter the fact that the interpretation of Isa. 7.14 by the New Testament and the early church as a prophecy of the birth of Jesus by the Virgin Mary is a specialized interpretation of the statement which as such goes beyond the horizons of Old Testament thinking. The text says nothing about how, why or by whom the 'maid' becomes pregnant. It is not even interested in her. One cannot infer more than that the passage is about the pregnancy of a woman with her first child. The citation of Isa. 7.14 in Matt. 1.18ff. is based on the one hand on the presupposition that the Old Testament is a prophecy of Christ and that therefore some details about his life can be found in it, and on the other hand on the conception which grew up in the Hellenistic world, out of earlier religious notions, of the divine conception of a child which comes about without the agency of a human father and in the end conveys simply that 'a certain person was given to the world by God'.[28] In fact this conviction forms the foundation of the existence and the proclamation of the Christian church. And the answer that Jesus is sent to us by God himself is necessarily given by one who, in the face of the proclaimed Jesus, crucified and risen, is aware of the goodness of God disclosed through him, Thus there is no reason for the church to guard over the traditional interpretation of Isa. 7.14, and no reason for the Christian to make fun of a historically conditioned attestation to the unique significance of Jesus for us men.

If we turn to the interpretations put forward in more recent

[24] Cf. H. G. Liddell and R. Scott., A Greek-English Lexicon, rev. H. S. Jones and R. McKenzie, Oxford 1940 (1961), 1339b s.v. parthenos, and C. T. Lewis and C. Short, A Latin Dictionary, Oxford [4]1907, s.v. virgo.

[25] Cf. W. McKane, Proverbs, OTL, London 1970, 658: 'The object of reflexion is the mystery of sexuality. . . . It is the way of a man with a woman and not with a virgin which is the topic of Prov. 30.19 . . .'

[26] Cf. also Rehm, Messias, 53. For the Ugaritic instances, which are essentially grounded in Hebrew linguistic usage, cf. J. Aistleitner, Wörterbuch der Ugaritischen Sprache, ed. O. Eissfeldt, BVSGW 106, 3, Berlin 1963, 248 no. 2150, and the evidence in R. E. Whitaker, A Concordance of the Ugaritic Literature, Cambridge, Mass. 1972, 515, s.v. ǵlmt.

[27] Cf. e.g. the objection by H. Lenhard, ' "Jungfrau" oder "junge Frau" in Jesaja 7.14?', Theologische Beiträge 7, 1976, 264ff. and also L. Köhler, ZAW 67, 1955, 50.

[28] E. Schweizer, The Good News according to Matthew, London 1976, 34.

scholarly exegesis, we find a confusing variety: individual and collective contemporary interpretations, claiming that the sign denotes salvation or disaster or both, not to mention messianic interpretations, fill the pages of a constantly growing mass of literature of the most varied kind.[29] Simply to list them and evaluate the patterns of their argumentation would go far beyond the possibilities of this account. So I shall limited myself to presenting the basic types and assessing them, as a way of marking out the course for my own interpretation. Perhaps in this way we shall also gain a further indication of the literary stratification of the chapter.

We can deal most simply with the *collective interpretations*, which see the sign either in the giving of the name or at the same time also in the further fate of the child. According to these, women who are pregnant at the time of the meeting between prophet and king will give their sons the name Immanuel at their birth for joy at the averting of danger, or dismay at the time of distress which has dawned. In that case, if they were to be a sign for the king, these children would have to meet Ahaz and remind him of the promises and admonitions given to him of which he had taken no notice.[30]

The *indeterminate individual* contemporary interpretation, according to which the prophet had referred to a particular woman nearby and had made the prophecy in question about her,[31] can be included in the criticism of the collective contemporary interpretations. The objection has rightly been made that, first, the sign is too indeterminate and that it is uncertain whether it is grasped by the king;

---

[29] Cf. the account of research and critical survey by E. G. Kraeling, 'The Immanuel Prophecy', *JBL* 50, 1931, 277ff.; A. von Bulmerincq, 'Die Immanuelweissagung (Jes 7) im Lichte der neueren Forschung', *Acta et Comment. Univers. Dorpat* B 37, 1, 1936, 1ff.; J. J. Stamm, *RTP* 32, 1944, 97ff.; *ZAW* 68, 1956, 46ff.; id., 'Die Immanuel-Weissagung und die Eschatologie des Jesaja', *TZ* 16, 1960, 439ff.; J. Coppens, 'L'interprétation d'Is. VII, 14, à la lumière des études les plus récentes', in *Lex tua veritas*, FS Hubert Junker, Trier 1961, 31ff.; id., *Le messianisme royal*, Lectio divina 54, Paris 1968, 65ff.; Rehm, *Messias* 83ff.; and R. Kilian, *Die Verheissung Immanuels*, SBS 35, Stuttgart 1968, 59ff.

[30] A collective interpretation of the sign of salvation has been given e.g. by Duhm, Marti, L. Köhler ('Zum Verständnis von Jes. 7, 14', *ZAW* 67, 1955, 48ff.) and W. McKane ('The Interpretation of Isaiah 7,14–25', *VT* 17, 1967, 213f.), and an indeterminate individual interpretation by K. Elliger ('Prophet und Politik', *ZAW* 53, 1935, 21 n. 28 = *Kleine Schriften zum Alten Testament*, ed. H. Gese and Otto Kaiser, TB 32, Munich 1966, 138f. n. 28). T. Leskow, 'Das Geburtsmotiv in den messianischen Weissagungen', *ZAW* 79, 1967, 177ff. has interpreted v. 14 as a sign of disaster: the name, given by an individual woman, has connotations of disaster. On the other hand G. Fohrer, 'Zu Jes. 7.14 im Zusammenhang von Jes. 7.10–22', *ZAW* 65, 1956, 54ff, has understood the giving of the name as meant positively and then refuted by the catastrophe which breaks in on Judah. E.g. Dillman-Kittel; Guthe (*Jesaja*, Religionsgeschichtliche Volksbücher II, 10, Tübingen 1907, 27, which is different from yet similar to Fohrer, HSAT(K)⁴, Tübingen 1922, ad loc.), and Kaiser¹ have interpreted this as a sign of salvation/disaster.

[31] Cf. the comments in Rehm, *Messias*, 87 n. 206.

second, instead of confirming the prophecies in vv. 5–9 for the meantime, it would be identical with their fulfilment; thirdly, the mention of an *ʿalmā* remains mysterious; fourthly, the form of the birth-oracle chosen in v. 14 suggests a particular mother; and fifthly – and this is at the same time the most important argument against any interpretation which thinks in terms of a pregnancy which has already begun at the time of the prophecy – the attributive meaning of the participle 'pregnant' (*hārā*) which would fit this significance would have required the repetition of the article. As things are, however, it is brought back into the same period of time as what follows, announcing the birth of the son.[32] Or, to put it another way, Hebrew syntax prevents us from assuming that the birth oracle refers to a woman who is already pregnant.

However, there are also comparable objections to the historical interpretations relating to a *specific individual*. According to an interpretation already known in Christian circles in the days of Jerome,[33] taken up again by the great Jewish scholars of the Middle Ages, Rashi and Ibn Ezra, and also put forward by distinguished scholars in this century, the boy Immanuel is none other than a further son of the prophet Isaiah.[34] The prophet is thought to have referred to the royal house with this boy and his symbolic name, and to the whole people with the 'Spoil-speed-prey-hasten' of 8.3f. The trust in God expressed in the giving of this name would then be substantiated by the interpretation in v. 16. Verse 15 is excluded as a later interpretation.

While in this context we can explain as we wish the family relationships of the prophet and the ultimately parallel involvement of his children, and also come to terms in one way or another with the psychology of the king, this interpretation comes to grief not only on the supposition of pregnancy, which contrary to the text is thought to be contemporaneous, but also on the fact that v. 16bβ,

---

[32] On the first two points see Kraeling, *JBL* 50, 281ff.; Coppens, *Messianisme royal*, 71; Kilian, *Verheissung Immanuels*, 85, and Rehm, *Messias* 89; thirdly, it should be remembered that a woman giving a name to her first child needs to have a reason for it. Kraeling and Budde have at least sought such a reason, Kraeling (286) by referring to the greater probability that young women who give birth for the first time conceive sons by older men, Budde, *Jesaja's Erleben*, 51ff., in that he finds here the announcement of a new generation of believers. For the fourth point cf. Stamm, *ZAW* 68, 1956, 52, and Kilian, *Verheissung Immanuels*, 86; for the fifth and last, Rehm, *Messias*, 88.

[33] Cf. Migne, *PL* 24, 112, and further reference in Rehm, *Messias*, 86, n. 201.

[34] Cf. e.g. G. Hölscher, *Die Profeten*, Leipzig 1914, 229f.; Stamm, 'Die Immanuel Weissagung, ein Gesprach mit E. Hammershaimb', *VT* 4, 1954, 33; id., *ZAW* 68, 1956, 53; *VT* 9, 1959, 333; *TZ* 16, 1960, 4; C. Kuhl, *The Prophets of Israel*, Edinburgh 1960, 78; E. Rohland, *Die Bedeutung der Erwählungstraditionen Israels*, Diss, Heidelberg 1956, 170 n. 2; N. K. Gottwald, 'Immanuel as the Prophet's Son', *VT* 8, 1958, 36ff.; Donner, *Israel unter den Völkern*, 17f.

which is preserved in this interpretation, is clearly a gloss: *ᵃdāmā*, farmland, is in no way a primarily political term. The two kings do not have *a* land, but two quite different lands. Here the historicizing editor has intervened and fundamentally misunderstood the significance of v. 16.[35]

It is not much better to refer the oracle to the birth of the future successor to the throne of Judah and son of Ahaz, namely Hezekiah, as has been done by significant exegetes in our own century, following a practice first found among Jews from the time of Justin.[36] In the end, this interpretation ultimately means that Ahaz is promised once again that the present distress will come to an end in the foreseeable future. We may arrange the chronology of the kings of Judah in the second half of the eighth century in such a way that they present no objections to this identification.[37] Nevertheless, we may ask whether after vv. 2f. a sign placed in the hand of the royal house itself is still credible. Furthermore, the same criticisms may be advanced against the presumption that the woman is already pregnant and against the use of v. 16bβ as a decisive element in the interpretation of the name Immanuel, as in the approach which refers the saying to a son of the prophet.[38]

As long as we suppose the scene to be historical, it is impossible to adopt the expedient of either making the prophet look towards an *unknown future* or making him look upon it as a *mystery hidden* even from him, that one day the *recipient of salvation*[39] or the *bringer of salvation*, Immanuel[40], will be born as representative of the remnant

[35] *Jesaja's Erleben*, 57; cf. also Procksch and Fohrer, ad loc; Kilian, *Verheissung Immanuels*, 41f., 101; id., 'Prolegomena zur Auslegung der Immanuelverheissung', in *Wort, Lied und Gottesspruch* II, Festschrift Joseph Ziegler, FzB 2, Würzburg 1972, 207ff.

[36] Cf. Justin, *Dialogue with Trypho* 43.8; 48.7; 71.3; 77.1. Further evidence from the early church in Rehm, *Messias*, 83 n. 193. Among more recent commentators cf. e.g. Bentzen, ad loc.; M. Buber, *The Prophetic Faith*, New York 1949, 139f.; J. Steinmann, *Le prophète Isaie*, Lectio divina 5, Paris 1950, 90; with specific stress on the elements from the royal ideology of the ancient near East; E. Hammershaimb, 'The Immanuel-Sign', *ST* 3 (1949), 1950/1951, 124ff.; with stronger stress on mythological elements; S. Mowinckel, *He That Cometh*, Oxford 1956, 110ff.; from the context of royal ideology or with the enthronement ritual, Lindblom, SMHVL 1957/1958, 4, 24; S. Herrmann, *Die prophetischen Heilserwartungen im Alten Testament*, BWANT 85, Stuttgart 1965, 139f.; Wildberger and Auvray, ad loc., are more restrained on this, as is Schedl, *Rufer des Heils*, 204f.

[37] See e.g. the dating of the birth of Hezekiah by V. Pavlovský and E. Vogt, 'Die Jahre der Könige von Juda und Israel', *Bib* 45, 1964, 342.

[38] Cf. Rehm, *Messias*, 85, and Kilian, *Verheissung Immanuels*, 67ff.

[39] Cf. e.g. Budde, *Jesaja's Erleben*, 52; id., 'Das Immanuelzeichen und die Ahaz-Begegnung Jesaja 7', *JBL* 52, 1933, 22ff., and esp. 24, 31.

[40] Cf. H. W. Wolff., *Frieden ohne Ende*, BS 35, Neukirchen 1962, 37ff., who has been followed by G. von Rad, *Old Testament Theology* II, London 1975, 173f., and most recently by Kilian, *Verheissung Immanuels*, 118ff. Cf. also A. H. J. Gunneweg, 'Heils- und Unheilsverkündigung in Jes 7', *VT* 15, 1965, 30ff.

that is returning. Whether or not he is regarded as the Messiah is in this case ultimately not a decisive matter.[41] If the sign extends into an indeterminate future, it loses its significance for Ahaz (cf. II Kings 20.19 par. Isa. 39.8). If at the same time we keep v. 16bβ, as do Wolff and Rehm, the mystery theory fares similarly, because now while the child must be born in the time-span defined by 7.5ff.; 8.3f., if its birth and its name are a secret, they must remain so, in order that these signs would not be incomprehensible only for the king.

Since the attempts at a solution indicated so far in this survey, which, while being simplistic, is all that is possible in the present context, have all proved to be problematical, we have to raise the fundamental question whether the difficulties are not the result of a misunderstanding of the literary character of the passage and of an over-hasty historicizing which follows as a result. So it is at least conceivable, if not understandable, that one should embark on a new way of attempting to solve the riddle of the Immanuel pericope. In what follows, I shall proceed in three stages, first investigating the significance of the sign without reference to its context, then looking at its position in this context, and finally considering the dates of the strata of the narrative which emerge from this investigation.

[7.13–17] The announcement of the Immanuel sign is to be found in vv. 13–17. To begin with, it can be divided into the rebuke in v. 13 and the prophecy proper in vv. 14–17. Here the rebuke serves as a reason for the following announcement, which is introduced by *lākēn*, therefore. Thus this is the announcement of a sign with a motivation. The prophecy itself is divided into the promise of the birth and naming of a child who is a mother's firstborn (v. 14), the prediction of the food that will be available to him at a particular point in his life (v. 15), and a depopulation of the land which will take place before this point in time (v. 16).[42] There follows in v. 17 a further announcement concerned with the destiny of the royal house and his people, which I took above to be a threat.[43] Scholars dispute whether and to what extent these verses form an original unity. A glance at the literature quickly shows that especially v. 15 (or vv. 15, 17), and also v. 16, can be regarded as redactional additions and excluded from a determination of the content of the Immanuel prophecy. Here some refer to the fact that v. 15 disrupts the necessary connection between the giving of the name and the explanation of

[41] Cf. the position taken by Rehm, *Messias*, 181ff., and the abundant evidence which he cites.
[42] For v. 16b$a_2\beta$, which for simplicity I cite as 16bβ, cf. above, 157f., and Kilian, FzB 2, 270ff.
[43] Cf. above, 153.

the name, and in so doing call on 8.3ff., whereas others by contrast see v. 16 as an addition inspired by 8.3f., which misunderstands the original significance of the prophecy.[44] Evidently commentators are continually irritated by the remarkable chronological restriction in vv. 15, 16 and the difficulties of inserting the complex of sayings which results into the literary and historical context without producing any tension.[45]

[7.14–16] For this reason alone it is worth first considering the next three verses by themselves and then making a separate investigation of their incorporation into their present context. [14] I shall begin with the detail mentioned first: in form this is a birth oracle reminiscent of Gen. 16.11abα.[46] In contrast to its Old Testament parallels, it is not addressed to the mother, but promises that a young, sexually mature girl will give birth to a son in the future and will give him a particular name.[47] As a woman is not called 'almā after her first pregnancy,[48] the son must necessarily be her first child. In so far as the text allows of any conclusion, by its formation the name Immanuel should be taken as a name expressing trust.[49] It therefore follows that a woman giving birth to her first child, a son, in the indeterminate future, will give him the name 'God with us', so expressing her trust. [15] About the further fortunes of this son we are told that when he has learned to distinguish between good and evil, he will eat cream and honey. Although in the Old Testament period the latter may have been understood to be wild honey,[50] there is no reason to regard cream and honey as food eaten in a time of distress. In Ps. 81.17, honey along with wheat is a food which Yahweh promises to his people if they obey him. And cream, which is a better translation

---

[44] Budde, *Jesaja's Erleben*, 56f.; *JBL* 52, 1933, 49; Gunneweg, *VT* 15, 1965, 31f., base themselves on v. 15. E.g. Duhm and Marti build on v. 16 and H. W. Wolff, BS 35, 10 n.q.; Wildberger, ad loc.; Kilian, *Verheissung Immanuels*, 114, on vv. 16, 17.

[45] There is an additional uncertainty in that after the rebuke in v. 13 one would expect a threat, but in the light of 7.4ff, it is imperative that what is promised there be not be put in question, Verse 16bβ seems to take account of this requirement, so that one has to pass over the arguments put forward against its authenticity.

[46] Cf. also Judg. 13.3; also Luke 1.13ff.; 1.31ff. Repeated reference has been made to the Ugaritic Nikkal text *CTA* 24 (Gordon 77), *7 hl ǧlmt tld bn*, which is thought to be a parallel with v. 14b. For this and other parallels in content cf. also Rehm, *Messias*, 47.

[47] Having rejected the hypotheses with which they are connected, we need not discuss the interpretations of *qr't*, cf. also above, 151 n. 8, as second person singular masculine in connection with the identification of Immanuel with the son of Ahaz, or even the change to a *qr'ty*, i.e. the first person singular common, used in addressing the child as son of the prophet.

[48] For the meaning of the word, cf. above, 154.

[49] Cf. above, 154.

[50] Cf; G. Dalman, *Arbeit und Sitte in Palästina* VI, Gütersloh 1939, 106ff., and VII, 1942, 294ff. Honey appears as a typical product of the country, and perhaps also as an export, in Gen. 43.11.

from the Hebrew *ḥemʾā* than buttermilk, butter or curds,[51] was evidently no bad hospitality for a princely guest (Judg. 5.25), even if the host was the wife of a wandering smith. Furthermore, Job 20.17 is evidence that cream and honey together were not regarded as emergency food or the food of nomads. There the wise man declares that both are withheld from the godless. Finally, it emerges clearly from 7.22 that cream is an enrichment of milk, and that presupposes that milk is available in abundance. That cream and honey are described in 7.22 as the food of those who survive the catastrophe need not be an announcement of a time of distress; it indicates a time of blessing.[52] Therefore we are compelled to understand v. 15a as an indication that the boy Immanuel will grow up in a time of salvation. The trust in God's support presupposed by his birth, namely that the boy will grow up under the protection of his God and that God will continue to be with him, will be justified in his life.

Of course there is again dispute as to how the similar information about the coming of the time of salvation in v. 15b is to be understood. In Gen. 2.9, 17; 3.5 (cf. esp. 3.22) it is a matter of the knowledge of good and evil, the useful and the harmful, man's capacity for autonomous decision.[53] On the other hand, Deut. 1.39, with its negated statement, is concerned with a lack of capacity to judge and thus a similar lack of responsibility (cf. also Num. 14.29). If that is the case, the present passage was not thinking of the still almost automatic reactions of the very young child to pleasant or harmful sensations from the outside world, or of the first conscious decisions of a young child, but of an age at which the child has become a sexually mature young man, capable of making decisions, who no longer needs a guardian. That will have been the case in the Old Testament world at the earliest between sixteen and eighteen, and as a rule at about twenty (cf. II Kings 15.2; 8.17, 26 with II Chron. 25.5; I Chron. 23.24).[54] Should the boy be one destined to rule (cf. above all the later interpretation in 8.8b), the passage would similarly imply his capacity to rule as evidenced by an ability to make legal judgments (cf. I Kings 3.9; Isa. 11.1f.; Ps. 72).[55] Therefore, summing

[51] Cf. also Dalman, VI, 307ff.

[52] To find here with Kilian, *Verheissung Immanuels*, 64, 'sparse meals and the devastation of cultivated land', can probably only be explained on the basis of the pressure of exegetical tradition that there is on this passage. For the content cf. also 177, nn. 22, 23, below.

[53] Cf. H. J. Stoebe, most recently *THAT* I, col. 659, and G. von Rad, *Genesis*, OTL, London and Philadelphia ²1972, 88f.

[54] Cf. F. Nötscher, *Biblische Altertumskunde*, HSAT E III, Bonn 1940, 75ff.

[55] To lower the definition of the age because of the context, as is done e.g. by Stoebe (n. 53) or Rehm, *Messiah*, 74, goes against my methodological postulate that the Immanuel prophecy must first be interpreted apart from the context, and will be shown to be justified in the further course of the investigation.

up the meaning of v. 15 as a whole, we can say that when the boy Immanuel has become a young man capable of making decisions, the trust in God expressed in his name will find its divine confirmation in the dawn of the time of salvation. In the last resort the Immanuel prophecy is the forecast of this coming salvation.

[16] In its original form, to be limited to abα$_1$,[56] this verse asserts that land previously worked and inhabited will be abandoned. This simply means that a violent catastrophe will precede the time of salvation. With this sequence of first disaster and then salvation, the Immanuel sayings in no way fit into the history of the Syro-Ephraimite war and the present narrative context: 7.5–9 and 8.3f. expressly predict a catastrophe for the enemy. If we are to take into account the consequences of v. 13, and not leave v. 9 aside, the lack of faith on the part of the king as the representative of the dynasty, manifesting itself in the refusal of a sign, would at any rate have had to be answered by a threat against his house. On the other hand, a further confirmation of the prophecy of vv. 5ff. could be omitted because it is adequately contained in v. 11. In fact it would continue to be in the sequence which goes against that of the Immanuel prophecy: first salvation and then disaster.

In the last resort, the numerous manipulations, beginning even in antiquity with glosses on the text, which try to harmonize the Immanuel prophecy and the text, show evidence of grasping this. If what I have said so far is correct, we must no longer feel compelled to interpret vv. 14–16 in terms of their own context and the contemporary historical circumstances which are presupposed by it, and rather see whether we can find within the eschatological expectations of Judaism a conception which accords with the sequence of times that we find here: first disaster and then salvation. If in resolving this question we are not to get ourselves lost in the broad and crevassed fields of the landscape of Jewish eschatology, we must first of all look at the immediate context. The end of ch. 6 already gives us the necessary indications: after the mention in v. 12 of the magnitude of the forsakenness of the land, v. 13 abα holds a further catastrophe in prospect for the tenth which has escaped the first one. Whatever avoids that will then, according to v. 13bβ, become the holy seed of the new Israel.[57] So a catastrophe coming upon the kingdom of Judah is to be followed by another catastrophe, and then the time of salvation. According to my interpretation, we find the same sequence of three stages in the history of the redaction of ch.

[56] Cf. above, 158 and 159 n. 42.
[57] Cf. above, 133.

1, which ultimately proves to be basic to the history of the formation of the collection which became Proto-Isaiah.[58]

Now of course the actual location of such a prophecy, which looks beyond a future second judgment to a time of salvation, is to be found after, rather than before, the catastrophe of 587. It is evident how similar the historical pattern of 6.12f. is to that of 7.15f. So we can confidently assert that according to 7.16 the eschatological catastrophe will take place in the time of Immanuel, and more precisely, during his childhood. Thus it is clear that the Immanuel verses leave the situation of Ahaz far behind. Whereas the basic text looked forward (from a narrative perspective) and back (in actual fact) to the ending in catastrophe of the policy begun by Ahaz, the Immanuel verses point to the future of the people of God. In this sense Immanuel is in fact the representative of the people of the holy remnant who survive the eschatological catastrophe.

Yet again, there is further dispute over the question whether this representative is an indeterminate figure or perhaps, more specifically, the king of the time of salvation, the Messiah. However, important arguments, which in my view are really decisive, can be advanced in favour of the second possibility: on this presupposition it immediately becomes clear why in this prophecy there is such a mysterious mention of a woman giving birth for the first time. The 'almā is the mother of the successor to the throne, and the successor to the throne is the first son of his mother. Here we need only recall the no less mysterious talk about the abandonment of the people to their enemies by Yahweh until the time when 'one who bears shall have given birth', to the yōlēdā yāl°dā of Micah 5.2,[59] to find this conclusion illuminated. So here the faithless house of David, represented by Ahaz and deposed from rule in the catastrophe of 587, is contrasted with the new royal house of the time of salvation, whose mother will trust in Yahweh by giving her son the name Immanuel, God with us, full of trust despite the clouds of the last catastrophe which is to befall Israel in its history, and who will not be put to shame in this trust.

The Immanuel prophecy does not keep to the requirements of the basic narrative in the stricter sense. Rather, it continues them in the perspective of its eschatological belief and so, by contrasting the transitory kingdom with the abiding kingdom that begins with Immanuel, brings it to a conclusion by surpassing it!

That this prophecy does not in fact belong to the basic narrative is

[58] Cf. e.g. 1.4ff.; 1.21ff.; 1.27f.; and 1ff., above.
[59] For the literary assessment of this promise cf. the references in Kaiser, *Introduction*, 227f. A. S. van der Woude, *Micha*, Nijkerk 1976, ad loc., is now among the supporters of authorship by Micah.

again evident if we consider the difficulties of the historical interpretations in terms of salvation or disaster which exclude vv. 15 and 16,
and see how incapable they are of deciphering the mention of a
woman giving birth for the first time without all kinds of speculations
about the family relationships of the particular figure who is chosen
for identification. Furthermore, the exclusion of vv. 15, 16bβ would
at the same time produce an ironical play on the name Immanuel,
which would be given to the child because the danger had apparently
been averted, without a realization of the true dangers of the
situation. We can hardly assume this to be the case within the solemn
framework of the birth oracle.

[21–22] In addition, the fact that the next two verses, which
correspond to 7.14–16, have only subsequently been incorporated in
their present context and are clearly distinct from the tenor of 7.18–
25, tells against the possibility that the verses which we have
recognized as an eschatological-messianic prophecy of salvation
belong to the basic text.[60] [13 + 14 + 17a] Therefore we may assume
that originally vv. 13 and 14a followed immediately after v. 17a. The
new sign, given by Yahweh himself, was therefore identical in the
basic narrative with the disaster that – in accordance with the time of
the narrative – was to break in upon the people and the ruling house;
according to the time of the narrator, this was something which had
already come about.[61] Here the strange list of the people affected by
it in v. 17, first the king, then the people and finally the dynasty,
shows that one of the members was inserted at a later date. As the
catastrophe which determined the duration of his house did not
come about in the time of Ahaz, but is to be identified with the
conquest of Jerusalem by Nebuchadnezzar in 587,[62] the mention of
the king, which should really have come immediately after the
mention of the dynasty, proves to be secondary. Here we can see
once again the hand of the historicizing editor.[63] In the present
instance he may be excused on the grounds that he could have felt
obliged by II Chron. 28.5ff. to make the addition. It is a remarkable
phenomenon that the eschatological extension of the text was later
subjected to a historicizing reinterpretation, and we have to ask
whether here we have an anti-eschatological tendency, an attempt
to neutralize the message of a further judgment, or a need brought
about by the circumstances of the time to conceal the expectations
directed towards the Messiah's future.[64] In fact, it was only the

[60] I am grateful to Christian Wildberg for a remark which prompted this analysis.
[61] Cf. also Isa. 37.30 and above, 147, below, 168.
[62] Cf. II Kings 25 and e.g. A. H. J. Gunneweg, *Geschichte Israels bis Bar Kochba*, TW
2, Stuttgart ³1979, 122ff.
[63] Cf. above, 158 and below, 170ff.
[64] Cf. also above, 4f.

insertion of the Immanuel prophecy into the basic narrative which brought about the ultimately permanent rounding off of the theme, by responding to the open question of the future of the people with a reference to the new kingdom of the believing dynasty which put its trust in Yahweh. In this way this insertion not only went beyond the prophecy of disaster in v. 17a, but also gave a new significance to the lay figure in this narrative, the prophet's son Shear-jashub: instead of signifying the inescapability of the judgment on the royal house of Judah and its people, he now points into the distance, to the remnant which will survive the final catastrophe and trust for ever in God's support. This is how the name is also to be understood in 10.20–23. And the representative of the remnant is to be Immanuel, the royal prince of the last days. The reinterpretation of 7.10–14a, 17a, was made easier for the eschatological editor by the fact that he could refer the announcement of judgment contained in v. 17a on the one hand to the downfall of the kingdom in 587, and on the other to the last judgment to come.

Having clarified all these preliminary questions, before we finally turn to the exegesis of 7.10–17, a further reference is needed to the derivation of the theme worked out in the narrative 7.10–14a, 17a. I have already pointed out above[65] that it is in fact concerned to depict the negative decision of the monarchy towards the divine message of 7.3–9, along with its consequences. I noted in connection with the investigation of 7.1–9 that the narrative about the offer of a sign as such has the purpose of describing king Ahaz as the antitype of his son Hezekiah, and has therefore derived its theme from the legend contained in II Kings 20.1ff.[66] There is no trace of a further need to take into account the revision of a popular tradition handed down orally, and in view of the distance in time between the period of the narrator and that of the story, which is more than four generations, this is hardly probable.

[7.10–14a, 17a] *The offer of a sign and the decision.* Verse 9b had presented the alternatives confronting the house of David, to trust and endure, or to refuse to believe and to fall. This underlies the promise of deliverance from the danger which threatens, namely of losing the throne if the plans of the confederate kings of Damascus and Israel succeed (cf. 6b). According to the political customs of the time, this would have meant at least deportation and imprisonment, if not the extermination of the members of the royal house.[67] So it is doubly in accordance with the logic of things that in 7.1–9 the

[65] Cf. above, 154.
[66] Cf. above, 143.
[67] Cf. e.g. I Kings 15.28f.; 16.11; II Kings 9.22ff., 30ff.; 10.1ff. with II Kings 23.33; 24.15; 25.6f.

narrator continues with the account of the offer of a sign to king Ahaz. First, this takes account of the need for reassurance which is understandable in the situation; and secondly, it demonstrates the king's lack of trust as the representative of his house by the rejection of a sign, at the same time clearly justifying the final threat. Had the house of David trusted in Yahweh, runs its believing interpretation of history (like the preceding narrative), and not refused the sign of his prophet, it would not have gone under.

[10] The fact that the narrative now introduces Yahweh as subject of the whole of the following conversation with Ahaz is surely the consequence of a revision; for the following dialogue makes it clear that Isaiah is really speaking here. In vv. 11, 13, 14a, 17, only he can speak in this way of Yahweh as 'your and my God' in the third person.[68] The change was meant to link the following scene more closely with what had gone before, the style of which still makes it a commissioning of the prophet of Yahweh, and at the same time to stress that Isaiah had this conversation of considerable theological import – as the meeting with the king in v. 12 shows – with the express legitimation of his God.[69] So the reader is to imagine that the prophet had been authorized to hold it by a divine commission, in the same way as had been the case in the previous narrative (v. 3).

[11] The offer of a sign mentions the heights of heaven as the upper limit and the depths of the underworld, Sheol,[70] as the lower limit, thus giving the king the whole world to choose from for his sign.[71] This extension gave him the chance to ask for a miracle, ruling out any possibility of doubt by its unusual character, of the kind that was requested and given in Judg. 6.17ff., more clearly in 6.36ff., and not least in II Kings 20.8ff. As I have already pointed out, the antitypical character of the scene emerges from the parallel in the book of Kings: the believing king Hezekiah ventured to ask the prophet for a miraculous sign to confirm the promise which had been given to him in his personal distress, and he received it; however, the faithless king Ahaz rejected the sign offered him by the prophet at Yahweh's command, and thus manifested his resolve to obtain human safeguards for himself and his house. Thus the narrator of the second narrative, like the narrator of the previous one, derives from the power of decision of the God who has control over fate and directs all human action to its end, the claim that God alone is effective in the protection of men. Here we have signs of an

[68] Cf. also above, 151 n. 1.
[69] Cf. also below, 167.
[70] For the meaning of the word cf. also L. I. J. Stadelmann, *The Hebrew Conception of the World*, AnBib 39, Rome 1970, 165f.
[71] Cf. also above, 154.

unhistorical quietism of the kind that can arise in communities which are forced out of active involvement in the political shaping of their lives, or have withdrawn from it in order now to live from the realm of inwardness. Such an attitude is quite understandable in the Judaism of the Persian period, which had been robbed of its political independence, but as a result in no way lost its seriousness, because instead of reminding the believer of his secular responsibility, it relieved him of it, and so replaced moral action, which included the political sphere, with the need to wait for a miracle, making belief a venture which called for constantly new trust in God. Thus the answer of the king in v. 12, disqualified by the abrupt tone of v. 13, an answer which goes back to Deut. 6.16 and is confirmed by Matt. 4.7 par. Luke 4.12 as being in accordance with a Christian understanding of faith, is fundamentally justified in the face of the attitude represented by the narrator. Behind it lies the hope of post-exilic Judaism that Yahweh has not ended his saving action with Israel in the catastrophe of 587, and will free his people from slavery by a great change in the world situation. In this sense the narrative reflects the extension of eschatological faith. And to the degree that it expresses the faith of those who, having arrived at the limits of all human possibilities, hope in God, it has about it a dialectical truth, even if that truth goes far beyond the narrative.

[12] In the eyes of the narrator, the king has failed because he was unable as it were to discern the spirits, and thus to distinguish the true prophets from the false. However, in our eyes the king behaved correctly, because he refused to challenge God to demonstrate his power by miracle and thus refused to replace the appropriate attitude of man before God, namely trust in his never-ending support and never-ending presence, with a certainty behind which God would necessarily have to fade into the background. For God discloses himself to mankind precisely in the light of their uncertainty about the future, as the foundation on which we are based, and can only be experienced in trust in his saving presence. As Gottfried Quell noted in connection with Deut. 6.16, and at the same time in connection with the present passage,[72] 'man feels where faith ends and experiment begins. The commandment means that he is to make room seriously for this feeling when the crisis comes upon him in which the opportunity arises for him to evade a decision easily without having done everything possible to discharge the obligation there is upon him. If a prophet comes and proclaims "Nothing is happening", that may be the case. But at the moment when the enemy advances, this fact is also a word of God. It would be folly to

---

[72] *Wahre und falsche Propheten*, BFCT 46, 1, Gütersloh 1952, 175.

evade it by asking for a sign.' Or, to follow Johannes Hempel, 'One's own action and piety are closely intertwined . . .'[73]

[13] In the present narrative, the prophet flares up at the king's answer. While in v. 11 he had described Yahweh to Ahaz as 'your God', he now explicitly stresses that he is 'my God', thus indicating that in rejecting the offer of a sign Ahaz has made his decision, refused the trust that is required, and brought about the break. So there can no longer be any talk of the future permanence of the dynasty, but only of its fall. The narrator sees weariness on the part of God in the rejection of the offer of a sign. It is for him the last and greatest in the series of actions of the house of David towards their people. As there is an allusion in v. 17a to the rebellion of the ten tribes from the house of David, we cannot rule out the possibility that the narrator had in mind the provocative conduct of king Rehoboam towards the assembly of the northern tribes (cf. I Kings 12.1ff.). However, he could also have thought of the charge made against Ephraim in Hos. 12.2f., and extended to Judah, of perfidious temporizing politics between Assyria and Egypt or Babylon and Egypt, which ultimately led to the downfall of both kingdoms.

[14a + 17a] The scorned king is now confronted with the God-given sign as a threat.[74] It will consist in a catastrophe exceeding the rebellion of the ten northern tribes from the house of David, which took place at the beginning of the last third of the tenth century, after the death of Solomon,[75] affecting both people and dynasty at the same time. Given his own point in time, the narrator is in fact referring to the destruction of the Davidic kingdom which took place in 587. Anyone who refuses to believe ends in catastrophe. The catastrophe reveals the lack of faith. In this way the mention of the sign which has become the strongest confirmation of the prophecy gains renewed significance for those who have escaped the catastrophe: for them this has become the authentication of the threat, and thus the God-given sign which warns them in their own time to keep faith and endure, or to reject the prophetic demand for faith which has now been made on them and go under. In this way, the mention of the sign receives its real justification from the situation of the narrator and his community.

[7.14b – 16bα] *The birth of Immanuel.* In view of the promise of the eternal dynasty as it had been formulated in II Sam. 7, as testimony

[73] *Das Ethos des Alten Testaments*, BZAW 67, Berlin ²1964, 95.
[74] For literary criticism cf. above. 164. For the threatening character of v. 14a cf. above 154.
[75] For the tradition cf. also J. Debus, *Die Sünde Jerobeams*, FRLANT 93, Göttingen 1967, 19ff.

to the hope of its return to rule on the throne of David,[76] the question
posed by the Judaism emerging out of the catastrophe which it had
survived by virtue of its perseverance in trust cannot be limited to
the future of the people; it continually led on to the answer that this
dynasty would in fact return.[77] So even the theologian with a concern
for an eschatological salvation, whose words we hear in the Immanuel prophecy, felt obliged at this point to express the hope that
beyond the last distress that was approaching and would overcome
the world and the people of God, there would be the renewal of the
kingdom in the time of salvation. In an obscure oracular style,
adapted to the context and by that very fact proving to be written
work,[78] he made the prophet promise the birth of the child Immanuel
in the hour of the decision leading to catastrophe and of the
separation between God and the ruling house of David (vv. 14b–
16bα). Here the already existing form of the birth oracle, really given
to a mother or father,[79] serves as the vehicle for his prophecy. He
shows the special royal character of the boy by describing the mother
as a woman who is giving birth for the first time.[80] A look at Micah
5.1 shows how popular such mysterious circumlocutions were at
this time. The fact that the hope is expressed in a less constrained
way in 9.1ff.; 11.1ff., suggests that the reason why the oracle has this
style is not political. The purpose is to give a late message the feel of
an early one, and so to make it seem more credible, by virtue of its
riddling obscurity, in the mouth of the long-dead prophet.

[14b] The name of the child, Immanuel, God with us, points to the
mother's trust in God.[81] We can infer from v. 16a that the birth and
the giving of the name come at a hard time. Presumably the
eschatological writing prophet thought of things in analogy in 7.1ff.:
in the face of the gathering darkness of the last time of distress, the
mother expresses in the naming of this child her firm trust in
Yahweh's support. So this again refers back, as an antitype, to the
behaviour of Ahaz. If this child is in fact destined to be the king of

---

[76] Cf. above 147.
[77] By contrast, in Isa. 55.3 the Nathan prophecy with its promises seems to have
been transferred to the people as the recipient. Cf. O. Kaiser, *Der Königliche Knecht*,
FRLANT 70, Göttingen 1959 (²1962), 125f., and C. Westermann, *Isaiah 40–66*, OTL,
London and Philadelphia 1969, ad loc.
[78] Cf. also the comment by G. Roux, *Delphi Orakel und Kultstätten*, 144; 'All authentic
oracles known from epigraphy which relate to controllable historical facts, are written
in prose. Plutarch, our most notable and most competent source, asserts that the
Pythia of his day prophesied only in prose. By contrast, the evidently mythical and
apocryphal oracles are always written in verse.' For the similarly obscure oracle of
Balaam and its ecstatic picture of the prophet, cf. also Kaiser, *Introduction*, 85.
[79] Cf. above, 160.
[80] Cf. above, 163.
[81] Cf. above, 154, 160.

the time of salvation, and if the name is not only an expression of trust and of the guarantee of permanence which lies in him, and consequently of the salvation which can be seen in his life and the life of his people through their preservation in the coming distress and the time of happiness which follows, then he is not only the recipient of salvation but also the bringer of salvation. Through him, God will be with his people.[82] **[15]** When he has attained an age when he is competent to make decisions and to rule (cf. Deut. 1.39; I Kings 3.9),[83] he will feed on cream and honey, the food of a blessed time of peace (cf. Ps. 81.7; Job 20.17).[84] **[16abα]** But before his reign of peace dawns, the land must endure a harsh visitation which will depopulate it. We find this expectation recorded not only in the book of Isaiah but elsewhere; it was current in groups from the later part of the fifth century with an eschatological concern which drew them to apocalyptic.[85] The connection between the end of the time of oppression and the birth of the Messiah child can also be found in Micah 5.2.[86] The oracle does not say expressly that the boy Immanuel is a child of David, so it must remain open whether the author of this prophecy thought of the Messiah as a direct descendant of the old royal house. In the shadow of 7.9b we should probably assume, rather, that in accord with 11.1 the boy was thought to descend from a collateral line from which the dynasty would be renewed.[87] If the author did not want completely to lose touch with probability, he could not attribute more than these obscure allusions to the prophet at the time when he met Ahaz and parted company from him.

[7.1*, 4b, 5b, 16bβ, 17b) *The historicizing revision.* We cannot overlook the fact that the narrative 7.1–17 was worked over by an editor with a concern to historicize it, who has also left evident traces elsewhere in the chapters that we have investigated.[88] As we can tell from looking at these traces all together, his concern was to insert the narrative even more clearly into its historical context. It will be best to ask whether it is possible to discern his underlying interest when we have first determined his way of working. In v. 1 he has rightly connected the general comment that the events took place in the reign of king Ahaz, on the basis of vv. 2a, 5a, 6–8a, 9a, with the report contained in II Kings 16.5 about the Syro-Ephraimite war, and thus added an appropriate point to the verse.[89] By the apparently

---

[82] Cf. also Rehm, *Messiah*, 64f.
[83] Cf. above, 161.
[84] Cf. also above, 160f.
[85] Cf. above 3f. and e.g. Joel 2.1ff.; Ezek. 38f.; Zech. 14.1f.
[86] Cf. below, 207.
[87] Cf. below, 254.
[88] Cf. below, 5f.
[89] Cf. below, 137 and n. 15.

slight change of the predicate of the second main clause from the third person plural masculine to the third person singular masculine, he attributed the main responsibility for the war to the king of Aram (along the lines of v. 5a of the present narrative), thus demoting the king of Israel as it were to being a collaborator. He certainly did not do this without casting an unfriendly glance at the mixed population living there in his time (cf. also II Kings 17.24ff.; Ezra 4.1ff., 6ff.; Neh. 3.33ff.).[90] By passing over the note about the siege of the king in Jerusalem from II Kings 16.5ba, thus leaving the reader unaware of the actual magnitude of the danger, he indirectly strengthened the negative picture of Ahaz.[91]

[4b] Here he felt it necessary to give an explicit explanation of the metaphors. So he did so in a rather pedantic way, saying that the two smoking brands were the blazing wrath of the enemy. However, his list is clumsy: how do 'Rezin, Aram and Ben Remalyahu fit together'?[92] In v. 5b, for the sake of completeness, and perhaps also to stress what one had to expect from these unloved neighbours, he thought it necessary to make express mention of the threat from 'Ephraim' and its king, without paying too much attention to the sentence construction. [8b] If this also comes from him, the question ultimately remains open whether here he had a historical source, unknown to us, perhaps already combined on the basis of Ezra 4.10, or whether he chose fifty as a symbolic figure for a calculable but not too brief time.[93] I referred above to the possibility that here we have a recollection of the reciprocal deportation of peoples undertaken by the Assyrian kings Esarhaddon and Assurbanipal.[94] This need not necessarily be based on a report handed down in writing, but could very well have been preserved in the area concerned. [16bβ] The expansion of v. 16ba by 16bβ has concealed the messianic and eschatological character of the Immanuel prophecy. With clumsy syntax, and perverse in content, the addition identifies the land abandoned by its inhabitants, mentioned in v. 16ba, with the territory of the two hostile kingdoms. Hence v. 16 is one of the main sources of confusion in the interpretation of the Immanuel prophecy. The assumption that the editor himself was the first to relate it to the birth of Hezekiah is at least within the realm of possibility. Indeed,

[90] Cf. above, 137 n. 11.
[91] Cf. also above, 137. The fact that the editor of II Kings 16.5b changed the concluding 'al-'$ahaz$ into an '$\bar{a}l\bar{e}h\bar{a}$ and repeated it again at the end of the verse, could indicate his concern to take over his model as far as it could be reconciled with his tendencies; it could also indicate that he saw the attack on the city of God as *a priori* at attempt doomed to failure, and therefore wanted to give it a more prominent position.
[92] Dietrich, *Jesaja und die Politik*, 65.
[93] Cf. also Schedl, *Rufer des Heils*, 196.
[94] Cf. above, 137.

he must have had some historical context in mind for the prophecy. **[17b]** Once embarked on this historicizing, the editor also changed v. 17a so that it did not look so far into the future. By means of the insertion of 'upon you' in v. 17aα he related his threat to Ahaz, and attached v. 17b with its reference to the king of Assyria as a pure gloss, which resists any syntactical and logical connection with what goes before. As we find a similar note only in the book of Chronicles (cf. II Chron. 28.20), he seems to come at least from the circles to which we owe the Chronistic narrative.

In contrast to those who had the courage to develop in writing the narrative which had come down to them, and thus to draw out the perspectives of faith which it contained in the light of the questions and hopes of their time, here we find a sober, matter-of-fact exegete who has either deliberately eliminated the statements with an eschatological orientation, or in good faith has brought them well back into the past, so as to clarify the meaning of the narrative. Perhaps here he was motivated by a desire thus to heighten the reputation of the prophet whose words had been fulfilled so soon as in a way which could be so easily verified.[95]

CHAPTER 7.18–25

The Great Devastation

18   **And on that day it will come about:**
      Yahweh will whistle
      for the fly from the end of the Nile
      of Egypt, and
      for the bee
      which is in the land of Assyria.
19   **They will come and settle**
      in the ravines of the valleys
      and in the clefts of the rocks
      and on all the thorn bushes
      and in all the thorn hedges.[1]

---

[95] Cf. above, 5f.

[1] The lexica give *nahᵃlāl* as a 'drinking place', but in view of the parallelism, the conjecture by G. Dalman, *Arbeit und Sitte in Palastina*, II, Gütersloh 1932, 323, based on Saʿadya, that *nahᵃlōlīm* can equally well be understood as thorn bushes, is to be preferred. Accordingly to Saʿadya, the *naᵃṣūṣīm* are Christ's Thorn, *Zizyphus Spina*

20   **On that day**
        the Lord will shave
        with the razor that is hired
        beyond the River,
        the king of Assyria,
        the head and the pubic hair,[2]
        and will also cut off the beard.

21   And on that day it will come about
        that each one will rear a heifer
        and two goats.[3]

22   And it will come about that because of the abundance of milk
        which they produce,
        [4]one will eat cream;
        yes,[4] will eat cream and honey,
        everything that is left in the land.

23   **And on that day it will come about.**
        Every place where a thousand vines grew,
        worth a thousand pieces of silver,
        thorns and thistles will grow there.

24   With bow and arrow men will go there,
        for all the land will be thorns and thistles.

25   And every hill which is hoed with a hoe
        one will not go there for fear of thorns
        and thistles.
        And it will become **a place for cattle to pasture,**
        a place for sheep to tread.

[7.18–25] The prophetic formulas 'on that day' or 'on that day it will come about' in vv. 18, 20, 21, 23 suggest that this section is not a formal unit. Analysis shows that it is not a literary unit either. Of the four sayings contained in vv. 18–19, 20, 21–22, 23–25, the first two in vv. 18, 20 clearly show traces of the historicizing revision which can also be found in 7.1–17.[5] This revision again interprets the announcements of disaster, against their original meaning (which emerges from their connection with v. 17a envisaging the catastrophe for the kingdom of Judah in 587),[6] in terms of the Assyrian peril in the eighth

---

Christi, and the *naᵉlōlīm* the sweet briar, *prosopis Stephaniana*. The former can be ten metres and the latter one metre high. *Zizyphus Spina Christi* is not to be confused with the *paliurus spina Christi*. For both see O. Polunin and A. Huxley, *Flowers of the Mediterranean*, London 1965, 122 and plates 350, 361 on p. 35.

  [2] Literally, hair of both legs.
  [3] Literally, cattle (dual).
  [4] The omission in LXX might have been caused by the copyist's eye slipping from the first *hem'ā* to the second.
  [5] See above, 170ff.
  [6] See above, 168.

century.[7] Furthermore, the third saying (vv. 21, 22) falls outside the context of the sayings about disaster because it looks forward to a time of salvation. Contrary to other suggestions, the two verses might be regarded as a single addition,[8] since v. 21 does not make any obvious sense in itself. Thus the slight new beginning in v. 22 might be regarded either as a sign of stylistic weakness or as a consequence of an attempt to give its own promise a broader effect in context. In fact, the insertion of the two verses may be connected with the Immanuel redaction in 7.14b–16bα. In accordance with the observations made in 7.10–17, we might therefore have to consider also in 7.18–25 that the historicizing redaction took place only after the insertion of the prophecy of salvation, though it did not interfere with this.[9] The last saying in vv. 23–25 poses a special problem: here thorns and thistles are mentioned three times (vv. 23b, 24b, 25aγ). It is difficult to discover with any certainty what is the basic text here and what is a later addition. Perhaps, however, the suggestion put forward here, that the original saying should be reconstructed via a natural break-up of the anacolouthon in v. 23a, to be continued in v. 25b (cf. also 5.5), is to be preferred to arbitrary cutting of the text, and is therefore more probable. We can then ask whether the expansions took place in one or more stages, and whether they go back to a redaction with an eschatology of disaster or, in connection with the insertion of vv. 21, 22, whether the Immanuel prophecy in 7.14b–16bα at least presupposes a devastation of the land preceding the time of salvation.

Thematically, the three sayings which form the basis of this section envisage a consistent historical sequence: the first, to be found in vv. 18, 19, prophesies in metaphorical language the complete occupation of the land by an enemy attack; the second, consisting only of v. 20, no longer envisages the enemy coming from Mesopotamia, and announces the depopulation of the land in no less metaphorical language, while the third (in the original sequence, and now the fourth, in vv. 23–25*) envisages the consequences for the cultivated land. As these announcements continue the content of both 6.11 and 7.17, we may wonder whether they were meant originally for their present position or as a continuation of 6.11. However, as ch. 6 looks beyond ch. 7 to ch. 8, and ch. 8 in turn seems to presuppose ch. 7, we should probably assume that the verses go back to the actual author of the so-called memorial.[10] If I have been right in recognizing that ch. 6 and 7.1–17 are texts which have been subse-

---

[7] See above, 5f.
[8] Cf. e.g. Kaiser[1], ad loc.
[9] Cf. above, 164f.
[10] Cf. above, 115.

quently transposed to the time of Isaiah, and which put on his lips these sayings oriented on the future, the literary content of the present verses absolves us from asking whether they were written by Isaiah and from interpreting them in appropriate historical terms. In fact they look back on the downfall of the kingdom of Judah.[11] Verses 21, 22, which were later inserted between the second and third sayings, connect the occupation, depopulation and desolation of the land which they announce (along the lines of 6.13abα and 7.16abα) with the visitation on the land in the last times, the survivors of which will participate in the messianic salvation.

[18] The use of the prophetic formula in the opening of the first and subsequent sayings suggests that from a literary point of view they are not independent, but are connected with what has gone before. So 'that day' is the time when Yahweh will depopulate cities and houses, and bring upon the people and the house of David a catastrophe going beyond the misfortune of the division of the kingdom (cf. 6.11; 7.17a). In a deliberately mysterious but sufficiently evident metaphor, Yahweh is imagined as a bee-keeper who, with a whistle, lures a swarm of bees to his hives hidden in a cleft in the rock. Perhaps the hives were jars, as in Homeric Greece.[12] [19] However, the continuation immediately excludes any idyllic bucolics: by massing not only in the ravines and in clefts of the rocks, but also on all the thorn hedges in virtue of its magnitude, the swarm of bees summoned here takes on a superhuman, giant and dangerous dimension. Thus the reader immediately understands that in truth this is a mighty army which will take possession of the land down to its last corner, advancing at Yahweh's behest and allowing of no escape (cf. also 5.26). The metaphor itself goes back to the observation of swarming bees which hound men in their flight, as periodically recurs in societies close to agricultural life. How popular a comparison this was to describe the irresistible massing of hostile enemy forces is evident not only from Deut. 1.44; Ps. 118.12, but also, in a particularly impressive way, from *Iliad* II, 86ff.

[20] The second saying makes Yahweh into a barber whom he hires – here, to heighten the mystery and at the same time increase the threat, the instrument is substituted for the man using it – to shave off the main hair, the hair between the legs (pubic hair), and the beard (i.e. the whole body) of an unnamed person. The special

---

[11] Cf. above, 145.
[12] Cf. Homer, *Odyssey* XIII, 103ff., and for the attracting of swarms of bees by sounds e.g. Ovid, *Fasti* III, 741ff., and Virgil, *Georgics* IV, 58ff. For bees swarming in clefts of a rock cf. Deut. 32.13; Ps. 81.18; Homer, *Iliad* II, 87f. In addition to the references on 160 n. 50 above, cf. also G. Schrot, 'Biene, Bienenzucht', *KP* I, cols. 898ff., and Wildberger, ad loc.

mention of the beard clearly points to the shameful dishonour involved in this action (as in II Sam. 10.4 par, I Chron 19.4). Nevertheless, the significance of the metaphor cannot be limited to this meaning.[13] The hair on the head and the pubic hair stand for all the hair on the body, which according to Lev. 14.8f. had to be shaved off for purification from a skin disease. Although it is not clear whether the poet is thinking of the land of Judah or, in a comparable way to 1.5f., of the body of the people, there can be no doubt about the purpose of his remark: Judah, occupied by the enemy, will be depopulated with the utmost dishonour.[14] And Yahweh will bring these enemies from beyond the River, i.e. the Euphrates. Against the background of 6.11; 7.17a, we have to understand them as including the Babylonians with their auxiliaries.[15] The poet's standpoint is clearly that of Palestine,[16] so here we have a valuable indication that he was at any rate active in Judah.

[23–25] These verses announce the forsakenness of the land as a result of the depopulation, primarily along the lines of 6.11 and then of 7.16abα. Now we have examples, instead of the metaphors which have prevailed hitherto. Land which would now fetch the greatest price imaginable, because of the grapes growing on it (v. 23a.),[17] will be used as pasture, like a field which has been fully harvested or which is uncultivated because of its worthlessness (v. 25b). One or more later hands have further elaborated the situation of the land after the expected catastrophe, which is presumably already understood to be eschatological. Because the whole land will then be covered with thistles and thorns (cf. also 5.6), people will only venture out into what once were vineyards after taking certain safety precautions against the wild animals living there (vv. 23b, 24).[18] Indeed, for fear of the thorns and thistles, whose spikes are so hard and sharp that they still go through our modern footwear, a further

---

[13] Cf. e.g. Gray, Procksch and Eichrodt, ad loc.

[14] In this connection also Delitzsch, Marti and Feldmann, ad loc., and with Marti also Ezek. 5.1ff.

[15] This rules out the view of e.g. Feldmann, Wildberger and Schedl, *Rufer des Heils*, 217, that in v. 20a there is an ironic reference back to II Kings 16.7f. Cf. also Duhm, ad loc.

[16] Cf. e.g. Josh. 24.2f. with II Kings 5.4 and on the last passage E. Würthwein, ATD 11, 1, 47, ad loc.

[17] There is a parallel to the details about price in v. 23 in Song of Songs 8.11. Rudolph, KAT² XVII, 2, Gütersloh 1962, 185, has rightly pointed out that here one should not suppose that we have true-to-life economic calculations. This is an imaginary price, the highest conceivable. The silver pieces are presumably meant to be silver shekels of 11.4g.; cf. Helga Weippert, *BRL²*, 93f., and, to get some idea of the purchasing power, Lev. 5.15.

[18] Cf. also Gen. 27.3.

reader conjectures that people will not even venture out on to the once-cultivated slopes of the hills (v. 25aβγ).

[21–22] However, in the eyes of the editor with an eschatology of salvation, this is not the last thing to be said to the people. The small group of survivors[19] will manage in a land of quite notable fertility[20] which, according to the logic of Old Testament thought, also means a land ruled in complete justice,[21] with a minimal amount of livestock, and thus save themselves the extra work and toil with a greater herd. They will get so much milk, and find so much honey in the land,[22] that, like their king Immanuel, they will eat the best that their land can offer, cream and honey.[23] That one day all toil will come to an end and that all fighting, disputing and judging will lie in the past is a hope needed by both the individual and mankind as a whole, if they are not to succumb helplessly in the distresses and struggles of everyday life, and in the end simply trouble and impede one another in despair. Even the hope of being able to make this earth rather better and more of a home for all of us presupposes a basic trust in God's never-ending presence. For at the same time it gives to those who hope enough composure not to force the fulfilment of their dreams through violence, and thus bring them to nothing.

As in 7.10–17, the historicizing editor has related the prophecies which reach out far into the future, under the impact of 7.1ff., to the danger which threatens from the Assyrians. Going beyond 7.17b he has also connected them with the Egyptians. Here sayings like Ex. 8.16ff.; Isa. 18.1, and at the same time II Kings 18.21 par. Isa. 36.6; Isa. 30.5, may have strengthened him in his depiction of the Egyptians as flies, who in comparison with bees are troublesome rather than dangerous insects.

---

[19] Cf. also 6.13; 10.20ff.; 4.3; Zech. 14.16.

[20] Cf. also 4.2.

[21] Cf. also e.g. Ps. 72; Isa. 30.23ff.; 32.15ff. Becker, *Isaias*, 57f., and Vermeylen I, 223, see in what is left behind, *hannōtar*, a reinterpretation of Immanuel in terms of the pious remnant of the community of the exile.

[22] Cf. also Hesiod, *Works and Days*, 225ff., and on the subject also O. Kaiser, 'Dike und Sedaqa', *NZST* 7, 1965, 251ff., and id., 'Gerechtigkeit und Heil bei den israelitischen Propheten und griechischen Denkern des 8.–6. Jahrhunderts', *NZST* 11, 1969, 312ff.

[23] Contrary to Gressmann, *Der Messias*, FRLANT 43, Göttingen 1929, 157, the ideal of a basically nomadic and chronically poor people is not to be found here. The relationship of milk and honey to the surplus prevailing in a land can be seen in the Ugaritic text *CTA* 6 (Gordon 49) III, 10ff., as well as in the instances noted above, 000 on 7.15. For this see also J. C. de Moor, *The Seasonal Pattern in the Ugaritic Myth of Ba'lu*, AOAT 16, Neukirchen and Kevelaer 1971, 218.

CHAPTER 8.1–4

A Clear Sign

1   Then Yahweh said to me,
       'Take a large tablet[1]
       and write upon it <with a stylus of disaster>[2]:[3]
       'One hastens[4] to spoil, speeds to prey[5]!'

[1] For the meaning of *gillāyōn* cf. B-L 498c with n. 1 and *HAL* s.v. For the subject-matter cf. also Isa. 30.8. In his article 'Tafel, Buch und Blatt', in *Near Eastern Studies in Honor of William Foxwell Albright*, Baltimore and London 1971, 221f., K. Galling repeated his proposal in *ZDPV* 56, 1933, 209ff. to read *gillāyōn gōrāl*, notice of common land, thus thinking of a legal action. The question is, however, whether one can help out the weakness of the text in this way.

[2] MT, LXX and V read 'stylus of a man'. If we suppose a metonymy in which the instrument takes the place of the product (cf. E. König, *Stilistik, Rhetorik, Poetik*, Leipzig 1900, 17f.), we could translate 'human writing' and explain it as a contrast to divine writing (cf. Ex. 32.16). One cannot exclude such a connotation in a context which envisages a sign from the heavens to the underworld. G. R. Driver, *Semitic Writing*, London [3]1976, 84f., interprets the expression as the opposite to the instrument of the professional scribe. As there is no good philological foundation for the proposal by H. Gressmann, *Der Messias*, FRLANT 43, Göttingen 1929, 239 n. 1, to insert an *'ānūš*, meaning 'hard', and therefore indelible, though it would fit well into the context, I differ from the first edition of this commentary in no longer taking it up. The attempt by F. Talmage, *HTR* 60, 1967, 465ff., to add an *'ānūš* with the meaning 'broad, flexible', referring back to the Akkadian *enēšu* and the Arabic, *'anuta*, 'be weak', seems problematical in this connection, though possible in the sense intended by Galling, *Near Eastern Studies in Honor of W. F. Albright*, 222, according to whom the 'weak' stylus would be a rush, which is in fact what Talmage also means. As MT, LXX and V are possibly mystifying things after the event, and in the OT *'ānūš* more usually means 'disastrous'. I follow Wildberger in taking this as the starting point. The mention of a 'stylus of life' in 1 QM 12.3 gives such a figure a degree of probability. Cf. also Schedl, *Rufer des Heils*, 224. The 'with clear writing' in T shows that it had already explained the text.

[3] For the *l*[e] *inscriptionis* cf. G-K[28] § 119u.

[4] The meaning of the name is also problematical. As the imperative of *ḥūš* is similarly *ḥūš* and not *ḥāš*, it is impossible to understand the verb-forms as imperatives, on which the usual translation 'speed spoil, hasten prey' rests. H. P. Müller, 'Glauben und Bleiben', SVT 26, Leiden 1974, 44, differs. In accordance with the parallelism, we have to interpret the *maḥēr* as a participle from which the participial prefix has vanished, as in Zeph. 1.14, cf. G-K[28] § 52a and B-L 217d. In that case it is still open whether the two nouns are subject or object. As the second possibility, among other things, fits the context better, and there is no evidence for a corresponding use of *mihar* (cf. I Kings 22.9 par. II Chron. 18.8; Esther 5.5), I prefer it to the other, according to which the translation should be: 'the booty speeds, the prey hastens'. S. Morenz, *TLZ* 74, 1949, cols. 697ff., agrees with Donner, *Israel unter den Völkern*, 19, in seeing an Egypticism. A. Jirku, *TLZ* 75, 1950, col. 118, wanted to connect the *maher* with the Ugaritic *mhr*, warrior, cf. Aistleitner, *Wörterbuch*, no. 1532, and also A. F. Rainey, *JNES* 26, 1967, 60, and translate, 'Warrior of the booty, hastening to spoil'.

[5] For the omission of the pausal lengthening, cf. G-K[28] §291.

2   <And I took>⁶ as a reliable witness
      Uriah the priest
      and Zechariah the son of Jeberechiah.
3   Then I went in⁷ to the prophetess
      and she became pregnant and bore me a son.
      Then Yahweh said to me:
      'Call him
      "One hastens to spoil, speeds to prey".
4   For before the young man can say
      "My father" and "my mother",
      the riches of Damascus and
      the spoil of Samaria
      will be carried before the king of Assyria.'

[8.1–4] The first verse of this narrative, which has come down as an account by the prophet in the first person, records in the style of 7.1ff. a divine commissioning of the prophet Isaiah. This time, however, there is simply a symbolic action taking the form of the production of an inscription. Verse 2 presupposes that the commission has been carried out and by way of supplement reports that the prophet took two witness to it (cf. also 8.16). Verse 3a reports how Isaiah slept with 'the prophetess', her subsequent pregnancy and the birth of a son (cf. also 7.14bα). In v. 3b the prophet receives the further commission to name his son in accordance with the wording of the inscription (cf. 7.14β). In v. 4 the inscription and name of the prophet's son are explained together (cf. 7.16abα). Without v. 2 one could simply see the narrative as an account of the commissioning of the prophet to perform two symbolic actions, but v. 2 with its supplementary report of how they were carried out gives it a certain mixed character which even the ancients tried hard to eliminate.⁸

   It emerges from v. 4 that the story relates to the outcome of the Syro-Ephraimite war of the years 734/32 and its consequences.⁹ Anyone who wants to attribute a historical nucleus to it must at all

---

⁶ The translations use either an imperative, 'and take as witness', cf.1 QIsᵃ (LXX and T), or the first person singular of the so-called consecutive imperfect, *wā'ā'īdā*, 'and I took as witness', cf. V. The former is possible in 7.3, the latter in 8.3. The consonantal text of MT requires the first person singular. The pointing presumably wants to understand it as an imperative, without noting as Qere this dogmatic correction, which makes the prophet seem even more markedly to be a mere divine instrument. But in that case v. 2 should stand between vv. 1a and 1b. Thus the reading of V is to be preferred. On the difficulty of reading the imperative with the following ethical dative, cf. G-K²⁸, § 119s.
⁷ For *qārab* as an expression for sexual intercourse cf. e.g. Gen. 20.4; Lev. 18.6; Deut. 22.14; Ezek. 18.6.
⁸ Cf. n. 6, and among the more recent exegetes e.g. Duhm, Marti, Gray, Procksch, Fischer, Ziegler ad loc, and Donner, *Israel unter den Völkern*, 18.
⁹ For the course of events see 148f. above.

events put it chronologically prior to the encounter of the prophet with king Ahaz as told in 7.1ff., and possibly even before the outbreak of any hostilities. However, despite the almost universal view of modern exegetes, it is not so certain whether we can indeed consider it to be historically reliable. In fact the narrative is evidently concerned once again to stress the king's guilt and at the same time to extend it to the people: the prophet had not just presented his message of certain rescue from the king of Damascus and the king of Israel once and by word of mouth; he had also confirmed it by a twofold symbolic action. 8.5ff. suggests that he also had no success with it in the case of the people. So the connection to the style of 7.1ff. as the prophet's commissioning may be a deliberate way of bringing out the relationship of the narrative to what has gone before. Certainly it would not be too much to discover in v. 2, with its array of witnesses, a reference forward to 8.16, and in view of the fact that the witnesses are court officials, a further reference back to ch. 7.

The commission given to the prophet to take a large tablet is probably an indication that the inscription was intended for public display. The involvement of the two high-placed witnesses, the senior priest of the Jerusalem temple, Uriah (cf. II Kings 16.10), and the father-in-law of king Zechariah (cf. II Kings 18.2), is evidently intended to guarantee the truth of the first sign, which occurs at least nine months before the second. In that case, to the first sign, consisting simply of the making (and publishing) of the inscription, is added the second, consisting of the name given to the prophet's son on Yahweh's instructions, which is to correspond with the inscription. If we want to suppose that the meaning of this first sign was revealed to the prophet in fact only in connection with the second, the first sign would simply bring out what was meant in the statement and help to implement it: this was originally the significance of a prophetic symbolic action.[10] Psychologically, it would then be an unconscious precognitive compulsive action anticipating the future. What was meant by the sign would have been incomprehensible to the prophet until he was called on to undertake the second action. However, if we keep to the mere wording of the narrative, even the second sign would have remained private, since the call to perform it is not connected with any command to make a proclamation. So we could regard both symbolic actions as bringing about the downfall of the two hostile kingdoms and at the same time making the prophet certain of their end.

[10] Cf. G. Fohrer, *Die symbolischen Handlungen der Propheten*, ATANT 54, Zurich ²1968, 31.

However, this reconstruction does not explain the fact that the prophet is to write the inscription on a *large* tablet. This feature of the narrative presuppose that the tablet is to be on public display. If the commentator wants to give the second action a public aspect, he must allow free rein to his imagination and suppose that word went around in Jerusalem that the prophet who had once set up this mysterious inscription had now given the name on it to his small son, and that after that, people asked him the relevant questions. The exegete is not happy with this kind of explanation, because he knows that with it he finds himself on the forbidden territory of fabrication. If he supposes that the narrator gave only once, for stylistic reasons, the interpretation that goes *a priori* with both actions, and puts this at the end to make the story tighter and more effective, it is still withheld from the public.

At all events, in this case the interpreter has to read into the story the notion that the prophet gave the interpretation publicly, or saw in some other way that it was made known. Only in connection with the previous narrative about the sign which the king rejected and the subsequent saying against the people does the story gain its kerygmatic significance, and its theological concern become clear. That concern is to put beyond doubt the fact that king and people should have known better and could have done better than they did in the decisive period of the Syro-Ephraimite war. The reader is encouraged to go beyond the chronological problems which already arise as a result of the connection of v. 1 with what goes before, and to consider how the subsequent narrative really fits into the chronological context of the Syro-Ephraimite war. He is to learn from the story that in a time of crisis Yahweh did not fail to give plenty of opportune and impressive public signs which guaranteed the downfall of the two enemy kingdoms, no matter how their significance was read by the people of Jerusalem. And this very indifference of the narrative to historical logic shows that it is a story which from the beginning has in mind this later reader, probably contemporaneous with the narrator, for whom the latter has donned the mantle of the prophet Isaiah.

So we can leave open the question of the relative ages of the prophet's two sons, Shear-jashub (cf. 7.3) and Maher-shalal-hash-baz. The narrator presumably did not ask himself this question, nor did he suppose that we would ask it of his story later. In the inscription and the name, which in English runs 'One hastens to spoil, speeds to prey',[11] we should read a barely disguised reference to the message contained in v. 4, which holds forth a prospect of the

[11] Cf. also above, 178 n. 4.

defeat of the two enemy kingdoms and the plundering of their capitals by the king of Assyria. This recognizes that the plea for help and the voluntary submission of the kingdom of Judah, in the crisis of the Syro-Ephraimite war, to the king of Assyria, with its distant consequences, ultimately leading to disaster, could have been avoided[12] had king and people trusted in Yahweh (in accordance with 7.9b) and believed the words of his prophet supported by such signs. So we should not ask, either, what particular institutional status underlies the designation of the mother of Maher-shalal-hash-baz as a prophetess, but take it that the woman whose children fulfil a symbolic prophetic mission herself partook in the prophetic quality of the father and her children.[13] Finally, we should not see the mention of the highly-placed witnesses to the prophet as a guarantee of the historicity of the report; rather, we should follow Hugo Gressmann in seeing the whole narrative as a legend which, with the duplication of the action, follows a favourite literary pattern and introduces highly-placed figures, known from history, to give it the appearance of authenticity.[14] The narrator was concerned that his insight into their own guilt in the downfall of the kingdom of Judah, and into Yahweh's power over history which was clearly evident at the heart of events, should give his fellow countrymen hope. Instead of counting in despair the earthly battalions which would always be superior to a people that had now become a province of the Persian empire, they should trust in Yahweh's faithfulness towards those who kept faith with him.

---

[12] See also above, 145.

[13] For this approach see most recently also Duhm, Marti, Gray, König, Feldmann, Fischer, Kissane and Herntrich, ad loc. There is of course no dispute over the fact that a prophetess was understood to be a charismatic (cf. Ex. 15.20; Judg. 4.4; II Kings 22.14 par. II Chron. 34.22; Neh. 6.14). Particular attention should be paid here to the parallel between 7.14b, 16aba and 8.3b, 4a, which extends even to the choice of words. According to my understanding of 7.10ff., the reason for this is that the author has taken the Immanuel prophecy as a model in 8.3f. Cf. also above, 144.

[14] *Der Messias*, 239 n. 1.

CHAPTER 8.5–8

Siloah and Euphrates

5 And Yahweh spoke again to me
and said:
6 'Because this people have rejected
the waters of Siloah which run gently
<and quaked>[1] before Rezin and the son of Remaliah,
7 <>[2]Therefore, behold the Lord is bringing up against them
the water of the River, mighty and powerful,
the king of Assyria and all his power.
And it will rise above all its channels
and go over all its banks
8 and sweep on towards Judah, <flooding and subsiding>[3],
reaching even to the neck.[4]
Then the span of its wings will[5]
fill the breadth of your land, Immanuel.'

[8.5–8] 8.5 follows 8.4 with the same formula as that which joins 7.10 to 7.9. However, the connection in content has a looser form, because unlike 7.9b, 8.4 contains no reference to the effect or the consequences of the acceptance or rejection of the prophetic message. In this section, too, we meet the author of the so-called memorial, whom scholars are unanimous in identifying with the prophet of the eighth century, but whose activity according to the view developed here falls only in the early Persian period.[6] In content the brief threat clearly presupposes 7.1–17*, but goes back beyond this passage to 6.10, where the prophet is commissioned to harden the heart of 'this people'. The immediate presupposition for it is the account contained in 8.1–4 of the twofold symbolic action which announces the defeat

---

[1] mśś occurs here for mss (cf. 10.18). For the construction of the infinitive construct cf. Davidson § 96 R 4.
[2] Delete the wᵉ as a dittography.
[3] With Huesmann, Bib 37, 1956, 287, read sāṭōp w ᵉʿābōr. For the construction of the infinitive absolute cf. G-K²⁸ § 113s.
[4] For the use of the so-called imperfect to denote a concomitative action, cf. Bobzin § 7, 1b.
[5] For the incongruency between subject and predicate with a preceding predicate cf. G-K²⁸ § 145o.
[6] Cf. above, 114ff.

of the enemies of the kingdom of Judah in the Syro-Ephraimite war.[7] In ch. 7 the admonition to the king with its unconditional threat was followed by the scene with the sign promised by Yahweh himself in response to the unbelief of the king, the announcement of the coming great catastrophe. In ch. 8 the narrative about the twofold prophetic symbolic action comes at the beginning and is followed by the threat, the basis for which shows that the people cannot but act like their king and thus were themselves responsible for their downfall.

In the rebuke of v. 6 and the threat of vv. 7f., in deliberately obscure oracular style, the poet compares the gently-flowing native waters of the Siloah with the strange waters of the River, the Euphrates, which dangerously overflow their banks.[8] The threat shows that the statement is meant metaphorically: the alien waters inundating the whole land are evidently the hosts of the Mesopotamian powers advancing over the Euphrates into Judaea. The tendency of the memorial is to think not only of the Assyrians, but also of the Babylonians, whose attack finally put an end to the kingdom of Judah in 587 (cf. II Kings 18.13ff., par. Isa. 36.1ff.; II Kings 24.10ff.; 25.1ff.; and not least Isa. 7.20). Here the geographical details alone confirm a metaphorical understanding. In the case of the rebuke in v. 6, on the other hand, we may ask whether it too is only to be understood metaphorically, or whether in a complicated stratification of thought a statement primarily meant to be taken literally is at the same time intended to have a symbolic value. The Siloah or 'sender' is to be understood as the canal which draws off the water of Gihon, now known as Mary's spring. As is well known, the present channel was first constructed by Hezekiah, King Ahaz's son and successor (cf. II Chron. 32.20).[9] We do not know whether this was known to the author of the memorial or not, and how he thought of things in a specific instance. At all events, we cannot completely rule out the possibility that he connected the place names in 7.3, which are meant typologically, with an inspection of the water supplies by the king on the occasion of the expected siege, and saw in Ahaz' offer to subject himself to Tiglath-pileser, and his request for help, the result of a widespread doubt among king and people as to whether the provisioning of Jerusalem would prove

---

[7] Cf. above, 179ff.
[8] Cf. e.g. Gen 31.21; Deut. 11.24; Gen. 15.18; also Isa. 7.20 and 11.15.
[9] Cf. also the builders' inscription in the Siloam tunnel, *DOTT*, 209f.; *TGI*[2] no. 58, p. 66, and *KAI* no. 189; also R. Amiran, 'The Water Supply of Israelite Jerusalem', in *Jerusalem Revealed, Archaeology in the Holy City 1968–1974*, Jerusalem 1975, 75ff. For the early aqueducts which brought the water along the eastern periphery of the city wall cf. Vincent and Steve, *Jérusalem de l'Ancien Testament* I, Paris 1954, 289ff.; Simons, *Jerusalem in the Old Testament*, Leiden 1953, 175ff.; M. Burrows, *ZAW* 70, 1958, 226.

adequate in the case of a lengthy siege by the enemy. However, as we should envisage that the rebuke was concerned with sin against Yahweh, it will have taken the lack of trust in the local streams which provided the city with drinking water as a symptom of lack of trust in Yahweh's promise of protection and thus ultimately as the rejection of the prophet's words by the people (cf. 30.12 and also 5.24). So it is questionable whether the saying (which points beyond metaphor to allegory, as the artificial embodiment of a particular situation, and in so doing betrays its literary character) is meant to be understood to such a complex way. Perhaps v. 6, too, is *a priori* intended in a similarly transferred sense: the people who have rejected the word of their God[10] have in him despised the source of their own life (cf. Ps. 36.10; Jer. 2.13), and as a result will be given over to their enemies. With his picture of the river bursting its banks and flooding the whole country, the poet succeeds in conjuring up the intimation of an uncanny and irresistible danger (cf. also 30.28). In 17.12f. the metaphor of the mighty waters will return in another way as a comparison for the swirling host in their onslaught against Jerusalem in the last eschatological battle of the peoples over the city.[11]

[8b] It is extremely difficult to assess both the form and the content of v. 8b. It is part of the logic of the literary stratification that can be traced right through the so-called memorial that at least the concluding 'God is with us', 'Immanuel', is to be regarded as an addition.[12] As a climax has in fact already been reached with v. 8a, one wonders whether the new beginning at the start of v. 8b contains a reference to an addition. Furthermore, the Hebrew word meaning wing differs from the Latin *cornu* in never being attested as a description for the extreme divisions of a battle line,[13] and its use to describe the tributaries of a river would be limited to the present passage. Thus in more recent scholarship people largely conclude that v. 8b goes directly into the image of a giant bird, so that the metaphor is then interpreted within the framework of the formula of the shadow of Yahweh's wings, as an expression of protection.[14] From a literary point of view, v. 8b would accordingly need to be understood either as an expansion of the threat with an eschatology of salvation or, less probably, as an introduction to the following prophecy of

---

[10] Cf. also Num. 11.20; I Sam. 10.19; 15.23, 26; Jer. 8.9; Hos. 4.6.
[11] For the formula cf. Ps. 29.3; 32.6; 93.4.
[12] Cf. above, 115ff.
[13] Wildberger has rightly made this objection to Kaiser[1].
[14] Cf. e.g. Ps. 17.8; 36.8; Mal. 3.20 and not least Isa. 31.5.

salvation.[15] However, in the case of the single appearance of a phrase, we have to be careful and take poetic licence into account: the poet was not prohibited from speaking of the wings of a stream any more than of the wings of a garment (cf. Hag. 2.12), nor within a metaphorical discourse was he prohibited from using a further metaphor to stress the result of the action.[16] Moreover, if one were to think in terms of Yahweh here, talk of 'his wings' would remain abrupt. Therefore it seems legitimate to incorporate the half-verse into the threat and understand the mention of 'your land Immanuel' as the result of the changing of a simple 'of the land', along the lines of 7.16abα. That, the editor wanted to say, is the distress facing the young Immanuel before the beginning of the change of fortunes promised in the next verses.

[6b + 7aβ] The historicizing editor, whose traces we have continually come across since 7.1,[17] wanted once again to refer v. 6a clearly to the situation of the Syro-Ephraimite war and to decipher the metaphor in v. 7. He was right in so far as the threat posed by the Assyrians to the kingdom of Judah in 701 was in fact a consequence of that country's politics in the Syro-Ephraimite war. Thus announcement and fulfilment come closer together, though at the same time they no longer indicate so clearly the fate of the kingdom. The eschatological dimension of the Immanuel revision is also blurred in this way and drawn back into the historical situation. At first glance one might attribute the insertion of 'and subsiding' in v. 8aα similarly to his honesty: in the true prophetic saying there must have been a mention of the outcome, in this case a reference to the departure of the Assyrian army (cf. II Kings 18.32ff. par. Isa. 37.33ff.).[18] However, we cannot exclude the possibility that the addition already derives from the eschatological editor, who in this way introduced a reference forward to vv. 9f.

The theological significance of this brief threat and the justification for it lies in the extension of the saying about trusting in God and enduring, or failing God and falling (7.9b), to the people as a whole. Perhaps even now it is still not out of date, though we inevitably have the same hesitations about its quietistic undertone as about the

[15] Cf. above all Cheyne, *Introduction*, 39f., who is followed, with variations, by e.g. Duhm, Marti, Gray, Procksch, Fohrer and Wildberger, ad loc., Dietrich, *Jesaja und die Politik*, 98, and Barth, *Jesaja-Worte*, 200ff.

[16] This has been stressed, with differing intent, by Feldmann, ad loc., and Budde, *Jesaja's Erleben*, 77. I have not gone into the phrase 'wings' or 'ends of the earth', since according to A. S. van der Woude, *THAT* I, cols. 835f., it is an adoption of the Akkadian *kippat erbetti* which misunderstands its derivation.

[17] Cf. above, 4f., 137.

[18] For the historical background see also *Isaiah 13–39*, 374f.

basic saying.[19] Responsible foreign policy cannot set itself above the realities; however, it could be that the believer has other perspectives which also take into account responsibility for foreign nations. On the other hand, it is certain that a people which is united in trust in God can overcome its internal and external crises in a different way from a people which ultimately understands itself only as a collection of interested parties, sees material security as its ultimate goal in life, and thus forgets its fundamental togetherness, grounded in a special community of descent and historical experience, and the even more fundamental togetherness that derives from its creatureliness. The former requires internal brotherly union; the latter, brotherly union which is outward-looking. To realize both calls for the courage to love in the face of real conflicts of interest. Faith could provide it, as a basic certainty and a basic assurance.

CHAPTER 8.9–10

God with Us!

9   <Mark it>,[1] you peoples, and be afraid.
       Hearken, all far places of the earth.
       Gird yourselves and be dismayed!
       Gird yourselves and be dismayed!
10   Make a plan – it will come to nothing!
       Discuss the matter – it will not come about!
       For God is with us!

[8.9–10] Recent commentators differ over their literary assessment of this passage. Saebø wanted to see the verses as an ironical prophetic imitation of a summons to battle, and to evaluate them as a saying of Isaiah deriving from the situation of the Syro-Ephraimite war,[2] as e.g. Duhm had done before him and as Wildberger and

[19] Cf. above, 147f.
[1] Because of the parallelism, read *de'û* with LXX. For the absolute use of *yāda'*, 'know', cf. Lev. 5.3. What is said in v. 10 is the logical object of the knowledge. But cf. Wildberger, who argues for *rā'â* II, 'agree together', with reference to A, Σ, Θ, V and T.
[2] Cf. M. Saebø, 'Zur Traditionsgeschichte von Jesaja 8, 9–10', *ZAW* 76, 1964, 132ff. He leaves the *rō'û* in v. 9 untouched and translates it as a derivative of *rū'*, 'Raise the war cry . . .' For the genre, cf. R. Bach, *Die Aufforderungen zur Flucht und zum Kampf im alttestamentlichen Prophetenspruch*, WMANT 9, Neukirchen 1962, 51ff.

Dietrich do after him.[3] Accordingly, the peoples addressed here would be the Aramaeans and Israelites who had conspired against Ahaz and Jerusalem.[4] However, Donner has rightly objected to this identification, because the peoples concerned are obviously a large group of nations. Therefore he has referred the saying to one of the anti-Assyrian coalitions of the years 734/33, 722/21, 720, 713/11 or 705/01.[5] Here he has overlooked the fact that the hesitations which he himself has about the mention of 'all the far places of the earth' can also be applied to his own proposal. Furthermore, the context in both directions requires a relationship to Jerusalem and Judah (cf. vv. 8,14). Though we may not share Wildberger's conviction that the prophet Isaiah made use of the symbolic language of the Zion ideology in the eighth century to interpret the specific situation,[6] we can only conclude that here as in 6.13bβ; 7.14b–16bα; 7.21f., we have a contribution which takes up the theme of hope presented in 8.17 and gives it eschatological form; for vv. 5ff*, 11ff., with their announcement of the coming catastrophe, do not allow of any blurring by a message of rescue.[7] The so-called memorial in 6.1–8.18 originally looked forward to the coming judgment of annihilation, and only at the end indicated that even then hope set on Yahweh would not be in vain.[8]

Thus both the present verses are an eschatological interpretation of the inundation of the land announced in 8.5–8* by the onslaught of the nations, rather than the armies of Mesopotamia, in which for the last time the world rises up against the city of God, only to be put to shame before its gates. In a way which recalls 17.12ff.; 14.24ff., in addition to 29.1ff.; 30.27ff., its author goes back to the belief in the inviolability of Jerusalem at the onslaught of the nations, a paradigmatic expression of which can be found in Pss. 46; 48 and 76. These Songs of Zion are attributed by the tradition to the Asaphites and Korahites, guilds of singers working in the Jerusalem temple in the post-exilic period.[9]

After v. 8 has prophesied supreme danger for the land, vv. 9,10 look forward to the unexpected change in the situation. Anticipating it, the poet summons the peoples called from the furthest areas of

[3] *Jesaja und die Politik*, 134.
[4] For the political situation of the Syro-Ephraimite war cf. above, 148f.
[5] *Israel unter den Völkern*, 26f.
[6] But against this see now especially Vermeylen I, 223ff.
[7] E. g. Marti, Gray and Fohrer, ad. loc.; Budde, *Jesaja's Erleben*, 79f.; G. Wanke, *Die Zionstheologie der Korachiten*, BZAW 97, Berlin 1966, 117; and especially F. Huber, *Völker* 69ff., have voted differently.
[8] Cf. above, 115.
[9] Cf. above, 52, and *Isaiah 13–39*, 86 n. b.

the earth[10] to acknowledge in terror that what they think is an assured plan to conquer the city of God by virtue of their incomparable numerical supremacy will come to naught because in the hour of decision God himself will be with it, as Ps. 46, 8, 10 acknowledges in anticipation.[11] The parallel between v. 10 and 14.24, 26f. is obvious: human plans which clash with God's purposes will necessarily come to nothing, even if they are implemented by an apparently overwhelming supremacy (cf. Ps. 33.10f.; Prov. 21.30; 19.21 and also Ps. 81.13).

This expectation is an expression of the experience that the future is dark not only for the individual but also for peoples and states, and no human art can provide a certain view of it. Here faith encounters God as the limit. That as the limit God is also the limitation of evil follows from the basic certainty of a belief which recognizes him as the other-worldly ground of being, while realizing an inescapable commitment in this world to the neighbour. Only when men wait in trust on God for the future which they cannot see, do they achieve a free community. And where that happens, God is always already present. However, in the conflict between faith and a force which excludes faith, the believer knows himself to be secure in the God who ultimately awaits him. The way of Jesus shows that despite the text, this trust in God's never-ending presence has no guarantee of survival. But faith is distinguished from fatalism in that it believes that God can save even in this world, and so at all events maintains its hope. One characteristic of this faith is that it does not fade with future generations, because like their fathers, believers experience that God is with those who hope in him.

CHAPTER 8.11–15

Just Measures

11   For Yahweh spoke thus to me,
        when his hand became strong,[1] and he warned me[2]
        not to walk in the way of this people, saying,

---

[10] For the phrase cf. also 13.5; Jer. 4.16; 5.15; also Isa. 46.11.
[11] Cf. also above, 168f.
[1] For this infinitive of ḥāzaq cf. B-L 348i.
[2] For the form of yāsar cf. B-L 379t.

12   'Do not call conspiracy
       all that this people calls conspiracy,
       and what it fears, do not fear
       and do not dread.
13   Yahweh Sebaoth, him <you shall regard as a conspirator>[3]
       and he shall be your fear and your dread.
14   For he will become a sanctuary[4] and a stone of offence
       and a rock of stumbling
       to both houses of Israel,
       and a trap and a snare
       to the inhabitants of Jerusalem.
15   And many shall stumble over them[5]
       and shall fall and be broken
       and shall be snared and taken.'

[11–15] In form and content, this is a complicated section. It begins
in v. 11 with a messenger formula which is expanded by a reference
to the special prophetic experience which produces the saying. In
vv. 12, 13 there follow three prohibitions or unconditional commands
to a number of people who are not more closely defined, and
commandments which correspond to them. Thus the admonition –
which is what we can take these two verses to be – does not make
use of the vetitive formula, the admonition and the advice, characteristic of didactic literature and wisdom, but expresses unconditional divine demands. Be that as it may, the group addressed in this
way is separate from 'this people' and connected in a particular way
with the prophet. The two concluding verses, 14 and 15, contain a
threat against Israel, the people of God, divided in its two houses or
kingdoms. In content, vv. 12, 13 provide the basis for the threat; the
conduct of the group addressed here is the way in which 'this people'
behaves.

    Nevertheless, one hesitates simply to regard the pericope as a
threat against Israel, along with the reasons for it, because this fails
to pay sufficient attention to the character of vv. 12, 13. We can
hardly go wrong in understanding the word *yissar*, instruct, warn,
which occurs in v. 11bα, as the key, and take the group addressed
here to be the prophet and his disciples mentioned in v. 16. Therefore
we can define 8.11–15 as prophetic teaching to disciples. In content
it sums up what has been said in the memorial so far. With this

    [3] The 'keep holy' of the tradition could be the consequence of an eschatological
reinterpretation. With Duhm, Marti et al. read *taqšīrū*, but cf. also Isa. 29.23.
    [4] The *leˀmiqdāš* may also be the consequence of reinterpretation, so we might
imagine an original *leˀmaqšīr*, 'to the conspirator'.
    [5] Or 'among them', cf. LXX and V, and 5.27.

function, it is indispensable for the real conclusion of the composition which follows. The characterizing mark of authentic prophetic disciples and pupils lies in a fear of God which takes Yahweh's rule of the world seriously, and accordingly fears him more than all earthly powers. It must also be pointed out that in the context of the general interpretation of the memorial put forward here,[6] those who are really being addressed are not the groups of disciples clustering round the eighth-century prophet, but the people of Jerusalem in the early Persian period who read this work, or are present when it is read. The people of God who have escaped the catastrophe must remember its cause, and draw the necessary conclusions from it for their own behaviour.

[11] It is in accord with this purpose that the challenge to and reckoning over the fate of the people, extending far on into time, should be given irrefutable authority by a reference back to the special connection which exists between God and the prophet. This relationship is mysteriously indicated, more than described, as a strengthening of Yahweh's hand. The closest parallel to the phrase is in Ezek. 3.14, and there are others in Ezek, 1.3; 3.22; 8.1; 33.22; 37.1; 40.1. In content, the formula that the hand of Yahweh comes upon the prophet, or falls on him, indicates that Yahweh has taken hold of him in a special way. In addition to the Ezekiel passages, I Kings 18,46; II Kings 3.15 suggest that contemporaries also thought that this involved a special state of mind.[7] However, here the concern is not to arouse curiosity but to make the teaching be taken seriously. The instruction extended to Isaiah by Yahweh himself demands to be taken seriously not only by him but by all those who hear it.[8] It has prompted the prophet to adopt another course and therefore to lead a life based on other standards than those of the mass of people who are handed over to God's judgment.[9] Those with faith will not be assimilated to the majority, but will exercise the freedom of their

---

[6] Cf. above, 114.

[7] Cf. also F. Haeussermann, Wortempfang und Symbol in der alttestamentlichen Prophetie, BZAW 58, Giessen 1932, 24: 'The coming of "the hand" designates the woes which precede the birth of the word', with I. P. Seierstad, Die Offenbarungserlebnisse der Propheten Amos, Jesaja und Jeremia, Oslo ²1965, 172, who notes: 'It (the term relating to the coming of the hand of Yahweh) merely has the task of attributing a particular extraordinary event explicitly to the activity of Yahweh.'

[8] For the use of the verb yāsar piel with the basic meaning 'chastise', cf. e.g. Prov. 19.18; Deut. 22.18; Prov. 29.18; with God as subject e.g. Ps. 6.2; 118.18; Jer. 10.24; with the meaning 'bring up', e.g. Prov. 31.1; Job 4.3; Isa. 28.26; with God as subject e.g. Hos. 7.15; Jer. 31.18; Deut. 4.36; 8.5. Cf. also M. Saebø, THAT I, cols. 738ff.

[9] For the formula hālak bᵉderek NN, walk in the way of NN, cf. e.g. II Kings 21.22; Isa. 57.17; Ps. 1.1; I Kings 15.26 etc.; II Kings 16.3.

most authentic insights. That comes about by taking God seriously, and can be maintained on this basis.[10]

[12–13] If the freedom of faith, as freedom from public opinion, that vague something for which all and none are responsible,[11] is also to express itself in a different assessment of political facts as well; if it is not to term a 'conspiracy' everything that is so named by public opinion, it cannot ignore public facts like, in the situation of the Syro-Ephraimite war imagined here, the alliance[12] and the intentions of the kings of Damascus and Samaria.[13] The continuation shows that the most important thing is the right estimation of such events. This comes about when those affected fear God first and foremost, instead of their earthly enemies (cf. also 29.13, 23);[14] God's transcendence over the world and his rule of it are presented through the deliberate choice of the title Yahweh Sebaoth.[15] Here alone lies Israel's future and therein its sole reason to hope that Yahweh himself will ultimately have mercy on those who escape his judgment (cf. 8.17).

[14–15] This prophecy is in truth a retrospective judgment on the causes of the decline of the 'two houses of Israel':[16] the northern kingdom, which ceased to exist in 722,[17] and the southern kingdom, which had followed its brother state in 587. According to the judgment made in agreement with the prophetic tradition, the depths of which are attained only in 31.3, both have failed in the fear of Yahweh through what in the end has proved to be their disastrous foreign policy, and with their fear of men have thus put his Godhead itself in question.[18] One can understand this concentration on foreign policy and the complete playing down of what is usually called the social criticism of the prophets[19] if one remembers that their own

---

[10] It should be observed in passing that this freedom is bought with solitude and hostility, and in this connection it is worth remembering the so-called 'confessions' of Jeremiah (15.15ff.; 17.14ff.; 18.19ff.; 20.7ff.; also Jer. 16.1ff.). Perhaps there is therefore of necessity a Gethsemane in the life of every man who follows God's way. There ought also to be a corresponding living Christian fellowship!

[11] Cf. M. Heidegger, *Being and Time*, London 1962, 165f.: 'Everyone is the other, and no one is himself. The *"they"* which supplies the answer to the question of the *"who"* of everyday Dasein, is the *"nobody"* to whom every Dasein has already surrendered itself in Being-among-one-another.'

[12] For this use of *qāšar*, conspire, cf. also II Kings 17.4; Neh. 4.2

[13] Cf. above, 148f.

[14] Cf. also J. Becker, *Gottesfurcht im Alten Testament*, AnBib 25, Rome 1965, 82f.

[15] Cf. above, 126.

[16] This phrase occurs only here in the Old Testament.

[17] Cf. e.g. A. H. J. Gunneweg, *Geschichte Israels*. TW 2, Stuttgart ³1979, 112ff.

[18] Cf. e.g. Hos. 5.13; 7.11; 12.2f.; Isa. 7.3ff.; 30.1ff., 15; 31.1ff. and Jer. 2.13ff., 36.

[19] Cf. e.g. O. Kaiser, *Gerechtigkeit und Heil bei den israelitischen Propheten und griechischen Denkern des 8.–6. Jahrhunderts*, NZST 11, 1969, 312ff.; G. Wanke, 'Zu Grundlage und Absicht prophetischer Sozialkritik', KuD 18, 1972, 2ff.; S. Holm-

political situation was the opposite of what the survivors had hoped for: how was the people of God, some of whom had been scattered to the winds, some of whom were in the province of Judaea and some in exile in Mesopotamia, firmly in the hands of the world powers, to escape this domination and regain their freedom? Only if it was accepted that this situation had been introduced by Yahweh himself and was his answer to the people's lack of trust could the survivors gain new hope in God and confidently look forward to his transformation of the situation.

What the author of the memorial ultimately impresses on his contemporaries is that Israel as a whole has been brought low by its God, and not by the world powers, whom he merely used as his instrument. The God who could have been Israel's rock of refuge in all dangers[20] has become, in what is probably a linguistic innovation, the equivalent of a stone of offence[21] or a stumbling block[22] to a blind man or a nocturnal traveller. And, as the poet puts it, perhaps alluding to the siege of Jerusalem laid first by the Assyrians[23] and then by the Babylonians,[24] he has become a snare[25] and a trap[26] which[27] has seized the inhabitants of the city.[28] An incalculable number of people[29] have been caught in them,[30] in fact by Yahweh, and delivered over to the whim of the victors.[31] So the victory won

---

Nielsen, 'Die Sozialkritik der Propheten', in *Denkender Glaube*, Festschrift for Carl Heinz Ratschow, Berlin and New York 1976, 7ff., and O. Kaiser, 'Der soziale Auftrag der Kirche im Spiegel seiner biblischen Begründung', *NZST* 18, 1976, 295ff.

[20] Cf. 17.10; Deut. 32.4; Ps. 18.3; 31.3f.; 42.10; 62.8; 71.3 and also D. Eichhorn, *Gott als Fels, Burg und Zuflucht*, Europäische Hochschulschriften XXIII, 4, Bern and Frankfurt 1972, 30ff.

[21] Cf. also Sir. 32.20.

[22] Cf. Lev. 19.14; Jer. 6.21; Ezek. 3.20.

[23] Cf. II Kings 18.13ff.

[24] Cf. II Kings 25.1ff.

[25] The formula also appears in 5.3; 22.21; Zech. 12.7f., 10; cf. Judg. 1.21.

[26] Cf. Prov. 7.23; Amos 3.5 and the illustration in *AOB*[2], no. 182, or *BHW* III, col. 2111.

[27] There is some dispute as to whether the Hebrew *môqēš* is a fall-trap (so e.g. G-B[17], KBL and HAL s.v.) or a throwing weapon (so e.g. Wildberger, ad loc.). Cf. H. S. Gehman, *JBL* 56, 1936, 277ff.; G. R. Driver, *JBL* 74, 1954, 131ff.; and for the discussion also H. W. Wolff, *Joel and Amos*, Hermeneia, Philadelphia 1977, 185f. On this question cf. also what Sennacherib says about the siege which he laid against Hezekiah in Jerusalem in 701 (Taylor Cylinder III, 20f.; *AOT*[2], 353; *ANET*[2-3], 288a and *TGI*[2] no. 39, p. 40: 'I shut him up in his palace in Jerusalem like a bird in a cage').

[28] For this pair of words cf. Ps. 69.23; 140.6; 141.9; Josh. 23.13 and Amos 3.5.

[29] In contrast to its English equivalents, the Hebrew *rabbîm* is not partitive but should be understood in a universal sense; cf. also J. Jeremias, *The Eucharistic Words of Jesus*, London [2]1966, 227ff., and O. Kaiser, *Der Königliche Knecht*, FRLANT 70, Göttingen [2]1962, 90.

[30] For the coupling of *kāšal* and *nāpal* cf. 3.8; 31.3; for *nāpal* and *šābar*, Jer. 51.8; cf. also Hos. 4.5; 5.5; 14.2, 10; Jer. 6.15, 21; 8.12; 20.11.

[31] Isa. 28.13 takes over the whole sequence.

by the enemy over Israel is in fact a victory of Yahweh rather than a defeat.

[13a + 14a] Presumably the editor with an eschatology of salvation, whom we last met in vv. 9, 10,[32] changed an original 'regard as a conspirator' in v. 13 into a 'keep holy', and in v. 14 a 'conspiracy' into a 'sanctuary'; this could easily happen, given the similarity of the words in old Hebrew writing. In this way he expressed his expectation that a remnant would survive the downfall of the people brought about by Yahweh's act of judgment and (in his view) announced here, and that they would respond to the holiness of their God with the reverence due to him, thus fulfilling the conditions for future divine protection and so experiencing the dawn of the time of salvation.[33]

In a unique way the apostle Paul understood v. 14 along with 28.16 as a messianic prophecy, and thus imagined that in both passages Israel itself was guilty before God in rejecting the righteousness which had been given through Jesus Christ (Rom. 9.33: cf. also Luke 2.34; II Peter 2.8).[34] One can indeed acknowledge or deny through one's action the unworldly God who supports the world, but one cannot win him over by such action. He discloses himself to those who, in the face of the fear which rises out of the realization of their own nothingness, allow themselves to fall into the divine abyss which is hidden behind them. There is no freedom from this anxiety in religious or other efforts, but only through basic trust in the God who remains man's transcendent source, companion and destiny, by whom we may know ourselves to be accepted without any cause, in accordance with the life and promise of Jesus.

CHAPTER 8.16–18

Waiting on Yahweh

16   I[1] will bind up the testimony,
        seal[1] the teaching

---

[32] Cf. above, 188f.
[33] Cf. also Becker, Gottesfurcht, 44f.
[34] Cf. also E. Käsemann, Commentary on Romans, Grand Rapids and London 1980, 279.
[1] In the rule which is also followed here, in more recent exegesis the two forms, both understood by the Massoretes as imperatives, ṣōr, to be derived from ṣārar (cf.

in the presence² of my disciples
17   and wait on Yahweh
      who is hiding his face
      from the house of Jacob,
      and hope in him.
18   Behold, I and the children
      whom Yahweh gave to me
      are a sign and a portent in Israel
      from Yahweh Sebaoth,
      who dwells on Mount Zion.

[16–18] These verses were originally the culmination and end of the memorial.³ The prophet's proclamation had brought about the object of his mission in accordance with its beginning in ch. 6. It had hardened the people's heart and thus led them inexorably to Yahweh's judgment (cf. 6.9ff.). The king and the people had not been willing to be deterred from their attempt to secure the dynasty and the nation by political means. They had rejected the sign which had been offered them (7.10ff.), or failed to heed the message of the symbolic actions which had been performed in their midst (8.1ff.). Thus they had failed to trust God as they had been required to do (7.9b; 8.6). Accordingly, the promise of rescue given in face of the threat from the northern kingdom and from the state of Aram even further to the north,⁴ was masked and overshadowed by the announcement of the inevitable annihilation (7.17, 18ff.; 8.7., 14f.). In his own way, God had to teach a dynasty and people who feared men more than God, to fear him, so that he could show himself to be God. The prophet, however, instructed by Yahweh himself (8.11f.), stands on God's side, and so do his sons and his disciples. He had done what he could. He had struggled with his people as though their salvation actually depended on him, had they not long been marked out as victims of their stubbornness. So the narrator in conclusion finally makes him concerned to preserve the words of God which have been addressed to him and the instruction he has been given. What according to 30.8 was the express consequence of

---

G-K²⁸ 67o), and *hᵃtōm* are understood as the absolute infinitives of *ṣūr* and *ḥātam* respectively, and accordingly a *ḥātōm* is read alongside *ṣōr*. Otherwise, there would be a divine address without introduction in v. 16, which would be followed immediately by v. 17. Furthermore, the *plene* writing of the imperative *hᵃtōm* would be astonishing. But for a different view, cf. most recently Schedl, *Rufer des Heils*, 241. The agonized literary-critical history extends from Budde, *Jesaja's Erleben*, 83ff., through Eichrodt, 93ff., to Dietrich, *Jesaja und die Politik*, 72f. It bears witness to the difficulties which arise from the autobiographical hypothesis.
² Another possible translation is 'in my disciples'. Cf. below, ad loc.
³ Cf. below, and above 114ff.
⁴ For the political situation which is presupposed cf. above, 148f.

a divine command is here seen to by the prophet of his own accord – that is, if I have understood the verb-forms in v. 16 correctly.[5] Along the lines of 30.8, we may see that the prophet is concerned to preserve his message because it is evidence of the power of Yahweh for the survivors after the catastrophe which he announced has taken place, and at the same time makes it possible to hope for a new future. None other than Yahweh, who had prophesied the misfortune long before it took place, as a punishment for their ancestors' lack of trust in God, had brought this catastrophe upon his people.

[16] In accordance with this, the memorial as a whole is meant to be understood as testimony in the strict legal sense (cf. also Ruth 4.7). The further mention here of *tōrāh*, instruction, may similarly be an evocative usage with an eye to 8.12f. The binding up of the document serves to preserve its content,[6] and the sealing is a guarantee of the authenticity of the memorial (cf. also Dan. 12.9).[7] To keep a writing with complete safety, one might put it in an earthenware jar and seal that as well, as is recorded in Jer. 32.14 and confirmed by the finds at Qumran and in the wilderness of Judah.[8]

The Hebrew preposition *b[e]*, which describes the way in which the disciples or pupils of the prophet are involved, is ambiguous. It can be understood in such a way that the whole statement is a metaphor for the handing on of tradition, without the actual sealing of a document being involved. What would be meant would be rather that the testimony was preserved in and through the disciples, who would in turn hand it on to their pupils and so on down the generations until the message had been fulfilled.[9] However, in the light of 8.2; Ruth 4.7, it seems more likely that the expression should be understood in legal terms, and that v. 16 should be connected with a real sealing of the memorial in the presence of the disciples,[10] who would be present as witnesses to this legal act. If the law was strictly observed, they would have had to sign the document in their

---

[5] Cf. n. 1.

[6] Papyrus 1349 of the State Museums of Berlin is evidence of securing by means of a ring; cf. H. Kayser, *Die ägyptischen Altertümer im Roemer-Pelizaeus-Museum in Hildesheim*, Hildesheim 1973, 31 no. G. 47. But cf also Wildberger, ad loc.

[7] Cf. Jer. 32.14; Isa. 29.11 and e.g. F. M. Cross, 'The Discoveries of the Samaria Papyri', *BA* 26, 1963, 4, 115 fig. 4.

[8] Cf. e.g. *BHH* I, col. 247 pl. 2.

[9] Cf. for this Wildberger, ad loc, and the supporters whom he cites from Gray to Leslie, to whom should now also be added Auvray, ad loc., Schedl, *Rufer des Heils*, 241, and Vermeylen I, 227 n. 3. G. Fohrer, 'Entstehung, Komposition und Uberlieferung von Jesaja 1–39', in *Studien zur altestamentlichen Prophetie*, BZAW 99, Berlin 1967, 140ff., thinks that in view of the different renderings in the ancient translations, *b[e]limmuday* is a gloss interpreted differently at different times, and so solves the problem by excluding it; as Wildberger points out, this is hardly convincing.

[10] Cf. also Barth, *Jesaja-Worte*, 278 n. 6.

capacity as witnesses (cf. Jer. 32.12). Here, too, the disciples take the side of the prophet and thus of his God.[11]

[17] The kerygmatic character of the statement, which is not interested in the development of the scene as such but in its significance, stands out brilliantly as soon as we remember that the section has not been formulated either as a report of such attestation of the sealing, or as an actual piece of documentary evidence, but as a declaration of intent. As such it contains an indirect appeal to the reader to act like the prophet, and like him to hope on Yahweh in an apparently hopeless situation. In terms of form, the expression of confidence to be found in the psalms of lamentation underlies v. 17.[12] Although Yahweh has turned his face from the people,[13] and accordingly will give them over to destruction without hearing their prayers,[14] the prophet will nevertheless wait and hope on him.[15] That in fact means that the prophet counts on the possibility that Yahweh will turn to them again with salvation beyond the catastrophe.[16] In this way the 'until the cities are laid waste, without inhabitants' of 6.11 takes on in retrospect the significance of an actual terminus for the divine intent to harden men's hearts and destroy them. However, according to 7.9b; 8.12f., whether this possibility becomes a reality depends on whether the survivors of the catastrophe fear their God more than the powers of this world, and accordingly trust him unconditionally. Here the group formed by the community of disciples, separate from 'this people', forms as it were the pledge for the remnant who will repent beyond the catastrophe.

[18] Thus the narrator makes his prophet look far into the future, and set his hope on an event which neither he nor his sons are to experience, though they point to it with their whole person, by testifying with their actions and their words, or with their names, to the power of God over the history of his people.[17] If the word of the prophet promising salvation was confirmed when the danger from

---

[11] For the intention of the narrator cf. below, 198f.

[12] Cf. H. Gunkel and J. Begrich, Einleitung in die Psalmen, HK II E, Göttingen 1933 (³1975), 232f.

[13] For the formula 'house of Jacob', cf. e.g. Isa. 2.5f.; 10.20; 14.1; 29.22; 46.3; 48.1; Jer. 2.4; 5.20; Ezek. 20.5; Amos 3.13; Obad. 17f.; Micah 2.7; Ps. 114.1.

[14] Cf. 1.15 and e.g. Ps. 13.2; 30.8; 44.25; 88.15; Isa. 64.6; 54.8 and F. Nötscher, 'Das Angesicht Gottes schauen' nach biblischer und Babylonischer Auffassung, Darmstadt ²1969, 131f. For the discussion of the meaning of v. 17 cf. also Vermeylen, 227f.

[15] Cf. Hab. 2.3; Ps. 33.20 or 25.5; 39.8; 130.5; Jer. 14.22; Isa. 33.2; also Ps. 40.2; Job 30.26.

[16] Cf. also 25.9; 26.8f.

[17] Cf. also above, 139f. and 181. For the coupling of 'sign and portent', cf. Deut. 4.34; 6.22; 7.19; 29.2; 34.11; Jer. 32.21; also Deut 13.2; 28.46, and for the subject-matter Zech. 3.8; Ezek 12.6.

Syria and Ephraim was averted and the hostile kingdoms were destroyed, and the fulfilment of his message of judgment is there for all to see, it is now in God's power to open a new chapter of history with his people. The name of one son, 'one hastens to prey, speeds to spoil' (8.1ff.), points to the lack of trust in the message of salvation, and that of the other son, Shear-jashub, 'only a remnant returns', to the judgment that has consequently become unavoidable. However, in retrospect the latter name becomes ambiguous, pointing beyond the judgment to the return of the remnant in a trust in God which merits the divine promise of enduring which extends beyond time (7.9b).[18]

If we want to know which groups composed this memorial, we must probably follow the traces of the prophet's disciples. Like the sons of the prophets, they have been supposed to be among the personnel of the temple.[19] Once we recognize that the memorial has a pseudepigraphical, epic character, and is in fact to be dated only in the early post-exilic, Persian period,[20] the most likely origin of its author is from among the levitical singers of the second temple who preserved the legacy of the cultic prophets.[21] 7.20 makes it certain that the work was composed in Palestine. This context in the history of tradition also explains the proximity of the writing to Deuteronomic and Deuteronomistic theology[22] and to that of the Psalms.[23] By coming before the community with the writing which they have composed in the name of the prophet Isaiah, they bear witness clearly and simply that the downfall of the two kingdoms of the people of Israel was neither a consequence of the weakness of its God nor the fault of its prophets (cf. e.g. Lam. 2.14; 4.14). The kings and the people of Judah could have let the fulfilment of the promise of rescue from danger in the Syro-Ephraimite war stand as a warning for all times that instead of continuing the course begun by Ahaz and following it to destruction, they should have feared Yahweh more than all human powers and trusted in him alone. But because Yahweh knew that his people would fail to heed the prophet's word, he had sent Isaiah to harden their hearts instead of to convert them, and in this way to bring about all the more certainly the catastrophe the consequences of which had now brought such unspeakable

---

[18] For the primary meaning of the name Shear-jashub see above, 140f.
[19] Cf. A. R. Johnson, *The Cultic Prophet in Ancient Israel*, Cardiff ²1962, 62; also Isa. 35.4, and on this G. Widengren, *Literary and Psychological Aspects of the Hebrew Prophets*, UUÅ 1948, 10, 115; but cf. also ibid., 69 n. 4.
[20] Cf. above, 2f.
[21] Cf. also A. Cody, *A History of Old Testament Priesthood*, AnBib 35, Rome 1969, 184ff.
[22] Cf. above, 141ff.
[23] Cf. also above, 27f.

suffering, and which nevertheless at the same time contained with themselves the offer of a new beginning, if people finally repented. Therefore it was now important, following the prophet and his disciples, to hope in the God whose omnipotence was once again recalled by his name Yahweh Sebaoth,[24] and whose presence on the temple mount of Zion among the community of the second temple was assured.[25]

CHAPTER 8.19–9.1a [8.19–23a]

Help through Spirits?

19 And when they say to you,
'Make enquiries of the spirits of the dead and the knowing ones who chirp and mutter!
Does not every people ask its gods,[1]
the dead on behalf of the living?'
20 To the teaching and to the testimony!
Truly,[2] one should speak according to this word
to him who cannot work magic.[3]
21 They will go through it,[4] oppressed and hungry.[5]
And when they hunger, they will be enraged[6]
and will curse their king and their God,[7]
and look upwards[22] and glance down at the earth.

[24] Cf. above, 126.
[25] Cf. Joel 4.17, 21; also Ps. 135.21 and 9.12. The 'mount of Zion' is mentioned in II Kings 19.31; Isa. 4.5; 10.12; 24.8; 31.4; 37.32; Micah 4.7; Ps. 2.6; 48.12; Lam. 5.18. For the subject-matter see also above, 000.
[1] Particularly in view of the parallelism, the reference is to the spirits of the dead as in I Sam. 28.13.
[2] For the use of the oath-formula as an asseverative particle, cf. G-K[28] § 149e.
[3] The usual translation (which was still followed in the first edition of this commentary), is, 'If they do not speak in this way, there is no dawn for them (the people).' However, with G. R. Driver, 'Isaianic Problems', in Festschrift for Wilhelm Eilers, Wiesbaden 1967, 45, and Wildberger, ad loc., we have to connect šaḥar with the verb attested in Isa. 47.11; it could virtually be translated 'magic'.
[4] I.e. the city of Jerusalem.
[5] For the construction cf. G-K[28] § 118n.
[6] For the vocalization cf. G-K[28] § 54k.
[7] With Driver, op. cit., 46, read a mēʿōp and derive the ʿōp from the Arabic ġāfa.

But there is distress, <inescapable>[8] darkness,
oppression and ineluctable night.
9.1A[23A] Yes, there is no escape[9] for him
who is oppressed by it.

[8.19–9.1a (8.23)] This section forms an appendix to the so-called
memorial on the activity of the prophet Isaiah at the time of the
Syro-Ephraimite war.[10] With v. 19, it is addressed to the disciples of
the prophet mentioned in v. 16, and in v. 20 it takes up the terms
'testimony' and 'teaching' mentioned there, but gives them in the
reverse order, thus showing that here teaching is understood to be
Torah, the written divine law.[11] The writer knows that he has the
law behind him in his polemic against necromancy, illuminating and
ascertaining the future by conjuring up of the spirits of the dead.[12]
There is unmistakably a break in thought between v. 20 and v. 21.[13]
Verses 19 and 20 require the pupils of the prophet in the present
(that is, those who read and hear the Isaiah scroll) not to be led astray
by resorting to conjuring up the spirits of the dead, and in so doing
refers to the prophetic heritage. The feminine entity mentioned quite
abruptly in v. 21 may be identified with the city of Jerusalem, as in
3.25; 5.14,[14] and in accordance with the parallels, the distress may be
seen as the expected eschatological visitation.[15] However, it is
striking that in the inextricable situation which is announced, people
are to curse not only their God but also their king. This might lead us
to see the verses as a *vaticinium ex eventu*, a prophecy after the event,
relating to the catastrophe befalling Jerusalem in 587, especially since
at that time, according to II Kings 25.3f., the city was ripe for capture
through starvation.[16] In that case we would have to understand the
verses as a contemporary preparation for the messianic prophecy in
9.1ff. However, it is not out of the question that the phrase 'curse

---

[8] With Driver, read *minnᵉdōᵃh*.
[9] For the derivation from *'ûp*, escape, cf. A. Guillaume, *JSS* 9, 1964, 290; Driver, op.
cit., 46, 49, and Wildberger, ad loc.
[10] Cf. above, 114ff.
[11] Cf. e.g. Deut. 28.61; 31.26 and 1.5; 31.9.
[12] Cf. below, on v. 19.
[13] Accordingly, Cheyne, *Introduction*, 42, already conjectured that a few lines had
fallen out here. Others, like e.g. Duhm, Marti, Gray, Fohrer, Wildberger and Aubrey,
ad loc., thought that they could regard vv. 21, 22 as an Isaianic fragment.
[14] To this effect cf. also Barth, *Jesaja-Worte*, 153. Otherwise one could think of the
earth.
[15] Cf. above, 82f., 97.
[16] Barth, *Jesaja-Worte*, 154, thinks it possible to date the saying soon after 587. In
view of my late dating of the so-called memorial I could not date the section as early
as this: cf. also above, 2f. Furthermore, the proximity of vv. 19, 20 to Deuteronomistic
and post-Deuteronomistic theology argues for a late dating.

their king and their God' is to be understood proverbially.[17] At all events, in the light of the parallels cited in 3.25; 5.14, it is more likely that the prophecy is meant eschatologically. In view of the loose construction of the eschatological prophecy 3.1–4,1*,[18] one might finally ask whether the section 8.19ff. is not to be taken as a unity.[19] We would then have to exclude only 9.1a [8.23a] as a summary explanation of v. 22.

[19–20] The fact that the editor has inserted his warning against conjuring up the dead, and his call to be faithful to the law and to preserve the prophetic word, in such a prominent place as the end of the so-called memorial shows how great the temptation was to the people of Jerusalem and Judah in the middle of the Persian period to seek an interpretation of the future from the spirits of the dead, in view of the fact that their God was silent and did not intervene. This corresponds with the evidence in the so-called Holiness Code, in which necromancy is punishable with death (though of course this is a later construction, cf. Lev. 20.6, 27;[20] Deut. 18.9ff.).[21] To avoid this danger, I Sam 28 has been worked over accordingly, and the controversy over the matter has been transferred by way of example to the late period of the monarchy ending in its downfall (cf. II Kings 21.6 with 23.24).[22] What was possible and usual among the nations[23] had therefore been long forbidden in Israel. As a consequence of the old separation between the powers of the world above and those of the underworld, and the impurity emanating from everything connected with the dead, anyone who had traffic with the spirits of the dead also became unclean (Lev. 19.31).[24] To the ears of later generations, the way in which the spirits of ancestors were designated 'gods', as in I Sam 28.13, may have also seemed an offence against the first commandment of the decalogue, against the 'Yahweh alone' which was the basic and decisive factor

---

[17] Cf. also Vermeylen I, 230 n. 3.
[18] Cf. above, 67f., 75f., 82f.
[19] Cf. also Vermeylen I, 229f.
[20] For a literary-critical assessment, cf. K. Elliger, HAT I, 4, Tübingen 1966, ad loc.
[21] For a literary-critical assessment, cf. R. P. Merendino, *Das Deuteronomische Gesetz*, BBB 31, Bonn 1969, 193ff.
[22] For the literary-critical assessment cf. E. Würthwein, 'Die Josianische Reform und das Deuteronomium', ZTK 73, 1976, 419.
[23] Cf. Gilgamesh Epic, tablet XII: B. Meissner, *Babylonien und Assyrien* II, Heidelberg 1925, 199ff.; A. Erman. *Die Religion der Ägypter*, Berlin and Leipzig 1934 (1968), 305. M. P. Nilsson, *Geschichte der griechischen Religion*, I, Munich ²1955, 169f.; II, ²1961, 548f., and as an example from shamanism, A. Fournier, 'A Preliminary Report on the Puimbo and the Ngiami: The Sunuwar Shamans of Sabra', in: *Spirit Possessions in the Nepal Himalayas*, ed. J. T. Hitchcock and R. L. Jones, Warminster 1976, 114ff.
[24] Cf. also 65.4, and on the principle O. Kaiser, in O. Kaiser and E. Lohse, *Tod und Leben*, Stuttgart 1977, 48ff.

for Israel's faith and life.[25] The attempt to master the future by means of the spirits of the dead is not energetically rejected because everything is supposed to end with death, but because people should wait for their future from their God, and in the meantime observe his will as it has been revealed. Verse 20b seems to say that deliverance and help do not come from spirits and those who conjure up spirits,[26] but only from Yahweh and from obedience to his will as it has been revealed.

[21–9.1a (8.23a)] Because of the brevity of the allusions, it is not clear whether the theologian who envisages the eschatological threat against Jerusalem wanted to understand the famine in the city as a consequence of the siege by the host of nations (cf. e.g. 3.25; 29.4), or as a cosmic drought expected in the end time (cf. 24.7ff.). Cursing of king and God, which was obviously prohibited according to Ex. 22.27 (cf. I Kings 21.10, 13), and was punishable by death, is at all events to be understood as an expression of insensate despair. In the utter perplexity in which no direction comes from above or below, from prophet or from those who conjure up the dead (cf. v. 21b, 22a),[27] people will curse the powers from which they expected protection and preservation, the political power represented by the monarchy and the God who has all powers under his control.[28] Verse 22b certainly goes back through 30.6 to the conception of the great Day of Yahweh, on which all the stars will cease to shine (cf. Amos. 5.8; Isa. 13.10; Ezek 32.7f.; Joel 2.10; Matt. 24.29).[29] It is the firm conviction of the eschatological prophet that a violent catastrophe awaits the people of God and the nations of the world, which no one can escape. However, in view of the prophetic word of hope in 8.17 and the promises standing over obedience to the law,[30] those who hear this message had to ask whether for a more faithful Israel there would be no hope for a new beginning beyond this catastrophe.

---

[25] Cf. Ex. 20.3 par. Deut. 5.7; 6.4.

[26] For this, cf. also H. Wohlstein, 'Zu den altisraelitischen Vorstellungen von Toten– und Ahnengeistern', *BZ* NF 5, 1961, 30ff.; F. Schmidtke, 'Traüme, Orakel und Totengeister als Künder der Zukunft in Israel und Babylonien', *BZ* NF 11, 1967, 240ff., and for *'ōb* the relevant article by H. A. Hoffner, *TWAT* I, cols. 141ff., *TDOT* 1, 130ff.

[27] Against a merely metaphorical interpretation, cf. also Wildberger, ad loc.

[28] For an understanding of the curse as a power-laden word which diminishes the life force cf. J. Hempel, 'Die israelitischen Anschauungen von Segen und Fluch im Lichte altorientalischer Parallelen', in *Apoxysmata*, BZAW 81, Berlin 1961, 30ff.

[29] Cf. also above, 61f. on 2.10ff., and *Isaiah 13–39*, 15f.

[30] Cf. e.g. Deut. 28.1ff. and Lev. 26.3ff.

CHAPTER 9.1b–7 [8.23b–9.6]

The Saviour of the People

9.1b [8.23b] As in the past he brought shame upon the land of Zebulon and the land of Naphtali, so later he has made glorious the way of the sea, the land beyond the Jordan, the circle of the nations.

2[1]   The people who walked in darkness[1]
        saw a great light.
        A light shone on those
        who dwelt in the dark[2] land.
3[2]   You made much <of the rejoicing>,[3]
        you made the joy great.
        People rejoice before you,
        like the rejoicing at the harvest,[4]
        as they rejoice
        at the dividing[5] of the spoil.
4[3]   For his burdensome[6] yoke
        and <the wood>[7] of his shoulders,
        the staff of his oppressor,[8]
        you broke as on the day of Midian.
5[4]   For every boot
        treading in tumult,
        and <every>[9] garment
        rolled in blood,[10]

[1] For the combination of a noun in the singular in a collective sense with a plural adjective, cf. G-K[28] § 132g.
[2] Following a tradition which can already be detected in LXX, the Massoretic pointing interprets this as 'shadow of death'. Presumably the noun was *ṣalmūt* cf. Akkadian *ṣalāmu*, be or become black, dark, *AHw* III, 1076.
[3] M: you made him many people. On *lō'* for *lō* cf. G-K[28] §103g. But the parallelism similarly requires a *haggīlā*, just as the context rules out a reference forward to the king.
[4] For the construct before a preposition cf. G-K[28] §130a.
[5] Literally, 'they . . . over their . . .'
[6] For the so-called *dagesh forte dirimens* cf. G-K[28] §20h.
[7] With *HAL*, 543 a s.v. *maṭṭe*, read *mōṭat*; cf. also Wildberger, ad loc.
[8] For the construction cf. also Ex. 5.6.
[9] A *kol* may need to be inserted here for the sake of the metre and for parallelism; cf. Duhm et al.
[10] For the use of the plural cf. G-K[28] § 124n.

became[11] a brand,
food for the fire.

6[5]   For to us a child has been born,
a son has been given to us,
and the government came
upon his shoulders,
and his name was proclaimed,
'He who plans wonders,
divine hero,
father of spoil,[12]
prince of peace[13]!'

7[6]   Great is the rule,
and of the peace no end
on the throne of David
and in his kingdom,
because he sets it up
and upholds it
with justice and righteousness,
from now to eternity.
The zeal of Yahweh Sebaoth[14]
will do this.

[9.1b–7(8.23b+9.1–6)] The interpretation of the messianic prophecy in 9.2–7 [1–6] has been necessarily overshadowed in recent decades by the brilliant interpretation produced by Albrecht Alt in 1950. Alt thought that he could see that 9.1b [8.23b] formed the original introduction to this oracle and it provided the key to his understanding. As this half-verse seems to envisage the special fate of the Israelite coastal province, Galilee and Gilead, areas which were separated from the state alliance making up the northern kingdom at the latest in 733/32, and were turned into Assyrian provinces (cf. II Kings 15.29),[15] the prophet was thought to prophesy their imminent liberation and the accession of a son of David who would fulfil

---

[11] For the verb construction, which, despite the comments of Lindblom, SMVHL, 1957/58, 4, 33, and Wildberger, ad loc., does not imply a future meaning, cf. G-K[28] §§ 112mm and 143d; for the congruence cf. ibid., § 146e.
[12] Cf. below on v. 5.
[13] There is still a dispute as to whether the l[e]marbē, written strangely with a final mēm, which has to be divided into an lm and a rabbā, should be regarded as a reference to a fifth throne name which has fallen out except for the lm (e.g. with K.–D. Schunck, 'Der fünfte Thronname des Messias (Jes. 9, 5–6)', VT 23, 1973, 108ff., expanding it to šōpēṭ 'ōlām, eternal judge), or whether we have a dittography of the preceding šālōm. Cf. also W. Zimmerli, 'Vier oder fünf Thronnamen des messianischen Herrschers von Hes 9,5b, 6', VT 22, 1972, 249ff.
[14] Cf. 37.22 with II Kings 19,31, where the Sebaoth is missing in the ketīb.
[15] Cf. above, 148f.

all the hope of the people.[16] Thus 9.2–3, 4–5 [1–2, 3–4] would vividly present 'in a series of pictures, loosely attached to one another', the process of the restoration of the 'honour and glory of the parts of the kingdom of Israel annexed by the Assyrians', as announced in abstract terms in 9.1b [8.23b].[17] From the mention of the day of Midian in v.4 [3], Alt drew the conclusion that there was a nocturnal act of deliverance, performed by Yahweh alone, the night of liberation, which according to vv. 6f. [5f.] was to follow the accession of a son of David in Jerusalem. In that case, in the two latter verses we would have 'the official message of the Jerusalem court' about the ceremonial acts of the change of rule and the programme of the new ruler, which the prophet would have been thought to have sent to the liberated provinces of the northern kingdom on the same day, as a herald's message.[18] Attractive though Alt's interpretation is – and not just at first sight – and right though he may be in directing the exegete's attention to the institutional background of the prophecy, in the long run he fails to allay hesitations about the Isaianic authorship of the section and to carry conviction with his view as a whole.

Without being aware of the fact, Alt himself has given one indication of the inadequacy of his interpretation when, referring to 7.8a, 9a, 8.4, he declared that Isaiah 'did not just consider the return of the liberated provinces into the alliance of the kingdom of Israel . . . since this remnant still stood under the threat of Yahweh's judgment'.[19] As soon as we begin to imagine this in historical reality, serious difficulties immediately arise, because we cannot see through whom and how the judgment is to be inflicted on Ephraim, the heart of the northern kingdom, now almost surrounded on all sides by the Davidic kingdom, since the Assyrians have been destroyed by a divine wonder.[20] In addition, however, the connection of 9.1b [8.23b] with 9.2ff. [1ff.] already rooted in the tradition of the Septuagint and the Vulgate, the Greek and Latin translations of the Bible, and not

[16] 'Jesaja 8, 23–9,6. Befreiungsnacht und Kronungstag', in *Festschrift Alfred Bertholet*, Tübingen 1950, 29ff. = *KS* II, Munich 1953, 206ff. He has been followed, e.g. by the first edition of this commentary, ad loc.; G. von Rad, *Old Testament Theology* II, London 1975, 171f.; J. Becker, *Isaias – Der Prophet und sein Buch*, SBS 30, Stuttgart 1977, 40; Wildberger and Auvray, ad loc.; Barth, *Jesaja-Worte*, 142f., though with a different placing and attribution of authorship; K. Koch, *The Prophets*, Vol. 1, London and Philadelphia 1982, 133; with some reservations also S. Herrmann, *Die prophetischen Heilserwartungen im Alten Testament*, BWANT 85, Stuttgart 1965, 132f., and W. Zimmerli, *Old Testament Theology in Outline*, Edinburgh 1978, 195.

[17] Op. cit., 38 = 214.

[18] Ibid., 45 = 221.

[19] Ibid., 46 = 222.

[20] One can sense a certain uneasiness in the apostrophizing of Alt's idea by Herrmann, op. cit., and the rejection of this notion in Becker, SBS 30, 24f.

least in Matt 4.12–16, is questionable. There is nothing in 9.2–7 [1–6] to suggest that the perspective of the prophecy is simply narrowed to the inhabitants of the former northern and eastern provinces of the kingdom. With its mention of the people, v. 2 [1] suggests, rather, its totality.[21] Moreover, 9.1b [8.23b], with its contrast between the former shame and later honour of the areas in question, seems to be formulated at a greater distance in time from the events reported than Alt assumes. Here the mention of the 'circle of the nations' shows that a mixed population has settled in Galilee, which came about as a consequence of the separation of the district from the Israelite alliance by virtue of the Assyrian policy of population displacement (cf. also I Macc. 5.15). Finally, it is questionable whether the 'way of the sea' is really a reference to the later Assyrian province of Dor; it seems, rather, to envisage in quite general terms the land extending to the west, as is suggested in I Kings 18.43; Ezek. 41.12.[22] Above all, there is nothing in the syntax to suggest that the first half of the statement should be understood historically and the second prophetically. As a purely prophetic interpretation is ruled out, 9.1b [8.23b] must necessarily be understood historically. Therefore in this half-verse we may once again have come up against the historicizing editor, traces of whom we have kept finding since 3.8. He probably attempted to interpret the prophecy in 9.2.7 [1–6] in the light of II Kings 15.29, and thus to neutralize it by regarding it as having already been fulfilled. However, as there is no event in later history, down to the fifth century, which justifies talk about bringing honour to this area,[23] we get the impression that this editor was concerned to remove the political offence that might be caused by these prophecies.

[9.2–7(1–6)] The genre of the oracle contained in this passage is not easy to define.[24] With its assurance that the zeal of Yahweh will bring about what is celebrated here, v.6bβ shows that we should

---

[21] For this cf. e.g. Marti ad loc., and Rehm, *Messias*, 139f.; H. Graf Reventlow, 'A Syncretistic Enthronement Hymn in Is 9,1–6', *UF* 3, 1971, 321f.; Dietrich, *Jesaja und die Politik*, 206 n. 38, and Vermeylen I, 237ff. Cf. also the criticism of Lindblom, SMHVL 1957/58, 4, 40, and H.-P. Müller, 'Uns ist ein Kind geboren . . . (Jes 9, 1–6 in traditionsgeschichtlicher Sicht)', *EvTh* 21, 1961, 408ff. As a further argument against the combination of 8.23 and 9.1ff. it is worth noting the point made by H. W. Wolff, *Friede ohne Ende. Eine Auslegung von Jes. 1–7 und 9, 1–6*, BS 35, Neukirchen 1962, 61, that in 9.1b [8.23b] there is a mention of Yahweh's action and in 9.2ff. [1ff.] an address to Yahweh.

[22] Cf. also Z. Meshel, 'Was there a "Via Maris"?', *IEJ* 23, 1973, 162ff., and the considerations advanced by Barth, *Jesaja-Worte*, 162ff.

[23] He could hardly have derived a corresponding time of honour under king Josiah from II Kings 23.

[24] Cf. also G. von Rad, 'The Royal Ritual in Judah', in *The Problem of the Hexateuch and Other Essays*, Edinburgh 1966, 222–31, and Lindblom, SMHVL 1957/58, 4, 34.

understand it as prophecy in the strict sense. Preferably we should regard it as a prophetic hymn of thanksgiving. With it, the poet expresses his certainty that the saving acts of Yahweh expected by him will really happen (cf. also 12; 25.1–5, 9–10a; 26.1–6). Instead of beginning with an invitation to praise God, the prophetic hymn in v. 1 begins with a metaphorical description of the deliverance of the people, and then goes on in v. 2, in language addressed directly to Yahweh, to speak of the joy that he has caused, and so to praise him. In this alteration to the form of the thanksgiving[25] we can see that the poet freely subordinates the heritage of cultic lyricism to his own prophetic purposes. In vv. 4–7ba [3–6ba] there then follow three reasons for this thanksgiving, introduced with *kī*, for, which explain why Yahweh has brought joy to his people. Their sequence may at the same time correspond to the actual course of events. Again in language addressed to Yahweh, v. 4[3] reports his victory over the oppressors; v. 5[4] reports the burning of the spoil; and vv. 6–7b [5–6b] the accession of a king to the throne of David.[26] We shall have to make a separate investigation below of the way in which the announcement of the birth in 6aa[5aa] fits into this connection.[27] If we look over vv. 4–7baa[3–6ba], the extent of the last member already indicates that the stress of the prophecy lies on the re-establishment of the David kingdom. Here we should not miss the fact that the reason given in v. 4[3] repeats the harmony of the praise of God struck up in v. 3 [2], and thus sets a mark on the two which follow, so that the primacy of Yahweh is preserved. Accordingly, it also stamps on the postlude to the whole hymn in v. 7bβ[6bβ] the message that the people has to expect only from Yahweh the salvation anticipated in the hymn.

[2–3(1–2)] *The joy of the redeemed*. As a traveller joyfully greets the sunrise after a long and sorry night, so the people will welcome the salvation given them by Yahweh. The light which shines on them and gives freedom and joy to illuminate their world is the very presence of God, which is reflected in his actions. Those who walk in darkness see nothing; they are anxious and afraid, and so according to Old Testament thought are already in the power and

---

[25] For the popular thanksgiving cf. H. Gunkel and J. Begrich, *Einleitung in die Psalmen*, HK E 11, Göttingen 1933 (³1975), 314ff.; C. Westermann, *Lob und Klage in den Psalmen*, fifth expanded edition of *Das Loben Gottes in den Psalmen*, Göttingen 1977, 61ff.; F. Crüsemann, *Studien zur Formgeschichte von Hymnus und Danklied in Israel*, WMANT 32, Neukirchen 1969, 155ff., and for the definition of the genre of the present text also Wildberger, ad loc. and Barth, *Jesaja-Worte*, 148ff. I cannot discuss Barth's position in detail in this commentary, as its literary-critical presuppositions are open to question along the lines mentioned on 215f. below.
[26] Cf. also below, 210ff.
[27] Cf. below, 212f.

the realm of the underworld and of death.[28] Their relationship with God is blotted out,[29] so they are far from him.[30] Conversely, those who are in the light can look around and make use of what they have been offered. Here men feel joy as beings who realize themselves through action. However, as the brightness of the world is threatened by the darkness of death, they need the presence and saving concern of God, so that they do not experience this world as a place of danger and this life as a burden, but rather see it as the place and possibility for free and happy activity (cf. Ps. 36.10; 43.3; Job 29.3; Ps. 112.4).[31] Thus God's presence is the source of the light which shines on the life of the individual (Ps. 27.1) or on the whole people (Ps. 89.16; Isa. 10.17; 60.1f.). **[3(2)]** Perceiving the hour of the great and final liberation of his people (cf. v. 7[6]), the poet turns in praise to his God, who will give this splendour to the people and thus bring about unending joy. The liberated people will gather before him for a festival of thanksgiving, in the temple at Jerusalem, the place of his presence.[32] The comparisons with joy over the harvest[33] and over the spoil[34] indicate the magnitude of the joy, but at the same time they demonstrate that the act of deliverance will give the people life and unexpected abundance.[35] At all events, it should be noted that vv. 2, 3 [1,2] seem to be a transposition of Ps. 89.16f.

[4–5(3–4)] *The liberation*. In accordance with the structural principle of hymns of praise, there follows in vv. 4–7 [3–6], in a threefold division building up to a climax, an account of the saving intervention of Yahweh on behalf of his people. This is the reason for the grateful praise.[36] Appropriately the poet mentions the destruction of alien rule first: only when the enemy are destroyed can a people who

---

[28] Cf. Job. 3.3ff.; 10.21; Ps. 143.3; 107.10.

[29] Cf. Ps. 6.6; 30.10; 88.11; 115.17f., and also O. Kaiser in O. Kaiser and E. Lohse, *Tod und Leben*, Stuttgart 1977, 48ff.

[30] Cf. Ps. 88.7; Job 19.8 and Lam. 3.2, and for the conceptions and thought forms also N. J. Tromp, 'Primitive Conceptions of Death and the Nether World in the Old Testament', *BibOr* 21, Rome 1969, 142ff., and C. Barth, *Die Errettung vom Tode*, Zollikon 1947, 91ff.

[31] Cf. also S. Aalen, *TWAT* I, cols. 175ff., *TDOT* 1, 147ff.

[32] Cf. Deut. 12.12, 18; 16.11, 14; 26.2, 10f., 27.6f.; Lev. 23.40; Ps. 107.10ff., and on the question W. Beyerlin, *Werden und Wesen des 107. Psalms*, BZAW 153, Berlin and New York 1979, 86ff., and on the present passage H. Graf Reventlow, *UF* 3, 1971, 322.

[33] Cf. Ps. 126.6 and Deut. 16.10f., 13f., and on the question, H. Guthe, *Palästina*, Bielefeld and Leipzig ²1927, 41: 'Life on the threshing floor is the happiest time of the year for the farmer and his family and indeed for the whole village'.

[34] Cf. Ps. 119. 162; Judg. 5.30; Ps. 68.12f.; Isa. 33.23.

[35] For H. J. Stoebe, 'Raub und Beute', in *Hebräische Wortforschung*, Festschrift Walter Baumgartner, SVT 16, Leiden 1967, 345, who sees here 'old sacral conceptions of the Holy War', along with the mention of the Midianites, cf. the new assessment of the basic problem by F. Stolz, *Jahwes und Israels Kriege*, ATANT, Zurich 1972, 210ff.

[36] Cf. also Gunkel-Begrich, *Einleitung in die Psalmen*, 318, and Westermann, *Lob und Klage*, 63.

have hitherto been captive occupy themselves with spoil and think of appointing their own king. Thus v.4[3] promises that Yahweh will put an end to the servitude of his people who are at present bearing it as an ox bears the yoke![37] they are at the mercy of the alien ruler and his underlings[38] in the same way that an animal or a prisoner is at the mercy of the whip of its driver.[39] This event of deliverance is compared with what happened on the day of Midian. On that occasion, according to the tradition, Gideon had inflicted a devastating defeat on the far superior army of the Midianites in a surprise night-attack with a small company, greatly reduced at Yahweh's command (Judg. 7; cf. also Isa. 10.26; Ps. 83.10f.). According to Judg. 8.22, this victory had brought Gideon the offer of a hereditary monarchy. So we may follow Feldmann in saying that the day of Midian is the 'type of a glorious victory which is achieved with God's power through insignificant human strength'.[40] If, with Duhm, we note that this was a victory over an enemy who had invaded the land, and if we remember that the victor is offered the crown, we may have the two elements which prompted the poet to his comparison.[41]

A people which, like post-exilic Judaism, was utterly in the power of a far superior world empire, and in addition expected the onslaught of the nations against Zion,[42] could expect its freedom only in analogy to such a decisive event brought about by Yahweh himself. However, despite the growing tendency in Judaism to stress that God acts alone, and to expect a change in the word from him, human collaboration is not to be ruled out *a priori*. If the king on the throne of David in v. 5 is designated 'divine hero' and 'father of spoil', he must have at least some warlike qualities. Therefore it is at any rate *possible* that he is even thought to have a share in the divine

---

[37] On this subject cf. G. Dalman, *Arbeit und Sitte in Palästina* II, Gütersloh 1932, 93ff., or F. Nötscher, *Biblischer Altertumskunde*, HSAT. E III, Bonn 1940, 175f., with plate 21, illustration 51. For the yoke as a symbol of foreign rule cf. Gen. 49.15; Lev. 26.13; Deut. 28.48; Jer. 27.8ff.; 28.2ff.; Isa. 47.6; the promises in Isa 10.27; 14.25 are the closest parallels; cf. Jer. 30.8; Ezek. 34.27. The metaphor occurs in the retrospect on deliverance from Egyptian slavery (Ps. 81.7).

[38] Cf. also Isa. 14.4f., 14.2; Zech. 9.9; 10.4; and Ex. 3.7; 5.6, 10, 13f.; Dan. 11.20.

[39] Cf. Job 39.7; Isa. 3.18.

[40] Cf. also Fischer, ad loc.

[41] It should particularly be pointed out here that Judg. 8.22f. only seems to go back to the latest Deuteronomist, DtrN. Cf. T. Veijola, *Das Königtum in der Beurteilung der deuteronomistischen Historiographie*, AASF B 198, Helsinki 1977, 100ff. For the strata of the Deuteronomistic history work cf. e.g. R. Smend, *Die Entstehung des Alten Testaments*, TW 1, Stuttgart 1978, 111ff., or Kaiser, *Einleitung in das Alte Testament*, Gütersloh [4]1978, 158ff. (not in the ET).

[42] Cf. also above, 5, 53.

victory, which in the eyes of his people, along with his descent, is to justify his claim to the royal throne.[43]

In contrast to, say, 29.1ff.; 30.27ff., how all this will come about is left in mysterious obscurity. **[5(4)]** The second reason for jubilation is that the defeat of the enemy will be annihilating. All the noisy military boots,[44] symbolizing the power of those who wear them, and the cloaks,[45] soaked, not just spattered, with the blood of those who had previously worn them, are already burnt in this imaginary situation (cf. 9.19[18]). Accordingly, the uniforms of the dead have been treated as spoil. The spoil of war belonged to the divine leader of the army.[46] The traces of occupation are wiped out.

[6–7b(5–6bα)] *The restoration of the kingdom of David*. With the third and last reason for the prophetic praise of God in these verses, we reach the climax of the prophecy. The people and land freed by Yahweh are again given their own king, and the kingdom of David is restored. The second person applied to God in vv. 3, 4[2, 3] and the 'it' concentrated on the event in v. 5[4] is now followed in v. 6aα[5aα] by 'us', in which the poet includes himself and his people. Once one gives up the special reference to the act of deliverance of the territories separated from the northern kingdom in the course of the Syro-Ephraimite war, conjectured by Alt,[47] there is no real reason to assume that in vv. 6[5] and 7[6] we should see the official message of the accession and the programme for the new king as given out by the Jerusalem court and proclaimed by heralds throughout the land, including the new territory.[48] Here the speaker is the same as in the preceding verses, but, as Albrecht Alt and Gerhard von Rad along with all their followers have rightly seen, he makes use of the language of the enthronement ritual of Judah, a recollection of which had been preserved among the circles of the Jerusalem priests and the temple singers who took up the legacy of the cultic prophets,

---

[43] For S. Mowinckel, *He That Cometh*, Oxford 1956, 107, it followed that v. 1 already referred to the birth of the royal child and liberation was to be seen as his task. As the sequence in vv. 4–7 [3–6] is chronological, and one of content, those who argue that v. 6aα[5aα] relates to the birth of the king usually exclude its reference to deliverance. Elsewhere, however, this notion is rejected, or noted with reservations, as is evident from a look at Alt, op. cit., 45f. = 222; Fohrer, ad loc.; H. W. Wolff, op. cit., 65; H.– P. Müller, *EvTh* 21, 1961, 413ff., and W. H. Schmidt, 'Die Ohnmacht des Messias', *KuD* 15, 1969, 18ff. Gray seems to imagine that the liberation will take place without any warlike activity. For the chronological position of v. 6aα[5aα], cf. below, 212.

[44] Cf. also Jer. 47.3; Nah. 3.2. In Isa. 5.27 the soldiers are said to wear *na'al* on their feet. According to *AHw* 1213b, the Akkadian *šēnum* would be used for sandals and shoes.

[45] Against Gray, who here refers to Isa. 63.3, we must use the partial parallel II Sam. 20.12 for interpretation.

[46] For the original significance of the ban, cf. Stolz, *Jahwes and Israels Kriege*, 192ff.

[47] Cf. above, 204f.

[48] Against Alt, 44f. = 221.

even through the period of catastrophe.[49] That mention of the coming king of the time of salvation had to be oriented on the primal image of the ideal king and therefore on the royal ritual which represents a binding promise is so illuminating a notion that, once expressed, it seems quite obvious **[6(5)]** Alt thought that he could find the key to the understanding of v. 6a[5a] in Ps. 2.7b, where mention of the birth of the king refers to the adoption or, as we should more accurately put it (in view of the absence of this legal institution in Israel), the legitimation of the king as the son of Yahweh on the day of his accession.[50] There the king himself refers to the authority to rule given to him by Yahweh in the so-called royal protocol: 'Yahweh said to me: "You are my son. Today I have begotten you".'[51] The fact that the present passage says that a child is given to us and a son is born to us could accordingly be regarded as the consequence of adapting the element taken from the enthronement hymn, and therefore the enthronement ritual, to the thanksgiving,[52] and we might follow Alt in referring the statement, even in its present form, and within the context demarcated for comment, to the accession of the king rather than to his birth. This interpretation has already attracted scholars because it makes it possible to maintain the temporal unity of vv. 6f.[5f.], so that here the whole passage would be related to the enthronement of the new king. In that case, historically speaking we would have to go back through the enthronement ritual in Judah to that of Egypt; in the last resort the formula of legitimation would derive from the Egyptian conception of the physical begetting of the successor to the throne by the God, who cohabits with the queen in the form of the king.[53] At all events, we should maintain the fact that the notion of the physical conception

[49] In terms of the history of tradition, this assumption poses no greater problem than that of the handing down of prophetic sayings. On the contrary, it may be supposed that liturgical and ritual material was better known, and therefore had a greater chance of surviving the catastrophe. It follows from I Kings 1.32ff.; II Kings 11.12 that the priests were involved in the enthronement. That is in the nature of things. Who else would have performed the anointing and the coronation? In this connection it can remain open whether the cultic prophets were involved only as singers. Cf. also A. R. Johnson, *Sacral Kingship in Ancient Israel*, Cardiff [2]1967, 14f.

[50] Cf. H. Donner, 'Adoption oder Legitimation? Erwägungen zur Adoption im Alten Testament auf dem Hintergrund der altorientalischen Rechte', *OrAnt* 8, 1969, 87ff., and esp. 113f., and G. Fohrer, *TDNT* 8, 349ff.

[51] Cf. also II Sam. 7.14.

[52] Vermeylen I, 236, sees in the 'us' an echo of the Immanuel, God with us, of 7.14.

[53] Cf. the account of the birth of Queen Hatshepsut in J. A. Breasted, *Ancient Records* II, nos. 196ff.; the account of the coronation, nos. 217ff., and Thuthmoses III on his election as king, nos. 138ff.; *AOT*[2], 99ff., or *ANET*[2-3], 446f., and on this G. von Rad, 'The Royal Ritual in Judah', (n. 24); S. Herrmann, *Die prophetischen Heilserwartungen*, BWANT 85, 131ff., and not least H. Brunner, *Die Geburt des Gottkönigs*, Ägyptologische Abhandlungen 10, Wiesbaden 1964, 190ff.

of a human being by God himself, even though he were the expected
king of the time of salvation, was out of the question, and instead
took the form of the formula of legitimation.[54]

The Egyptian mythological idea that the king was the son of God
characterized him as God's representative on earth who, in God's
place, had to sustain *Ma'at*, the legal ordering which embraced the
cosmos and society.[55] According to Ps. 2; 89.27f., in Jerusalem the
title 'son' seems to have conveyed pretensions to world rule, and at
the same time to have suggested a special protective relationship
existing between father and son.[56]

If the way in which Alt related v. 6aα (5aα) to the enthronement of
the king still continues to seem possible in principle, the question
remains whether this view has not judged the statements here too
much in the light of their background in the cult, and not enough in
terms of their prophetic function. In the latter perspective, it is quite
possible to distinguish between the promise of the birth of the
Messiah in v. 6aα [5aα] and that of his accession.[57] It should not
trouble us that chronologically v. 6aα [5aα] lies before the liberation
celebrated in vv. 2–5 [1–4] (cf. also 7.14–16bα); it follows from what
has been said above about the involvement of the Messiah in God's
act of liberation that he emerges out of secrecy only by virtue of this
event. Only now is the sceptre placed on his shoulders as a sign of
the rule over the world that is transferred to him here by means of
the rather remarkable coronation procedure[58] (cf. Ps. 110.2). **[6b(5b)]**
What is to be expected from him as ruler is indicated by his great
throne-name which, unlike the five-element title given to the king of
Egypt, consists only of four elements.[59] In the context of the ritual in

---

[54] In this connection Gen. 6.1ff. is really an alien body in the Old Testament. For its
place in the history of religions cf. now R. Bartelmus, *Heroentum in Israel und seiner
Umwelt*, ATANT 65, Zurich 1979.

[55] Cf. also H. Frankfort, *Kingship and the Gods*, Chicago 1948 (1955), 42f.

[56] We may prudently leave open the question how far influences from Mesopotamian royal ideology are to be found in the second element. Cf. Frankfort, *Kingship*,
299ff. H. W. F. Saggs, 'Mesopotamien', *Magnus Kulturgeschichte*, Essen 1975, 531,
stresses that the king was called God there only when he played the role of the god in
the 'sacred marriage'.

[57] Cf. also Rehm, *Messias*, 145, and H. Gese, 'Natus ex Virgine', in *Probleme biblischer
Theologie*, Festschrift Gerhard von Rad, Munich 1971, 84f. = *Vom Sinai zum Zion*,
BEvTh 64, Munich 1974, 141f., and e.g. Budde, *Jesaja's Erleben*, 110ff., and H.
Gressmann, *Messias*, 242f.

[58] Cf. Ps. 21.4; II Kings 11.12.

[59] For the Egyption royal titles and the bestowing of them cf. A.H. Gardiner,
Egyptian Grammar, Oxford ²1950, 71ff.; Frankfort, *Kingship*, 46f.; Breasted, *Ancient
Records* II, nos. 142ff., 228ff., 239 and on them G. von Rad, 'The Royal Ritual in Judah';
Herrmann, *Prophetische Heilserwartungen*, 135. For the problem of a fifth throne-name
for the Messiah in this passage cf. above, n. 13 and Gese, 'Natus ex virgine', 83 = 140
n. 28.

Judah it had been preserved in the royal protocol which was handed on to the king in God's name in the celebration of the accession.[60] The first name characterizes the ruler as a man who, like God, can make extraordinary resolves[61] and then carry them out.[62] Illuminated by Yahweh himself, he needs no counsel from others (cf. I Kings 3.9; Prov. 16.10; 21.1).[63] The second name stresses his abundance of power, calling men to their God;[64] this makes it possible for him to translate his resolves into action, because no one can withstand him (cf. also 11.2).[65] Elsewhere in the Old Testament the king is designated God only in Ps. 45.7.[66] However, these two instances may be enough to show that the Egyptian influence on the royal ritual was deeper than the tradition generally wants to suggest.[67] Thus the king is the representative and viceregent of God on earth, who, as the one endowed with this spirit (cf. 11.1), shares in his nature and his will. A tradition going back to the old versions interprets the third name as 'eternal father', an interpretation which has notable advocates even today, and according to which, in hyperbolic court language, the king is promised a long life.[68] However, as the notion of the length of his reign is expressly mentioned in v. 7[6] and the logical development which can be observed up to this point in the names, from the plan, through victory to its consequences, would be interrupted, the other translation, 'father of spoil', which is equally possible (cf. Gen. 49.27), is to be preferred. Given the

[60] G. von Rad, 'The Royal Ritual in Judah', cf. *Old Testament Theology* I, London 1975, 310, connected the *'ēdūt* from II Kings 11.12 with the royal protocol. S. Yeivin, *IEJ* 24, 1974, 17ff., shows that the discussion of its significance has not been concluded, though his interpretation seems problematical to me.

[61] Cf. Ps. 88.13; 77.12, 15f.; 78.12; 89.6; Isa. 29.14 and also R. Albertz, *THAT* II, cols. 413ff.

[62] Cf. 25.1; 28.29, and on the question also S. Mowinckel, *ZAW* 75, 1961, 297f.: ' "Counsel" is part of the spiritual equipment of the ruler; he has "counsel" in himself, uses it in his work and asserts it, sees that it continues to exist.'

[63] For the last-mentioned passage cf. W. McKane, *Proverbs*, OTL, London 1970, 559f., and the Mesopotamian parallels produced by Rehm, *Messias*, 149.

[64] Cf. Deut. 10.17; Isa. 32.18; Neh. 9.32; Isa. 10.21; and not least Ps. 45.4, 8; for the translation see Gressmann, *Messias*, 245; McClellan, *CBQ* 6, 1941, 276ff.; H. Wildberger, 'Die Thronnamen des Messias Jes 9, 5b', *TZ* 16, 1960, 316f., and Rehm, *Messias*, 149ff.

[65] Cf. also Ps. 20.7; 21.2.

[66] After the comments made in n. 56, it is particularly worth noting that Ps. 45 is a wedding song. Cf. G. Widengren, *Sakrales Königtum im Alten Testament und im Judentum*, Stuttgart 1955, 78, and A. R. Johnson, *Sacral Kingship*², 30 n.1.

[67] Cf. also Rehm, *Messias*, 153, and H. Graf Reventlow, *UF* 3, 1971, 324.

[68] Cf. Wildberger, ad loc. This interpretation is to be preferred to the reference to a caring fatherly concern that I put forward in the first edition of this commentary, because it follows directly from the wording (cf. also e.g. Ps. 72.5; I Kings 1.31). An impressive account of the position I have rejected has again been put forward by Rehm, *Messias*, 156ff. J. Coppens, 'Le roi idéal d'Is. IX, 5–6 et XI, 1–5, est-il une figure messianique?', in *Mémorial A. Gelin*, 1961, 98 n. 37, refers to the length of the dynasty.

participation of the king in Yahweh's act of deliverance, the old theory of the honorific names would only have gone wrong insofar as it related all these names to future actions of the ruler rather than to actions already performed, and mistook the ritual background. The task with which he is confronted for the future is indicated by the fourth name: he is to secure external peace for the people,[69] and care for law and righteousness throughout his kingdom, without which in the conviction of the Old Testament there can be no salvation on this earth.[70]

[7abα (6abα)] This verse sums up what the throne-names have promised, with their characterization of the ruling ability, wisdom and power of the expected king: the newly-founded kingdom of David will remain unshaken during his reign and – we may add, because he is still mortal – during that of his successors. There can be no resistance which will disrupt his peace. Because the centre of the kingdom, the throne of David as the symbol of the kings from his family which sit upon it and reign from it,[71] remains unshaken, so too does the kingdom. And that is the case with both, because the king and all his successors have made justice and righteousness[72] the support of the throne.[73] Their rule is legitimated by their capacity to deal with the conflicts of interest which arise in their kingdom, to remedy injustices that have been suffered and to prevent new ones. To the degree to which it achieves this, it will not produce a desire for changes. The groups whose voice we hear in this passage, against the background of the second temple, hoped that despite the failure of the dynasty which lost its throne in the catastrophe befalling the kingdom, it would be renewed according to their ideal of kingship,[74] because with their limited experience they could not imagine any other form of government that could achieve a comparable result over the problems which arose within the realm and outside it. They

---

[69] Wildberger stresses in an illuminating way that in accordance with the context, but not exclusively, the name envisages peace in the sense of freedom from foreign occupation and as the opposite to war. For the connection with the ideal of the king in Judah and the ancient Near East cf. H. H. Schmid, šalōm. *'Frieden' im Alten Orient und im Alten Testament*, SBS 51, Stuttgart 1971, 73f. Cf. also ibid., 13ff., 30ff., 70ff., and especially Ps. 72. At all events, it should be noted that G. Gerleman, THAT, cols. 927, 930, suggests that šālōm should be translated 'recompense' and that the title should be rendered 'prince of recompense' or 'of tribute'.

[70] Cf. also O. Kaiser, 'Gerechtigkeit und Heil', NZST 11, 1969, 312ff.

[71] Cf. I Kings 2.12, 24; Jer. 13.13; 22.2, 4, 30; 29.16; 36.30 and esp. Jer. 17.25 and 33.21; II Sam. 7.12f.; Ps. 132.11f.; 89.4f., 30.

[72] Cf. Jer. 22.3, 15; 23.5; 33.15; Ezek. 18.5, 19, 27; 33.14ff., and further I Kings 10.9 par. II Chron. 9.8.

[73] Cf. Prov. 16.12; 20.28; 25.5; 29.14; and not least Ps. 97.2, and on it H. Brunner, *VT* 8, 1958, 426ff.

[74] Cf. below, 254.

did not picture a utopian world free from any form of rule, because they knew that in any human society there is need of an ordered state and authority to resolve the conflicts of individuals and nations. And perhaps their affirmation of order is the presupposition for any advance, in that it diminishes the actual power of the state. If a state wanted to renounce this potential, it brought about its own breakdown.

[7bβ(6bβ)] The end of the oracle, whether it is original or from the hand of a redactor,[75] is a formula which recurs in II Kings 19.31 and Isa. 31.31. In all these passages it is an assurance that the promise will in fact be fulfilled because Yahweh will support it with his 'zeal', i.e. here, probably, with all his strength.[76] In 26.11f. it is said that his zeal for his people will annihilate the enemy and bring peace to the people. In fact belief in the election of Israel and that of the Davidic dynasty is the unexpressed presupposition for the divine help which is expected.[77] As the zealous God, Yahweh is the one who has chosen Israel for his own possession.[78] By delivering the people and re-establishing the Davidic kingdom, he will observe this reservation. It is certainly no coincidence that here, as in 37.11, the divine name is extended to include the epithet Sebaoth, which recalls Yahweh's omnipotence.[79] In its political impotence and servitude, Israel can look for liberation and deliverance only from the almighty power of its God and the raising up of the man whom he will make his instrument in the hour of decision.

Derivation. If we trace the interpretation of this passage over the last century, we can see two basic views of the origin of the oracle. According to one, it derives from the prophet Isaiah, and according to the other it comes only from the exile or the post-exilic period. It is possible to distinguish a whole series of variations of the former hypothesis. According to some scholars, the prophecy was given by the prophet himself as a conclusion to the memorial on the Syro-Ephraimite war,[80] or was added not too long afterwards.[81] Others again see Isaiah as a cultic prophet who either composed the prophecy on the occasion of Hezekiah's accession[82] or in whose literary remains it would have been found as a piece of liturgical tradition.[83] The time of Sennacherib has also been considered a

---

[75] Cf. Vermeylen I, 239f.
[76] Cf. H. A. Brongers, *VT* 13, 1963, 279.
[77] Cf. also Isa. 42.13; 43.15; 59.17; 63.15; Zech. 1.14; Ezek. 36.5.
[78] Cf. Ex. 20.5; 34.14; Deut. 4.24; 5.9; 6.15 and on this Brongers, *VT* 13, 280ff.
[79] Cf. above, 126.
[80] Cf. e.g. Budde, *Jesaja's Erleben*, 119.
[81] Alt, 47f. = 223; H. W. Wolff, BS 35, 63.
[82] Becker, *Isaias*, 22ff.; id., *Messiaserwartung*, 40; cf. also Schedl, *Rufer des Heils*, 255.
[83] H. Graf Reventlow, *UF* 3, 1971, 324f.

possible period for it.[84] Duhm sought to relieve the tension between the prophet's proclamation of judgment and his proclamation of salvation by regarding this oracle as teaching to disciples which was not intended for public proclamation. Finally, some scholars have simply attributed it to the prophet and not tried to be more specific about the date.[85] In recent decades the early date of the psalms and the prophecy of Nathan seemed to provide the necessary basis in the history of tradition for attributing the oracle to Isaiah, because it promised to support an earlier date for the election of the Davidic dynasty and of Zion.[86]

Because those who support Isaianic authorship have necessarily differed in their attempts at dating the passage after breaking the connection between 9.1 [8.23] and 9.2ff. [1ff.], inevitably other scholars have stressed that the expectations expressed here would be more understandable against a later background, when catastrophe had already befallen the kingdom of Judah. In fact v. 2[1] presupposes that the whole people has lost its freedom, and accordingly the prophecy in vv. 6f. [5f.] is also to be connected with the restoration of the monarchy. As linguistic statistics present a particularly complex problem in this context, I shall leave them out of account as support for one view or the other.[87] Instead, the argument from content can be supported by an observation of form. In this book, we continually find that promises have been inserted later at the end of a succession of announcements of judgment (cf. e.g. 2.1ff.; 4.2ff.; 11.1ff.).[88] These objections to the traditional attribution

[84] Cf. e.g. B. Duhm, ad loc.; Gressmann, *Messias*, 244; H.-P. Müller, *EvTh* 21, 1961, 414; T. Lescow, 'Das Geburtsmotiv in den messianischen Weissagungen', *ZAW* 79, 1967, 186f., doubts that the text comes from Isaiah, but supposes it to have been composed after 701. S. Mowinckel, *He That Cometh*, 109f., suppose pupils of Isaiah to have written it. Barth, *Jesaja-Worte*, should also be mentioned in this connection; he supposes that the oracle relates to the birth and enthronement of king Josiah (172ff.); similarly Vermeylen I, 244f.

[85] Cf. e.g. Feldmann and Eichrodt, ad loc., and the careful comments made by O. Eissfeldt, *The Old Testament. An Introduction*, Oxford 1965, 318f., and W. H. Schmidt, *Einführung in das Alte Testament*, Berlin and New York 1979, 219f., though in fact they support Isaianic authorship.

[86] Cf. G. von Rad, *Old Testament Theology* II, 'As a result of this study, it can be said that the whole of Isaiah's preaching is based on two traditions, the Zion tradition and the tradition about David' (p. 174), and further E. Rohland, *Die Bedeutung der Erwählungstraditionen Israels für die Eschatologie der alttestamentlichen Propheten*, Diss. Heidelberg 1956, 145ff., 234ff.; S. Herrmann, *Heilserwartungen*, 130ff., 141ff. The first edition of this commentary and Wildberger adopt this position.

[87] Cf. J. Vollmer, 'Zur Sprache von Jesaja 9, 1–6', *ZAW* 80, 1968, 343ff.

[88] Cf. e.g. B. Stade, *Geschichte des Volkes Israel* I, Berlin 1887, 596 n. 2; H. Hackmann, *Die Zukunftserwartungen des Jesaja*, Göttingen 1893, 133ff.; Cheyne, *Introduction*, 45f.; Marti, ad loc.; G. Hölscher, *Die Propheten*, Leipzig 1914, 347ff., and esp. 362f.; E. Balla, *Die Botschaft der Propheten*, ed. G. Fohrer, Tübingen 1958, 474; G. Fohrer, ad loc., and id., 'Komposition und Überlieferung von Jesaja 1–39', in *Studien zur*

of the text to the prophet Isaiah could already be taken up in the present commentary because I believe that I have demonstrated that even the basic text of the so-called memorial in 6.1–8.18, to which 9.2ff.[1ff.]. was finally attached by the bridge of 8.19ff., 23a, represent a piece of post-exilic prophetic theology with a kerygmatic concern.[89] In such circumstances, very strong reasons would have to be advanced for demonstrating that the text added by a redactor was substantially earlier than its context.

Finally, in favour of a post-exilic dating of this passage, it may be pointed out that the prophets Haggai and Zechariah, who emerged in the last third of the sixth century and therefore after the catastrophe which befell the kingdom of Judah and the end of the exile, show signs of the cherishing of messianic hopes, and in the second half of the fifth century these seem to have been associated with the governor Nehemiah.[90] Accordingly, we may assume that the prophecy here falls in the period delimited by these dates and comes from the group of guilds and singers in the second temple, among whom the recollection of the royal liturgy of Judah may have been preserved. If the messianic interpretation advanced above, with all caution, is an apt reading of the Immanuel prophecy in 7.14–16*,[91] we cannot exclude the possibility that the incorporation of the present prophecy is to be ascribed to the author of that prophecy along with the relevant additions in ch. 8 which in the last resort correspond with it in content.

9.2–7[1–6] as a prophecy of the birth of Christ. The commentary so far has shown that here a divine act and a king were expected, who would decisively alter political conditions on this earth and bring about freedom for the oppressed Jewish people for ever. If the Christian church once again finds the birth of Jesus prophesied in this text, though in a different way from Matt. 4.21ff., it must be clear about the presuppositions on which it can do this, so as to meet the demands of intellectual honesty and of the purity of the gospel with which it has been entrusted. There is obviously a difference between the king of the time of salvation depicted here and the Christ whose kingdom is not of this world (John 18.36). If that is overlooked, it can happen that the expectation expressed here

---

alttestamentlichen Prophetie, BZAW 99, Berlin 1967, 235; M. Treves, *VT* 17, 1967, 464ff., though with his dating in the Maccabaean period he may be putting it too late; J. Vollmer, *ZAW* 80, 1968, 342f.; Dietrich, *Jesaja und die Politik*, 206f., and finally the restraining voices of H.-J. Hermisson, *EvTh* 33, 1973, 57 with n. 13, and R. Smend, *Die Entstehung des Alten Testaments*, TW 1, Stuttgart 1978, 150.

[89] Cf. above, 114ff.
[90] Cf. Hag. 2.21ff., Zech. 4.6f., 11ff.; 6.9ff. and K. Elliger, ATD 25, ad loc.; Neh. 6.5ff. and U. Kellermann, *Nehemia*, BZAW 102, Berlin 1967, 147.
[91] Cf. above, 168ff.

overlays Christian hope and thus falsifies it by turning it, among other things, into a political programme. This would obviously put at risk the expectation of salvation brought about by God himself.

Before the church recognizes in this text a prophecy of Jesus of Nazareth as the Christ, it has already recognized him as the pioneer of a trust in God that does not end even in death. Because it is convinced that all human hope can be seen and recognized as what it truly is only from this perspective, it supposes that all expectation of a freer and fuller life as expressed in any particular form of expectation really represents deliverance from anxiety and death.[92] Wherever this liberation comes about, it recognizes the dawn of the kingdom of God and the presence of the salvation which he has brought about. By asserting that such salvation is only to be expected from God, and that the way to him is opened by the words and work of Jesus, it relegates all plans for living constructed by individuals and all political programmes to the realm of a penultimate state of the world. Because they are within the limits of a life which is under the shadow of death, they cannot remove the threat which that poses in terms of anxiety and all the consequences which follow, disturbing the life of the individual and the nations and caring only for the well-being, not the salvation, of man. Conversely, anyone who sees the brotherly dimensions of salvation will also be concerned for the welfare of others. Here, in view of their common immediacy towards God, he will know that in his concern for the well-being of others he may not simply make his own plans and allow or deny to others a claim to their freedom and life only in accordance with his own presuppositions. Thus, rightly understood, the freedom of the church and the freedom and worth of the individual over against society depend on a distinction between salvation and welfare. For this reason, in view of the Christmas message and the hope which goes with it, the church may not plan for the perfection of the world in the same way as a political movement. It must constantly see that its political task of warning against the destruction of human society through oppression and violence is at the service of its real task, to announce God's salvation to all men.

---

[92] Cf. M. Heidegger, *Being and Time*, 228ff., 304ff.

CHAPTER 9.8[7]–10.4

Yahweh's Outstretched Hand

9.8[7] The Lord[1] sent a word against Jacob,
        and it fell upon Israel.
9[8]   And all[2] the people became aware of it,
        Ephraim and the inhabitants of Samaria,
        <that boasted>[3] in arrogance
        and haughtiness[4]:
10[9]   'If bricks fall, we shall build with dressed stones,
        If sycamore (beams) are shattered,
        we shall replace them with cedars.'
11[10] Then Yahweh strengthened the adversaries *of Rezin*[5]
        and goaded[6] his enemies.
12[11] Aram before and the Philistines behind,
        that they might eat Israel with open mouth.
        For all that his anger was not turned away,
        and his hand was stretched out still.

13[12] But the people did not turn to him who smote them,
        and did not seek Yahweh Sebaoth.
14[13] Then Yahweh cut off from Israel head and tail,
        shoot and reed in one day.
15[14] The elder and nobleman were the head,
        and the prophet who preaches lies was the tail.
16[15] And the leaders of this people led them astray,
        and those who were led by them were blinded.
17[16] Therefore the Lord did not <spare>[7] his young men
        and had[6] no compassion on their fatherless and their widows.
        For they were all godless and wicked,
        and every mouth spoke only folly.
        For all that his anger was not turned away,
        and his hand was stretched out still.

[1] Presumably the 'Lord' replaces an original Yahweh: cf. also 10.12, 16, 23, 24.
[2] For the emphatic heightening of meaning provided by a following *kōl*, cf. G-K[26] § 127b.
[3] With Procksch, read *hammitga'ᵃwe*. There is probably an omission by haplography.
[4] Literally greatness (= haughtiness) of heart.
[5] Presumably we should follow Budde in assuming an original *ṣōrᵉrāw*, his oppressors.
[6] For the so-called imperfect to denote a concomitant action cf. Bobzin, § 7.1b.
[7] Instead of the *yiśmaḥ* read a *pāsaḥ* or *šāmaḥ*, cf. Arabic *šamuḥa*, be gracious, generous. The imperfect is here a sign of a change of meaning to the future.

18[17]   Yes, the evil burned like fire,
           that consumes[6] thorns and thistles,
           and kindled the thicket of the wood,
           so that it rolled up high in smoke.
19[18]   Through the wrath of Yahweh Sebaoth
           dark[8] was the land,[9]
           and for the people it was like consuming fire,
           none spared[6] his brother,
20[19b]   each one devoured[6] the flesh of his arm.[10]

20a[19a]   They snatched on the right and remained hungry,
           and devoured on the left and were not satisfied.
21[20]   Manasseh Ephraim and Ephraim Manasseh,
           and both against Judah.
           For all this his anger was not turned away,
           and his hand was stretched out still.

10.1   Woe to those who decree iniquitous decrees,
           and write regulations of suffering.
2   To suppress the claim of the weak
           and to rob the oppressed of my people of their right,
           so that widows become their spoil
           and that they may therefore[6] plunder the orphans.
3   What will you do on the day of visitation,
           in the storm which comes from afar?
           To whom will you flee for help,
           and where will you leave your wealth?
4   Only at the place of the captives will they crouch down
           and so[6] fall at the place of the slain.
           For all this his anger was not turned away,
           and his hand was stretched out still.

[9.8[7]–10.4 + 5.25–29] This poem, with its refrain about the outstretched hand of Yahweh, proves a difficult area for the commentator.[11] It is obvious that the wording as it has come down to us and
the present division of the poem are the result of a process of
redaction which is hidden from us, and which perhaps we shall
never completely succeed in illuminating. The song now presents
itself as a complex which extends from 9.8 [7] to 10.4; the refrain in
9.12b[11b], 17b[16b], 21b[20b] and 10.4b, and the strophes each
constructed of seven lines, keep the poem formally together within

---

[8] Cf. Arabic 'atama II, make dark, and 'atmat^un, dark. For the incongruency of the
following feminine subject cf. G-K[28] § 150o.
[9] Or, the earth.
[10] The zᵉrōʿō in the tradition troubled even the translators of the early versions.
There is better parallelism if we follow T in reading rēʿō, his neighbour.
[11] For discussion cf. also Barth, Jesaja-Worte, 109ff.

these limits. However, that this is a problematical division is evident simply from the fact that the fourth strophe consists of a woe which culminates in paraenesis. As according to v. 91aβ[8aβ] the poem seems to be addressed to the northern kingdom, the question in 10.3, which is evidently part of a conversation with the reader and hearer, is amazing. The problem is further complicated by the fact that another strophe of three lines ending in the refrain appears in 5.25. This is followed in 5.26–29* with a seven-line announcement of judgment, syntactically connected with the refrain in v.25b, which can evidently be regarded as the closing strophe of the whole poem. As it now comes at the end of the series of woes in 5.8–23(24), we may assume that the last woe was exchanged with the closing strophe of the refrain poem during a revision of the book, and at the same time adapted to its new context.[12]

Turning to the remaining three strophes in 9 8–21[7–20], we find that the difficulties are just as great. The question, vigorously discussed in older scholarship, whether these sayings are a prophecy or a retrospect, can easily be decided in favour of the latter, in view of the parallels in Amos 4.6–13 and the chronological structure. In their present form, these strophes are to be regarded as a retrospect on a history of disaster which ends in the announcement of an annihilating judgment to come (5.26ff.). In the first strophe, the mention of the oppressor Rezin in v. 11[10] is the first disruption. Here we evidently have an intervention of the historicizing editor whose hand we have been able to detect almost continuously since 3.8.[13] Presumably here he envisages the Assyrians as the destroyers of the Aramaean kingdom[14] and the state of Israel. It is obvious that this distorts the chronological sequence. It is also striking that the whole people of God referred to in vv. 8[7] and 9aα[8aα][14a] are limited to Ephraim and Samaria in v. 9aβ[8aβ] and therefore to the heart and the capital of the northern kingdom. Presumably here again we have the work of the historicizing editor,[15] who was evidently concerned to relate the poem specifically to the northern kingdom.

In v. 14[13] the second strophe evidently describes a blow which affects the whole people. According to v. 17[16], this is a severe military defeat. But v. 15[14] interprets the metaphors of v. 14[13] only in terms of the secular and prophetic leadership, and therefore cannot in any way be original.[16] If we exclude v. 15[14], however,

[12] Cf. above, 111.
[13] Cf. above, 5ff.
[14] Cf. above, 149f.
[14a] Cf. 8.17f., 2.3, 5, 6; 10.20f.; 14.1; 17.4; 27. 6, 8; 29.22f.
[15] Cf. also Vermeylen I, 178f.
[16] For vv. 15–17 [14–16], cf. also Vermeylen I, 180ff.

the seven-line construction of the strophe is damaged. That this strophe has been changed substantially is also evident from the fact that at least v. 17aα [16aα] may have originally stood in front of v. 14[13]. We should also consider whether v. 16[15] is to be moved. In the third strophe, according to vv. 18, 19abα[17, 18abα] a catastrophe is expected which will exceed the visitation of the second one. If we may refer the specific characterization of the remnant to an eschatological famine accompanied by anarchy (cf. 3.5; 24.1ff.), we would have such a development. That, however, would disrupt the chronological structure and presumably be a misunderstanding of v. 21[20], which is probably meant to point beyond, to historical controversies among the two tribes which make up the northern kingdom and between that kingdom and the southern kingdom. If this is in fact another subsequent historicization, the editor would have so thoroughly obliterated the traces that any other reconstruction would seem rash.

If we try to put the events referred to in the first three strophes into a historical sequence, we have further difficulties. They can be avoided in the first strophe by interpreting the mention of the Aramaeans and Philistines, made from a geographical perspective, in historical terms in such a way that the reference is to the threat posed by the Philistines in the time of Saul (cf. I Sam. 13f.; 31). Later, the Philistines were more the neighbours of the southern than of the northern kingdom. Here might be above all a reference to a possible collaboration between the Philistines and the Aramaeans at the time of king Joash of Judah (cf. II Kings 12.8).[17] In other respects, the Aramaean kingdom at any rate posed a permanent threat to the northern kingdom in the second half of the ninth century.[18]

According to v. 14[13], the second strophe calls for an annihilating military defeat. It is not enough to identify it with Jehu's revolution (cf. II Kings 9f.), because essentially the descendants of Omri, and not the whole people, were affected by that. Furthermore, that interpretation would clash with the present third strophe.[19] So we have to decide to put the second strophe after the third; that makes the development of the content comprehensible: oppression of Israel (either the whole of the people of God or, as the historicizing editor intends, the northern kingdom) by its neighbours or by external difficulties; controversies among the main tribes of the northern kingdom in the time of the judges (cf. Judg. 6.35; 8.1; 12.1.4ff.) down

[17] Cf. also J. Gray, *I & II Kings*, OTL, London and Philadelphia ²1970, 588f.

[18] Cf. e.g. A. H. J. Gunneweg, *Geschichte Israels bis Bar Kochba*, TW 2, Stuttgart ³1979, 59ff., 109ff.

[19] Against e.g. Fohrer, Eichrodt, Wildberger and the first edition of this commentary, ad loc.

to the overthrow of king Pekahiah by Pekah and his followers coming from Gilead, who were thus members of Manasseh (cf. II Kings 15.25), and then the battles between the two brother kingdoms at the beginning of the eighth century (cf. II Kings 14.8ff.) and finally in the Syro-Ephraimite war (cf. II Kings 16.5ff.; Isa. 7.1ff.). Verses 13–17 [12–16] would then look back on the annihilation of the northern kingdom by the Assyrians. At the same time this means that the old final strophe (5.26ff.) cannot have had in mind the advance of the Assyrian army, but refers to the coming either of the Babylonians or of an eschatological enemy. The mere fact that there seems to have been a clash between his troops and those of the Assyrian king Tiglath-pileser III during the last years of the reign of king Azariah Uzziah of Judah[20] tells against the assumption that the prophet Isaiah could at any time have announced the coming of the Assyrians in such a mysterious way as in 5.26ff. We must now recall that according to v. 9aα[8aα] the people of God described in v. 8[7] as Jacob and Israel are to experience all together the word of God sent against them. Accordingly, at any rate in the final strophe we have an extended application to the southern kingdom which had been prepared for by v. 21[20]. It makes the prophet predict the annihilating judgment inflicted by the Babylonians in the way that we can observe in the so-called memorial.[21] The editor who added 10.1–4 may be responsible for the transposition of the second and third strophes of the poem. It would at least be conceivable that he was moved by a desire to put together both strophes which were concerned with inner conflicts among the people.

[8–12 (7–11)] *The word of Yahweh and the visitation by neighbours.* Inevitably the difficulties over context which arose in the preceding analysis recur in the exegesis. Thus as early as v. 8[7] the reader wonders whether the poet is thinking of a word of Yahweh proclaimed by the prophet which accompanies the whole history of Israel, constantly renewed, or the word in 5.26ff. which stands at the end of the whole poem and contains the announcement of the victorious approach of the people from afar. It is indeed striking that there is further mention of the visitations of Yahweh, but not of the prophetic word which precedes them and follows them. So it would be conceivable that the antithesis between the word which certainly achieves its goal, bringing about the annihilation of the people of God, and the arrogant self-certainty of the people, refers to the time at which the announcement of judgment goes forth. It thus, in full accordance with 6.10f., only increases the stubbornness of a people which has already been demonstrated adequately in history by their failure to respond with their conversion to any of the blows inflicted by Yahweh. **[9(8)]** The announcement that one day the whole people will experience the effect of this word takes place within the context of the conviction that a prophetic saying in fact legitimated by Yahweh participates in the effective power of the divine word itself, so that this word is not mere communication but a creative word (cf. 55.10f.; Jer. 23.29; Hos. 6.5; Ps. 107.20; 33.9). If despite what has gone before, the historicizing editor gives it a special application towards Ephraim and Samaria, and therefore towards the nucleus of the northern kingdom and its capital, he is clearly concerned to fit the poem more clearly in with the time of Isaiah and refer to the authentication of the word provided by the fate of the northern kingdom, which – as is well known – did not survive past the year 722. **[10(9)]** This arrogant self-assurance is clarified with a saying which could have had a proverbial character.[22] It says that people will respond to the destruction of the old houses by building imposing new ones. The usual building material, clay bricks (cf. Ex. 5.7f., Gen. 11.3) and beams of wood from mulberry trees,[23] will be replaced by hewn stones and beams of cedar, of the kind used in building the royal palace and the temple (cf. I Kings 6.36; 7.11; Amos 5.11).[24] The people's self-awareness has not been shattered by the blows inflicted by Yahweh. Neither the Philistine wars in the early period, which almost destroyed them,[25] nor the Philistine and Aramaean wars late on in the ninth century, made the people repent, so that the wrath of Yahweh would have been turned aside[26] and he could have withdrawn his hand stretched out to strike.[27]

[13–17(12–16)] *The annihilating blow.*Furthermore the second strophe (in my view originally the third)[28] begins with the express statement that these blows have not moved the people to repent.[29] Had they repented, they would have 'sought' Yahweh, i.e. turned to him and kept his will (cf. Deut. 4.29; Amos 5.6, 14; Hos. 10.12; Jer. 29.13). **[17aα (16aα)]** To begin here, it is clear that the mention of the

[22] Cf. also H. W. Wolff, 'Das Zitat im Prophetenspruch', *Gesammelte Studien zum Alten Testament*, ThB 22, Munich ²1973, 97, who relates the saying to the expectation of the people of Jerusalem.

[23] Cf. also J. Feliks, *BHH* II, col. 1177.

[24] Instead of the interpretation which I put forward earlier, it is preferable to follow Wildberger in referring the passage to the replanting of felled trees (cf. Deut. 20.19).

[25] Cf. above, 222f.

[26] Cf. II Kings 23.26; Jer. 2.35; 4.8; Hos. 14.5.

[27] Cf. the formula 'the strong hand and outstretched arm of Yahweh', Ex. 6.6; Deut. 4.34; 5.15; 7.19; 26.8; and the reverse order, the outstretched hand and strong arm of Yahweh, Jer. 21.5.

[28] Cf. 223 above.

[29] Cf. II Kings 23.25; Amos 4.6, 8, 9, 10, 11; Jer. 18.8; Ezek. 33.14,

young men[30] refers to the able-bodied youth of the people, who will not be spared by Yahweh and thus will fall in battle (Amos 4.10). Whether Yahweh's failure to have mercy on the widows and fatherless rests on the fact that they only become widows and fatherless as a result of Yahweh's action – which is one way in which one might prefer to interpret it – or is because he removes from them the protection accorded to them in a general catastrophe which affects them particularly (cf. Deut. 10.18; Ex. 22.21ff.) is unclear. [14(13)] At all events, Yahweh responds to the failure to repent with a blow which completely annihilates the people. As the comparison with Deut. 28.13, 44 shows, the head and tail of the people are its rulers and the subjects who serve them. If one removes the central stem and leaves from a plant, it is destroyed completely above the ground.[31] At all events, it is clear that if we do not want to regard the strophe in its present form as a retrospect on the catastrophe of 587, from which the eschatological understanding of 10.1–4 is to emerge more completely, we can relate it only to the decline of the northern kingdom in 722. [15(14)] Remarkably enough, the editor responsible for this verse wants to see the judgment as a blow only against the elders, the men of reputation at court[32] and the false prophets.[33] Only with this limitation is it possible to think in terms of events in the ninth century like the slaughtering of the prophets of Baal (cf. I Kings 18.40) and the extermination of the dynasty of Omri (cf. II Kings 9f.). [16(15)] This echoes 3.12b and takes over the derogatory use of the term 'this people' which is characteristic of the memorial.[34] In content, along with v. 17a[16a] it justifies Yahweh's act of annihilation of his people, whose leaders have failed by leading the people on a false path, while the people have incurred guilt by allowing themselves to be led.

[17(16)aβb] Thus the people as a whole had shown themselves to be apostates in religion (cf. 10.6),[35] and evil in their conduct (cf. 1.4;31.2).[36] That their conduct was opposed to the will and ordinance of Yahweh is reflected in the fact that all their words were foolish, i.e., not in tune with the ordering and reality of this world as determined by God (cf. Ps. 14.1f.; Isa. 32.6f.).[37] Whether this strophe is now related to the events of the year 722 or those of 587 remains

---

[30] For attestation of the word *bāḥūr* cf. Vermeylen I, 182.
[31] Cf. also 19.15.
[32] Cf. II Kings 5.1; Isa. 3.3; Job 22.8.
[33] Cf. Jer. 14.14; 23.25; also Jer. 23.32; 27.10, 14, 16; 29.21.
[34] Cf. 6.10; 8.6, 11f.; 28.14; 29.13f.; and Jer. 6.19, 21; 7.16, 33; 8.5; 9.14, etc.
[35] Cf. also 33.14 and Job 8.13; 20.5; 27.8.
[36] Cf. also Prov. 17.4; Ps. 37.9.
[37] Cf. also M. Saebø, *THAT* II, cols 27ff.

immaterial for the understanding of the refrain, as now (at any rate) it refers to a further divine action relating to Judah.

[18–21(17–20)] *The fratricidal dispute.* The strophe which is third in its present context but second in the sequence[38] in terms of content is concerned with internal disputes as a consequence of the divine wrath. **[18(17)]** With its direct mention of evil, this already seems to presuppose v. 17[16] in the present position. So it once again becomes clear that editorial work has been done on the poem. The author of this verse is by no means sure of his style, but he is a poet concerned with the effect of his images; in the second half he has already forgotten that he has spoken in his metaphor of the fire kindled in the dry scrub. He produces the impressive picture of the burning of the undergrowth which makes clouds of smoke whirl skywards. Thus the reader gets the impression of the immeasurable harm that has been done by evil in Israel. The closeness of v. 18aα(17aα] to Num. 11.13 is as striking as the fact that v. 18a[17a] has influenced 10.17b.[39] **[19(18)]** If I understand this verse rightly, it indicates that the effect of human wickedness is at the same time, and above all, an effect of the divine wrath.[40] That wrath is ultimately responsible for the clouds of smoke from the great fire bringing darkness over the land and harassing men with their flames. Right at the end of the image the poet reminds us again that he has spoken metaphorically.[41] In reality – according to the present context – this is about a *bellum omnium contra omnes*, a struggle of each man for himself, which ran through the history of Israel, in which each person fell in insatiable greed upon the other[42] and thus (if we follow the Massoretic text) devoured his own arm, or (if we follow the emendation) the flesh of his neighbour, without becoming full, i.e. without finding new satisfaction. I have already indicated (cf. also 8.21) that these statements can be related more easily to the consequences of an eschatological famine and the consequent anarchy than to a fratricidal war.[43] **[21(20)]** In the light of the next verse, however, we are to refer the talk about merciless and greedy eating back to the people and understand it as a metaphor for the fratricidal

---

[38] Cf. above, 223.
[39] For the formula 'thorns and thistles', cf. 5.6; 7.23–25; 27.4.
[40] Cf. 13.13; 10.6 and Jer. 4.4; 21.12; 7.20; Lam. 2.2.
[41] For the 'devouring fire', cf. 9.4.
[42] For v. 19bβ[18bβ] and v. 20b[19b] cf. also Jer. 23.35; 31.34 and Isa. 30.14. For the formula referring to right and left hands cf. e.g. Gen. 24.49; Num. 20.17; Deut. 2.27, and as a closer parallel Zech. 12.6. For the combination of eating and being full, cf. e.g. Deut. 31.20; 6.11; 8.10ff.; 14.29; 16.12.
[43] Cf. above, 222.

dispute which first raged in the northern kingdom and then led to an attack on the southern state of Judah.[44]

[10.1–4] *Woe to the lawbreakers!* As though the editor had referred vv. 19b, 20[18b, 19] to the oppression of the humble people, he adds a woe which is directed specifically against this wrong. There is some dispute as to what we should specifically understand 'iniquitous decrees' to be. On the one hand this has been thought to be a reference to changing the existing law, which allowed the pledging and dispossession of land and house belonging to an overdue creditor, thus depriving him of his legal rights or even making him a slave;[45] on the other hand the reference has been thought to be to judgments put into writing which disregard the rights of the weaker members of society.[46] In both instances reference can be made to the use of the Hebrew *ḥōq*: in Gen. 47.26 it denotes a general regulation, while in Job 23.14 it seems to refer to an individual judgment. As we know hardly anything about state laws either before or after the exile,[47] it is probably better to opt for the second possibility and see the woe directed against those who twist the legal claims[48] of the humble people who are not entirely without possessions, the *dallīm*,[49] and the widows and fatherless who had to seek an advocate for their claims at law because as women and minors they had no rights of their own. This is therefore a matter of exploiting one's own economic power and social position to the disadvantage of the insignificant members of society standing on its periphery. Because of the especially precarious position of such people, they were under the special protection of Yahweh (cf. Prov. 22.22f.; Ex. 22.21ff.). We can therefore understand the question as to where the lawbreakers will turn when the day of visitation comes[50] and disaster suddenly breaks on them from afar like a storm[51] (cf. 2.12ff.; 5.26). There will be no help before the onslaught of Yahweh and the people whom he

[44] Cf. above, 222f.

[45] Thus e.g. Procksch, Hans Schmidt, Kaiser[1] and C. Schedl, *Rufer des Heils*, 266f.; more cautiously, Wildberger, ad loc. Duhm, followed by Dillman-Kittel, Marti, Feldmann, Fischer, Ziegler and Fohrer, ad loc., thought of legal prescriptions which laid heavier burdens on the common man and hindered processes at law.

[46] Thus e.g. Gray, Penna and Auvray, ad loc.

[47] Cf. also M. Noth, *The Laws in the Pentateuch*, Edinburgh 1966, 18ff., and G. C. Macholz, 'Zur Geschichte der Justiz-organisation in Juda', *ZAW* 84, 1972, 314ff., and P. Welten, *Geschichte und Geschichtsdarstellung in den Chronikbuchern*, WMANT 42, Neukirchen 1973, 184f.

[48] For *dīn* with the meaning 'legal claim' cf. e.g. Deut. 17.8. Here *mišpāt*, literally 'the decision', may have almost the same meaning, cf. also Ecclus. 50.19.

[49] For the combination of *dallīm* and *ʿanīyyīm* cf. 11.4; 26.6; further also Amos 2.7. For the social position of the small farmer, cf. H.-J. Fabry, TWAT II, cols. 232f., TDOT 3, 208ff.

[50] Cf. Hos. 9.7; Micah 7.4.

[51] Cf. e.g. 47.11; Ps. 35.8; Prov. 3.25.

summons from afar (cf. 31.1f.), and no hiding-place in which riches can be concealed. Instead of this, points out the eschatological editor who has adapted the woe to the verse and its refrain, the powerful and the rich will be made to fall upon their knees before their captors and suffer merciless execution (cf. II Kings 1.13; 25.18ff.). In its present position the refrain should really be translated, 'for all that his anger cannot be turned away', because in this strophe there is no further mention of a visitation which has already taken place; everything is referred to the last visitation to come. In accordance with the context, the reference is to the judgment accomplished by Assyria as Yahweh's rod of chastisement, in which Assyria itself will be broken. What is discussed here and the way in which it is discussed may seem very far from the present. However, perhaps the question what use riches will be, whether justly or unjustly gained, at the hour of a man's death, reaches down through all merely historical presentations to our own time and our own lives (cf. Luke 12.15ff.).

CHAPTER 10.5–15

Woe to over-confident Assyria

5   **Woe to Assyria, the rod of my anger,**
     <and the staff of my wrath>,[1] which <in his hands>[2]
6   **I send him against an apostate people**
     and thus command[3] him against the tribe of my wrath,
     to take spoil and to seize plunder,
     and to tread them down like refuse in the street.
7   **But he does not so imagine it,**
     and has[3] other things in his mind;[4]
     for his intention[4] is to destroy
     and to root out nations not a few.

[1] Read *ūmaṭṭē zaʿmī*.
[2] Deletion would be the simplest solution if the metre allowed it. So instead of 'in their hands' we should read *bᵉyādāw*. Vermeylen I, 254f., points to the possibility that the phrase is a secondary interpretation along the lines of 10.20, 24.
[3] For the use of the so-called imperfect to denote a concomitant action, cf. Bobzin, 7 § 1b.
[4] Literally, 'heart'.

8   *For he thinks:*[5]
    'Are not my princes all kings?
9   **Was not Calno like Carchemish**
    or Hamath like Arpad,
    or Samaria like Damascus?
10   *As my hand found*
    the kingdoms of the idols –
    and their graven images were greater
    than those of Jerusalem and Samaria –
11   *Can I not do what I have done*
    to Samaria and her idols,
    to Jerusalem also and her images?'
12   And it will come about that when the Lord has finished all his work on Mount Zion and on Jerusalem, 'I will punish the fruit of the arrogant boasting of the king of Assyria and the proud splendour of his eyes!'
13   **For he thinks,**[6]
    'By the strength of my hand I have done it,
    and by my wisdom, for I have understanding.
    <I have removed>[7] the boundaries of nations,
    and have plundered their treasures

    ....

    <And have cast down>[8] like a hero[9] those who sat on thrones,[10]
14   **My hand found like a nest**
    the wealth of the peoples;
    and as one gathers eggs that have been forsaken
    I have gathered the whole earth.
    And there was no one who moved a wing
    and opened its beak and chirped.'
15   **Does the axe vaunt itself over the one who hews with it,**
    or the saw magnify itself against the one who uses it?
    As if a rod should wield the one <who lifts it>[11]
    or a staff should lift that which is not wood.

[10.5–15] By the standards of the sayings of classical prophecy, the

[5] Literally 'says' – people thought aloud.
[6] Literally 'said'.
[7] Read *wā'āsir*.
[8] Read *wā'ōrid*.
[9] Read *kᵉ'abbīr*. V. seems to have read *bᵉ'āpār*, in the dust.
[10] V: *residentes;* LXX: inhabited cities. The text is evidently corrupt, and a line has fallen out. In view of this I shall not attempt my own reconstruction, but instead give Duhm's expansion: 'and make their cities sink into ashes and their rulers into the dust'.
[11] For the so-called *waw* explicative, cf. G-K²⁸ § 154a n. 1b and J. A. Soggin, *Old Testament and Oriental Studies*, BibOr 29, Rome 1975, 232f. Barth, *Jesaja-Worte*, 23, has referred to the *pluralis majestatis* used to clarify the relationship with Yahweh. The reading will originally have been *mᵉrīmō*.

woe against Assyria is a remarkable construction. It resorts to the means of dramatic presentation by taking up the thoughts – which for this period means the words – of the party threatened, and ends with a series of didactic questions, instead of in a clear announcement of judgment. The strangeness of it emerges once again if we compare it with a normal woe: in the ideal case the woe is a short saying in which the woe itself contains the announcement of coming disaster and the address contains the accusation (cf. e.g. 5.20–23). Here the elaboration of the address makes it possible to justify the accusation in more detail (cf. 5.8f., 11f., 18f.). Finally, an independent announcement of judgment can also be added (cf. 5.9f., 13).[12] If the place of this announcement is taken by a question, as in 10.3, one can speak of a didactic variation on the form.

If we investigate the present woe against this background we find that even if we leave out of account the announcement of judgment in 10.16–19 as a secondary addition, which goes beyond the didactic conclusion in v. 15,[13] the remaining eleven verses make it unusually long. This impression is confirmed by analysis. The address in vv. 5, 6 contains no accusations as such, but indicates the divine control over the one affected by the woe, and in so doing raises a claim to acknowledgment and submission. In v. 7a the accusation at first merely brings out the difference between the commission and the self-understanding of the one to whom it has been given. According to the text as it has come down to us, the accusation contains a threefold grounding in vv. 7b, 8ff., 13f., before two didactic double questions bring the section to an end. Verse 12 comes between the second and third groundings. It falls outside the poetic structure which is otherwise characteristic of the woe, and in v. 12a contains details of the situation and in v. 12b a brief divine discourse,[14] without citation formula, which has the character of an announcement of judgment. Despite recent attempts to extract from the verse a nucleus which will have belonged to the basic text,[15] it is worth keeping to the old exegetical insight that the whole of v. 12 is an addition. It has in turn been occasioned by the insertion of vv. 10, 11: the blasphemy of Yahweh contained in them seemed to require a direct answer.

A striking formal feature of vv. 10, 11 is that v. 10 interrupts the

[12] The expression 'address' should not prove troublesome. What is meant is the outcry of those concerned: we know very well that this will originally have been in the third person. For the problem of the genre cf. the literature mentioned above, 96, nn. 19, 21, or the brief mention in Kaiser, *Introduction*, 332f.

[13] Cf. below, 238f.

[14] LXX has the third person.

[15] Cf. B. S. Childs, *Isaiah and the Assyrian Crisis*, SBT II, 3, London 1967, 43, and Barth, *Jesaja-Worte*, 23f.

WOE TO OVER-CONFIDENT ASSYRIA 231

series of questions beginning in v. 8b and introduced by $h^a l\bar{o}'$, 'is not?', which are taken up in v. 11. Furthermore, v. 10 ends in an anacolouthon. It is continued only in v. 11b, without it being made clear that v. 11a does not contain the organic protasis to v. 11b. So we may conclude that v. 10 has been inserted into the poem later than v. 11. However, v. 11 itself introduces a notion which is alien in comparison with vv. 8f., by quoting his thoughts: vv. 8,9 demonstrate the arrogance of the great king who believes all the kingdoms of the earth, without distinction, to be within his grasp, as is later expressly stated in vv. 13f. Thus v. 11 interrupts the development. It produces an explicit focus on Jerusalem and with its late polemic against idolatry looks like a coarse version of the thinking to be found in II Kings 18.33ff. par. Isa. 36.18ff. It has been suggested that the reference to the idols has been introduced into the verse subsequently, which would make it possible to arrive at a basic element which was part of the original poem.[16] However, operations of this kind are open to suspicion as long as the simple solution of omitting the whole verse provides a more satisfactory structure and a more coherent meaning. As further investigation will show, both of these results follow in the present case. Verses 13, 14 attach to vv. 8.9, which provide the material for the assertion in v. 14. Now, however, there is tension between the charge made in v. 7b that Assyria is concerned to annihilate many peoples, and the picture offered in vv. 8.9 and 13, 14, since v. 8, like v. 13 later, stresses the blindness of the Assyrian. Furthermore, in the end v. 15 culminates in precisely this charge. However, in contrast to the position in v. 11, it remains questionable whether we should exclude v. 7b in consequence,[17] since it provides the key word for the narrative in v. 9. In turn, there is no reason for excluding vv. 8, 9, since they prepare for vv. 13, 14.[18] It is further supposed that there is tension between v. 6b and v. 7b which calls for a literary solution. Thus vv. 7b, 6b, instead of being a commission to annihilate, seem to be a commission to chastise.[19] However, even this observation is not yet sharp enough: the charge made in v. 7b is directed against the fact not just that Assyria is out for annihilation – according to v. 6b that is irrefutably part of its business and could not be misunderstood – but that over and beyond the task which has been assigned to it, it is out for the annihilation of *many* nations.[20] And precisely that makes up the arrogance and

[16] Childs, op. cit., 42ff., and Barth, op. cit., 23.
[17] Cf. K. Fullerton, 'The Problem of Isaiah, Chapter 10', *AJSL* 34, 1917/18, 170ff., who limits the oracle to vv. 5–7a, 13–15. Huber, *Völker*, 41ff., by contrast limits it to vv. 5, 6a, 7a, 13–15 and then immediately adds 14.24–25a, 26–27. Cf. below, 232f.
[18] Against Fullerton and Huber.
[19] Cf. Fullerton, op. cit., 183.
[20] The 'nations' are the objects of both verbs!

self-glorification of Assyria (or its king) as it has been exemplified hitherto. Therefore there might not be sufficient reason to remove v. 6b or v. 7b, even if v. 6b has evidently been composed with an eye to 8.1; 5.5b (cf. also Micah 7.10).[21]

If the poem so far has proved to be a unit in thought, we have to ask whether the excision of v. 15b$\beta\gamma$ is in fact required, as has recently been once again proposed.[22] If we exclude the argument that the *pluralis majestatis* in b$\beta\gamma$ is the result of a secondary intensification,[23] it remains the case that instead of the rejection of the self-glorification of the instrument in abα, in b$\beta\gamma$ we have a rationalistic stress on the absurdity of the event.[24] But in that case in the end a decision becomes a question of taste as to whether such rationalism is to be attributed to the poet. Perhaps it is enough for the moment to ask in return whether the whole poem, with its weakening of form, and at least a couple of didactic questions at the end, is not ultimately to be regarded as a witness to religious rationalism. If we exclude the quotation formula in vv. 8a, 13aα_1[25] as later interpretative elements, and consider that the textual criticism of v. 13bβ suggests that we must suppose that a line has fallen out, we eventually have additional confirmation of the correctness of our literary-critical decisions: The verses which I have taken as belonging to the basic material now total exactly fifteen lines and can be divided into either two (vv. 5–7, 8b–9 and 13a$\alpha_2\beta b$, 14–15) or three strophes (vv. 5–7, 8b–9, 13a$\alpha_2\beta b$ and 14–15).

The woe-poem with the preceding cry of woe in 10.1–4 is connected not only externally but also thematically by means of the notion of a judgment which befalls the godless people. The day of visitation announced in v. 3 is seen by the author of vv. 5ff. as the day on which Assyria invades the country. Thus 10.5–15 could only have been given its present place when the final strophe of the poem with the refrain referring to Yahweh's outstretched hand in 5.26–29 had been separated from 9.7–20 and exchanged for the last woe now extended by 10.1–4.[26] Perhaps the break-up of the earlier compositions and the insertion of this woe was a single process. Through it the enemy from afar, announced in 5.26 and expected in 10.3, is

---

[21] Considerations of Isa. 8.1 may hardly be ruled out because the phrases *šālal šālal* and *bāzaz baz* only appear elsewhere, apart from these passages, the first in Ezek 29.19; 38.12f. and the second in Isa. 33.23. In this case the argument from metre does not seem to me to be so certain. In literary criticism in the first instance one should be cautious about the criterion of an Isaianic vocabulary.

[22] Cf. Wildberger, ad. loc., and Barth, *Jesaja-Worte*, 23. Vermeylen I, 255 cf. 258, regards the whole verse as an expansion contemporaneous with 10.12.

[23] Cf. n. 11.

[24] Barth, *Jesaja-Worte*, 23.

[25] The insertion of this formula was necessitated by the insertion of v. 12.

[26] Cf. also above, 111f.

connected with Assyria in a remarkable act of apparent rehistoriciz-
ing, and thus referred back to the historical situation in the time of
Isaiah, in which at the last moment Jerusalem had escaped conquest
by the Assyrians.[27] This process reflects the significance which the
survival of Jerusalem and the Davidic kingdom in 701 had gained as
an antitype for the catastrophe of 587.[28] However, it would be over-
hasty to see this merely as a historicizing process: as a counterpart to
the events of 587, the deliverance of Jerusalem in 701 was at the same
time the archetype for the city of God preserved in the eschatological
onslaught of the nations. So it is by no means necessary to suppose
that these texts arose, if not during the lifetime of Isaiah, at least
during the existence of the Assyrian kingdom.[29]

An examination of 14.24–27, or more exactly 14.24, 25a, 26–27,
adds additional support to these considerations. The way in which
this announcement of the destruction of Assyria in Yahweh's own
land, introduced with a divine oath, goes with the present woe, has
been recognized on many occasions.[30] It manifestly belongs with
this woe not only because of its theme of 'Assyria and Yahweh's
purpose', but also because of its five-line strophe and a double
question which again stands at the end. Here the questions at the
end of 10.5–15 are given a decisive answer. Verse 26 indicates that
Assyria has become the type of a world power, and judgment on it
has become the archetype of the expected judgment upon the world.
The severing into two parts of what originally belonged to one poem
may be in accordance with the wish of a later editor who did not
want to lose a saying against Assyria among the oracles on foreign
nations, hidden under the prophecies directed against Babylon in
chs. 13, 14. This in fact produced a gap after v. 15, which is now filled
by the announcement of judgment in vv. 16–19.

This conclusion is more significant for the understanding of the
present text than might appear at first sight. If it is correct that 14.24–
27 is a piece of literary prophecy, the same is also true of 10.5–15.[31]

[27] Cf. also *Isaiah 13–39*, 374f.
[28] Cf. also O. Kaiser, 'Geschichtliche Erfahrung und eschatologische Erwartung',
NZST 15, 1973, 272ff. = *Eschatologie im Alten Testament*, ed. H. D. Preuss, WdF 480,
Darmstadt 1978, 444ff.
[29] S. Mowinckel, *Komposition des Jesajabuches Kap 1–39*, AcOr 11, 1933, 281f., arranges
the texts in Isaiah relating to the Assyrians on the basis of this presupposition, and
the basic work by Barth, *Jesaja-Worte*, is in principle along the same lines.
[30] For an argument to this effect cf. Cheyne, *Introduction*, 79; Dillmann-Kittel and
Procksch, ad loc., and Vermeylen I, 253f.; with caution also Auvray, ad loc. By
contrast cf. e.g. Marti ad loc. and Childs, op. cit., 38f.
[31] For the secondary character of 14.24ff., cf. Kaiser, *Isaiah 13–39*, ad loc., and Barth,
Jesaja-Worte, 117ff. G. Beer, 'Die Zukunftserwartungen Jesajas', in *Studien zur semi-
tischen Philologie und Religionsgeschichte*, Festschrift Julius Wellhausen, BZAW 27,
Giessen 1914, 26; G. Hölscher, *Die Profeten*, Leipzig 1914, 363f.; and S. Mowinckel,
op. cit., have already argued against the Isaianic authorship of 10.5ff.

Therefore we should remove 10.5–15 from the list of sayings which go back to the prophet Isaiah himself, and discard as immaterial questions as to whether the saying belongs to the period of rebellion against Assyria under the leadership of Ashdod in the years 713–711, or only to the time of the rebellion, with moderate support from Judah, which took place in 703–701.[32] If at the end of these preliminary considerations we also remember the complicated construction of the text, which goes against traditional categories of form criticism, and in the end virtually ends up in a wisdom 'dispute fable',[33] we shall find here a confirmation of the argument that the present woe is purely a literary construction.

[10.5–7] *Yahweh's woe over Assyria.* It is a characteristic feature of the audacity of Israel's assurance of God that it saw in its own impotence, and the way in which it was delivered-over to the world power of its time, evidence that the latter was Yahweh's instrument by which he acted on his own people and at the same time gained glory in the world. Thus Jeremiah is said to have declared that Yahweh himself had given rule over the world to his servant Nebuchadnezzar (Jer. 27.5ff.), and Second Isaiah saw the Persian king Cyrus, who conquered the kingdoms of Media and Lydia and the Neo-Babylonian empire, as the anointed one (Messiah), called by Yahweh for the sake of his people Israel and his own glorification over the people of this earth (45.1ff.). From the fundamental belief that the deity stands behind all the fortunes and misfortunes of the individual and the nation, and therefore decides on victory or defeat in war, in time there developed out of the helplessness of Israel a theology of history according to which Yahweh deliberately goaded the enemies of his people against his own people (cf. 9.11 [10]), and summoned them from afar to annihilate his faithless people (5.26; 7.18f., 20). In this way the defeated people assured themselves of the power of their God in the past for the sake of his future. The present woe against Assyria should also be seen against the background of this theology of history, which understands Assyria as the punitive instrument of Yahweh to annihilate his apostate people (according to 9.16, this means the people of God). As v. 6 envisages a present event and vv. 9, 13f. show that the northern kingdom, Israel, had already been destroyed, Assyria's task on this occasion involves Jerusalem and Judah, as now the authentic Israel. Its ravaging (cf. Ezek. 29.19; 39.10; also Isa. 8.1ff.; 33.23) and annihilation (cf. 5.5; 28.18; Micah 7.10) are in accordance with God's purpose.

---

[32] For dating in the early period of Sargon II (722–705), see Procksch, Ziegler, Kaiser[1], Wildberger and Schedl; for dating in the reign of Sennacherib (705–681), e.g. Duhm, Marti, Steinmann, Fohrer, Eichrodt and Auvray.

[33] Cf. the detailed discussion in Whedbee, *Isaiah and Wisdom*, 68ff.

However, the great king, who is named simply after his God and his kingdom, does not understand himself as an instrument of Yahweh, but sees the possibility offered to him of incorporating yet another kingdom simply as a confirmation of his arrogant self-understanding. He believes that he can subdue any kingdom he likes and incorporate it into his empire. Thus the divine instrument of punishment has turned into the tyrant concerned for the annihilation of all peoples.

[10.8–9 + 13*] *The ungodly ruler of the world.* To illustrate this arrogant attitude of the ruler of the world, the poet allows the reader to share in the thinking of the king who, in seeing all his officials and officers as kings, puts himself on earth in the position of God. In its contemptuous rhetorical questions, the list of subjected kingdoms in v. 9 expresses the arrogance of the king and at the same time provides the specific background for the boasting in vv. 13, 14. In content, this passage is not oriented on the historical course of events, but on the approach of the Assyrian army from crossing the Euphrates at Carchemish to the frontiers of Judaea. Carchemish, present-day *Ǧerāblus*, lies on the west bank of the central Euphrates. As the last resort of Hittite colonial culture, it paid for the attempt to cast off the yoke of Assyria in 717 with the loss of its freedom. The strategic significance of the city is evident from the fact that here in 605 the decisive battle for the possession of Syria and Palestine took place between the Egyptian Pharaoh Necho II and the Babylonian king Nebuchadnezzar (cf. Jer. 46.2).[34] Calno, in cuneiform Kullani, situated in the plain east of Antioch, was conquered as early as 738 by Tiglath-pileser III (cf. also Amos 6.2).[35] In the Old Testament, Arpad is always mentioned alongside Hamath, with which it alternated during the eighth century in its rule over northern Syria.[36] It was situated on Tell *Rfād* north of Aleppo (cf. II Kings 18.34; 19.13 par. Isa. 36.16; 37.13; Jer. 49.23).[37] Involved with Samaria and Damascus in the rebellion of Jaubidi of Hamath, it shared Samaria's fate in 720. Hamath itself is to be identified with present-day *Ḥama* north-west of Homs (cf. II Sam. 8.9; Gen. 10.18; Isa. 11.11; I Macc. 12.25).[38] Damascus had lost its independence at the end of the Syro-Ephraimite war in 732 and Samaria its independence in 722/21.[39] The experience of Assyria that all these kingdoms without distinction were in its power is in accordance with its feeling that it

[34] Cf. R. Borger, *BHH* II, cols. 933f.
[35] Cf. M. A. Beek, *BHH* II, col. 922.
[36] Cf. A. Jepsen, *AfO* 14, 1941/44, 170.
[37] Cf. K. Elliger, *BHH* I, col. 132.
[38] Cf. J. D. Hawkins, *RLA* IV, 67ff.
[39] Cf. above, 149f. and for the end of Samaria also H. Tadmor, 'The Campaigns of Sargon II of Assur', *Journal of Cuneiform Studies* 12, 1958, 2ff., 77ff.

owed the fact solely to its own strength and its own competence.[40] The boasting attributed to it is presumably put in deliberate contrast to the woe in 5.21 (cf. also Jer. 9,22; Isa. 29.14b). Instead of recognizing Yahweh's commission and disposition in the facts, Assyria attributes its success solely to its own competence, supposing that it alone is responsible for the fact that the frontiers of the nations do not hold up (cf. Deut. 32.8) and kings fall from their thrones.

[10.14–15] *The blindness of human boasting.* The boasting and blindness of Assyria reaches its climax in the comparison of its victorious course, which secures for it the treasures of the nations and rule over the world, with the easy, carefree assembly of a debauched feast.[41] Denying the resistance which is in fact offered by the peoples, it claims to be the absolute Lord of the earth; and with this confidence it will also launch an attack on Jerusalem. While the experience may justify its own conviction, Assyria has nevertheless transgressed the limits imposed on human beings and overlooked the fact that even the mightiest is only an implement in the hands of a superior power. Taking his reality into account, the imposing behaviour of the ruler of the world is transformed into an almost laughable over-estimation of itself. The didactic rhetorical questions, which invite the judgment of the reader and hearer, have their closest parallel in the sayings of Ahikar, a wisdom poem presumably going back to an Akkadian original, which was found among the ruins of the Jewish military colony in Elephantine in Upper Egypt. There the subordination of the courtier to the will of the king is stressed with the triple rhetorical question: 'Does wood dispute with fire? Or flesh with the knife? Or a man with the "king"?'[42] Assyria is in fact a rod in Yahweh's hands and no more (cf. also 29.15f.). If it forgets this limitation and dependence, it inevitably falls victim to the divine wrath. Thus the divine woe delivered on the arrogant Assyria is a comfort to all the oppressed who suffer under an alien power. 14.24ff. will show that Assyria is doomed to destruction in Yahweh's land. What happened before the gates of Jerusalem according to the legendary tradition, in the year 701, the mysterious destruction of the Assyrian army (cf. 37.36), gave the poet justification for his woe (cf. 37.36). Every period could see this ruler as the embodiment of its tyrants and could ask whether it had been chosen once again to inflict Yahweh's wrath on his own people and thus meet its downfall, to the glory of his name.

The reader may not ask whether the picture drawn here corresponds with the Assyrian king's own understanding of himself. If we look through the annals of this ruler, we shall find, for example

[40] Cf. below, 255f. on 11.2.
[41] Cf. also Deut. 22.6.
[42] Line 104, cf. *AOT*², 459, or *ANET*²⁻³, 429a.

in those of king Esarhaddon (680–669), almost a mirror-image of the role assigned to Assyria in v. 5: the only difference is that his own god, Assur, has taken the place of Yahweh. As he boasts to his own glory, the gods themselves have sent him against any land which had sinned against Assyria. Assur himself had called him to extend the frontiers of his kingdom. And the great cosmic gods, the moon god Sin, the sun god Shamash, Marduk the king of the gods, Nergal, who as king of the underworld was omnipotent among the gods, and Ishtar, the queen of battle, had made possible his victorious course by bestowing on him strength, boldness, praise, fear which casts men down, and weapons which reach their mark.[43] So this woe is not concerned with 'Assyria', but with those world powers which have taken its place, smugly regard themselves as being superior to the tiny people of God, and will ultimately fall before the gates of Jerusalem, as did once, according to legend, the army of Sennacherib. Thus those who are really addressed by this woe are not Assyria but the people of God who suffer under the rule of that pagan power, who take comfort in a dark present from the future liberation which is reflected in the former act of deliverance performed by their God.

[10.10–12] *The additions.* Verse 12 explicitly asserts that Yahweh will punish the arrogance of the heart[44] and the haughtiness of the eyes[45] of Assyria, now explicitly identified with its king, when he concludes his historical action[46] on Zion.[47] Verse 11 extends the line of the kingdoms enumerated in v. 9 by including Samaria with Jerusalem in the context of a Judaism which feels itself superior to the religions of the nations. 37.12 may be the stimulus to this. Here the person responsible for the addition makes Assyria reverse its own thinking about the gods of the nations, and speak in derogatory fashion about the nonentities, the gods of Samaria and the idols of Jerusalem,[48] in this way directly blaspheming Yahweh, the true God worshipped in both the northern and the southern kingdom. The editor whose work we find in v. 10 tries to take account of the comparison of Yahweh made there with the gods of the nations, whom he regards as idols (cf. Ps. 96.5). Here he takes delight in the thought that the magnitude of the divine protection is related to the number of idols. Judaism, which worshipped its God without idols,

---

[43] Cf. *AOT²*, 357, or Luckenbill, *Ancient Records* II, § 507f.
[44] Cf. 9.8 and 3.10; 27.9; Jer. 6.19; Isa. 13.19.
[45] Cf. also Prov. 21.4; also 2.11, 17.
[46] Cf. 5.12, 15; 28.21; Ps. 66.6; 107.24; 118.17.
[47] Cf. Isa. 38.12; Job 27.8; Lam. 2.17.
[48] Cf. 2.8, 18, 20; 19.1, 3; 31.7; Ps. 96.5; 97.7; also I Sam 31.9; II Sam. 5.21; Isa. 46.1; Jer. 50.2. In the light of Hos. 4.17; 8.4; 13.2; 14.9; Micah 1.7, we cannot rule out the possibility that the poet thought the charge against Samaria apt.

was aware that in so doing it was provoking the amazement of all nations and at the same time felt itself to be superior to all those who worshipped their gods in the form of images.[49]

CHAPTER 10.16–19

Yahweh's Punitive Judgment on Assyria

16   Therefore the Lord[1] Yahweh Sebaoth will send
        wasting sickness against his fat ones.[2]
        Instead of his splendour a burning will be kindled
        like the burning of a fire.
17   Then the light of Israel will become a fire
        and his Holy One a flame,
        which will kindle and devour
        his thistles and his thorns in one day.
18   The splendour of his forests and his gardens
        will be destroyed[3] from the soul to the flesh,
        and it will be as though a sick man wastes away.[4]
19   The remnant of the trees of his forest will be so few
        that a child can write them down.

[10.16–19] In view of the typological significance which the legendary annihilation of the Assyrian army before the gates of Jerusalem in 701 acquired for the fate of the powers of the world in the expected eschatological onslaught of the nations upon the city of God,[5] we can understand why people were still preoccupied with this theme in the later post-exilic period.[6] Thus it seemed important to the editor whose words we have here to follow 10.15 with an unmistakable announcement of the annihilation of Assyria, and in this way to

---

[49] Cf. also 2.8, 20; 31.7; 40.19f.; 41.7; 44.9ff.
[1] Like the *ᵃdōnāy* in vv. 23, 24, the *hā'ādōn* could be taken as a later insertion. However, in view of the late character of the section, we should also reckon with the possibility of a primary accumulation of divine epithets.
[2] The plural is meant to indicate the fat parts of the body.
[3] LXX and V read a passive.
[4] For the problems in translating v. 18b cf. Barth, *Jesaja-Worte*, 29f. The half-verse interrupts the connection between v. 18a, and v. 19, has no parallel half-line, and thus looks suspiciously like a gloss.
[5] Cf. above, 233.
[6] Against Barth, *Jesaja-Worte*, 34.

close the gap which arose from the transposition of 14.24ff.[7] The external occasion for the insertion of vv. 16–19 may have been the incorporation of 10.20–27 and the consequent isolation of 10.5–15 from 10.28–34, which in the meantime was understood as a threat directed against the world power.

There are two particularly striking features in a literary evaluation of the eschatological prophecy which expects Yahweh's last judgment upon the world power: first the restless and inconsistent shift of images, and secondly the affinity with other passages in the proto-Isaianic collection made up of chs. 1–39. This is probably to be interpreted as a consequence of literary dependence. Verse 16 presents Assyria as a stout and imposing man[8] who is being weakened by fever. In v. 17 the fever is replaced by the light of Yahweh, which becomes fire. At the same time, instead of a man we have mention of his crops. However, in v. 18, instead of this, we again have mention of his splendid forests and orchards, to which anthropological concepts are now applied along the lines of v. 16. Therefore at least v. 19 carries through the metaphors of v. 18a.

Before we are led aside into an allegorical interpretation, and see the weeds and the trees of the forest as common men overrunning Judaea, and the orchards as the officers of the great king, we must note the literary references as far as we can. The decisive parallels in construction and content are to be found in the announcement of judgment against the northern kingdom of Israel in 17.4–6: here too the personification of the people as a stout and imposing man appears at the beginning. Here, too, he is threatened with thinness. Two comparisons taken from the harvest then follow, to clarify the process of judgment. At the end, the result of the judgment is again described with a comparison taken from agriculture. Here the meaning of this prophecy is quite clearly that only a very few people will escape the annihilating judgment to come. This corresponds very closely to the statement in 10.19, which was certainly not formulated without a knowledge of 11.6. In addition, for subsidiary elaborations borrowed from elsewhere one might refer to 9.18[17] and 14[13] for v. 17, in addition to 11.6 for v. 19. Like Israel in the fictitious prophetic situation of 17.4–6, Assyria is now to fall victim to Yahweh's wrath. We cannot rule out the possibility that with these references the prophet, well-versed in written tradition, wanted to indicate that the action of the world power would ultimately rebound against it, by virtue of the divine ordinance.[9] If

---

[7] Cf. also above, 232f., Barth, op. cit., 34, and Vermeylen I, 252 and especially 259f.

[8] With Barth, op. cit., 28f., who has thus refuted the other interpretations of the verse.

[9] Cf. Barth, op. cit., 31f.

we add that Yahweh is the light of Israel as the salvation and help of his people (cf. 60.1; Micah 7.8; Ps. 27.1; Isa. 9.1) [10], and a devouring fire as the God who watches zealously over his people (cf. Deut. 4.24; 9.3),[11] we can see the theological significance of the prophecy; the God who is the helper of his people Israel ultimately guards over his possession by destroying powers which are hostile to them.

CHAPTER 10.20–23

Only a Remnant will Return

20   In that day it will come about:
      the remnant of Israel will no longer lean,
      nor the survivors of the house of Jacob
      upon him who smote them,
      but will lean upon Yahweh,
      the Holy One of Israel, in faithfulness.[1]
21   Only a remnant will return,
      a remnant of Jacob,
      to the mighty God.
22   Yes, though your people, Israel,
      were like the sand of the sea,
      only a remnant of them will return.
      Destruction is decreed,
      overflowing righteousness.
23   Yes, the Lord[2] Yahweh Sebaoth
      will carry out the decreed destruction
      in the midst of the whole earth.

[10.20–23] The prophetic formula 'on that day it will come about' shows that the present prophecy is a literary expansion. As evidence that it cannot be attributed to the prophet Isaiah, Duhm's observation about the behaviour of the two kings of Judah in whose reign Isaiah's activity falls is still relevant: 'According to II Kings 16, Ahaz relied on

---

[10] Cf. also S. Aalen, TWAT I, col. 175, TDOT 1, 147.

[11] For the connection with the conception of a theophany cf. also Ps. 50.3.

[1] The added be'emet is perhaps a later addition, but we can also follow Wildberger in seeing it as having been put at the end of the clause for greater emphasis.

[2] It is hard to decide whether the 'adōnāy is redactional or comes from the author of the verse. Cf. also above, 238 n.1.

Assyria and was not defeated; Hezekiah was defeated, but did not rely on Assyria.'[3] In fact the text, with hardly any metric structure, proves to be a skilful compilation of formulae and reminiscences of Isaiah and other parts of the Bible. A section composed in such a mosaic style may be regarded as primarily the product of scribal activity, and can hardly have been produced before the fourth century. [20] If we compare this verse with II Kings 10.30f. par. Isa. 37.31f., we recognize that it is about the remnant of the people of God[4] and the people of Jerusalem who escape the expected onslaught of the world power on Zion, a world power which, maintaining the fiction of Isaianic authorship, is designated Assyria.[5] A look at 10.27ff., which describes the breathtaking and terrifying advance of the enemy, shows that this interpretation is correct. The phrase 'him who smote them' has been taken from the refrain poem about the outstretched hand of Yahweh (9.13[12]) and transferred from Yahweh to Assyria (cf. also 10.5). The contrast between the remnant relying on Yahweh and those relying on the world power has presumably been formulated as a variation of the charge made against king Asa of Judah (II Chron. 16.7).[6] The fact that Yahweh is addressed as the Holy One of Israel gives the saying an Isaianic stamp.[7] It cannot be asserted that the 'in faithfulness' is taken from 16.5, though that possibility cannot be excluded.

[21] Here the scribe works with the name of Isaiah's son Shearjashub, 'only a remnant returns' (7.3), and in the case of the hero god, with one of the throne-names of the Messiah from 9.6f[5f.]. However, the last-mentioned might be a reference to Yahweh rather than to the king of the time of salvation. [22] If this is addressed to the ancestors of Israel, it echoes the promise given in Gen. 32.13 that their seed will be as numerous as the sand of the sea.[8] Again, the existing notion is turned into its opposite: even if the descendants of the patriarch Jacob-Israel were as numerous as the sand of the sea, only a remnant of them would be left, because the annihilating judgment of Yahweh summoned up with reminiscences of 28.17,

[3] Schedl, *Rufer des Heils*, 290, asserts, 'King Ahaz had relied on the power of Assyria and had been shattered on it', but the evidence for this assertion is lacking. The attempt by Steinmann to transfer the saying to the year 738, in which Menahem of Israel had to pay tribute to Tiglath-pileser III, comes to grief, as Wildberger rightly points out, on the fact that at that time there was still no occasion to speak of a remnant of Israel. Apart from that, literary evidence outside this chapter tells against the attempt. It should be noted that K-D. Schunck, *VT* 14, 1964, 323, and Auvray, ad loc., have once again argued for Isaianic authorship.
[4] For the evidence for the formula 'house of Jacob', cf. above, 56 n. 30.
[5] Cf. also above, 237.
[6] Cf. also 30.12; 50.10; II Chron. 13.18; 14.10; 16.8.
[7] Cf. the evidence in 22 n. 36.
[8] Cf. also Gen 22.17; Hos. 2.1; Isa. 48.49.

22, is inexorable. **[23]** The next verse then goes directly back to 28.22, so as to adapt the quotation only slightly to the requirements of its new context.

In content, the announcement here of the decimation of the people of God in the last onslaught of the nations (cf. 6.13abα; 7.16abα), which must happen before the nucleus of the new Israel emerges (cf. 6.13bβ), rightly comes after the announcement of the plans made by Assyria to attack Jerusalem, which are doomed to failure because of their arrogance (10.5–15), and before the announcement of the attack on the city in 10.27ff. Presumably in that case 10.24–26, with its no less 'scribal' invitation not to fear 'Assyria', was then inserted first.[9] Its exclusive character of promise seemed to require the qualification contained in 10.22–23, that even the people of God will not be spared in the imminent judgment, but will be measured by God with the measure of righteousness, and thus judged anew. Yet in the end the 'scribal' prophet is not concerned with this judgment as such, but with the remnant emerging from it which will finally put its trust in Yahweh and thus fulfil the condition of enduring expressed by the prophet according to 7.9b; 30.15. What could not be brought about by the divine visitations in the past and the prophetic preaching to repent will be achieved by the last great crisis of history with its unexpected divine help, annihilating the powers of the world like a spectre: the return of the remnant to Yahweh. After he has demonstrated his superiority to the power of the world in the deliverance of Jerusalem, the temptation to trust in their help rather than his will be removed for ever (cf. also II Kings 16.7ff.; Isa. 30.1ff.; 31.1ff.). However, judgment stands like an inexorable doom before repentance. So we may draw conclusions from this for the verdict of the scribe on this own time: evidently in his eyes it fails to trust Yahweh as it should.

Does his verdict still apply today? Is it still the case that we take God as seriously as he means to be taken only when we have no other expedient? And does this justify hope for peace among the nations before they have experienced the hopelessness of their politics of power and violence?

---

[9] One may well hesitate over deciding whether in the insertion, 10.5–15 had already been expanded by vv. 16–19. For a literary assessment cf. also Barth, *Jesaja-Worte*, 17ff., and Vermeylen I, 262, who regards 10.20–22aα and 24–27 as a self-contained section which was put before 10.15–19.

CHAPTER 10.24–27

Do not Fear Assyria

24　　Therefore thus says the Lord,[1] Yahweh Sebaoth,
'Have no fear, my people
who dwell in Zion, of Assyria,
when it smites you[2] with a rod
and lifts up its staff against you
as Egypt did.
25　　For in only a little while,
wrath is exhausted
and my angry concern for their annihilation will be finished.[3]
26　　Then Yahweh Sebaoth will swing the scourge against them
as he smote Midian at the Rock of the Raven,
and will lift his rod over the sea,[4]
as he did against Egypt.

27　　On that day it will happen that
his burden will disappear from your shoulder
and his yoke from your neck
and the yoke will be shattered for fat.[5]

[10.24–27] 10.24–26, like the previous prophecy in 10.20–23[6] (though that prophecy was presumably only inserted later), is a prophecy

---

[1] It remains open to question whether the *'adōnāy* is an expansion or original. Cf. also 10.16, 23.

[2] For the form cf. G-K[28] § 58i.

[3] So M, which I follow Delitzsch and Dillmann-Kittel in keeping, in view of the problems of conjectures. For the proposal of G. R. Driver, *JTS* 38, 1937, 38, to read a *wᵉ'appī 'al-tēkel yittōm*, 'and my wrath is completely exhausted', cf. J. A. Soggin, *Old Testament and Oriental Studies*, BibOr 29, Rome 1975, 232f. For the suggestion by S. D. Luzzato, *Il Profeta Isaia volgarizzato e commentato ad uso degl'Israeliti*, Padua 1867, ad loc., also supported by Soggin, of a reading *wᵉ'appi 'al-tēbēl yittōm*, 'and my anger over the earth is at an end', cf. already Gray, ad loc.

[4] H. Winkler, *Alttestamentliche Untersuchungen*, 1892, 177, made the attractive conjecture that we should read *ᵃlēhem*, against them.

[5] In the form in which it has been handed down, v. 27b looks like a gloss, which is concerned with the sudden strengthening of the people of God as indicated in 9.3f. Usually nowadays attempts are made to find a parallel to v. 28a behind the text as transmitted. So conjectures are made e.g. of an *'ālā mippᵉnē rimmōn*, or *šomrōn, bēt 'ēl, šāmōl, ṣāpōn* or *yᵉšīmōn*: 'he went up from Rimmon', or Samaria, Bethel, the north or the wilderness, without finding any secure ground. Schedl, *Rufer des Heils*, 292, and Auvray, ad loc., keep to M.

[6] Cf. above, 242.

created *a priori* for its present place in the book. Verse 27 is an addition to it. After the madness of the world power, named 'Assyria' to maintain the fiction of Isaianic authorship, has been called in question in 10.5–15 and its downfall has been announced in 10.16–19, the present text turns to address the people of Jerusalem as the nucleus of the people of God, the part of them which is particularly affected. It tells them to trust in Yahweh's name with tranquillity in the face of the expected onslaught of the world power and assures them that its days are numbered. The prophet of comfort derives the authority of his message from the study of scripture:[7] he formulates the address to the people of God dwelling on Zion on the basis of 30.18. Both 10.5 and 30.31 are used in the characterization of Assyria. He could have taken the reference to servitude in Egypt from 30.18. When he wrote v. 25 he had 29.17 and 26.20 in mind. Moreover, there is also influence from 10.5. Verse 26 may echo 28.15, 18, but exploits the ambiguity of the Hebrew word *šōṭ*, which in the one passage means 'flood' and in the other 'scourge'. 9.3 provided him with the comparison with the victory over the Midianites. However, in accordance with 10.5ff. he concentrates on the annihilation of the leaders (cf. Judg. 7.25). Verse 26b is problematic.[8] In content it works with the antithesis, Yahweh will do to Assyria what Assyria did to the people of God.[9] Perhaps this half-verse is a later addition which sought to affirm the annihilation not only of the princes but also of the whole of the enemy host.

[24] Because Assyria and especially its king have vaunted themselves and in so doing invited their destruction (cf. 10.5ff., 16ff.; 30.27ff.), the scribe can comfortingly assure the people of Jerusalem, as the nucleus of Judaism[10] threatened by the world power, in the name of the almighty Yahweh Sebaoth,[11] that they need not fear. In so doing he resorts to the old formula of reassurance with which Yahweh introduced his oracle of salvation when the lament of the suppliant was heard (cf. Lam. 3.57).[12] Against the background of the failure of its attack on Jerusalem in 701, Assyria has become a code name for the world power (cf. 10.5ff.; 14.24ff.; 30.28ff.; 31.4ff.). What once happened, according to legend (cf. II Kings 19.35 par. Isa. 37.36), will be repeated in the face of the eschatological onslaught of the peoples on Jerusalem: they will meet their end before the gates of the city! [25] The brooder who recalls 29.17; 26.20 here is convinced

---

[7] Cf. also Vermeylen, I, 264.

[8] Cf. n. 3.

[9] Cf. above, 239.

[10] In the Persian period Jerusalem was the religious centre of Judaism and at the same time the centre of its eschatological expectations.

[11] Cf. above, 126.

[12] Cf. J. Becker, *Gottesfurcht im Alten Testament*, AnBib 25, Rome 1965, 52.

that the shift in the fortunes of the people is imminent: the wrath of Yahweh which was once poured out against his own people in the threat to the city of God will soon be over, and will be directed – if I am right in suggesting that the text should be kept as it has come down to us –[13] towards the annihilation of the 'Assyrians'. **[26]** If Yahweh goes against them with the whip or the goad, they will no longer offer him further resistance, but will be completely routed. Of course the goad is not a normal weapon of attack. It was occasionally used by the Persians to urge on their own soldiers.[14] The Romans later made isolated use of it as an instrument of torture in connection with crucifixion (cf. II Macc. 7.1, 13, 15; Matt. 27.16).[15] The victory of Yahweh over the enemies assembled before the walls of Jerusalem is compared with that over the Midianites at the Rock of the Raven (cf. also 9.3). There, according to Judg. 7.25, the Israelites had captured and executed two Midianite princes. The ruler of the world, hostile to God, will not escape the future wrath of God, and his army will perish with him, so that the country will see a repetition of the annihilation of Pharaoh and his army as it once took place at the Sea of Reeds (cf. Ex. 14.27ff.).

[27] This verse is an addition. Referring back to 9.3, it maintains that this victory signifies the liberation of the people from its servitude (cf. also 14.25b).

CHAPTER 10.28–34

The Enemy from the North

28   He comes from Aiath,
       passes through Migron,
       he[1] directs his baggage train towards Michmash.
29   They cross over[2] the pass:

---

[13] Cf. n. 3.
[14] Cf. Herodotus VII, 56 and 103.
[15] Cf. also B. Reicke, *BHH* I, col. 534.
[1] For the use of the so-called imperfect to denote a concomitant action, cf. Bobzin § 7b.
[2] 1Q1s[a], LXX and S read the singular. It is hard to discover who has altered what in which direction.

'Let Geba be our quarters for the night.'
Ramah trembles,
Gibeah of Saul flees.

30   Cry aloud, daughter of Gallim,
Hearken, Laishah,
<Answer her>[3] Anathoth!

31   Madmenah is in flight,
the inhabitants of Gebim hide.

32   This very day he is in Nob,
he raises his hand against the mount of the daughter of Zion,
the height of Jerusalem.

33   Behold the Lord[4] Yahweh Sebaoth
lops the boughs with terrifying power.
The great in height are felled,
and the lofty sink low;[1]

34   The thicket of the wood is cut down with iron
and Lebanon <with its mighty cedar>[5] will fall.

[10.28–34] In the present context we must see the enemy whose
unstoppable advance is depicted in vv. 28–32 as Assyria, the world
power which Yahweh has called up against his own people as a rod
of chastisement, yet which is doomed to certain destruction because
of its folly (cf. 10.5ff., 16ff., 24ff.; 14.24ff.). Accordingly the wood cut
down by Yahweh seems to refer to the hostile army storming against
the city of God, to find an end before the gates of the city. However,
presumably this interpretation suggested by the present context
does not catch the original meaning of the remarkable poem, the
style of which, working throughout with mosaic stones taken from
the Bible, differs markedly from late additions like 10.16ff., 20ff.,
24ff.; 11.10ff., and can hardly have been the continuation of 10.5–15
+ 14.24–27. If we remember that the last strophe of the refrain poem
about Yahweh's outstretched hand in 5.26–29 once took the place of
10.1–4, and that at any rate 10.5–15 was only inserted at a later point,
it becomes clear that this section takes up the theme of the unstoppable march of the enemy begun in 5.26–29 and applies it specifically
to Jerusalem. This hardly happened at the same time as that poem,
but rather in connection with the conception of the onslaught of the
nations breaking ominously over Jerusalem and Judah in the shade
of the expectation of judgment upon the world, as it has found

---

[3] Read *ᵃnīhā, second person feminine singular imperative of the qal of *ᶜanā,
answer, with the suffix of the third person singular feminine.
[4] The *hā'ādōn can just as well be original as a secondary addition. Cf. also v. 16.
[5] With D. L. Christensen, 'The March of Conquest in Isaiah 10, 27c–34', *VT* 26,
1976, 392, read a *bᵉ'erez 'addīr. Cf. Ezek. 17.23. M can be explained as a haplography.

expression in 3.1–4.1.[6] Accordingly, vv. 33–34 originally dealt more with the fortunes of those under attack than those attacking them.[7]

Dramatic though the description of the advance in vv. 28–32 may be, it is not formally an independent literary unit: it has no introduction developing as an exposition of the historical context and giving the name of the enemy, nor does it have a conclusion. Given the context, it is less probable that this is a fragment of a lament from a real historical situation like that of the Syro-Ephraimite war[8] or a later otherwise unattested violation of the territory of Judah by an Assyrian army[9] than that here we have a redactional construction along the lines characterized above.[10]

If we adopt this assessment of the section, we cannot attribute it to Isaiah. Among recent scholars, Duhm and Marti had above all challenged aesthetic arguments and at the same time pointed to dependence on Micah 1.10ff., a prophetic lament which our eschatological poet seems to have exploited for the notion of the dramatic outcry of various places in the face of the misfortune descending upon them. He also made much of paronomastic word-play, sadly impossible to reproduce in English, which works on the relative sounds of words. However, this view found little following, so that even today a place is sought for the saying in the context of Isaiah's preaching. Thus for example Donner sees the present verses as a description of the advance of the allied army of Aramaeans and Israelites against Jerusalem in the so-called Syro-Ephraimite war.[11] In this view, v. 33 corresponds with the announcement of the destruction of the two hostile kingdoms handed down in 7.1ff.; 8.1ff. That seems to be a sufficient explanation of the striking advance, which at any rate was not made by the Assyrians in 701.[12] However, as here there is neither a mention of two peoples, nor has the passage been handed down in the context of the so-called memorial from the time of this war (6.1–8.18), Wildberger, like e.g. Feldmann and Procksch before him, thought in terms of the period of the Philistine rebellion under the leadership of the city of Ashdod against Sargon II of Assyria, between 713 and 711. Wildberger thought that he could infer from the text that at that time the king of Assyria had organized an advance by his troops stationed in Samaria

[6] Cf. above, 3f.
[7] Cf. Vermeylen I, 266, with n. 3 and Barth, *Jesaja-Worte*, 64ff., of whom the former refers to the attackers and the latter to Jerusalem under attack.
[8] Cf. below.
[9] Cf. also Vermeylen I, 266f.
[10] Cf. also Barth, *Jesaja-Worte*, 64ff.
[11] For this cf. above, 248.
[12] *Israel unter den Völkern*, 30ff., and also the more precise geographical details in 'Der Feind aus dem Norden', *ZDPV* 84, 46ff.

to the northern frontier of the kingdom of Judah, without the expected attack actually taking place.[13] Others, like e.g. Fohrer, Kaiser and Auvray, have got over the argument used against dating the passage in 701, that on that occasion Sennacherib did not attack the city from the north but from the south,[14] and that 10.28–32 could not therefore be connected with this event, by regarding the text as a prophetic prediction.

If we leave vv. 33, 34 out of account, the dramatic poem can be divided into three strophes, each with five lines or two and a half stanzas. The first consists of vv. 28, 29a and reports the advance of the enemy from Aiath to Geba. The second, in vv. 29b, 30, is concerned with the panic which is caused in the cities in front of Jerusalem. The third, in vv. 31, 32, reports the beginning of flight from these places and the imminent appearance of the enemy before the gates of the city. In time, the poem spans an afternoon and the following night up till dawn, the time when an attack was usually launched (cf. Josh. 6.15; 8.9ff.; Ps. 46.6; Isa. 17.14). Stylistically, the unconnected clauses, put one after the other, usually made up of between two and four words and ultimately of seven, give the impression of reports from messengers being poured out one after another. I have already referred to the use of paronomasia, a word-play using terms which reflect the names of the places; this is particularly evident in v. 29a. In addition, the fact that there are seven places reached or aimed for by the enemy and seven cities which respond to the advance indicates that the report is a polished composition.[15]

[10.28–29a] *The enemy advance.* The poet makes his reader share in the advance of the eschatological host on Jerusalem as reflected in a series of breathtaking messages of disaster. It is not surprising that he has details of exact locations which he can imagine as the places from which the messages emanate. Thus he makes the enemy advance in a circle towards the east instead of taking the main route which runs roughly along the watershed from Bethel via Mizpah and Nob to Jerusalem.[16] The route described here takes the army back on to the main route after Nob, having crossed over the *wādi es-suwēnīt* by side roads. Despite the detour, this saved time, because it by-passed the fortress of Mizpah (*tell en-naṣbe*) (cf. also Neh. 3.14–19). At the same time, the reader in Jerusalem would be

[13] Cf. also Dillman-Kittel, ad loc., and Vermeylen I, 266ff.
[14] Cf *TGI²* no. 39, 67ff., and II Kings 18.3f., 17.
[15] Nevertheless, I have suspicions about the attempt by Christensen, *VT* 26, 1976, 395ff., to reduce the poem to a more even structure.
[16] As the enemy from the north advances south and passes Ai, he must earlier have come through Bethel. For the attempts at reconstructing v. 27b in the interest of incorporating the half-verse into the existing poem, cf. above, 243 n. 5.

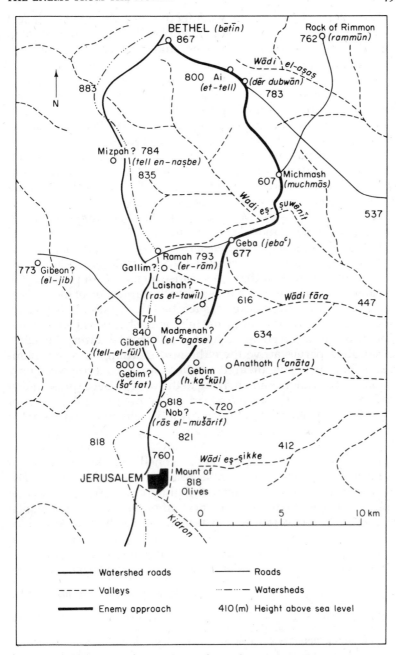

The northern approaches to Jerusalem after Dalman, *PJ* 12, 1916, 37, amended by Donner, *ZDPV* 84, 1968, 51.

left wondering for a moment whether the enemy would now in fact advance on Zion or at the last moment bend round into the Jordan valley. The stretch between Bethel and Michmash, present-day *muḥmās*, a distance of about five miles, could be covered in about two hours. First of all the army would come up against Aiath, presupposing that this is to be identified with the biblical Ai, Arabic *et-tell*, both meaning 'ruined place' (cf. Josh. 7.2; 8.9; Neh. 11.31).[17] The moment it turned towards Migron,[18] and shifted its weapons and equipment to Michmash, evidently a particularly suitable place for such a purpose (cf. I Sam. 13.16; I Macc. 9.73),[19] the force could clearly be seen to be directed towards Jerusalem. If Geba (present-day *Ǧebaʿ*) was to serve as night-quarters, this frontier fortress had to be occupied by a surprise attack (cf. I Kings 15.22), which meant first reaching the pass of Michmas (cf. 13.25), on the upper course of the *wādi es-ṣuwēnīt*, under cover of darkness.[20]

[10.29b–30] *The outbreak of panic on the outskirts of Jerusalem.* The fact that the appearance of the enemy in places outside Jerusalem creates such panic means that this is a surprise attack which prevents the inhabitants taking refuge in time under the protection of the walls of Jerusalem. Now the attacker has reached the frontier of Judaea by nightfall, and no one knows what the coming hours will bring. If the enemy columns can go through these small towns during the night, or scouting parties arrive there the next morning, foraging, plundering and damaging them, the outlook for all concerned can only be bad. Accordingly Ramah, lying to the west of Geba (present-day *er-Rām*),[21] has good reason for fearing that in view of the report of the advance against the frontier fortress of Geba, at least parts of the army might return past it to the main route during the night,[22] so as to arrive at their marshalling-point of Nob more quickly by by-passing Mizpah. People evidently reckoned with this possibility in Gibeah of Saul, that king's former residence on present-day *Tell el-Ful* (cf. I Sam. 10.26; 11.4), and took flight in order to escape the cruel conqueror who might murder, carry off or enslave its inhabitants. The cries of terror move from Gallim via Laishah to Anathoth, perhaps not only because the troops are expected to march through, but also because advance detachments suddenly appear at the gates. Of the three places we can identify only Anathoth with any certainty

---

[17] Cf. G. Dalman, 'Palästinische Wege und die Bedrohung Jerusalems Jesaja 10', *PJB* 12, 1916, 46, and Donner, *ZDPV* 84, 48.

[18] The location is uncertain. Dalman, op. cit., 47, and Donner, op. cit., 51, with different degrees of certainty vote for *Tell el-ʿAskar*.

[19] Cf. the description of the situation in Dalman, op. cit., 48.

[20] Cf. Dalman, op. cit., 48f.

[21] Cf. Elliger, op. cit., 50.

[22] Cf. Donner, op. cit., 50.

(cf. Jer. 1.1); this once lay south of present-day *'Anāta* on *Ras el-harrūbe*.[23] Perhaps Donner is right in arguing that the reference to the other places mentioned here at the same time evokes the three ways open to the conqueror from Geba to Nob. If we take it that the list would naturally progress from the north southwards, Gallim could be *hirbet erha* south of Ramah and Laishah *hirbet Rās et--Tawīl*; if we take into account the places Madmenah and Gebim mentioned in the next strophe, these could be identified with *hirbet Ka'kūl* and *hirbet el-'Adase* respectively. However, that can be regarded as little more than a probability.[24]

[**10.31–32**] *The way lies open to the target!* Still during the night, the flight towards Jerusalem overtakes Madmenah and Gebim, places which lie immediately in front of the city. If the enemy was expected soon, the utmost speed was necessary were the refugees were to reach the walls of the capital before him under protection of darkness. Nob, on present-day Mount Scopus, was a marshalling point immediately in front of the gates of Jerusalem. The poet has such accurate knowledge of his homeland that he almost makes us forget that he comes to us not as a war correspondent, but in the guise of a prophet who is predicting the unstoppable course pursued by the victorious eschatological army on its way to Jerusalem.

[**10.33–34**] *Yahweh's judgment.* What was later related to the intervention of Yahweh on behalf of his city at the last moment (cf. 10.16ff.), originally envisaged, rather, the accomplishment of his annihilating judgment. With fearful violence Yahweh falls upon the city of Jerusalem, as a woodcutter falls upon his trees, to destroy high and low alike (cf. 2.12ff.). Here the undergrowth (cf. 9.17) may have signified for him the common people, and the cedars of Lebanon the great men of Zion.[25]

---

[23] Cf. A. Alt, *PJB* 22, 1926, 23f.

[24] Cf. Donner, op. cit., 50ff.

[25] Cf. 2.13. Ezek 17.22ff., cf. vv. 3f., shows that the cedar could be referred allegorically to the royal house of David, and Ezek, 31.3, that it could be referred to Assyria. The use in the plant fable of II Kings 14.9 contrasts it with the thorn and thus stresses the difference between high and lowly. Barth, *Jesaja-Worte*, 57f., excludes v. 33a as the introduction to 11.1 and regards vv. 27b–32 as a bridge text, in which vv. 33b and 34 serve to link it with the messianic prophecy. Here he provides a variation to the interpretation first put forward by Herder and then, following this, by Kaiser[1]. However, it is questionable whether we can separate vv. 33a and 33bf. so sharply and connect v. 33a and 11.1 as closely as Barth proposes. Some tensions are characteristic of the texts with an eschatology of disaster, from 3.1ff. on.

CHAPTER 11.1–9

The King of Peace

1   Then a shoot will come forth from the stump of Jesse,
     and a stem <spring forth>[1] from his ròots.
2   And the spirit of Yahweh shall rest upon it,
     a spirit of wisdom and understanding,
     a spirit of counsel and might,
     a spirit of knowledge and the fear of Yahweh.
3   <>[2]He shall not judge by what his eyes see
     nor decide by what his ears hear;
4   but with righteousness shall he judge the poor
     and decide with equity for <the bowed down>[3] of the land.[4]
     With the staff of his mouth he will smite <the oppressor>[5]
     and kill[6] the wicked with the breath of his lips.
5   Righteousness will be the girdle of his waist
     and faithfulness <the band>[7] about his loins.

6   Then the wolf shall dwell with the lamb,
     and the panther lie down with the kid,[6]
     and the calf and the lion cub shall <feed>[8] together
     and a little child shall lead them.
7   And the cow and the bear <shall be friends>[9]
     their young shall lie down together[6]
     and the lion shall eat straw like the ox.
8   The suckling shall play at the hole of the cobra,[10]

---

[1] With LXX, A, Σ, Θ, T and V read *yipraḥ* for the *yprh*, 'will bear fruit', of M. For the so-called imperfect to denote a concomitant action, cf. Bobzin, § 7.1b.

[2] 'And his delight is in the fear of Yahweh and' is a half-line which arose through dittography of v. 2bβ, and in view of the absence of a parallel half-line cannot be rescued even by more elegant translations.

[3] Read ᵃ*nīyyē*, cf. 10.2.

[4] Or 'the earth'. Subsequent expansion is not excluded, cf. v. 10.

[5] M: 'my land', is to be regarded as a mishearing of the primary *'ārīṣ* because of the lack of parallelism in v. 4b.

[6] For the use of the so-called imperfect to denote a concomitant action, cf. Bobzin, §7, 1b.

[7] With Driver, *JTS* 38, 1937, 39f., read *'ēsūr* to avoid the repetition of a word.

[8] With 1Q1sᵃ read *yimrᵉ'ū* instead of M *wᵉmᵉrī*, and cattle.

[9] Instead of the *tir'ēnā* of MT, 'they pasture', read *tērā'ēnā*.

[10] Cf. Ps. 58.4f. This identification is made on the basis of the present use of the *Naya haye* in snake charming cf. W. F. Ferguson, *Living Animals of the Bible*, New York nd, 69.

while[6] the weaned child shall roll[11] stones on <the hole>[12] of the viper.[13]

9   They are not evil and do not destroy
       in all my holy mountain,
       for the land is full of the knowledge of Yahweh
       as water covers the sea.

[11.1–9] If ch. 10 was dominated by the thought of the judgment inflicted by Assyria on Jerusalem and at the same time by Yahweh on Assyria,[14] ch. 11 directs attention to the coming time of salvation. That it is not a unity is most evident from vv. 10ff.: the new beginnings in vv. 10, 11 show that a series of additions begins here.[15] However, the remaining verses (1–9) are not of a piece either:[16] v. 9 is a mixed quotation from 65.25b and Hab. 2.14. The second half of it cannot refer to the animals mentioned in vv. 6–8. As a whole it stands in some tension to vv. 1–5, as the perfect righteousness of the people promised here makes superfluous royal protection for the weak members of society.[17] There is also a comparable difference between vv. 1–5 and 6–8: the need for the king to ensure social peace among men is not at first matched by the universal peace in the realm of nature. Clear though it is that we should understand peace in nature as a consequence of the unconditionally righteous rule of the new monarchy, and the perfect righteousness of the people as the effect of this rule, after what has been said it seems advisable to exclude not only v. 9 but also vv. 6–8 as thematic extensions of the nucleus of the oracle in vv. 1–5.[18] As v. 10 refers back to vv. 1–5,[19] we cannot rule out the possibility that vv. 6–8(9) were inserted only after

[11] With J. Reider, *VT* 2, 1952, 115, read *y^edahdē*, cf. Arab *dahdah*, since 1. there is no reason to put the object, *yādō*, first in the connection, and 2. the *hadā* is syntactically impossible in this position.

[12] Read *m^e'orat*. The *m^e'ūrat* of M might well be the result of a mishearing.

[13] *Vipera palaestinae*, cf. Ferguson, 69.

[14] Cf. above, 5f., 6f.

[15] Cf. above, 262.

[16] For the demarcation cf. also above, 251 n.25.

[17] Cf. also Barth, *Jesaja-Worte*, 60.

[18] To this effect cf. implicitly, Becker, *Isaias*, 27ff., with the restriction of the oracle to 11.1–5; explicitly, O. Eissfeldt, *The Old Testament. An Introduction*, Oxford 1965, 319f.; H.–J. Hermisson, 'Zukunftserwartung und Gegenwar skritik in der Verkündigung Jesajas', *EvTh* 33, 1973, 59f.; Barth, *Jesaja-Worte*, 60f., and Vermeylen I, 275f., more briefly T. Lescow, 'Das Geburtsmotiv in den messianischen Weissagungen', *ZAW* 79, 1967, 188. The traditional view of the unity of 11.1–8 (9) has most recently been put forward emphatically by Kaiser[1-4]; Rehm, *Messias*, 185ff.; Wildberger, ad loc., and K. Seybold, *Das davidische Königtum im Zeugnis der Propheten*, FRLANT 107, Göttingen 1972, 94.

[19] But cf. Becker, *Isaias*, 62, who refers the 'root of Jesse' in v. 10 to the post-exilic community.

the addition of v. 10. But if we notice the lameness of vv. 15, 16 after vv. 12ff., we can also see that this conclusion is by no means certain. Contrary to what it is still a widespread view, we cannot recognize a prophecy of Isaiah even in the basic material of the oracle which can thus be limited to vv. 1–5. Since the saying about Immanuel in 7.14b–16bα has turned out to be an addition, with an eschatology of salvation, to what has proved in turn to be a post-Deuteronomistic narrative, and the messianic prophecy in 9.1–6 is similarly to be taken as a prophecy which came into being after the downfall of the Davidic empire,[20] we have no literary focal point for such an attribution. Furthermore, the beginning of the oracle in v. 1 shows that it is to be understood as a continuation, presumably in fact of 10.33–34.[21] At all events, the expectation of the renewal of the kingdom from the roots of the dynasty points to a time at which the David dynasty had ceased to rule.[22]

[11.1–5] *The renewal of the kingship.* If the annihilation of the Davidic monarchy had been brought about by Yahweh himself in the catastrophe of 587,[23] this was nevertheless not to be the last word on the matter. Rather, he would call a collateral line, stemming from the roots of the dynasty, to succeed to the throne and endow it with his spirit, so that it could fulfil all the claims made on a king. If we want to reduce the picture of the king drawn in the present prophecy to an impressive formula and at the same time bring out the difference with 9.2[1]ff., we can say with Theodor Lescow that here we have an eschatological Solomon (cf. I Kings 3.4ff., 16ff.), and there an eschatological David.[24] While in 9.2[1]ff. expectations are primarily directed towards liberation from the yoke of the enemy, here they are turned inwards. At the same time the passage develops as it were the theme of the righteousness of the rule of the one to come which was begun in 9.7[6]. In fact it will emerge that here too the ideal of the king and the kingship ritual in Judah are to be found in the background.[25]

---

[20] Cf. above, 163f.

[21] Cf. also Vermeylen I, 271. Presumably the same hand is responsible for the insertion of 11.1ff as also incorporated 9.1ff. into the Isaiah scroll.

[22] That Isaiah is the author of the prophecy has been disputed by e.g. H. Hackmann, *Die Zukunftserwartungen des Jesaja*, Göttingen 1893, 149; Cheyne, *Introduction*, 63ff.; Marti, Gray and Guthe, ad loc.; Budde, *ZAW* 41, 1923, 189; the *Introductions* by R. H. Pfeiffer, New York 1941 (1948), 438; O. Eissfeldt, 319, with reference to 11.6ff.; also S. Mowinckel, *He That Cometh*, Oxford 1956, 17; J. Lindblom, *Prophecy in Ancient Israel*, Oxford 1962, 281 n. 100; M. Treves, *VT* 13, 1963, 205; T. Lescow, *ZAW* 79, 1967, 188ff.; G. Fohrer, ad loc., and in his *History of Israelite Religion*, Lonfon 1973, 349f.; Vollmer, *Geschichtliche Rückblicke*, 180ff., and Vermeylen I, 269ff.

[23] Cf. above, 115.

[24] *ZAW* 79, 1967, 189.

[25] Cf. also above, 214f.

[1] The Davidic dynasty is compared with a tree, all that is left of which is a stump. Just as this can again send forth shoots, so too the royal family will renew itself from a further group of descendants of Jesse, the father of King David (I Sam. 16.1ff.).[26] Just as David once suddenly emerged from obscurity, so now after the apparently final abdication of the house of David from its people, a second David will arise from the stock of their ancestor. In Micah 5.1, we hear mysteriously and yet ultimately in the same way that someone is to arise from Bethlehem to be ruler over Israel, 'whose origin is to be sought in the past, in distant times'. We should probably be cautious in answering the question raised in most recent scholarship as to whether the metaphor of the shoot springing from the stump was chosen solely for the clarity of the comparison, or whether we should see behind it a special reference to the king as the tree of life.[27] It is neither an *ad hoc* metaphor nor a reference back to a mythical conception of the king, but the adopting of the conception, evidently widespread also among Semitic peoples, of a clan as a tree the strength of which lies in its roots.[28] So it is quite understandable that here, as in Jer. 23.5; Zech. 3.8; 6.12, the Messiah is understood as a shoot from his family tree.

[2] This verse addresses the coming king, and with him his descendants,[29] as bearer of Yahweh's spirit. The influence of that spirit is developed in three couplets. First, it will give the king wisdom and understanding. The word translated 'wisdom' really means specialized knowledge or, in other words, 'skill and knowledge for the purpose of practical action'.[30] 'Understanding' is a capacity for discernment.[31] The ruler needs both gifts if he is to make his decisions fairly, and judge in peace and righteousness. Thus according to I Kings 3.9 Solomon asked Yahweh for a wise and understanding heart. And when he discovered the truth in the prostitutes' fight over the child it was recognized – so we are told – in Israel that God's wisdom was in him to speak justly (I Kings 3.28). Furthermore, he is to be endowed with counsel and understanding[32]

---

[26] Cf. also Job 14.8f.; Dan. 11.7.
[27] Cf. I. Engnell, *Studies in Divine Kingship in the Ancient Near East*, Uppsala 1943 = Oxford [2]1967, 28ff., and G. Widengren, *The King and the Tree of Life in Ancient Near Eastern Religion*, UUÅ 1951, 4, Uppsala 1951; id., *Sakrales Königtum im Alten Testament und im Judentum*, Stuttgart 1955, 56, with the criticism of Mowinckel, *He that Cometh*, 453ff.
[28] Cf. the references in Barth, *Jesaja–Worte*, 70.
[29] Even the king of salvation does not live for ever; cf. II Sam. 7.12ff.; Ps. 89.30ff.
[30] G. Fohrer, 'Die Weisheit im Alten Testament', in *Studien zur alttestamentliche Theologie und Geschichte*, BZAW 115, Berlin 1969, 243.
[31] Cf. H. Ringgren, *TWAT I*, cols 621ff., TDOT 2, 201ff.
[32] Cf. above, 213.

and might.[33] Planning is intellectual and volitional preparation for action; in this context, the king's capacity to make an appropriate judgment. To carry this out, he needs the necessary power. In this connection the Assyrian general mockingly asks king Hezekiah whether in war he regards mere words as counsel and might (II Kings 18.20 par. Isa. 36.5). Of course both capacities are needed not only in war but also in peace, since there is no rule without potential power.[34] The thought and will of the king sent by God are connected with the spirit of God, so that his rule does not serve the purpose of self-glorification, but the will of God in implementing righteousness on this earth.

Thus it is no coincidence that the last pair of terms to describe the effect of the spirit are the knowledge and fear of Yahweh. Here is to be found the self-limitation of knowledge and power in the recognition of the fact that even the mightiest upon earth are still subject to God. For the Hebrew, knowing and knowledge are not merely intellectual processes or achievements; they include the whole person, so that they are realized in appropriate involvement with what is known.[35] Thus the knowledge of God is at the same time practical acknowledgement of God which is implemented in thought and action. In this connection, too, the fear of God is not merely numinous awe, but moral conduct:[36] because people have grasped the supremacy and punitive force of God's deity, they are afraid to act against his will (cf. Prov. 3.7). This endowment with wisdom and understanding, will and power, in the knowledge and recognition of God, whose is the supreme power and authority, is to be given to this monarchy for ever. Unlike that of Saul, from whom the spirit of Yahweh departed (cf. I Sam. 11.6 with 16.14) or that of the house of David, which ultimately came to grief at the hands of Yahweh, this kingship will never be taken away.

The idea that the king ultimately needs the support of the spirit of Yahweh for his rule is clearly one of the notions which is firmly bound up with the monarchy in Judah. This is evident not only from the passages about the possession of the spirit by Saul and Solomon, which have already been mentioned, but also from a text like II Sam.

[33] Cf. above, 212f. on 9.6 [5].
[34] Cf. above, 214f.
[35] Cf. W. Schottroff, *THAT* I, col. 690, and for the knowledge of God, still G. J. Botterweck, 'Gott erkennen' im Sprachgebrauch des ATs, BBB 2, Bonn 1951, 97, to know God 'means to "refrain" from idolatry and sin, to "turn" to Yahweh and seek him, "follow" him and "fear" him, practise love, justice and righteousness'. Cf. also R. Bultmann, TDNT 1, 696ff. and S. Mowinckel, *Die Erkenntnis Gottes bei den alttestamentlichen Propheten*, Oslo 1941, 5ff.
[36] Cf. J. Becker, *Gottesfurcht im Alten Testament*, AnBib 25, Rome 1965, 258f., 222 and e.g. Prov. 1.7, 29, and not least Prov. 9.10.

23.2ff., the so-called 'last words of David', a section which at all events has been preserved in the style of a hymn to the glorification of a king of the kind transmitted to us in Ps. 2.7ff.[37] The fact that v. 3b says,

'Whoever rules in justice over men,
rules in the fear of God',

echoes v. 2bβ here. Because the king possesses the spirit of Yahweh, it can be said of him that as judge he gives authentic oracles (Prov. 16.10), or that Yahweh directs the heart of the king, like streams of water, where he wills.[38] In terms of ritual the king's endowment with the spirit was connected with his anointing (cf. II Sam. 23.2f.; I Sam. 16.13; Isa. 61.1). Thus the ideal of the king filled with the spirit in fact proves to be rooted in the kingship ritual.

[3–5] The connection between v. 2 and the following verses is closer than might appear at first sight: vv. 3, 4 mention the judgments of the king. Verse 3 ascribes to him the capacity not to be deceived by what is submitted to him on whatever pretext. So we should be reminded not so much of the admonition not to judge by the appearances of a person as handed down to us by e.g. Prov. 18.5; 24.23,[39] as rather of statements like I Sam. 16.7; Prov. 16.10; 20.8, which give the king a share in God's capacity to see through the disputes which are presented to him, and therefore to arrive at a just judgment. [4] In purely human legal proceedings, the reputation and influence of the person concerned all too easily play a decisive role. Therefore it is the declared duty of a ruler to help even the most insignificant to obtain justice in their struggle with the powerful. In this context I need not stress that this is something quite different from a lawless, partisan support for the underprivileged. That goes without saying.[40] The fear of God comes into play in the recognition of the rights of the weaker members of society, because it makes people shrink back in awe from the divine avenger and thus treat even their cases in an unpartisan way (cf. Prov. 22.22f.; Ex. 22.21f.).[41]

Verse 4b has a mysterious ring to it: this king 'needs no sceptre, no

[37] For the age of II Sam. 23.3ff. cf. A. R. Johnson, *Sacral Kingship in Ancient Israel*, Cardiff [2]1967, 16ff., with T. Veijola, *Die ewige Dynastie*, AASF B 193, Helsinki 1975, 106; for the wording and translation cf. P. A. H. de Boer, SVT 4, Leiden 1957, 47ff., and Kaiser, *Der Königliche Knecht*, FRLANT 70, Göttingen 1959 = 1962[2], 22ff.

[38] Prov. 21.1. Cf. W. McKane, *Proverbs*, OTL, London 1970, 559ff. H. Gese, *Lehre und Wirklichkeit in der alten Weisheit*, Tübingen 1958, 48, differs.

[39] Cf. also 3.9.

[40] For the terms *dal* and *'ani* see above, 227.

[41] Cf. also I.15ff.; 5.1ff., 8ff.; 10.1ff. For the duty of the king to maintain law among his people cf. e.g. Ps. 72.2; also Ps. 45.8; 101; for the duty to give support to the weak cf. Ps. 45.5; 72.4, 12f., and Isa. 32.1f. I would add: any state shows itself to be a just state in so far as it respects the rights of its weakest member.

bodyguard, no headsman, to implement his verdict; one word from his mouth is enough to kill the evildoer immediately'.[42] The king's word is not just a report or an indication of his will; it participates in the power of the creative word of God and of the prophet (cf. Ps. 33.6; Hos. 6.5; Jer. 23.29; Isa. 55.10f.).[43] [5] The 'girdle' is probably not to be thought of as a sword-belt, but as the apron worn under everything else which preserved a man's modesty even when all other garments had been removed, and which gave the person who wore it considerable freedom of movement if other garments were tucked up into it.[44] That the king makes justice and faithfulness or constancy[45] the girdle of his loins means that his constant and inviolable righteousness do him honour and give him freedom to act.[46]

Israel was not the only nation in its environment to have this understanding of the kingship as the authority which was called to preserve justice on this earth. One can cite parallels from the world of the Sumerians, Babylonians and Assyrians, the Egyptians and even the Canaanites. In this connection Israel had not created any special ethos for the monarchy.[47] Rather, along with the institution it had also taken over from its neighbours the ideal and ritual of kingship (cf. also I Sam. 8.5).[48] Therefore, as far as we know, the unique and special feature of Israel was that after the downfall of its monarchy it looked for the foundation of a new kingship which lived up to the divine will not only ideally, but also in reality. Messianic faith is the special instance of this.[49] In the present text we find this expectation in a remarkable blend of elements from the old tradition of kingship in Judah and from wisdom thinking. Perhaps this should

[42] H. Gressmann, *Der Messias*, FRLANT 43, Göttingen 1929, 247.

[43] Cf. also W. H. Schmidt, *TWAT* II, 127ff., *TDOT* 2, 94ff.

[44] Cf. *HAL* 26b s.v. *'ēzōr* and M. Metzger, *BHH* I, col. 615.

[45] For *ṣedeq*, righteousness, cf. above, 42 on 1.21; for *'emūnā*, reliability and steadfastness, cf. e.g. Ex. 17.12.

[46] Cf. also the formula describing righteousness as the support of the throne, whether of the king (e.g. Prov. 16.12) or of Yahweh (e.g. Ps. 89.15; 97.2).

[47] Cf. E. Hammershaimb, 'On the Ethics of the Old Testament Prophets', SVT 7, Leiden 1960, 75ff., and for a similar understanding of kingship among the Sumerians, S. N. Kramer, *The Sumerians*, Chicago and London 1963 (1972⁵), 83f.; in Mesopotamia, A. L. Oppenheim, *Ancient Mesopotamia*, Chicago and London 1964 (1965), 102; among the Egyptians, R. Frankfort, *Kingship and the Gods*, Chicago 1949 (1955), 51ff., and among the Canaanites, J. Gray, *The Legacy of Canaan*, SVT 5, Leiden 1957, 160f. = 1965, 221.

[48] Cf. also above, 212ff.

[49] For the prophesying of Neferti, *AOT*², 46ff., cf. H. Brunner, *Grundzüge einer Geschichte der altägyptischen Literatur*, Darmstadt 1966, 53ff. The prophesying of a potter under a king Amenophis im Greek, *AOT*², 49f., belongs to another group of themes.

be enough to make us not too hasty to connect it with the enthronment of a king of Judah.[50]

[11.6–9] *Universal peace*. It is striking that the expectation of the return of primal peace, embracing both men and animals, is limited in the Old Testament to this passage, the way in which it is briefly taken up in Isa. 65.25, and perhaps also Hos. 2.20. Alongside it stands another notion, that in the time of salvation Yahweh will destroy all wild animals (cf. Ezek. 34.25; Isa. 35.9). This was also taken up later in Lev. 26.6b.[51] The notion that in primeval times human beings and animals did not hurt one another, but were content with vegetarian food, in accordance with a divine command (cf. Gen. 1.29ff.), as evident in the Priestly creation story, shows the connection between this conception and a fundamental ascetical-vegetarian view. The same connection is also characteristic of Greek parallels.[52] Here too we find the roots for the incorporation of the notion of peace among animals into the idea of the transmigration of souls.[53] Furthermore, it is here again that this idea has connections with the doctrine of the ages of the world.[54]

We cannot uncover the roots of the Old Testament instances with such clarity. If we look at the Priestly doctrine of primal vegetarianism, it can hardly be reduced to a mere search for security projected back into the primal period. We should rather assume that here we have the expression of a sensibility which is aware of the primal guilt in all life, which can only survive through the death of other life. Going further, we can at any rate ask (though not discover with any certainty) whether underlying the Priestly chronology, which looks back to a year 4000,[55] we do not have a doctrine of world ages treated as esoteric knowledge, so that here too we could reckon with the expectation of a return of the primal period, however much this seems to contradict Gen. 9. However, this consideration necessarily also recalls the difference between the philosophical Greek doctrines of the ages of the world, with their expectation of periodic change,

[50] Against M. B. Crook, 'A Suggested Occasion for Isa. 9.2–7, 11.1–9', *JBL* 68, 1949, 213ff.; Becker, *Isaias* 28. Cf. also Vermeylen I, 274f.

[51] Cf. Elliger, *HAT* I, 4, Tübingen 1966, 365; also Virgil, *Eclogues* 4,22, 24.

[52] Cf. B. Gatz, 'Weltalter, goldene Zeit und sinnverwandte Vorstellungen', *Spudasmata* 16, Hildesheim 1967, 155f., 171.

[53] Cf. e.g. Empedocles, fr. 130D with fr. 136 and 137D; also Porphyry, *Vita Pythagorae* 19; Iamblichus, *De vita Pythagorica* 24, 17f., and on them W. K. C. Guthrie, *A History of Greek Philosophy* 1, Cambridge 1962 (1971), 155; Aristophanes, *Pax* 1075f.; Plato, *Politicus* 271 d. 6ff.; 272 d. 9ff.; *Laws* 782c: Horace, *Epodes* 16,50ff.; Ovid, *Metamorphoses* I, 101ff.; XV, 96ff., *Fasto* IV. 395ff.

[54] Cf. e.g. Empedocles fr. 17, Plato, *Politicus* 269–74.

[55] Cf. P. R. Ackroyd, *Exile and Restoration*, OTL, London 1968, 91. For esotericism in late Judaism cf. Joachim Jeremias, *The Eucharistic Words of Jesus*, London ²1966, 125ff.

as already expressed in the famous fragment 30D of Heraclitus,[56] and Jewish eschatology. It looks forward to a reign of peace which will finally dawn, the duration of which is guaranteed by the Lordship of the spirit of Yahweh itself (cf. v. 2; 9.6 and *Or. Syb.* III, 767ff., 785ff.).

In the end, the present text merely expresses the longing for a life with no danger. The fact that the beasts of prey feed with domestic animals means that the farmer will no longer have losses among his herds. If a young child can look after the flocks, being a shepherd has become a peaceful idyll. Yet it would not be enough to consider this section only from the perspective of a future freedom from harm, and to want to stress those features in it which envisage a real change in the nature of animals. In this world the lion which eats straw is an unnatural, sick phenomenon. It cannot chew cud alongside the cow, but must follow its nature in attacking the bull. And if suckling and little child play with the most poisonous snakes, without their mother finding them dead, the old enmity between the seed of the woman and the seed of the snake has been removed (Gen. 3.15). Thus the text probably says less than it knows. Therefore it remains for us to ask whether it has not been extracted from a wider context and inserted here.

[9] With its quotation from Isa. 65.25b, v. 9a reduces the expectations expressed in vv. 6–8 to the notion of the future removal of harm and danger, by which, incidentally, the Sumerian conception of the peace among animals prevailing in paradise seems already to have been governed.[57] Verse 9b goes back to Hab. 2.14 and thus expressly makes a connection between the expectation of the future ruler concerned for utter righteousness in the land – or should we say, on earth – and that of peace among the animals, by ensuring that true knowledge of God prevails everywhere. We have seen above that doing right accords with this.[58] Accordingly the threat posed to men by animals is understood as the consequence of human guilt and divine punishment (cf. Lev. 26.22).

It is easy to reduce the text to silence by genetic arguments and to

---

[56] 'This world-order [*kosmos*], the same for all, none of the gods nor of men has made, but it was always and is and shall be: an ever-living fire, which is being kindled in measures and extinguished in measures' (Guthrie, I, 465; cf. also Guthrie I, 454ff.). Cf. also e.g. Plato, *Politicus* 269–74, and on this K. Gaiser, *Platons ungeschriebene Lehre*, Stuttgart ²1968, 205ff.

[57] Cf. the Dilmun myth in the epic of Enki and Ninhursag, *ANET*²⁻³, 38a; German text and commentary in H. Gross, *Die Idee des ewigen und allgemeinen Weltfriedens im Alten Orient und im Alten Testament*, TTS 7, Trier 1967, 17ff., and the epic of Enmerkar and the Lord of Aratta 136ff., ibid., 23ff.; also the theme of the wild man living in peace with the animals in the Gilgamesh epic, table I, in *ANET*³, 74.

[58] Cf. above, 256f.

condemn it as mere wishful thinking, in so far as it is based on the conception of a happy primal period, while at the same time calling upon nations and every individual to do all in their power to make sure that there is at last more justice on this earth and that nature loses its terrors. If we ask how both these things can in fact be achieved, we are confronted with a choice between spirit-inspired anarchy and a totalitarian state. The former presupposes the miracle of the endowment of all men with a new heart and a new spirit, and is thus overshadowed by vv. 1–5, even if it would like to do away with all rule. Without human renewal, anarchy can only be chaos and will not produce any lasting world peace. Until this eschaton, therefore, we must soberly keep to a policy of small steps, the attempt to become personally more just and do more justice to our own world. For those who have thought things through to the end, with Aldous Huxley's *Brave New World*, a totalitarian world is a daydream. To the degree to which it is inevitable as a result of technical pressures and an increasing population, the important thing is to regain a feeling for the primal vitiation of our lives, to recognize that our own life is always made possible by the sacrifice of other life and is fulfilled only by surrender to other people. The result of this would be a new reverence for life, primarily for the life of other people, and then, by virtue of the ultimate unity of all life, reverence also for the life of animals. That alone could set clear limits to what we do with the life of others.[59] So it could succeed in making sure that the life of animals and of human beings continued to be worth living.

However, with this we have not arrived at the horizon of the ultimate future which confronts us all. The question where our life comes from, on what it is grounded, along with all our world, and in which direction it is going, is still as open as ever. Has it been demonstrated that God is no longer the goal of the common origin of life or our own goal, and at the same time the transforming power which he already shows himself to be to those who receive their days in trust from him?[60]

---

[59] Albert Schweitzer's plea for reverence for life, cf. *Kultur und Ethik, XXIf.*, Munich 1960, 328ff. is not an expression of nostalgia but of the awareness that because of the unity of life, once the life of animals is no longer respected, respect for that of human beings also disappears. For the place of the animal in human religious thought and action cf. also E. Rudolph, *Vertrieben aus Eden*, Munich, 1979.
[60] Cf. Rom. 8.18ff.

CHAPTER 11.10–16

Aspects of the Time of Salvation

[11.10–16] Here we have at least three, and presumably four, additions which expand from various perspectives the picture of the messianic time sketched out in 11.1–9. The new beginning with the prophetic formula 'on that day it will come about' in vv. 10,11, together with the change of theme, shows that here an independent addition has begun. Verse 10 promises that the king of the time of salvation will also be acknowledged as supreme lord by the peoples of the world. Verses 11 and 12 promise the gathering and homecoming of the scattered remnant of the people of God. Verses 13 and 14 envisage the restoration of its inner unity and that of the external dimensions of its kingdom, and so perhaps represent a supplement to the two preceding verses. With their announcement of the preparation of the way for the homecomers, vv. 15 and 16 go behind vv. 13 and 14, and by virtue of that show themselves already to be independent additions.

CHAPTER 11.10

The Signal for the Nations

10   And on that day it will come about:
      the root of Jesse, which stands as a signal for the people,
      for him shall the nations seek,
      and his dwelling shall be glorious.

[11.10] This verse is closer to 11.1ff. than those which follow. However, unlike 11.1, it does not speak of the shoot from the root of Jesse, but of the root of Jesse itself. It is best to leave open the question whether this is a deliberately mysterious circumlocution for the Messiah as such, or whether the author had in mind the whole new dynasty in the never-ending succession of its rulers, rather than the individual king.[1] In content the distinction is relatively insignificant, as what is said of the one king at all events also applies to his successors, and what is promised of the dynasty at all events applies to all its neighbours, namely the signal[2] set up by Yahweh for the nations, to be the place to which they are to go in search of a decision in all matters of dispute.[3] The world-wide recognition of the kings from the stem of Jesse, David's father (cf. I Sam. 16.1ff.), would finally fulfil what had been promised to the kings in Jerusalem since days of old (cf. Ps. 2.8; 18.41ff.; 72.8ff.).[4] In this connection, the resting place[5] is either the royal palace and the temple (cf. I Kings 7.1ff), or the whole city of Jerusalem. We can hardly go wrong if we connect the glory promised to the new kingdom with the gifts which the nations and the kings are to bring to the ruler on the throne of David (cf. Ps. 72.10; 68.30; also Isa 60.9ff.). The riches of the world come together in the royal city in which Yahweh's earthly representative rules. This is an expression of the fact that all the world is drawn towards him, and recognizes him for who he is. What is promised in 2.2ff., the pilgrimage of the nations to Zion, has here been focussed specifically on the king.

CHAPTER 11.11–14

The People of God Reunited

11   And on that day it will come about:
      again the Lord will <lift up> his hand[1],
      to redeem the remnant of his people,
      which is left from Assyria and from Egypt,
      from Pathros and from Cush and from Elam,
      from Shinar and from Hamath and from the islands of the sea.
12   And he will raise up a signal for the Gentiles
      and will assemble the scattered ones of Israel

[1] Becker, Isaias, 62, understands the root of Jesse to be the post-exilic community. He has been followed by Barth, Jesaja-Worte, 59, and Vermeylen I, 277.
[2] Cf. 18.3; 49.22; 62.10; 13.2. Cf. also v. 12.
[3] Cf. e.g. Ex. 18.15; II Kings 8.8; Deut. 19.17ff.
[4] Cf. the echo of this expectation in Ps. Sol. 17.30ff.
[5] The $m^e n \bar{u} h \bar{a}$, resting place, is of course originally the stopping place for a herd (Ps. 23.2) or a caravan (Num. 10.33). In a metaphorical sense the promised land is the resting place of the people of Israel (Deut. 12.9; Ps. 95.11; cf. also Isa. 28.12), and the temple that of the ark (Ps. 132.8, 14).
[1] Instead of $\check{s}\bar{e}n\bar{\imath}t$, for the second time, read $\check{s}^{e'}\bar{e}t$, cf. LXX, and v. 12a; 49.22.

and bring in the dispersed ones of Judah
from the four ends of the earth.

13   Then the jealousy of Ephraim will depart
and the oppressors of Judah will be[2] exterminated.
Ephraim shall no longer be jealous of Judah
and Judah shall not oppress Ephraim.

14   Then they shall fly <on the slope>[3] of the Philistines towards
the sea,
and together they shall plunder the sons of the East.
Edom and Moab will be in the <grasp>[4] of their hand
and the Ammonites shall obey them.

[11.11–12] *The homecoming of the Diaspora.* The knowledge that the
greater part of the Jewish people in the post-exilic period lived in
exile in Mesopotamia and in a dispersion which ran round the coasts
of the Eastern Mediterranean with its focal point in Egypt, the
Diaspora, led one well-read reader to make an addition announcing
this people's homecoming; for to the Jews, part of the time of
salvation in the fullest sense was the complete restoration of the
people of Israel in its own land and, as vv. 13, 14 show, the restoration
of the kingdom as it was in the time of David.[5] Accordingly, this
scribal prophet affirms that Yahweh will once again deliver what
remains of the people, divided into two kingdoms, and after their
downfall scattered throughout the world,[6] as he once delivered them
from Egypt.[7] As Israel had been deported by the Assyrians (cf. II
Kings 17,6; Ezra 4.2, 10), and Judah by the Babylonians, one might
expect the mention of Assyria and Babylon rather than of Assyria
and Egypt. Perhaps the author is dependent on the Chronicler's
account for this change; according to him, the exiles from Judah
returned home under the Persian king Cyrus (cf. II Chron. 36.23;
Ezra 2.1ff. par. Neh. 7.5ff.). At all events he had to take account of
the extensive Egyptian Diaspora,[8] about whose origin Jer. 42ff. gives
a no less tendentious account.[9]

[2] For the use of the so-called imperfect to denote a concomitant action, cf. Bobzin,
§ 7.1b.
[3] Instead of the absolute, read the construct *ketep.*
[4] Read *mišlōᵃh.*
[5] For the train of thought and its parallels in Obad. 19ff.; Micah 7.7ff.; Zech. 10.3ff.,
cf. Barth, *Jesaja-Worte,* 58.
[6] The verb *qānā* here, like *pādā,* no longer envisages the act of purchasing or
redeeming e.g. terms. Cf. Hos. 7.13; Jer. 31.11; Ps. 44.27; and esp. e.g. Deut. 9.26;
Neh. 1.10.
[7] For the four ends of the earth cf. also Job 37.3; 38.13; Isa. 24.17; Ezek. 7.2.
[8] It should be conceded that the mention of two centres at the same time accords
with the political reality of a Judaism enclosed between the Seleucid kingdom
(Assyria) and that of the Ptolemies (Egypt), and can be regarded as an indication that
this addition was composed in the early Hellenistic period.
[9] Cf. K. Pohlmann, *Studien zum Jeremiabuch,* FRLANT 118, Göttingen 1978, 245ff.

He could take up the message of the homecoming of the people of God from all over the world from Deutero- and Trito-Isaiah (cf. 49.22f.; 60.4; 43.5ff.). As Yahweh once gave the enemy the signal to attack the city of God, and will do so once again in the last time (cf. 5.26), so he will give the Gentiles the signal to bring his own people home.[10] It is hard to see the principle by which the list has been made of the places in which the dispersed people of God are to be found (v. 11ba₂β); it may be an addition. Presumably it takes account of the circumstances of the time. The list begins with Egypt, which has been mentioned immediately before, and which it understands as Lower Egypt, and then, going from north to south, mentions first Upper Egypt[11] and then Nubia.[12] Now moving over to the east, after that it mentions Elam, the district lying to the east of Babylon, providing access to the high country of Iran. The palace of the Persian kings was in Susa, the capital of Elam, and there was a strong Jewish group there. After it had fallen into the hands of Alexander the Great, it remained in the possession of the Seleucids until the area broke away from the empire after the death of Antiochus III, and then came under Parthian rule.[13] The fact that now Babylon finally appears, under its old name Shinar,[14] pays the necessary tribute to history and to the present. We do not know why Hamath in particular has been selected from among the cities of Syria.[15] One can only assume that at the time this prophecy was composed there had been a particularly strong Jewish colony there. The mention of the islands of the sea hardly restricts the perspective to the coasts of Syria and Phoenicia (cf. 20.6; 23.2), but refers to the Jews living round the eastern and northern coasts of the eastern Mediterranean, the Aegean and its islands.[16] At least as reflected in religious literature, the geographical details of this area remained remarkable indefinite to the mother country (cf. Sir. 47.16; also Rev. 16.20).[17]

[11.13–14] *The restoration of Israel and its kingdom.* It is quite understandable that a prophetic book which alludes as clearly as does the

[10] Cf. also above, on 11.10.
[11] For its designation as Pathros cf. O. Kaiser, *BHH* III, col. 1400, and Gen. 10.14; Jer. 44.1, 15; Ezek. 30.14.
[12] For the Nubians, designated, in Egyptian fashion, as Cush, cf. Ezek. 29.10; Gen. 10.6, 8; Isa. 18.1; 43.3; 45.14, and T. Schlatter, 'Mohrenland', *CBL*⁵ᐟ², cols 913f.
[13] For Elam cf. 22.6; Ezra 2.7; Neh. 7.12; Acts 2.9; for this subject cf. also W. Hinz, *BHH* I, cols. 389f. For Susa, cf. Neh. 1.1; Dan. 8.2; Esther 1.2, 5; 3.15; and J. Duchesne-Guillemin, *KP* V, col. 437.
[14] Cf. Gen. 10.10f.; 11.2ff.; Zech. 5.11; Dan. 1.2; and e.g. G. Wallis, *BHH* III, col. 1805.
[15] This is present-day *hama* on the Orontes. Cf. K. Elliger, *BHH* II, cols 629f., and Gen. 10.18; II Sam. 8.9; II Kings 18.34 par. Isa. 36.19; Isa. 10.9; Zech 9.2; I Macc. 12.25.
[16] Cf. also Gen. 10.5; Jer. 47.4; Ezek. 27.6; also Ex. 27.15 and not least Joel 4.6.
[17] Cf. also A. Schwarzenbach, *BHW* II, col. 767.

Isaiah scroll in chs. 7 and 8 (and presumably also in 9.20) to the enmity between the brother empires and peoples of Israel and Judah could move a reader to express his thoughts about the relationship between them in the time of salvation. Hope for a gathering together of the remnant of the people by Yahweh, as expressed in the two previous verses, made such a consideration inevitable. We may suppose that the problem was not just a historical one, posed by scripture, but also a current and topical one, in view of the fact that the relationship between the community of Jerusalem and the remnant of the population of Israel in Ephraim was tense even in the Persian period,[18] and was disturbed further after the Ephraimites built their own temple on Gerizim in the time of Alexander.[19] A real schism between the Jews and the Israelites, who now understood themselves as Samaritans, came about only in the second half of the second century BC.[20] The claim of the north to be the real Israel and to have the right to pre-eminence, which was rooted deep in history (cf. Gen. 49.22f.; Deut. 33.13ff.), had constantly led to jealousy of the south and had developed into acts of violence like the Syro-Ephraimite war.[21] On the other hand, Judah had also exploited the weakness of the brother nation. With the dawn of the time of salvation, the enemies of Judah will be exterminated in Ephraim; enmity between the two peoples will die out, so that instead of tearing each other apart they can present a united front to their old enemies in the neighbourhood. As in Ezek 34.23; 37.15ff., and not least in Jer. 3.18; 31.31ff., here once again we have an expression of the hope for a greater Israel.

[14] The expectation of the restoration of the empire of David is in accord with this. So the combined nations are going to swoop down on their neighbours like an eagle on its prey (cf. also Hab. 1.8). This first involves the overthrow of the Philistines (cf. II Sam. 8.1), who had retained their language until the fifth century BC (Neh. 13.24) and could evidently maintain their own way of life even in the framework of the Persian satrapy, mentioned by Herodotus in fifth place[22] (cf. I Macc. 5.68). Accordingly, the united brother kingdoms are to advance eastward through the inhabited regions into the

---

[18] Cf. also R. C. Coggins, *Samaritans and Jews. The Origins of Samaritanism Reconsidered*, Oxford 1975, 80f.

[19] Cf. H. G. Kippenberg, *Garizim und Synagoge*, RGGV 30, Berlin and New York 1971, 57ff., and Coggins, op. cit., 100, 113.

[20] Cf. Kippenberg, op. cit., 85ff.; Coggins, op. cit., 113ff.

[21] Cf. above, 148f.

[22] Herodotus III, 91; cf. O. Leuze, *Die Satrapieneinteilung in Syrien und im Zweistromlande von 520–320*, SKGG 11, 4, Halle 1935 = Hildesheim 1972, 100ff.

wilderness of Syria and Arabia,[23] to seize their spoil here. We should imagine here the treasures from caravan cities like Tadmor/Palmyra, and not just the possession of herds (cf. Job 1.3). These plundering forays presuppose, as is explicitly stated in v. 14b, that Edom (cf. II Sam. 8.14),[24] Moab (cf. II Sam. 8.2),[25] and Ammon (cf. II Sam. 12.26ff.)[26] will again be subject to them. It hardly need be pointed out that there is an unbridgeable contrast between this very earthly hope of the kingdom and that of Christianity.

CHAPTER 11.15–16

The Way for Those Returning Home

15   Then Yahweh will <dry up>[1] the tongue of the sea of Egypt
      and will raise[2] his hand against the River[3]
      with his violent[4] storm
      and will smite it into seven channels
      and make it passable for people wearing sandals.
16   Then there will be a highway for the remnant of his people
      which is left from Assyria,
      as it arose for Israel
      when it came up out of the land of Egypt.

[11.15–16] The picture of the time of salvation comes to a comforting conclusion with the adopting of the theme, familiar from the prophecy of Deutero-Isaiah, of the preparation of a way for the people[5]

[23] For the sons of the East cf. Gen. 29.1; Judg. 6.3, 33; 7.12; 8.10; Jer. 49.28; Ezek. 25.4, 10; and on this also O. Eissfeldt, *KS* III, 296ff.
[24] For the fate of the Edomites in the post-exilic period cf. J. R. Bartlett, 'From Edomites to Nabataeans: A Study in Continuity', *PEQ* 101, 1979, 53ff.
[25] For the decline of the Moabites cf. A. H. van Zyl, *The Moabites*, POS 3, Leiden 1960, 137ff., and *Isaiah 13–39*, 64.
[26] For the fate of the Ammonites cf. F. Schmidtke, *LTK*[2] I, col. 443.
[1] Instead of w^eheh^erim, 'and he will put to the ban', read w^eheh^erib. The mistake came about through a misreading of *m* and *b*.
[2] For the meaning of *henip* cf. J. Milgrom, *IEJ* 22, 1972, 34f.
[3] As in 8.7, this means the Euphrates.
[4] The derivation of $^{a}y\bar{a}m$ is obscure. For attempts at its interpretation cf. the criticism by Wildberger, ad loc. It seems most likely that we should conjecture $^{\prime}\bar{o}sem$. LXX, T and V at any rate show that this is a reference to the power or violence of the divine storm.
[5] Cf. 40.3; 41.17ff.; 42.15ff.; 43.1ff. and 35.1ff.

returning home from captivity: Yahweh himself will remove the natural obstacles so that those returning home have a free passage. In accordance with the typology bound up with this expectation, according to which Yahweh's future saving action will correspond with that in primal times, the way for the Egyptian Diaspora is again to lead through the sea,[6] for which in the changed conditions of the time of salvation there will no longer really be any occasion. For this purpose it will again be dried up.[7] In a similar way Yahweh will lift up his hand[8] threateningly against the Euphrates and divide it by an east wind[9] into seven (i.e an indeterminate number)[10] tributaries, so that people can cross it without even taking off their shoes. This creates the prior conditions for the return home of the remnant of the people living in the East (cf. v. 11), for whom a special way is built, certainly (as in 40.3) with other-worldly help.[11]

The fact that the prophecy in v. 16 concentrates on the people of God left by Assyria is certainly not as it were a mechanical consequence of the reference to v. 11; it is either a sign that the poet is artificially putting himself back into the historical situation of the prophet Isaiah, or an indication that like the author of Ezra 6.22 he lived in the early Hellenistic period.

CHAPTER 12.1–6

The Thanksgiving of the Redeemed

12.1   On that day you will say:
        'I praise you, Yahweh,
        for after you were angry with me,
        your anger <turned aside>[1]<and you comforted>[2] me.

⁶ The phrase, which only occurs here, might mean the Red Sea, cf. Ex. 13.18; 15.4; Num. 14.25; Ps. 106.7; 136.15, etc. For the subject-matter cf. also Barth, *Jesaja-Worte*, 19 n. 9.
⁷ Cf. 50.2; 51.10; II Kings 19.24 par. Isa. 35.27; Nah. 1.4; also Ps. 106.9.
⁸ Cf. Job 31.21; Isa. 10.32; 19.16.
⁹ Cf. Ex. 14.21; Isa. 40.7.
¹⁰ Cf. Eccles. 11.2
¹¹ Cf. also 49.11; 62.10 and further 19.23.
¹ Despite Wildberger's arguments for the precative forms of M, they must be regarded as a consequence of secondary alteration of the text by a later generation which was still waiting for salvation, and in accordance with the context we should read *wayyāšab*.
² We should read *watt^enaḥ^amēnī* here, for the reasons mentioned in n. 1.

2   Behold, God[3] is my help,
       I trust and am not afraid.
       For my power <and my strength>[4] is Yah,<,[5]>
       and he has become my help.
3   Then you will draw water with joy
       from the wells of salvation.
4   And will say on that day,
       'Praise Yahweh, call upon his name,
       make known his deeds among the nations,
       recall that his name is exalted.
5   Sing to Yahweh,
       for he has done great things.
       Make this known[6] in all the world!'
6   Shout and sing for joy, you citizens of Zion,
       for great in your midst is the Holy One of Israel.

[12.1–6] The recollection of the exodus from Egypt in 11.15f. led the editor to whom we owe at least the final form of the collection known as Proto-Isaiah, extending from ch. 1 to ch. 39, to make the redeemed people sing an eschatological hymn of thanksgiving as they did once when delivered from the sea (cf. Ex. 15). Thus he transports his own community, that of the second temple, still suffering as a result of the exile, to the moment in which the prophecies given in 10.5–11.16 have been fulfilled. The world power has been destroyed, the kingdom of the king of peace has dawned, and the scattered people of God have returned to a homeland freed from foreign rule. With the insertion of this hymn he provided a powerful conclusion to the prophecies about his own people contained in chs. 1–11, which set them apart from the following chapters 13–23 (33), with their sayings about foreign nations.[7]

    In v. 1aα the hymn is introduced by an introductory quotation formula expanded by the prophetic formula 'on that day'. It is

[3] IQIs[a] read 'el 'ēl, with God, which is possible, but is suspect as a possible dittography.

[4] With the Samaritan text on Ex. 15.2, LXX and V read zimrātī. We must reckon on the possibility of a technical haplography of the y before the divine name. For the evidence in IQIs[a] cf. also S. Talmon, VT 4, 1954, 207. For the meaning of zimrā II cf. Zorell, KBL and HAL s.v. As all the versions translate it 'song', however, we must ask whether at the time when it was taken into the present text, the formula was still understood in its original meaning. Cf. also S. Loewenstamm, VT 19, 1969, 464ff.

[5] The Yāh has been preserved as a form of the name contained in old cultic calls and formulas; Yahweh, in accordance with Ex. 15.2; Ps. 118.14, is to be regarded as an addition. For the discussion cf. also M. Rose, Jahwe ThSt(B), 122, Zurich 1978, 41; W. H. Schmidt, 'Der Jahwename und Exodus 3,14', in Textgemäss, Festschrift Ernst Würthwein, Göttingen 1979, 126.

[6] Read mūda'at with the Qere.

[7] Cf. also Becker, Isaias, 52, and Vermeylen I, 280.

followed in v. 1aβb–2 by a short hymn of thanksgiving. Its subject is the 'remnant of the people' mentioned in 11.16. The transition to an address in the second person masculine plural in vv. 2–5 shows that this is in fact meant to be a collective entity. We cannot rule out the possibility that the choice of the first person singular in vv. 1 and 2 has been affected by the fact that in Israel only the individual thanksgiving was a special genre, while the role of the popular thanksgiving was played by the hymn in praise of God. The only two popular thanksgivings contained in the Psalter, Pss. 124 and 129, would accordingly need to be understood as imitations of the individual genre.[8] Verse 3 is a reference to a prophetic liturgy and at the same time a background metaphor. At the latest with v. 3b, the reader becomes aware that the poet has taken up the word $y^e\check{s}\bar{u}\,{}^c a$, help, three times, in v. 2a and b and now here. So we should consider whether this is a deliberate allusion to the name of the prophet Isaiah, 'Yahweh has helped'.[9] Perhaps we should go so far as to say that that at the time when the prophecies are fulfilled and the community reads this book again, it will discover Yahweh as the source of its salvation and so attribute something of the same quality to this book. In v. 4, we should first note that here the quotation formula has been incorporated into the parallelism. The dominant form of v. 4aα₂b and v. 5a, with their invitations to praise God, is the imperative hymn. In v. 4b there is the insertion of a herald's instruction (cf. Jer. 4.16).[10] Verse 5 concludes the artistic composition with a summons to joy of the kind that belongs to the prophetic promise of salvation (cf. e.g. Zeph. 3.14f.; Zech. 9.9f). Thus the prophetic-eschatological quotation formula in v. 1aα, the liturgical instruction in v. 3, and the concluding borrowing from the promise of salvation[11] in v. 5 show that the poem is a prophetic composition which the community finds to have the property of a promise of salvation. The lateness of the composition is evident from its mosaic style, its character and its thought, made up of quotations and allusions to other hymns in the Old Testament and words from the book of Isaiah.[12] This indicates once again that it has been composed by an editor for its present place in the book.

[1–2] The poet directs the thoughts of his community towards the

---

[8] Cf. F. Crüsemann, *Studien zur Formgeschichte von Hymnus und Danklied in Israel*, WMANT 32, Neukirchen 1969, 174.

[9] Cf. also above 7.

[10] Cf. also Crüsemann, op. cit., 56.

[11] Cf. Crüsemann, op. cit., 56ff.

[12] Thus Ps. 118.21a underlies v. 1. aβ; v. 1b alludes to the 'for all that, his anger is not turned away' in Isa. 5.25; 9.12, 17, 21[11, 16, 20]; 10.4. For v. 2a we might recall Ps. 88.22 and further e.g. Ps. 25.5b; whereas Ex. 15.2; Ps. 118.14 clearly stand behind v. 2b. Verse 4 aα₂ takes up Ps. 105.1a; v. 4aβ Ps. 105.1b. Verse 4b cites Ps. 148.13aα₂, but perhaps had Isa. 2.11, 17 in mind. The invitation in v. 5aα corresponds to Ps. 9.12a;

day on which it will be free from the burden of its present servitude and from being scattered among the nations as an expression of the divine anger, and Yahweh himself has comforted it by creating all-embracing salvation. The Hebrew word translated 'comfort' really means that one allows a person who has a severe spiritual or external burden to breathe again, thus removing what has caused him distress. To generalize, comforting means removing the burdensome pressure from someone and thus ultimately helping them (cf. Ps. 23.4; 71.21; 86.17). In grateful confession (cf. Ps. 118.21), the poet makes the community bear public witness to the tangible help (as evidenced by the 'see') which Yahweh has given it, as used to happen in Israel on the occasion of thank-offerings (cf. Ps. 66.13ff.).[13] In so doing he attributes to the community a brief hymn of thanksgiving or a narrative praise of God which contains the basic elements of the genre: the introduction, which expresses the resolve to utter praise and therefore always contains the name of Yahweh, and the narrative proper, introduced by 'for', which gives the reason for the praise.[14]

[3] We have information about the rite noted here from remarks in the Tractate of the Babylonian Talmud called Sukkah, Tabernacles, which refers expressly to this passage. According to it, on the night between the sixth and seventh days of the Feast of Tabernacles, with the whole city lit up, there was a water procession from Siloam though the Water Gate to the temple courtyard, accompanied by the singing of psalms, music and the blowing of trumpets, in which the high priest on this day came before the people in his full array and solemnly poured the water on the altar (cf. Sukkah IV, IX; V, IIIff. and Josephus, *Antt.* XV, 50f.). It is said of that event: 'He who has not seen the delights of the water procession has not seen any of the pleasures of life' (Sukkah, V, II). As according to v. 27, Ps. 118 seems to have been sung at this festival, the appeal to it by the poet in vv. 1,2[15] is certainly not coincidental.[16] The rite itself must be seen in

30.5a; however, we might also think of Isa. 26.10b; Ps. 93.1a. Verse 5b might look back to Isa. 37.20bα par II Kings 19.19bα. Verse 6a can hardly fail to have Isa. 54.1abα and 24.14 in mind, and in addition is perhaps also composed of Zeph. 3.14a. Despite the divine designation 'the Holy One of Israel', which runs through the book of Isaiah from 1.4 and is deliberately taken up here, cf. the reference above, 22 n. 36, verse 6b is to be compared with Zeph. 3.15b; Ps. 99.2a and finally also with Isa. 9.1aβ.

[13] Cf. Crüsemann, 227ff.

[14] Cf. Gunkel-Begrich, *Einleitung in die Psalmen*, 7, 3 and 4; Weiser, *The Psalms*, OTL, London and Philadelphia 1962, 52ff., 35ff.; C. Westermann, *Lob und Klage in den Psalmen*, Göttingen ⁵1977, 20ff., and Crüsemann, 263ff.

[15] Cf. above, n. 12.

[16] Cf. P. Volz, *Das Neujahrfest Jahwes* (Tabernacles), SGV 67, Tübingen 1912, 6f., 42f.; S. Mowinckel, *Psalmenstudien* II, Kristiania 1922, 100f.; id., *The Psalms in Israel's Worship* I, Oxford 1962, 123 n. 58; 130f.

connection with the ancient New Year Festival celebrated in the autumn and now coinciding with the Feast of Tabernacles, at which it represented the rain and the fertility dependent on it. To this extent the mention of the 'springs of help' was perhaps at first related quite realistically to the spring of Gihon which fed the channel of Siloam (cf. I Kings 1.38, 45).[17] But according to v. 2, Yahweh himself is the help of his people or, as Jer. 2.13; 17.13 puts it, the 'source of living water'. Thus with his reference to the eschatological festive procession and its great thank-offering, the poet is probably pointing to God who is the help of his people, through whom they will continue to live, and will recognize his helping power when they again read of it in the prophecies of this book whose prophet bears the name 'Yahweh helped'.

[4–6] The brief hymn which ends in an invitation to rejoice assures the community that the day will in fact come when they confess in praise of God the deeds of Yahweh before the nations,[18] in order to bestow on his name[19] the honour which is really always due to him, but thanks to his help is now manifest for Zion and the remnant of Israel.[20] The people of Jerusalem, who in the present suffer in grievous servitude because their God is hidden from the world, will then truly shout and sing for joy, because Yahweh now dwells in their midst in all his splendour, which the world can no longer ignore (cf. 40.9; 52.7f.; 60.1f.). His epithet 'the Holy One of Israel' contains the mystery of the election of the people, which consists in the fact that the God who is set above all the world will make use of this shattered Israel to manifest himself before the peoples.

It is a strange accentuation of this paradox, which will not be resolved before the eschaton, that Christianity confesses that this revelation of God has taken place in the crucified one (Phil. 2.5ff.), at the point where the meaning of life turns into meaninglessness and God not only suffers in and through men but also discloses himself as the infinitely gracious ground of this life, of whom human beings become aware when they come to the end of their capacities, leave the world and all their own wishes behind them, and lean upon him in trust.[21]

[17] Cf. Mowinckel, Psalms I, 131; Wildberger, ad loc.
[18] Cf. e.g. Ps. 9.12ff.; 57.10ff.
[19] For understanding the name as representative of the person cf. A. S. van der Woude, THAT II, cols. 947ff.
[20] Cf. also Isa. 43.8ff.; 44.6ff.; 45.18ff.; Ezek. 36.33ff.
[21] Cf. also Plotinus VI, 9(9). 24f., 28.